ARCHAEOLOGICAL INSTITUTE OF AMERICA
Monographs New Series, Number 6

The Orientalizing Bucchero from the Lower Building at Poggio Civitate (Murlo)

ARCHAEOLOGICAL INSTITUTE OF AMERICA
Monographs New Series, Number 6

The Orientalizing Bucchero from the Lower Building at Poggio Civitate (Murlo)

Jon Berkin

Published for
Archaeological Institute of America
Boston, MA

by
THE UNIVERSITY OF PENNSYLVANIA MUSEUM
of Archaeology and Anthropology
Philadelphia, PA, 2003

Design and production
Publications
University of Pennsylvania Museum of Archaeology and Anthropology
Philadelphia, PA

Library of Congress Cataloging-in-Publication Data
Berkin, Jon M.
The orientalizing bucchero from the lower building at Poggio Civitate (Murlo) / Jon Berkin.
p. cm. -- (Monographs / Archaeological Institute of America ; new series, number 6)
Includes bibliographical references.
ISBN 1-931909-03-2 (alk. paper)
1. Poggio Civitate Site (Italy) 2. Bucchero (Pottery) 3. Pottery, Etruscan. 4. Etruscans--Italy--Murlo. 5. Murlo (Italy)--Antiquities. 6. Excavations (Archaeology)--Italy--Murlo. I. Title. II. Monographs (Archaeological Institute of America) ; new ser., no. 6.

DG70.P64B47 2003
738.3'0937'5--dc21 2002043709

Printed in the United States of America.
10 9 8 7 6 5 4 3 2 1

To the memory of Abbeyleix Collins,
fellow excavator and friend

Contents

List of Figures

List of Plates

Plates appear at the end of the book, after figure 31.

List of Tables

ACKNOWLEDGMENTS

The present study of the Orientalizing Bucchero from the Lower Building at Poggio Civitate (Murlo) represents an outgrowth of my dissertation of the same name completed at Bryn Mawr College in 1993. There are many people who have contributed toward the realization of this monograph and to whom I owe my appreciation. I begin by thanking my advisor, Dr. Erik Nielsen, for giving me the opportunity to study the bucchero from the Lower Building and for allowing me to participate in the excavations at Poggio Civitate (Murlo). I also thank my co-advisor at Bryn Mawr, Professor Gloria F. Pinney, for her support and helpful suggestions. Special gratitude goes to Dr. Jean Turfa, who provided me with invaluable help and assistance throughout this project, and to Professors Brunilde S. Ridgway and James C. Wright, who encouraged me to publish this study. The Alwyn M. Cotton Foundation and the Cummer Fund provided financial support for the work, and for this I am most grateful. In addition, several members of the Soprintendenza Archeologica per la Toscana were very helpful while I was in Italy conducting research. In particular, I thank Dr. Benedetta Adembri, Dr. Elisabetta Mangani, and Dr. Anna Rastrelli for their cooperation and assistance; also Dr. Maria Grazia Celuzza, who allowed me to see the bucchero in the Grosseto Museum; and Dr. Edilberto Formigli, with whom I shared many enjoyable hours working at Murlo. I also thank Sharon Herson for her editorial assistance.

My good friends Steven, Julia, Olivia, Nicole, Mara, and Rob Briskin offered hospitality and encouragement. And finally, I owe a special debt of gratitude to my parents, Brian and Sandy Berkin, and to my brother, Adam Berkin, who have been a continual source of support in all my endeavors.

All the illustrations were drawn by Georgie Grentzenberg and Stephanie Gleit Weinstein. All photographs were taken by Chris Williams, and the graphics were drafted by Lynn Berg and Joseph Flannery. Margarita Gleba provided research assistance. My appreciation and thanks extend to each of them.

Introduction

Overview

This study of the bucchero pottery from the Lower Building at Poggio Civitate represents the first comprehensive presentation of this ceramic type from the site. It is also one of the first investigations of a large assemblage of bucchero from a nonfunerary context and, in addition, one of the few typological examinations of bucchero from northern Etruria.

The majority of the material from the Lower Building is unpublished or has been presented only briefly in excavation reports or exhibition catalogues. The current study commences with a discussion of the history and development of bucchero pottery. Chapter 1 consists of a general review of the excavations at Poggio Civitate. Chapter 2 contains a discussion of the excavation, stratigraphy, and chronology of the Lower Building, along with a brief survey of the other published materials found in the same building. Chapter 3, a catalogue of the 139 bucchero vessels and vessel fragments recovered from the Lower Building, includes a detailed discussion of the typology and comparanda for each vessel type identified in the Lower Building bucchero assemblage. Fourteen vessel shapes with forty-five distinguishable types and subtypes were represented in the deposit. In Chapter 4, a total of thirty-three decorative motif types and subtypes, as well as three inscriptions, are identified on the bucchero and discussed in detail. Chapter 5 presents the conclusions of the study, beginning with a review of the nature and limitations of the deposit, followed by a consideration of the vessel typology and decorations. This discussion also includes an analysis of the relationship between vessel shape and decoration, and a review of the distribution of parallels recovered elsewhere at the site, outside of the deposit. On the basis of the typology and comparanda, the possible place of manufacture of the bucchero is discussed and an attempt made to distinguish locally produced items from imported ware. The excavators have already suggested that some of the bucchero was produced on the site. The present study confirms this and also identifies a few likely imports.

A determination of the stylistic and typological orientation of the Poggio Civitate bucchero is also made to document whether this material is allied more closely with bucchero from northern Etruria or with that from the south. Since previous typological studies of bucchero were developed principally from material found in southern Etruria, their applicability to bucchero from the north has remained uncertain. The present investigation reveals the bucchero from the Lower Building to be, for the most part, typologically different from that of the south. While the shapes of the vessels are somewhat similar to those of Chiusi and Vulci, and while their decorations are similar to those found on bucchero from Chiusi, Vetulonia, and Roselle, as well as a number of sites in southern Etruria (most notably Cerveteri), the majority of vessel shapes and decorations nevertheless are not identical and represent either variant or unique types.

An overview of bucchero production both at Poggio Civitate and other sites within northern Etruria during the Orientalizing period follows. A review of this material indicates that during the latter half of the Orientalizing period the production of bucchero in northern Etruria was less of an "industry" than in the south. There were more local workshops involved, and, consequently, a much greater stylistic diversity.

The chronology of the bucchero from the Lower Building is then discussed and its place in the general development of bucchero pottery assessed. Since few sizable deposits of chronologically secure bucchero pottery have been identified in northern Etruria, establishing the chronology of the Lower Building bucchero is important for documenting the spread, as well as the initiation of production, of bucchero pottery in the north: while a few vessels in the deposit may date as early as the third quarter of the seventh century, the date for the majority of the bucchero lies within the last quarter of the seventh and first quarter of the sixth centuries B.C.

The bucchero from the Lower Building is then compared with that included in contemporary funerary assemblages, and the deposit is examined to determine whether or not it sheds any further light on the function of bucchero, particularly in relation to the banquet and the service of wine. Analysis reveals that, in fact, the Lower Building bucchero formed part of an elaborate banquet service, the only one of its kind known from Etruria. A comparison of the shapes present in this banquet service with those recovered from contemporary tomb assemblages, commonly thought to include the equipment for the funerary banquet, shows a great deal of overlap, as well as some notable differences. Many of the differences are attributable to the domestic nature of the deposit and the consequent need for a greater variety of shapes. In addition, the absence of several types standard in bucchero, especially jugs and amphoras, suggests that some shapes may have been present in metal. Finally, the study assesses whether or not the analysis of the bucchero helps to determine the function of the Lower Building itself.

HISTORY AND DEVELOPMENT OF BUCCHERO POTTERY

Bucchero pottery is a common feature at most early Etruscan sites.[1] Bucchero first appeared in the first quarter of the seventh century in burials at Cerveteri in southern Etruria.[2] This early bucchero, with its extremely thin walls and often shiny, almost metallic appearance, is considered by many to be of the finest quality. During the second half of the seventh century B.C., the production of bucchero spread to other centers of southern and central Etruria, and also became established in the north (Rasmussen 1979:159).[3] Beginning in the last quarter of the seventh century B.C., and throughout the first half of the sixth, bucchero production expanded to areas outside

[1] For a general survey of the literature on bucchero, see Bouloumié 1982:773–84. For the origin of the name "bucchero," see G. Mazzoni, *StEtr* 8 (1934):165–67. The two principal studies of bucchero are those of Ramage 1970 and Rasmussen 1979, although they deal primarily with the bucchero of southern Etruria. For reviews of Rasmussen's study, see S. Wisseman, in *AJA* 84 (1980):546–47; Bartoloni 1981:386–91; Strøm 1981:789–92. For more general discussions of bucchero, see D. Lollini, s.v. "Bucchero" in *EAA* 2 (1959):203–10; Camerini 1985; M. Cristofani, s.v. "Bucchero" in *Dizionario della civiltà etrusca* (Florence, 1985):45–48; Cottier-Angeli 1991:292–94; Gran-Aymerich 1982:37–38; Gran-Aymerich 1992:31–32; Gran-Aymerich 1993; Gran-Aymerich 1995; De Puma 1986:8–13; Nijboer 1998:82–195. For more specialized treatments of different topics concerning bucchero, see *Bucchero nero* and Bonghi Jovino 1993.

[2] Rasmussen 1979:3–5, 158; Bartoloni 1981:388–89; Gran-Aymerich 1979; Gran-Aymerich 1995:49; Nijboer 1998:154–59. Gran-Aymerich has divided the production of bucchero into six chronological phases, beginning within the first quarter of the 7th century B.C. and continuing into the 4th century B.C.; see Gran-Aymerich 1993:20–23 and note 2.

[3] The earliest known, securely datable context for the appearance of bucchero in northern Etruria appears to be the Tomba del Duce, Vetulonia, Groups 2 and 4. Although Camporeale originally dated these deposits to the last quarter of the 7th century B.C., Strøm, Rasmussen, and Cristofani have argued convincingly for their redating; see Camporeale 1967:63–65, 78, 115–26, 134; Strøm 1971:178–80; Rasmussen 1979:4–5; and Cristofani, *StEtr* 38 (1970):277. Strøm has proposed a date in the second quarter of the 7th century B.C. for Group 2 and a slightly later date, toward the middle of the 7th century B.C., for Groups 4 and 5. Rasmussen has suggested a date for all three groups in the third quarter of the 7th century B.C., more specifically, soon after 650 B.C. Cristofani has also dated Group 4 around the middle of the seventh century (not later than 640 B.C.). In addition, although it was originally believed that the bucchero in the tomb was not locally produced but was imported from southern Etruria, most

Etruria proper, and the ware was also widely exported not only to the rest of Italy, but throughout the Mediterranean world.[4] The shapes of the exports, however, were very limited and consisted predominantly of kantharoi. Further, the places of manufacture of exported bucchero appear to have been few and were associated with other industries, especially the trade in wine.

Bucchero is predominantly a wheel-made ware fired in a reducing atmosphere so that both surface and core are black (Rasmussen 1979:2; Camerini 1985:3; Cottier-Angeli 1991:292–93).[5] The bucchero from Poggio Civitate is generally composed of well-levigated clay and displays a high degree of surface polish. Its ceramic paste and homogeneous color distinguish it from the local buccheroid, another early Etruscan fabric; in the latter, only the surface is black, while the black color of the core is less homogeneous and the ceramic paste more micaceous than in true bucchero.

The bucchero from the Lower Building comes from a problematic deposit. The conflagration that destroyed the building burned much of the pottery, including the bucchero, which had originally been fired in a reducing environment. The subsequent oxidation of the fabric in an open fire changed all or much of the surface color of many of the pieces to a mottled orange, tan, or reddish brown.[6] Since the usual standard for identifying bucchero, namely a fabric possessing a uniformly black surface and core, cannot be applied to many of these pieces, the following criteria have been adopted:

1) the surface and the biscuit are black, or
2) a substantial part of the surface is black and the biscuit is black, or
3) the surface is mottled orange-brown, tan, or red, and the biscuit is black or nearly so.

Bucchero as a material appears to have evolved principally from the Italic impasto tradition and represents a purely Etruscan phenomenon.[7] Many of the earliest bucchero shapes are derived from prototypes in impasto, and numerous impasto vessels display a black surface reminiscent of bucchero (Ramage 1970:4, 9–10;

Note 3 continued

likely from Cerveteri (L. Banti *Il mondo degli etruschi.* [Rome,1969]:291–2, 10c; Camporeale 1967:115–122; Ramage 1970:2,29; Rasmussen 1979: 109, 115), it has also been argued that at least some of the bucchero vessels in the tomb were locally manufactured (Bonamici 1972: 110–113; Bagnasco Gianni 1993:207–216). Camporeale (1995:77, note 15), however, has found the arguments for the production of the bucchero kyathos (Florence 7082) and kantharos (Florence 7081) from Group 4 of the Tomba del Duce by a local, northern Etruscan potter unconvincing. He has suggested, instead, that these vessels may have been produced by an itinerant potter from Cerveteri working in northern Etruria. Camporeale (1995), in the same study, has similarly proposed that an itinerant potter from Cerveteri produced several Orientalizing bucchero and buccheroid vessels found at Massa Maritima.

Rasmussen (1979:159) initially placed the date of the initiation of production of bucchero in northern Etruria in the last quarter of the 7th century B.C. However, the reevaluation of the bucchero in the Tomba del Duce, as well as other, more recent research, has indicated that production of bucchero in northern Etruria may actually have begun around the middle of the seventh century B.C.; see Bagnasco Gianni 1993:210–211 and note 19.

[4] For discussions of the trade and commercialization of bucchero, see Bouloumié in *Bucchero nero*:111–23; Gras 1985; Rasmussen 1979:143–56; Shuey 1983:116–52; Turfa 1986:73–74; Villard 1962:1625–35; Bouloumié 1982:780–82; Rizzo 1990; Gran-Aymerich 1993:34–35; Swaddling, Walker, and Roberts 1995.

[5] As Cuomo di Caprio has noted (1993:217), in most ancient ceramic kilns the process of firing normally involved a continual alternation between reducing and oxidizing phases as fuel was successively introduced and consumed. Maintenance of either a sustained reducing or oxidizing environment would not have been possible. Thus, the potter, in order to maintain a continuous reducing environment, must have modified either the kiln structure or the firing technique. See also Cottier-Angeli 1991:293.

For the purposes of this study I have utilized the definitions of the ceramic wares from Poggio Civitate, most specifically those for bucchero and buccheroid, developed by the excavators (see Nielsen and Phillips 1977a:87, note 5; Tobey, Nielsen, and Rowe 1986:116–17). For a discussion of the diverse usages and meanings of the term buccheroid, see Ramage 1970:3–4; Gran-Aymerich 1993:27–28.

[6] Several orange-colored burned bucchero fragments were included among the ceramic material from the site tested by neutron activation analysis. Unfortunately the published results of these tests do not specify in which fabric cluster the burned fragments appeared (Tobey, Nielsen, and Rowe 1986:117). Visual analysis by a ceramicist from Alfred University of fragments of discolored pottery from the Lower Building has confirmed that the surface color of this burned pottery was originally black (personal communication from Dr. Nielsen).

[7] Edlund 1980:45–46; Rasmussen 1979:157; Gran-Aymerich 1979; Gran-Aymerich 1995:49; Nijboer 1998:82.

Camerini 1985:8–9; Gran-Aymerich 1979).[8] As Rasmussen has noted, "Bucchero may be distinguished from the dark impasto out of which it develops by the finer levigation of the clay, by the greater reduction in firing, and by the shapes used" (Rasmussen 1979:2). In addition, several early bucchero shapes are derived from ceramic and metal vessels imported from Greece and the Near East.[9] The influence of metallic vessels also is clearly evident in many of the decorative techniques and motifs displayed by bucchero (Gran-Aymerich 1995:49–50; Nijboer 1998:83). That this is the case for several bucchero vessels from the Lower Building will be shown in Chapter 4 .

Gran-Aymerich has illuminated the complex relationship between Etruscan impasto and bucchero vases and vessels of more precious materials, particularly metallic vessels (Gran-Aymerich 1995).[10] The connection between bucchero vases and those in other media, especially metal and ivory, has long been acknowledged. The formal and decorative similarities between bucchero and metallic vessels suggested to many scholars that bucchero may in fact have represented an imitation of more expensive locally made and imported metal vessels. In addition, following this reasoning, the relationship was generally considered to have been one-sided with bucchero always serving as the recipient of influences of vessels in more precious materials.

Gran-Aymerich, however, has conclusively demonstrated that the relationship between Etruscan bucchero vases and metallic and ivory vessels was in fact much more complex. There existed a dynamic, fluid relationship between potters and workers in metal and ivory. This relationship was reciprocal, with shapes and decorations freely transferred among the various media. Moreover, far from representing an imitation of metal vessels, bucchero vessels constituted important luxury and prestige items in their own right.[11] Finally, Gran-Aymerich has also quite rightly noted that the development of bucchero must be seen within the larger context of the changing social-cultural conditions among the aristocracy during the Orientalizing period, especially the trade in luxury goods, the adoption of banqueting, and the service of wine.[12]

These points all directly apply to the Lower Building bucchero. Their lavish decoration and ornate character suggest that these vessels almost certainly represented prestige goods. As will be shown in Chapter 5, the deposit of bucchero in the Lower Building also constituted a banqueting service. Moreover, the similarity of some bucchero decorative motifs to decoration on metal and ivory objects manufactured at the site demonstrates the close interaction of local artisans working in different materials.

A growing body of literature exists concerning the technical aspects of bucchero production.[13] Research has largely concentrated on determining the process by which bucchero obtained its uniform black color. Studies have now shown that the deep black color results from both the reduction of iron oxides in the clay and the combustion of carbon (Leoni and Trabucchi 1962:257–66; Francaviglia, Minardi, and Palmieri 1975:230; also Rasmussen 1979:2). It is still a matter of debate, however, whether organic material, the source of the carbon, was originally present in the clay, or, alternatively, was introduced by the potter.[14] It has

[8] It should be noted that the production of impasto vessels did not cease with the introduction of bucchero. Impasto vessels continued to be manufactured well into the 6th century and later. Numerous impasto vessels have been recovered from the excavations at Poggio Civitate. The published examples from the Lower Building will be presented in Chapter 2.

[9] Ramage 1970:4–11; Gran-Aymerich 1972; Strøm 1981:792; Gran-Aymerich 1993:21.

[10] For a brief review of Gran-Aymerich's article, see J.P. Small, in *JRA* 10 (1997):408–409.

[11] According to Gran-Aymerich (1995:60), "Les vases en bucchero ne doivent pas être envisagés come des imitations bon marché des vases métaliques, comme de simple substituts des vases de prestige, mais comme des objets spécifiques, correspondant á demande et á fonctions nouvelles, d'un société étrusque qui se transforme et évolue rapidemente... " This point has also been made by Nijboer (1998:188).

[12] As Gran-Aymerich (1995:53) notes, the majority of bucchero vases are directly tied to the service of wine. Banqueting in Etruria will be discussed in more detail below in Chapter 5.

[13] For a survey of the literature on bucchero production, see Cuomo di Caprio 1993:218–20; Bouloumié 1982:777; Camerini 1985:4–6; Gran-Aymerich 1995: 48 and note 22. See also Wadsworth 1983:65–68; Wisseman 1978:45–60; Cottier-Angeli 1991:292–94.

[14] For different suggestions: A. Flamini, O. Graziani, O. Grubessi, and P. De Lorenzo in *Bucchero nero*:72–78; Wadsworth 1983:65–68; Cottier-Angeli 1991:293–94.

also been suggested that, in the case of some examples with particularly fine surfaces, a slip rich in organic materials, or a purified solution of the clay itself, may have been added before firing (Rasmussen 1979:4; Cottier-Angeli 1991:294).

Cuomo di Caprio (1993:217–21), in a review of the major theories on bucchero production, has pointed out a number of technical deficiencies in many of the hypotheses regarding bucchero production. Utilizing evidence gathered from both her own experiments and a study of the work of modern producers of imitation bucchero vessels, she has suggested an alternate method of producing bucchero. According to her theory, the potter would have placed the future bucchero vessel into the kiln in a sealed container filled with reducible, carbonaceous substances. These reducible materials could have consisted of sawdust, wood shavings, or some similar substance. During firing, the consequent reduction of these materials would have created a strongly reducing atmosphere saturated by the gases produced by the dry distillation of the wood within the sealed container. The carbon would have then permeated the body of the vessel, causing it to turn black. Thus, the carbon, instead of being added to the clay before firing, as previously suggested, actually would have been introduced during the firing process.

It is clear that a number of bucchero styles developed during the course of its production, and a variety of terms have been used to describe them.[15] Montelius (1889:79–106) originally proposed a tripartite classification scheme for the development of bucchero; it was based mainly on the appearance of the ware's ceramic paste and the decorative techniques employed in its production. The descriptive terms employed by Montelius included: bucchero *sottile*, *normale* or *regolare*, and *pesante*.[16] In subsequent years, the definition of these terms was further refined, and they were ascribed a chronological significance.

It has become apparent, however, that the application of these terms is often highly subjective, and, given the diversity of bucchero production, they are much too limiting. Thus, without precise contextual information, the characteristics that these terms denote cannot alone be utilized as temporal indicators. In fact, in more recent studies, the tendency has been to avoid them altogether.[17]

Gran-Aymerich (1993:22–26), in a discussion of the production and diffusion of bucchero, has rightly noted that bucchero does not display uniform characteristics throughout Etruria. The evidence indicates that not long after bucchero appeared, distinct regional classes developed as its production spread throughout Etruria and surrounding areas. Gran-Aymerich's regional and local classifications are based on chronological, typological, and stylistic criteria. He distinguishes four major regions of production: Etruria proper, non-Etruscan central Italy, Campania, and the northern Apennines. Gran-Aymerich further subdivides the bucchero of Etruria into three major geographic areas: southern Etruria, northern Etruria, and central, interior Etruria.

The area of southern Etruria includes the cities of Cerveteri, Tarquinia, Veii, Vulci, and their respective territories. This area produced the earliest, and eventually, the most widely exported bucchero. The area of northern Etruscan bucchero production extends from the Maremma to the Arno valley. The major Etruscan centers at Roselle, Populonia, and Vetulonia are included in this territory, as are a number of smaller sites. Finally, the area of central, interior Etruria consists of Orvieto and Chiusi, and smaller sites in their vicinities.

Additional studies will be necessary before these regional classes of bucchero can be confidently assigned to specific workshops and places of production.[18] The present investigation of the Orientalizing bucchero from the Lower Building represents one such, and as excavation of other Etruscan settlements continues, new studies will doubtless follow.

[15] Hayes (1985:62), for example, has spoken of the existence of bucchero "traditions."

[16] For a detailed discussion of Montelius's tripartite classification of bucchero, see Gran-Aymerich 1993:20–21. See also De Puma 1986:8–9.

[17] For example, Rasmussen (1979:3) retains only the term bucchero *pesante*. See also Edlund 1980:45.

[18] Nijboer has recently presented the evidence for the production of bucchero at several Etruscan sites, including Poggio Civitate, see Nijboer 1998:143–95.

I

The Site of Poggio Civitate

The site of Poggio Civitate is located on a small hill approximately twenty-four kilometers southwest of Siena[1] (Fig. 1). The site is strategically placed on the Crevole River, a tributary of the Ombrone, linking it with the major Etruscan coastal centers at Roselle, Populonia, and Volterra. Since 1966, excavations have been concentrated on Piano del Tesoro, a small plateau on the northeastern part of the hill. To date, excavations on Piano del Tesoro have revealed the remains of at least five structures, comprising at least two successive phases of construction and dating to the late Orientalizing and early Archaic periods (Fig. 2).[2]

The early excavation campaigns brought to light the remains of a monumental complex of the Archaic period. This structure, known as the Upper Building, was square in plan and consisted of four wings of rooms, each approximately sixty meters long, defining an open, porticoed, central courtyard.[3] Two additional rooms projected off the northeast corner of the building. While porches were placed along the south, east, and north sides of the central court, a small, rectangular structure was built directly off the central room of the west wing. The Upper Building had a foundation of large, tightly packed stones of irregular shape, pisé walls, and a tiled roof. It was lavishly decorated with a full program of architectural terracottas, including lateral and raking simas, human and animal akroterial statuary, antefixes, and frieze plaques. In addition, more recent excavations in the area around the Upper Building have also revealed the existence of an elaborate system of fortifications associated with the structure, including fossas and fortification walls (Nielsen and Phillips 1986:15–16; Nielsen 1991:245–50).

For reasons still unknown the entire Archaic complex was destroyed and systematically dismantled sometime during the third quarter of the sixth century B.C.[4] In the process, the majority of the materials were removed from the rooms of the building. Some of the architectural terra-

---

[1] The excavations at Poggio Civitate are currently being directed by E. O. Nielsen and A. Tuck under the auspices of Franklin University, Switzerland, and the University of Evansville. For a general discussion of the site, including bibliography, see *Case e palazzi*:64–154 and Phillips 1993. For more recent studies of the site and its associated material, see Damgaard Andersen 1990; De Puma and Small 1994; Edlund 1987:87–92; Edlund-Berry 1992; Nielsen 1987; Nielsen 1993; Phillips 1989a; Nijboer 1998:164–71, 277–81; Nielsen 1998.

[2] For a general discussion of the chronology of the site, see Nielsen and Phillips 1977a:99–100; Nielsen and Phillips 1977b:465; Phillips, in *Case e palazzi*:74–75; Phillips 1980:202–6; Phillips 1993:80. See also Phillips 1989a:29–42.

[3] For a discussion and plan of the Upper Building and a presentation of a selection of its associated material, see *Case e palazzi*:66–69, 98–154 and Phillips 1993:5–49.

[4] For a recent reconsideration of the diverse theories regarding the destruction of the site, see Edlund-Berry 1994:16–28.

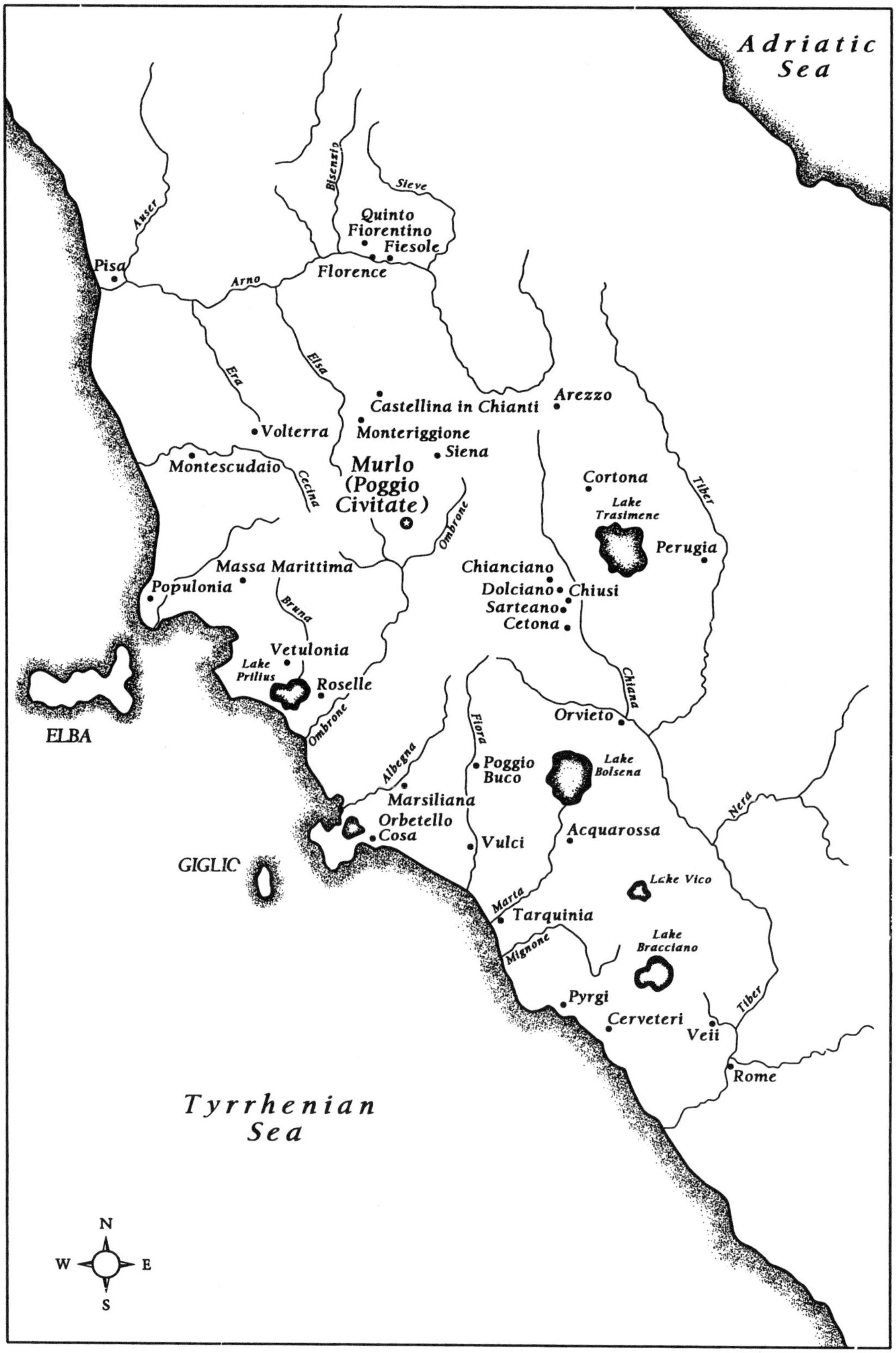

Figure 1. Map of Etruria. (L. Berg)

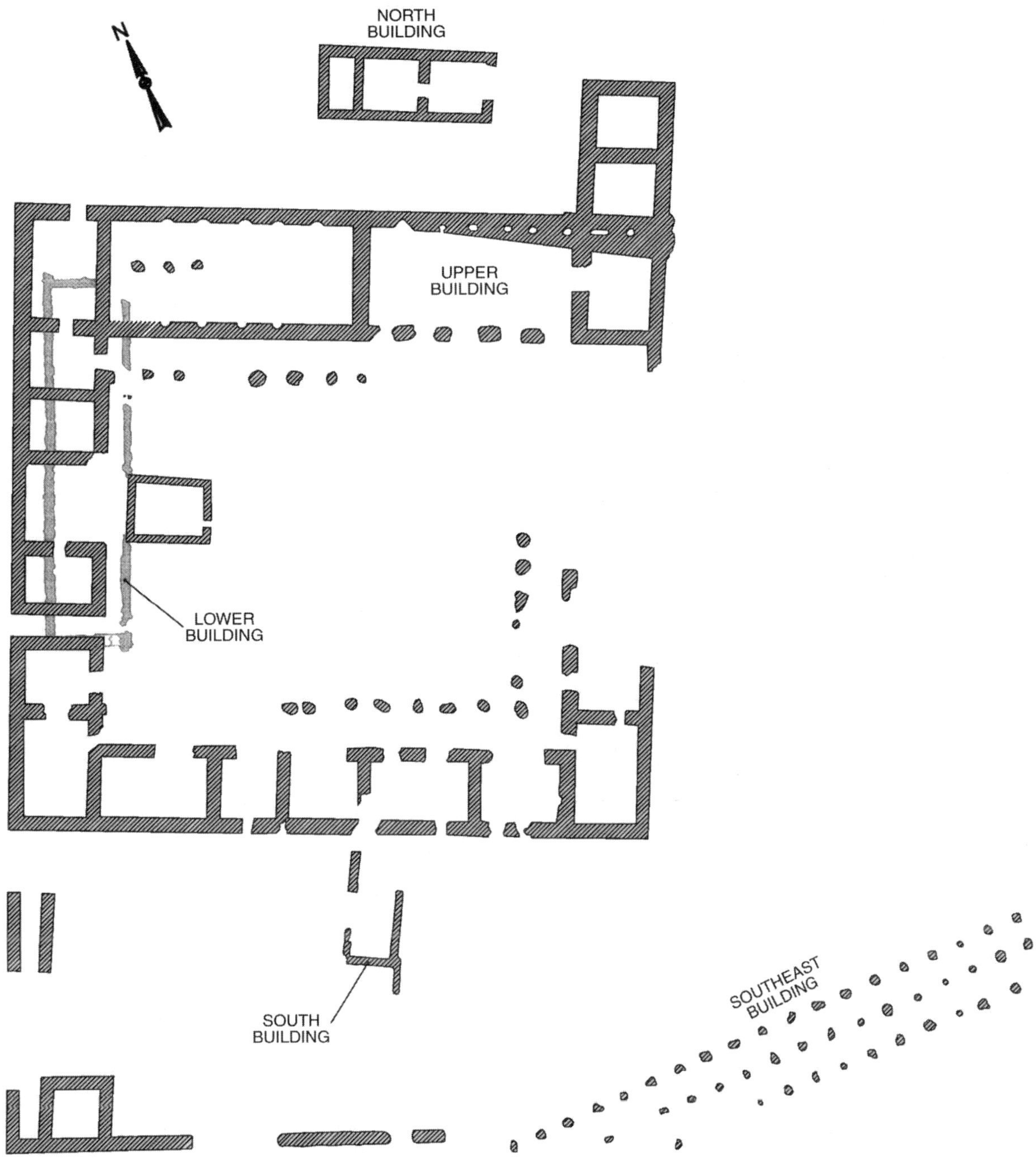

Figure 2. Structures on Piano del Tesoro (not to scale) (drawn by L. Berg after D. Peck)

cottas were gathered and thrown into the pits to the north and west of the complex, which were then sealed with a cap of stones and earth. Others were either carried farther to the west, where a large dump was created, or buried in smaller pits in other locations around the site. Finally, the entire site was scraped, and a large earthen mound, or agger, was formed over the west flank of the Upper Building, covering the western wing of rooms and projecting fortification walls, and possibly extending around other portions of Piano del Tesoro as well (Phillips 1993:49).

Excavations in the early 1970s revealed the existence of a structure of the Orientalizing period beneath the west wing of the Upper Building. This structure, dubbed the "Lower Building," was rectangular in plan with dimensions of 8.50 × 35.80 m and may have consisted of two storeys (Fig. 3).[5] Since no indication of subdividing cross-walls has been found, it would appear that the structure consisted of a single long room. The Lower Building employed the same manner of construction as the Archaic building, though the walls are slightly thinner, including a foundation of tightly packed local stones and walls of pisé and mud brick. The structure also possessed a tiled roof (Phillips 1980:202–6; Wikander 1990:288)—one of the earliest known in Etruria—which was decorated with an imaginative series of cut-out animal and vegetal akroteria (Rystedt 1983). The building was destroyed by a fire and collapsed upon itself, forming a sealed deposit.[6]

Notable among the contents of the Lower Building was a varied assortment of imported and locally made luxury objects, including fine ceramics, gold and silver jewelry, bronzes, amber and carved ivory, antler, and bone.[7] These luxury goods are consonant with those found in many of the wealthy burials of the period, the so-called *tombe principesche*, and certainly can be associated with persons of high rank (Rystedt 1984:367–71). In addition, seven large pithoi, which had been set into the floor, were uncovered in the northern portion of the structure.[8] These pithoi were presumably utilized for the storage of foodstuffs. The Lower Building has been tentatively identified on the basis of its contents and imposing dimensions, as well as its elaborate architectural decoration, as a residence and the possible seat of a small northern Etruscan league[9] or the residence of a wealthy Etruscan, perhaps the local chieftain or ruler (Damgaard Andersen 1990:79; Rystedt 1984:367–76).

Further investigations of the area immediately adjacent to the Upper Building have revealed the existence of two small structures of uncertain date to the north and south (Fig. 2). The first, the North Building, lies a short distance away from the north flank of the Upper Building (Nielsen and Phillips 1986:10–15). It was rectan-

[5] For a discussion of the Lower Building and a presentation of its associated material, see *Case e palazzi*:69–98; Nielsen and Phillips 1986:5–10; Phillips 1993:51–78. Phillips, in his most recent discussion of the structures on Piano del Tesoro, referred to the Lower Building as the "Orientalizing Long Building."

[6] The existence of additional structures of the Orientalizing period has been mentioned in several publications. Phillips noted the presence of poorly preserved walls, perhaps for a series of small rooms, below Rectangles 14–16 of the south flank of the Upper Building (see *Case e palazzi*:69; Phillips 1993:54). In addition, Rystedt, in her publication of the cut-out akroteria, has pointed out the existence of a wall below Rectangle 5 of the northeastern wing of the Upper Building. She refers to this wall as Lower Building 2 and to the remains mentioned above, below the south wing of the Upper Building, as Lower Building 3 (see Rystedt 1983:87). From my examination of the trench notebooks regarding these remains, I have concluded that the evidence is not secure enough to identify the remains beneath Rectangle 5 as a foundation wall. Alternatively, an identification of the remains beneath the south flank of the Upper Building remains inconclusive since this area has never been completely excavated. Anthony Tuck has informed me that this area is currently being investigated. The results of this excavation will undoubtedly provide more definitive evidence regarding the possible existence of an Orientalizing structure in this area.

[7] For a presentation of a selection of this material, see *Case e palazzi*:74–98. See also Phillips 1993:72–76. It is important to note that not all the finds that Phillips (1993) illustrated in his discussion of the Lower Building were actually found inside the building. This material will be discussed in greater detail in Chapter 2.

[8] These pithoi were located in Rectangles 5, 6, and 7. Two have been published; see *Case e palazzi*:146, nos. 641 and 642.

[9] This identification is also based upon an assumed continuity of function between the Lower and Upper Buildings; see Nielsen and Phillips, in *Case e palazzi*:65; Phillips 1993:79–83; also Edlund 1987:87–92.

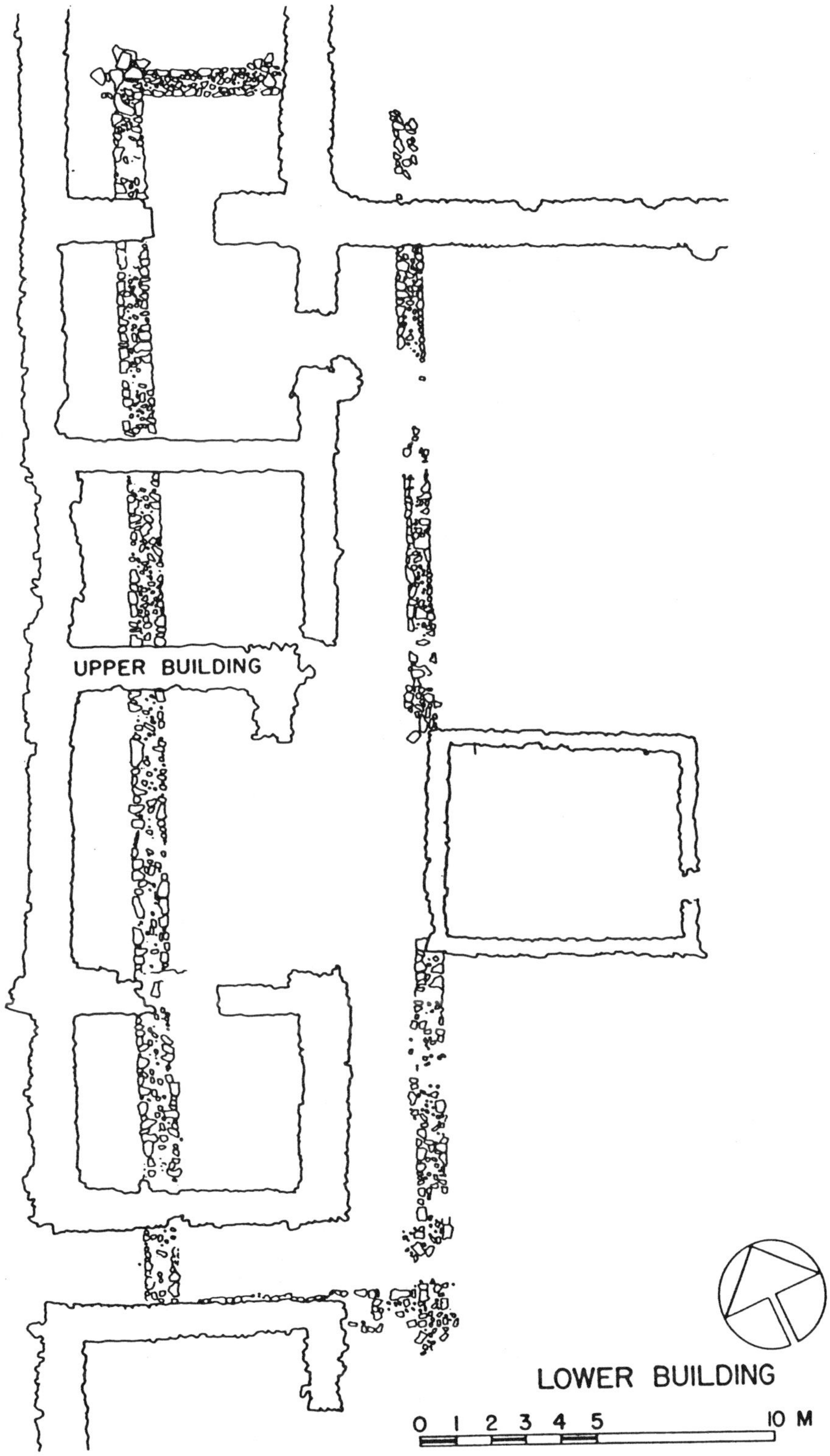

Figure 3. State plan of the Lower Building. (Nielsen and Phillips 1986, drawn by H. Linden)

gular in plan with dimensions of 16.25 × 7.00 m and was divided into three rooms. The relation of this building to the other structures on the site remains uncertain. Examples of pottery recovered from under its foundation walls are similar to those that were discovered within the Lower Building, indicating that the North Building was erected after the destruction of the former structure (Nielsen and Phillips 1986:15).

A second small rectangular structure, the South Building, has been uncovered to the south of the Upper Building (Nielsen and Phillips 1986:23–24). Its complete plan and date are not yet known, since it is still under excavation. The excavators have observed, however, that the building appears to have been sited and aligned with respect to the small North Building. They have postulated, therefore, that these two structures may have functioned as a complex prior to the existence of the Upper Building or were contemporary with it.[10]

The possible existence of a production facility to the south of the Upper Building was indicated by the discovery of numerous pieces of ivory, antler, and bone in various stages of preparation (Nielsen 1984a:333–48). Apparent confirmation has come with the recent discovery of a workshop complex situated in the southeast corner of Piano del Tesoro, approximately twenty meters southeast of the Upper Building (Fig. 2).[11] This large shedlike structure, the Southeast Building, had a hard-packed clay floor and was apparently unwalled. Its tiled roof was supported by three rows of columns, presumably wooden, resting on cut stone bases of irregular shape. To date, forty-five bases have been uncovered, representing a structure with minimum dimensions of 50 × 6 m. The roof of the building, moreover, also appears to have been decorated with a lateral sima and cut-out akroteria. The discovery of a large number of unfired cover tiles stacked on the floor of the building, of a terracotta mold for a "canopic"-type antefix head, and of several unfired revetment plaques supports the identification of the structure as a tile workshop. In addition, the presence of a discard dump of small worked pieces of bone, antler, and ivory off the northeast flank of the building, and of several bellows fragments, crucibles, nozzles, and braziers at its eastern end as well as in the surrounding vicinity indicates that other craft activities also took place there.

The determination of the chronological relationship between this structure and the Upper Building remains problematic. The situation is complicated by the sparseness of the topsoil in the area, which resulted in lack of clear stratigraphy, and by the thoroughness of the final destruction of the site, which disturbed the original deposition of material and produced a mixture of Archaic and Orientalizing levels. Erik Nielsen has noted, however, that the orientation of the two structures is quite different and, more importantly, that the architectural terracottas found on the floor of the Southeast Building stylistically predate those of the Upper Building (Nielsen 1987:116–19; Nielsen 1989b:509–16; Nielsen 1991:257). He has proposed a date of ca. 630 B.C. for the construction of the Southeast Building (Nielsen 1987:116–19; Nielsen 1989b:509–16) based on a stylistic analysis of these decorative terracottas. Nielsen has also suggested the likelihood that the same fire destroyed both the Lower Building and the Southeast Building, constituting a single horizon of destruction.[12]

The available evidence suggests that the Southeast Building represents a workshop for

[10] The excavators initially suggested that the Lower Building was earlier than the North Building since pottery found under the foundation walls of the North Building was similar to that found in the Lower Building. They later proposed an alternative interpretation, suggesting that the North, South, and Lower Buildings may have existed at one time prior to the Upper Building and functioned as its predecessors (Nielsen and Phillips 1986:10, 24). Phillips, however, later returned to his initial proposition and stated that the North and Upper Buildings might be contemporary (Phillips 1989a:30 and note 10) or, at least, that the North Building was erected in the period between the destruction of the Lower Building and that of the Upper Building (Phillips 1993:56 and note 132).

[11] Nielsen, in *Case e palazzi*:194; Nielsen 1987:91–119; Nielsen 1989b:509–16; Nielsen 1991:253–58; Nielsen 1993:29–30; Nielsen 1994a:319; Nielsen 1996:380; Nielsen 1998:95–107; Nijboer 1998:167–68, 277.

[12] The contemporaneity of the Lower and Southeast Buildings is also suggested by parallels between some of the carved objects in ivory, antler, and bone found in the Lower Building and others discovered in a dump adjacent to the Southeast Building (see Nielsen 1991:255, 257).

attached specialists.[13] This is suggested by both the setting of the structure and the materials recovered during its excavation. According to Brumfiel and Earle (1987:5), "attached specialists produce goods or provide services to a patron, typically either a social elite or a governing institution."Attached specialists can be contrasted with independent specialists, "who produce goods or provide services for an unspecified demand crowd that varies according to economic, social, and political conditions" (Brumfiel and Earle 1987:5). Attached specialists generally are nucleated in order to produce near their patrons. There is a close physical association between patrons and the specialists who produce goods for them. As Costin notes (1991:25), "The workshops of attached specialists most often are physically associated with elite domestic structures or government facilities." The close proximity of the Southeast Building to the other, elite structures on Piano del Tesoro is consistent with this situation.

In addition, attached specialists produce items integral to the political economy and the status, power, or control structure of the society (Brumfiel and Earle 1987:5; Costin 1991:11). "These include luxury and wealth items, weaponry, and wealth-generating goods" (Costin 1991:11). As noted above, the materials recovered both from within and immediately around the Southeast Building suggest that the artisans were predominantly producing luxury goods. The paucity of materials manufactured at Poggio Civitate that to date have been found elsewhere in Etruria suggests that these luxury goods were primarily produced for local consumption.

Finally, recent excavations conducted elsewhere on the site indicate a more extensive occupation of Poggio Civitate than previously suspected. A series of test trenches distributed over a large area on Poggio Civitate have produced ceramics and architectural terracottas in several locations (Nielsen 1989a:258). The recovery of this material suggests the existence of other structures, perhaps contemporary with those on Piano del Tesoro, elsewhere on Poggio Civitate. In addition, two small ovens associated with the production of metal recently were uncovered during testing on the north slope of Poggio Civitate (Nielsen 1993:33–34; Nielsen 1996:380). Limited excavations have also been conducted on Poggio Aguzzo, the small hill located directly adjacent to Poggio Civitate (Nielsen and Phillips 1974:265–66). These excavations uncovered nine fossa tombs, dated in recent studies by Anthony Tuck to the middle of the seventh century (Tuck 1996a and 1996b:399–400).

The function of the buildings on Piano del Tesoro, particularly that of the monumental Upper Building, remains unclear. Their interpretation is complicated by the completeness of the final destruction of the site, which included the removal of most of the material from the rooms of the Upper Building and dispersion of the remaining material about the area. The apparent isolation of the site, most specifically the ostensible lack of an associated settlement, together with the size of its buildings and the unprecedented wealth of their architectural decoration, have given rise to diverse theories of identification: the complex has accordingly been identified as the seat of a small northern Etruscan league (Colonna 1973: 69–70; Nielsen and Phillips, in *Case e Palazzi*: 68–69; Phillips 1993: 79–83), a residence and political and religious sanctuary (Edlund 1987:87–92; Edlund-Berry 1992:196–215; Edlund-Berry 1994:26),[14] or a "princely" residence.[15] Implicit in these identifications is the notion of a functional

[13] The concept of "attached" specialists was originally defined by T. Earle ("Comment on P. Rice, Evolution of Specialized Pottery Production: A Trial Model," *Current Anthropology*, 22.3:230–31). For subsequent, and more detailed, discussions of attached specialization, see Brumfiel and Earle 1987 and Costin 1991. Additional discussions of attached specialization can be found in the contributions contained in *Craft Specialization and Social Evolution: In Memory of V. Gordon Childe*, ed. B. Wailes (Philadelphia, 1996).

[14] Edlund-Berry's interpretation of the function of the site does not contradict that proposed by Nielsen and Phillips, but, rather, represents an amplification of their theories. She emphasizes that the complex of buildings at the site undoubtedly served a variety of purposes: as a Meeting Hall, residence, and *templum*. As a result, there is no specific term that encompasses all its functions. In addition, as Rathje aptly notes (1989:75–76), clear distinctions separating the political, religious, and civil spheres may not have existed in Etruria during the late Orientalizing and early Archaic periods. Thus, the complex of buildings on Poggio Civitate may have fulfilled functions in all these areas. See also Jannot 1988:95–96; Edlund-Berry 1989:30 and note 37.

[15] Cristofani 1975:9–17; Torelli, in *Case e palazzi*:26–30; Torelli 1983; Damgaard Andersen 1990:79; Nijboer 1998:171.

continuity between the Orientalizing and Archaic phases of the site, especially between the Lower and Upper Buildings. But the recent discovery of a monumental, "attached" workshop of the Orientalizing period, the Southeast Building, and the clarification of the elaborate system of defense associated with the Upper Building, the evidence of possible additional structures and industrial areas elsewhere on the site, and the publication of the Poggio Aguzzo tombs may, in fact, require a revised interpretation of the evidence.

II

THE LOWER BUILDING

EXCAVATION AND STRATIGRAPHY

The Lower Building was discovered during excavations beneath the floor level of the western wing and adjacent courtyard area of the Upper Building (Fig. 4). During excavation, each room of the Upper Building was designated as a "Rectangle" and provided with an independent meter square grid determined by the area of its walls. Separate grid units were also given to the courtyard, to the doorway between Rectangle 7 and the courtyard, and to the doorway between Rectangles 6 and 7. In addition, the southern and western walls of Rectangle 7, which were both removed, were also each provided with a grid. The Lower Building was located beneath portions of Rectangles 5–11 and the northwest edge of the courtyard of the Upper Building. While in retrospect this grid system may appear cumbersome, it should be noted that it was originally established for the excavation of the individual rooms of the Upper Building. Only later, after the grid system had been implemented, was it discovered that a structure, i.e., the Lower Building, lay beneath the foundations of the Upper Building.

Unfortunately, the documentation available from the excavation of the Lower Building does not allow a comprehensive examination of the distribution of finds, including the bucchero, within the structure. Finds were provenienced solely by stratum, not by individual depth measurements. While stratigraphic changes were noted by the excavators, the depths of the individual strata cannot be determined with precision since measurements were not all taken from a single, common datum point. No consistent sectional or horizontal plan has been produced of the complete building. In addition, many finds were designated by larger segments of the meter grid system rather than by precise individual plotting.

A further complicating factor is the disturbance of portions of the Lower Building by the subsequent construction of the Upper Building. The foundations of this later structure cut into the remains of the Lower Building. Excavation records indicate that the foundations for the walls of the Upper Building were found lying either directly on top, or within a few centimeters, of the remains of the walls of the Lower Building. Disturbance is further attested by joins made between several fragments of pottery found within the Lower Building and other fragments found within the foundation walls and the pavement of the Upper Building (Fig. 5).[1] Other

[1] The displacement of material from the Lower Building during the construction of the Upper Building has been previously noted by the excavators in their presentation of the Ionic bowls from the Lower Building (see Nielsen and Phillips 1974:268–70; Phillips 1989a:40, note 15; Phillips 1993:54). Winter (1977:22) has also noted a similar distribution pattern for a Lower Building akroterion. Joins have been made between bucchero fragments found within the Lower Building and other fragments found within the foundations of the south (**14**, **40**, **48**, **123**) and west (**27**, **43**) walls of Rectangle 7 of the Upper Building, as well as in the Upper Building pavement (**80**, **118**, **124**).

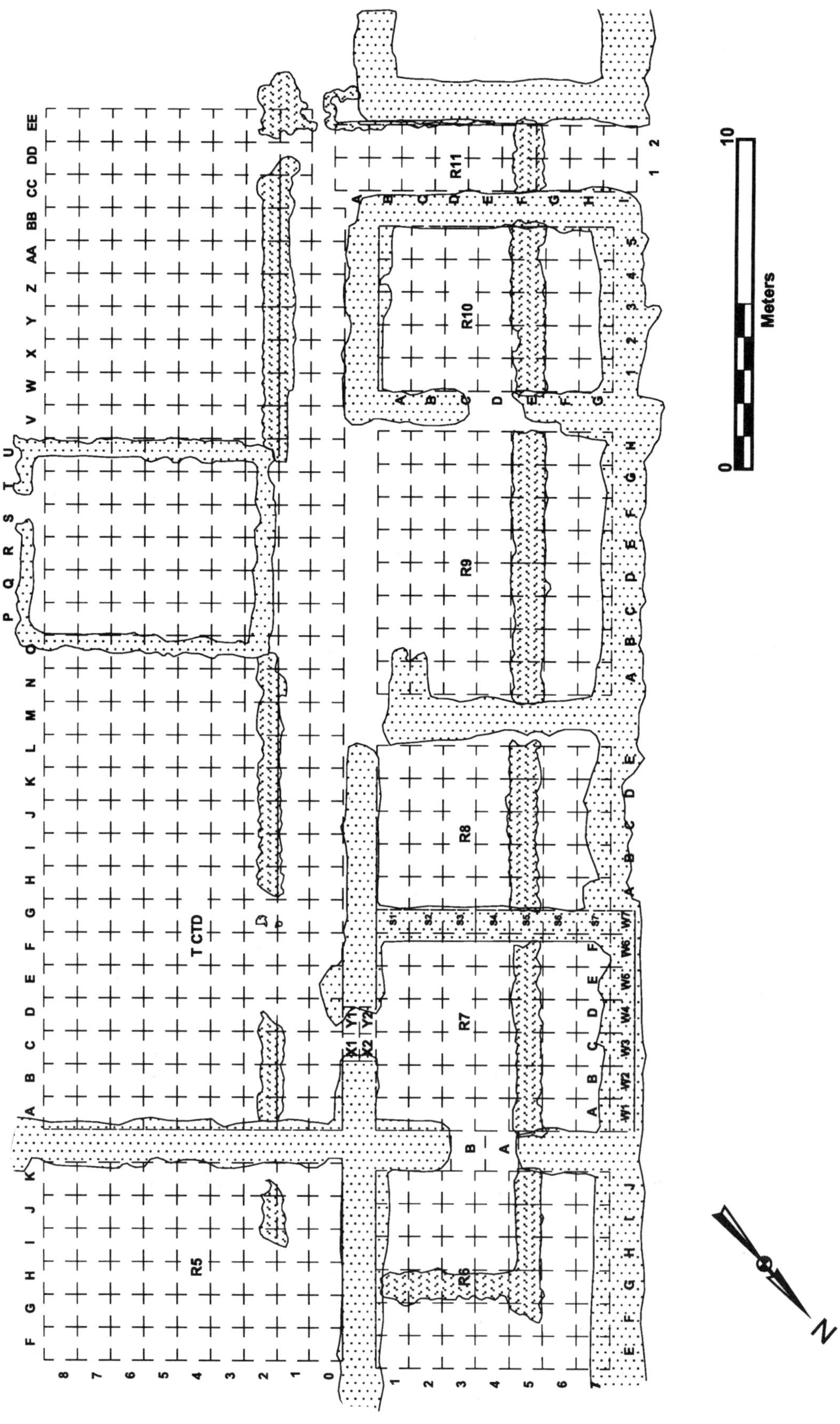

Figure 4. Gridded plan of the Upper and Lower Buildings. (J. Flannery)

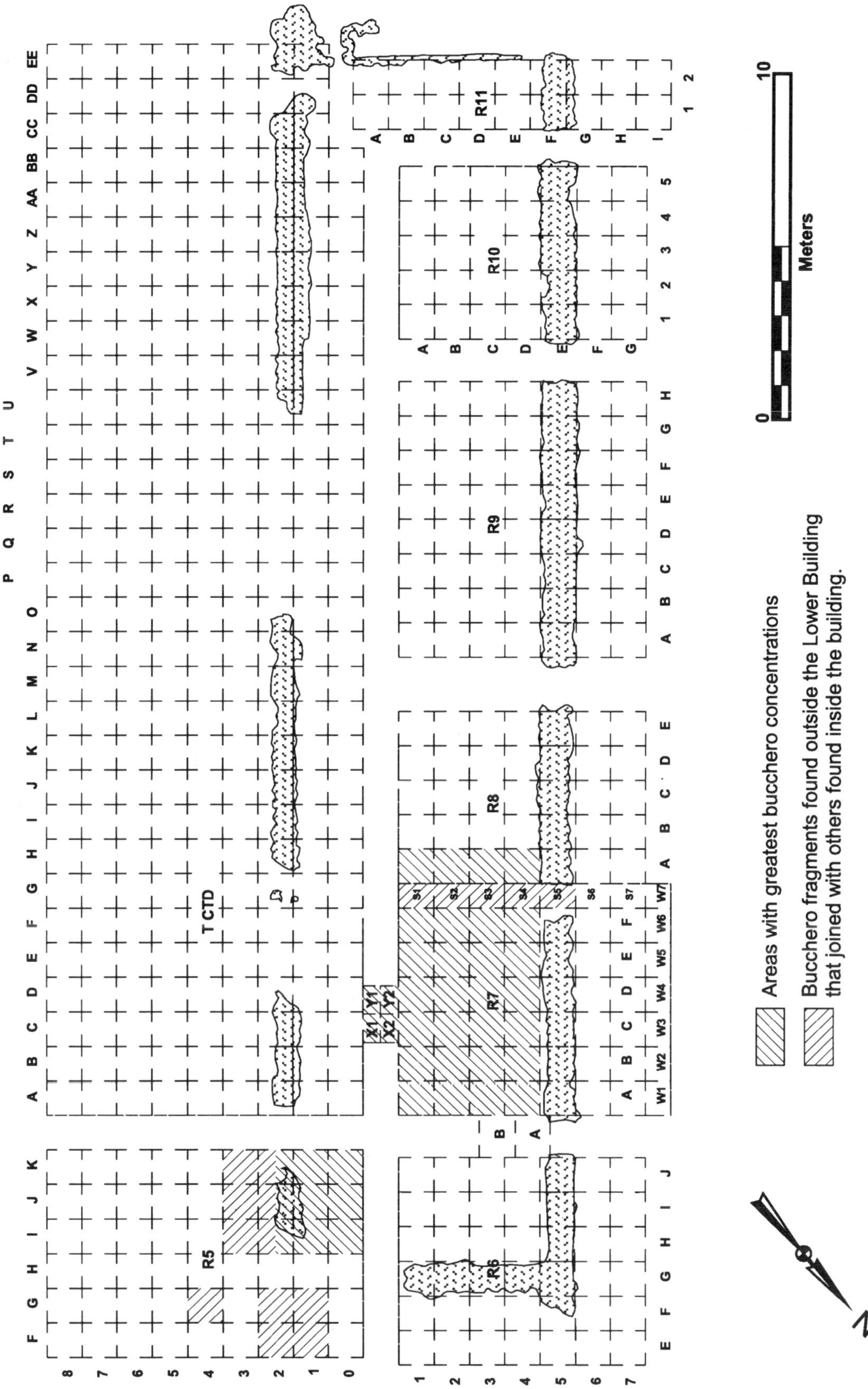

Figure 5. The Lower Building as excavated. (J. Flannery)

joining fragments, which were found outside the walls of the Lower Building below Rectangles 5 and 7, however, appear to have been deposited during the destruction and collapse of the Lower Building, since they were discovered in a burn layer sealed beneath the pavement of the Upper Building (**58**, **59**, **67**, **80**, **92**, **94**, **124**). Recently, a fragment joining a vessel recovered from Rectangle 7 of the Lower Building was found ca. 90 meters to the southeast within the destruction debris of the Southeast Building.[2] As a result, the extent to which the recoverable distribution of material from the Lower Building represents a primary deposition or the result of subsequent disturbance during the building's destruction or the construction of the Upper Building is unclear.

Three stratigraphic layers have been associated with the Lower Building. The uppermost layer, varying in thickness from 10 to 15 cm and composed of light gray-brown soil with admixtures of plaster, constituted the pavement of the Upper Building. This layer would have been created during the construction of the Upper Building, when the area previously occupied by the Lower Building had been leveled and a floor of plaster was laid in the rooms of the Upper Building. This pavement also formed a seal for the deposit below.

The second layer consisted of a thick stratum of dark black- and-red burned soil that contained a high concentration of carbon and is associated with the destruction of the Lower Building. This burned layer, 30 to 60 cm in thickness, was both the blackest and the most uniform in coverage in the northern half of the building, whereas in the south it was found only in sporadic patches. In addition, in most areas the burned stratum was found to extend up to a distance of two meters in all directions beyond the walls of the Lower Building.[3] The virtual absence of both the burned layer and any material in the interior of the southern half of the building beneath Rectangles 9–11, while both were present outside the walls in this area, would appear to suggest that the burned layer originally extended throughout this area as well. If this were the case, the area must have been disturbed by subsequent activity during either a cleanup of the building or the construction of the Upper Building. This possibility is strengthened by the finding of a large deposit of burned pottery buried without reference to any architectural feature both below and around the North Building in Trench 18 (Fig. 6).[4] Although no joins have yet been found between pottery in the Lower Building and this deposit, and there is as yet no clear stratigraphical evidence linking the two areas, their contemporaneity is suggested by the recovery from both locations of two figured bucchero handles and two kyathoi drawn from the same two molds.[5] In addition, there is a great deal of overlap between the two deposits in vessel typologies as well as in decoration (Phillips 1973a:324–25; Nielsen and Phillips 1986:15). It thus appears possible, as the excavators too have suggested, that the burned pottery and other material recovered from Trench 18 could originally have come from the Lower Building (Phillips 1973a:324; see also Nielsen and Phillips 1977a:100). In fact, no other likely source for this material is known at this time.[6]

---

[2] Excavation along the northern flank of the Southeast Building in Trench 26 produced a fragment of a tripod vessel (Murlo no. 92-42) that joined to a bowl (Murlo no. 72-354; **51**) recovered from Rectangle 5 of the Lower Building.

[3] Bucchero and other materials of the same type as those found in the Lower Building were discovered in the burned stratum that continued outside the walls of the Lower Building. In order to preserve the integrity of the deposit, however, it was decided not to include this bucchero in this study.

[4] For discussions of the excavation and finds from this area, see Phillips 1973a:324–25; Nielsen and Phillips 1974:277; Nielsen and Phillips 1975:362–66; Nielsen and Phillips 1977a:86–95, ill. 1; Nielsen and Phillips 1986:10–15.

[5] For a discussion of the two kyathos handles, see Nielsen and Phillips 1977a:90–92, Murlo. nos. 73-239, 71-562 (**36**). In addition, I have noted that the body of kyathos **25** was drawn from the same mold as that of a kyathos recovered from Trench 18 (Murlo no. 73-286). For this latter kyathos, see *Case e palazzi*:81, no. 76. See also Nielsen 1987:118 and note 41. It should be noted that the area of Trench 18 has not yet been completely excavated.

[6] Adding the bucchero excavated from Trench 18 to that found in the Lower Building would more than double the size of the original deposit. Alternatively, should excavation of the area below the south flank of the Upper Building confirm the existence of the Orientalizing structure tentatively identified by Phillips in this location, then presumably some of the bucchero from Trench 18 could have come from this building as well. See Chapter 1, footnote 6.

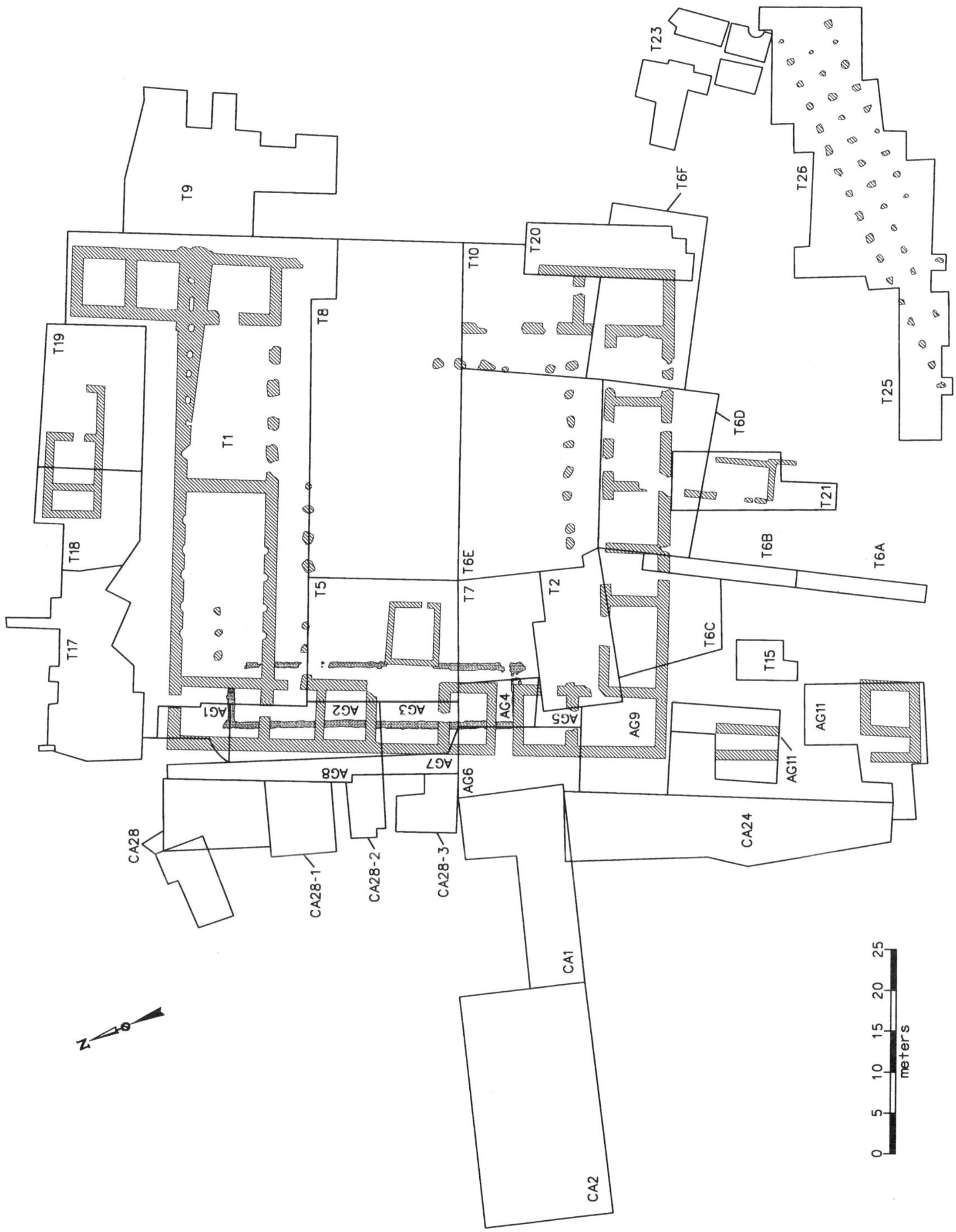

Figure 6. Trench plan of Piano del Tesoro. (L. Berg)

The third layer to be distinguished was a thin stratum of sandy-gray claylike soil, which seems to have formed the pavement of the Lower Building. This layer was uneven in many places and at certain points lay directly above the bedrock. Like the burned layer, it was much less distinct in the southern half of the building.

The majority of bucchero, as well as the other material recovered from the Lower Building, was found in the burned stratum bounded by the Lower Building walls and, thus, is securely associated with that structure. Smaller amounts of material were also found in the pavement stratum of the Upper Building, where they presumably were amalgamated with paving material prepared in proximity to piles of Lower Building rubble. In addition, while some of the material was apparently found resting directly on the floor of the Lower Building, nothing can be securely located either within or below its pavement level. One fragment (**110**) was found in a preserved portion of the pisé wall of the Lower Building. It is not clear, however, whether this fragment was actually built into the wall or became lodged in it during the destruction of the building.

Almost all of the material recovered from the Lower Building, including the bucchero, was found scattered in the northern half below Rectangles 5–8 and the northwest corner of the courtyard.[7] Several fragments of bucchero vessels were found inside pithoi sunk into the floor below Rectangles 5, 6, and 7. A few of these fragments joined others found in the immediate area around the pithoi (**45** and **80**). Joins have also been made between bucchero fragments found up to six meters apart inside the area of the building. Only one vessel, a small bowl (**65**), was found nearly intact. The remaining material was found in fragmentary condition, although several complete vessels have subsequently been reconstructed.

Despite the limitations imposed by both the later disturbances of the area and the documentation available from excavation of the building, some patterns in the distribution of the bucchero pottery in the Lower Building do emerge. The bucchero was found concentrated in two major areas, one below Rectangle 7 and the other below Rectangle 5 (Fig. 5). Smaller quantities of bucchero were also discovered below Rectangles 6, 8, and 9 and the northwestern corner of the courtyard.[8] In addition, an analysis of the identifiable vessels reveals that within the two areas of major concentration there appears to be some typological division of the bucchero (Table 1).[9] While all the oinochoai, the alabastron, and most cups, jars, and lids were found in the area below Rectangle 7 and the northernmost meters of Rectangle 8, the majority of plates and bowls were found in the area below Rectangle 5. The published finds of imported pottery, including Ionic, Corinthian, and Laconian cups, and Etrusco-Corinthian plates, show a similar distribution, all having been found below Rectangles 6–8.[10] Notably, none of the lids, with one possible exception, belonged to the cups or jars, although the cups and lids were found together (**114**, a lid, may have belonged to **48**, a jar).

The excavators originally hypothesized that the pottery and precious materials found in the Lower Building, most of which were discovered widely and apparently randomly scattered

[7] **138**, discovered below Rectangle 9, represents the only fragment of bucchero found in the southern portion of the Lower Building.

[8] The quantities for Rectangles 6, 8, 9 and the courtyard are as follows: Rectangle 6, four fragments: **7**, **42**, **82**, **93**; Rectangle 8, two fragments: **45**, **117**; Rectangle 9, one fragment: **138**; Courtyard, three fragments: **73**, **131**, **132**.

[9] I have used the maximum possible number of each vessel type in calculating the distribution. Rim and appliqué fragments **80–89** are not included because it is uncertain whether they belonged to broad-rimmed plates or bowls. These fragments display the following distribution: Rectangle 5, two fragments (**80**, **83**); Rectangle 6, one fragment (**82**); Rectangle 6/7 Doorway, one fragment (**84**); Rectangle 7, six fragments (**81**, **85–89**).

[10] The quantities and find spots of the imported pottery are as follows: one Corinthian skyphos (Rectangle 8); five Ionic cups (three from Rectangle 7, two from Rectangles 7 and 8); eight Laconian cups (one from Rectangle 6, one from Rectangles 6/7 Doorway, one from Rectangles 6/7 Doorway and Rectangle 7, one from Rectangles 6 and 7, one from Rectangle 7, one from Rectangles 7 and 8, two from Rectangle 8); three Etrusco-Corinthian plates (two from Rectangle 7, one from Rectangles 7 and 8); one Etrusco-Corinthian aryballos (Rectangle 7). For publications of the imported pottery see the references in Table 2; for Murlo numbers see the section on Imported Pottery later in this chapter. Since the majority of the impasto pottery from the Lower Building remains unpublished, it is not possible to plot its distribution.

TABLE 1: DISTRIBUTION BY LOCATION OF IDENTIFIABLE BUCCHERO VESSELS AND VESSEL FRAGMENTS FOUND WITHIN THE LOWER BUILDING

Vessel Type	Rec.5	Rec.6	Rec.7	Rec.7/Rec.8	Rec.8	T.CTD
Oinochoai	—	—	4	—	—	—
Alabastron	—	—	1	—	—	—
Cups						
1) Kantharoi	—	1	15	—	—	—
2) Kyathoi	4	—	11	1	—	—
3) Cups	—	1	4	1	—	—
4) Chalices	1	—	1	—	1	—
Totals	5	2	31	2	1	—
Jars	—	—	1	1	—	—
Bowls						
1) Tripod	2	—	1	—	—	—
2) Footed	3	—	—	—	—	—
3) Phiale	—	—	1	—	—	—
4) Broad-Rimmed	12	—	1	—	—	—
5) Lug-Handled	8	—	1	—	—	—
Totals	25	—	4	—	—	—
Plates						
1) Broad-Rimmed	17	1	5	—	—	1
2) Miscellaneous	1	—	1	—	—	—
Totals	18	1	6	—	—	1
Lids	3	—	14	—	1	1

among the pithoi set into the floor and adjacent area below Rectangles 5–8, had fallen from living and banquet rooms located in an upper storey (*Case e palazzi*:69; Nielsen and Phillips 1974:270; Phillips 1993:56). It should be noted, however, that there is no architectural evidence to support this theory. It is equally possible that the building consisted of only a single storey and that the pottery and other materials were being stored, perhaps on shelves, which collapsed onto the pithoi below during the destruction of the building. Either way, the recoverable distribution pattern would suggest that the bucchero was grouped together by type—as perhaps was the imported pottery—probably in storage, and was not in use when the building was destroyed.

CONTENTS

In order to understand more clearly the context of the bucchero pottery recovered from the Lower Building, this section presents an overview of the published materials by material type. A great deal of material, however, still remains unpublished. Therefore, this catalogue is not complete. The majority of the fine impasto pottery, all of the glass, and many of the ivory, bone, and antler objects, the amber, and some of the metal objects from the building still await publication.

METAL ARTIFACTS

More than fifty metal objects were recovered during excavation of the Lower Building.[11]

[11] Many of the metal finds from Poggio Civitate, including the majority recovered from the Lower Building, have been studied by Warden (1985). For a selection of the metal objects recovered from the Lower Building, see Warden, in *Case e palazzi*:88–92, nos. 134–185 and references cited.

As Warden has noted, very few of the objects from the deposit are functional in nature; they are primarily luxury or decorative items.[12] The objects consist of personal ornaments, decorative objects, implements of common use, utensils, hardware, metal vessels and metal-vessel attachments, and chariot gear. Warden and others have suggested that the majority of the metallic objects found at the site were locally produced.[13]

The objects categorized as being for personal adornment include gold, silver, and bronze fibulae, a single gold-and-silver jewelry fragment, a single silver and eight gold jewelry fragments, a bronze bulla, two bronze pendants, two bronze pins, and two small bronze rings.[14] All of the gold jewelry fragments were discovered below Rectangle 8. De Puma, in a study of a selection of this material, has reconstructed six of the gold fragments as a single piece of gold jewelry.[15] He has suggested that the six fragments may have originally formed part of a fibula clasp or an articulated bracelet. The gold-and-silver fragment is more difficult to reconstruct (Murlo no. 71-721; Nielsen and Phillips 1974:273–75, ill. 11, pl. 58, fig. 18; De Puma 1981:85-86, no. 6, fig. 7; pl. 26, 1 and 2). A gold tenia with rosettes from the Quinto Fiorentino tholos tomb offers the closest parallel for this piece. The remaining gold fragments, which include a small, hollow tube with incised lines and a fragment of a gold tube or bead, are too fragmentary to reconstruct.[16] Finally, the silver consists of a small section of thin wire (Murlo 71-194; Warden 1985:59, no. 67, pl. 9a).

The tools consist of a curved iron blade (Murlo no. 71-523; Warden 1985:90, no. 50, pl. 21c), perhaps representing a sickle, and an iron adze (Murlo no. 70-197; Warden et al. 1982:33, figs. 13a–c; Warden 1985:90–92, no. 151, pl. 21a, b, fig. 26). The hardware includes large and small nails, and rivets. While most of the nails are manufactured solely of either bronze or iron,[17] there is a group of small nails with bronze shafts and silver foil-covered heads,[18] at least a single example with a bronze shaft and gold foil-covered head (Phillips 1973a:322, pl. 56, fig. 9; *Case e palazzi*:91, no. 169), and several large nails with iron shafts and bronze heads.[19] By contrast, the

[12] This disparity between luxury and functional objects applies not only to the Lower Building, but also to the metal assemblage of the site as a whole; see Warden 1985:147.

[13] Warden et al. 1982:26–35; Warden 1985:147–53; Warden et al. 1991:151–56; Warden 1993:41–51; Nielsen 1993:29–40; Nielsen 1995:19–26; Nielsen 1998:103–104; Nijboer 1998:277–80.

[14] Fibulae: Murlo nos. 71-133, 71-274, 71-618, 71-669, 71-705, and 75-55; De Puma 1981:86–87, nos. 7, 8, fig. 8, pl. 26, 3, 4; Warden 1985:30–32, nos. 24, 27–29, 39, 49, 50, pls. 5a, b; Warden, in *Case e palazzi*:89, nos. 134, 137; De Puma, in *Case e palazzi*:93, nos. 186, 187; De Puma, in *Cento preziosi*:65, 135, nos. 90, 91. Gold-and-silver jewelry fragment: Murlo no. 71-721; Nielsen and Phillips 1974:273–75, ill. 11, pl. 58, fig. 18; De Puma 1981:85–86, fig. 7, pl. 21:1, 2; De Puma, in *Cento preziosi*:65, 134-35, no. 88. One silver and eight gold jewelry fragments: Murlo nos. 71-194, 71-317, 71-400, 71-721 *bis*, 71-721 *ter*, 71-722, 71-723, 71-724, and 72-2; Nielsen and Phillips 1974:273–75, ill. 11, pl. 58, fig. 18; De Puma 1981:78–85, nos. 1–5, figs. 1–3, pls. 22:1–4, 23:1–4; Warden 1985:59, nos. 67–69, pl. 9a, b; De Puma, in *Case e palazzi*:93, nos. 188–190a–f; De Puma, in *Cento preziosi*:65, 133-35, nos. 87a–f, 89. Bronze bulla: Murlo no. 71-120; Warden et al. 1982:34, fig. 16; Warden 1985:69, no. 11; Warden 1985:51, no. 58, pl. 7d. Two bronze pendants: Murlo nos. 75-53, 75-80; Warden 1985:53, no. 60, pl. 8c, d; 55, no. 66; Warden, in *Case e palazzi*:89, no. 141. Two bronze pins: Murlo nos. 71-645 and 71-679; Warden 1985:64–65, nos. 81, 82, pl. 9c. A third bronze pin (Murlo no. 72-185), probably also associated with the Lower Building, was recovered from the south wall of Rectangle 7 of the Upper Building; see Warden 1985:67, no. 93, pl. 10d. Two bronze rings: Murlo nos. 75-62, 75-100; Warden 1985:76, nos. 114, 115, pl. 13b, c. Warden speculated that these small rings may have been utilized as buckles or as permanent fasteners for two or more straps.

[15] Murlo nos. 71-721 *bis*, 71-721 *ter*, 71-722, 71-723, 71-724, 71-400; De Puma 1981:78–89; De Puma, in *Cento preziosi*:65, 133-34, no. 87a–f; De Puma, in *Case e palazzi*:93, no. 190a–f.

[16] Murlo 72-2 and 71-317; Warden 1985:59, no. 68; De Puma, in *Cento preziosi*:65, 135, no. 89; De Puma, in *Case e palazzi*:93, no. 189.

[17] Because of their large quantity, only a selection of the nails from the Lower Building have been published; see Warden 1985:94–105; Warden, in *Case e palazzi*:90–92.

[18] Warden (1985:101–2) notes that 36 of these nails were recovered from a small area within Rectangle 8 of the Lower Building. For examples of these nails see Warden 1985:100–101, nos. 179–182, pls. 23g, h, 24a; also Warden, in *Case e palazzi*:91, nos. 158–169.

[19] For examples, see Warden 1985:99, no. 126, pl. 23d; Warden, in *Case e palazzi*:92, nos. 171–175.

rivets were manufactured entirely from bronze (Warden 1985:106). Warden has suggested that these nails and rivets would have been primarily decorative in function (1985:104–5; *Case e palazzi*:89). For example, the small nails or tacks could have been used to affix ivory inlays and appliqués to furniture or to fasten metal attachments. The large nails, too, may have been used in the construction of furniture or on wooden doors, and the rivets may have decorated a large metal vase (Warden 1985:104).

A small bronze figural group, portraying two wrestlers and an umpire, constitutes one of the more impressive metal finds from the Lower Building.[20] This group most likely was attached to an elaborate bronze vessel. Two bronze handles for vessels were also discovered.[21] The only recovered vessels are two large bronze cauldrons and two bronze vessel body fragments.[22]

The remaining metal finds consist of objects of common use. They include a number of small bronze "files," which may have functioned either as cosmetic implements or tools, bronze needles, bronze fishhooks, a bronze blade, an iron handle revetted with bone, perhaps representing a knife handle, and at least two bronze arrowheads.[23] Finally, a bronze shaft decorated with a fragmentary bull protome constitutes one of the more interesting metal finds from the Lower Building.[24] Warden has demonstrated that this piece, along with a fragment of an iron wheel (Murlo no. 71-99; Warden 1985:120, no. 237), belonged to a cart or chariot. Other metal fragments recovered from the Lower Building include an iron rod, and several bronze strips and pieces of bronze sheeting.[25]

IVORY, ANTLER, AND BONE OBJECTS

The numerous carved objects in ivory, antler, and bone form the most spectacular, and certainly the most well known, group of artifacts recovered during the excavation of the Lower Building.[26] More than 130 ivory, antler, and bone pieces were discovered in the destruction debris associated with the building (Nielsen 1984a:

[20] Murlo nos. 71-105 and 71-106. One of the wrestlers is preserved only by his lower wrist. For a discussion of these pieces, see Phillips 1973b:177–82, figs. 1–15; Warden 1982:233–38, pls. 33–35; Warden 1985:89, pls. 18 and 19. See also Warden, in *Case e palazzi*:90, nos. 145, 146; Phillips 1993:52–53, figs. 57–59.

[21] Murlo nos. 71-270 and 71-273. Warden, in *Case e palazzi*:90, no. 144; Warden 1985:88, nos. 146, 147, pl. 17a, e, f. Warden speculates that one of the handles may have belonged to a bucket or pail, and the other to a large open vessel, possibly a cauldron.

[22] Cauldrons: both, found on the floor of the Lower Building below Rectangle 7, are unpublished; see Warden 1985:86. Bronze vessel fragments: Murlo nos. 71-446 and 71-843; Warden 1985:86, nos. 139, 140. Warden notes that a large amount of sheet metal, some of which may have belonged to vessels, has been excavated from both 7th- and 6th-century contexts at the site.

[23] Bronze tools: Murlo nos. 70-428, 71-119, and 71-127; Warden 1985:81, no. 129, pl. 16a; 83, nos. 136, 137, pls. 15g, 16e; Nielsen and Phillips 1986:9–10, fig. 3d–f. Nielsen has suggested that these implements were used in the production of the carved ivory, antler, and bone objects found at the site; see Nielsen 1984b:399, note 6 and Nielsen 1995:21, note 23. Bronze needles: Murlo nos. 71-109 and 71-131; Warden 1985:79–80, nos. 123, 124, pl. 15c. Bronze fishhooks: Murlo nos. 71-129 and 71-130; Nielsen and Phillips 1975:360–61, pl. 63, figs. 7, 8; Warden 1985:111–12, nos. 210, 211, pl. 26e–f, figs. 30, 31; Warden, in *Case e palazzi*:92, nos. 181, 182. Bronze blade: Murlo no. 71-90; Warden 1985:108, no. 203. Iron handle with bone revetment: Murlo no. 71-137; Warden 1985:109, no. 206. Bronze arrowheads: Murlo nos. 72-262 and 77-231; Warden 1985:110, no. 209, pl. 26c; Warden, in *Case e palazzi*:92, nos. 183, 184.

[24] Murlo no.71-706; Warden et al. 1982:32, fig. 11; Warden 1985:120–22, no. 238, pl. 30a–d, fig. 38; Warden, in *Case e palazzi*:92, no. 185.

[25] Iron rod: Murlo no. 71-452; Warden 1985:93, no. 158, pl. 22c. Bronze strips: Murlo nos. 71-276 and 72-336; Warden 1985:117, nos. 225, 226. Bronze sheeting: Warden 1985:118-119, nos. 228–230, 235, pl. 28d. Three additional metal fragments of uncertain function recovered from the Lower Building also were published by Warden (1985:128–29, nos. 252, 256, 257, pls. 30e, 31c, and 32b, c).

[26] A group of 111 of the antler, ivory, and bone objects recovered from the destruction debris of the Lower Building were studied by Erik Nielsen for his Bryn Mawr dissertation ("The Murlo Ivories," Bryn Mawr, 1974). I thank him for allowing me to consult his dissertation during the course of the present study. For other discussions of the ivory, antler, and bone objects recovered from the site, see Nielsen 1984b:397–99; Nielsen 1984a: 333–48; Nielsen, in *Case e palazzi*:94–98; Nielsen 1995:19–26; Nielsen, in *Cento preziosi*:61-64, 126-33, nos. 75–86; Phillips 1993:75–78.

335–37). Nielsen, in his study of this material, has demonstrated that the majority of the antler, ivory, and bone objects recovered from Poggio Civitate were locally produced.[27]

The sheer quantity of antler, ivory, and bone objects recovered from the Lower Building precludes a detailed discussion of this material here. In the course of the conflagration that destroyed the Lower Building, many of the ivory, antler, and bone objects were burned and badly fragmented. Fortunately, the majority of the objects could still be identified. Nielsen has separated the material into three general categories: furniture inlays, pyxides, and objects of personal ornamentation (Nielsen 1984a:337; Nielsen, in *Case e palazzi*:94).

FINE IMPASTO

Most of the fine impasto pottery recovered from the Lower Building remains unpublished. The published material consists only of two oinochoai, a footed bowl, and a deep cup, or "skyphos," with vertical handles (Murlo nos. 71-320, 71-232, 71-321, and 71-215; *Case e palazzi*: 86–88, nos. 120, 126, 127, 130).

COARSE IMPASTO UTILITARIAN POTTERY

A large number of coarse impasto utilitarian vessels were recovered from the Lower Building. A total of 23 of these vessels has been published.[28] Bouloumié (*Case e palazzi*:138) has divided this material into two categories: tableware, and cooking and serving/storage vessels.

Nine coarse impasto tableware vessels were recovered from the Lower Building. They include: four small deep bowls with either a disk or ring foot, a shallow carinated bowl with a conical foot, two rounded deep bowls with conical feet, a one-handled cup with a flat base, and a two-handled cup with a flat base.[29] The cooking and serving/storage vessels consist of: ten ollas of various sizes, two large pithoi, and two cooking lids.[30]

IMPORTED POTTERY

The imported Greek and Etrusco-Corinthian pottery recovered from the Lower Building will be reviewed in greater detail below in the discussion of chronology. This material is presented here for the sake of completeness. The imported Greek pottery consists of a single Early Corinthian skyphos (Murlo no. 71-793; Phillips 1989a:30–31, fig. 2), five Ionic bowl fragments,[31] and eight Laconian II bowl fragments (Murlo nos. 70-236, 71-767–71-769, 72-408, 74-30, 74-31, and 74-33; Phillips 1989a:32 and notes 25–28). Three Etrusco-Corinthian plate fragments (Murlo nos. 71-726 and 71-727 [two joining fragments], 71-777, and 71-778; *Case e palazzi*:78–79, nos. 54–56) and a single Etrusco-Corinthian aryballos (Murlo no. 71-779; *Case e palazzi*:79, no. 57, pl. 3-57) constitute the Etruscan imports.

[27] In his dissertation, Nielsen initially speculated that many of the ivory, antler, and bone objects found at the site were manufactured locally (see Nielsen 1974). Conclusive evidence appeared later when numerous fragments of both unworked and partially worked pieces of ivory, antler, and bone objects were recovered from various locations on the site (Nielsen 1984a:333–48; Nielsen 1993:30; Nielsen 1994a:319; Nielsen 1995:19–26; Nielsen 1996:380; Nielsen 1998:103–104; Nijboer 1998:280).

[28] For a discussion of this material, see B. Bouloumié in *Case e palazzi*:138–47. The coarse impasto from the Lower Building was not included in the study of this ware published by A. Bouloumié-Marique (1978); her study was limited to material associated with the Archaic occupation of the site.

[29] Deep bowl with disk foot: Murlo no. 71-419; *Case e palazzi*:139–40, no. 536; Bouloumié Form B1. Deep bowl with ring foot: Murlo nos. 70-326, 71-146, 71-395; *Case e palazzi*:139–40, nos. 538–540; Bouloumié Form B2. Shallow carinated bowl with conical foot: Murlo no. 71-80; *Case e palazzi*:140, no. 547; Bouloumié Form C2. Rounded deep bowls with conical feet: Murlo nos. 71-185 and 71-212; *Case e palazzi*:140, nos. 554 and 555; Bouloumié Form E1; see also Bouloumié-Marique 1978: 62, note 10. One-handled cup: Murlo no. 71-125; *Case e palazzi*:142, no. 590. Two-handled cup: Murlo no. 71-148; *Case e palazzi*:142, no. 591.

[30] Ollas: Murlo nos. 70-337, 70-419, 71-79, 71-87, 71-216, 71-317, 71-322, 71-396, 71-887, 73-128; *Case e palazzi*:143-46, 148, nos. 600–602, 607, 623, 625, 626, 629, 635, and 665. Bouloumié Forms L, M2, and M_b. Pithoi: Murlo nos. 70-345, 70-346; *Case e palazzi*:146, nos. 641, 642. Cooking lids: Murlo nos. 71-397, 71-398; Bouloumié 1978:126, nos. 1180, 1183, pl. 4; *Case e palazzi*:147, no. 653.

[31] Murlo nos. 71-742–71-745 and 71-748; Phillips 1989a:31–32 and references cited. Phillips notes that the total number of Ionic bowls in the Lower Building could have been 20 or more.

TABLE 2: IMPORTED DATABLE POTTERY ASSOCIATED WITH THE DESTRUCTION OF THE LOWER BUILDING (ADAPTED FROM RYSTEDT 1983)

Ceramic Types and Quantities	Date	References
Ionic Bowl (5)	620–600 B.C.	Nielsen and Phillips 1974:268–70, pl. 55, figs. 6, 7, pl. 56, figs. 4, 5; Phillips 1989a:31–32, figs. 11, 12; *Case e palazzi*:75-76, nos. 31–35, pls.3-31, 3-34; Phillips 1989b:101, note 4.
Corinthian Skyphos (1)	Early or (Early) Middle Corinthian, ca. 600 B.C.	Nielsen and Phillips 1977a:98–99, ill. 17, figs. 35–37; Phillips 1989a:29–30, fig. 2; *Case e palazzi*:75-76, no. 30, pl. 3-30.
Laconian Cup (8)	Laconian II, 620–580 B.C.	Phillips 1971:261, pl. 62, fig. 40; Nielsen and Phillips 1977a:97–98, figs. 31–34; Phillips 1989a:32, figs. 21–26; *Case e palazzi*:76–77, nos. 36–43, pls. 3-36, 3-40.
Etrusco-Corinthian Plate (3)	600-580 B.C.[a]	Phillips 1973a:322–24, pl. 57, figs. 10, 11; Nielsen and Phillips 1974:271, pl. 56, figs. 8, 9; *Case e palazzi*:78–79, nos. 54–56; pl. 3-54.
Etrusco-Corinthian Aryballos (1)	600–?[b]	*Case e palazzi*:79, no. 57, pl. 3–57.

[a] J. G. Szilágyi originally attributed these plates to the American Academy Painter and dated them to 590–570 B.C.; see Nielsen and Phillips 1974:271, pl. 56, figs. 8, 9. He subsequently reanalyzed this identification and attributed all the works of the American Academy Painter to the Pescia Romana Painter. In his most recent study of this material, Szilágyi redated the black-figure works of the Pescia Romana Painter, which include the three plates from the Lower Building, to 600–580 B.C., principally on the basis of the date given by the excavators for the destruction of the Lower Building (see Szilágyi 1992:212; also *Case e palazzi*:78–79; for a discussion of the dating of the Lower Building, see the chronology section in Chapter 5).

[b] Etrusco-Corinthian globular aryballoi of this type imitate Corinthian aryballoi of Type B2. Unfortunately, the examples with simple linear decoration, as in the present case, are not easily datable. Their production begins at the start of the 6th century B.C. and continues well into the century (see Szilágyi 1981:44–45, pl. 12.8; Mangani 1986:40, pl. 50.8; Cimino 1986:26–27; Cherici 1988:120–21, cat. no. 109). In response to a letter I sent to Professor Szilágyi, he replied: "I think this type was made in more than one center of manufacture in South Etruria; actually, I cannot propose a date more precise than the first half, or, rather, first quarter, of the sixth century." I thank Professor Szilágyi for his helpful comments.

CHRONOLOGY

The numerous finds of both imported Greek and Etrusco-Corinthian ceramics found in the burned stratum provide a secure *terminus ante quem* for the destruction of the Lower Building (Table 2).[32] These examples, which include an Early Corinthian skyphos, several Ionic bowls, and

[32] For a discussion and presentation of this material, including previous bibliography, see *Case e palazzi*:74–79; Phillips 1989a:29–39.

Laconian II cup fragments, as well as an Etrusco-Corinthian globular aryballos and several plates, indicate 620 and 580 as the upper and lower limits respectively.[33] Within this range the excavators have tentatively proposed a median date of 600 B.C. for the destruction of the building.[34]

The dates of the construction and subsequent life of the building are less secure. Originally the excavators proposed a *terminus post quem* of 650 B.C., thereby placing the floruit of the Lower Building between 650 and 600 B.C.[35] They based this date on the stylistic analysis of the carved bone and antler objects found within the building, a "canopic"-type head antefix found on the site, and the building's architectural terracottas. While more recent studies of the excavated material have generally agreed with the date proposed by the excavators for the destruction of the building, these same studies have not substantiated their suggested *terminus post quem* of 650 B.C. for the construction. In a study of the ivory and bone objects, Nielsen has demonstrated that several of these pieces find close parallels with material from the Montagnola tomb at Quinto Fiorentino, which has been dated to the last quarter of the seventh century;[36] De Puma has presented parallels between two pieces of gold jewelry from the Lower Building and gold jewelry from this same tomb (De Puma 1981:82, 86); and more recently, Mangani has noted the close similarity between several pieces from the Lower Building and a number of carved ivories recovered from a chamber tomb at Poggione, in the area of Castelnuovo Berardenga, dated to the beginning of the sixth century.[37] In addition, the "canopic" antefix head is now more closely associated with the Southeast Building (dated by Nielsen to 630 B.C.) since a mold for this type was found on the floor of this structure.[38] Rystedt, in her study of the akroteria from the Lower Building, has dated her earliest group to the period 625–600 B.C. on the basis of both style and archaeological context (Rystedt 1983:151–53). Finally, as will be seen, the examination of the bucchero pottery that can be securely associated with the building indicates that the bucchero generally falls within the range of the other chronologically diagnostic materials recovered from the deposit, as well as the date for the destruction of the building originally proposed by the excavators; while a few vessels in the deposit may date as early as the third quarter of the seventh century, the date for the majority of the bucchero lies within the last quarter of the seventh and first quarter of the sixth centuries.

[33] Phillips, in *Case e palazzi*:75; Nielsen and Phillips 1977a:99; Nielsen and Phillips 1977b:465; see also Rystedt 1983:151.

[34] Nielsen and Phillips 1977a:100; Phillips 1980:204. A date of 600 B.C. for the destruction of the Lower Building has also tentatively been accepted by Rystedt (1983:151).

[35] Nielsen and Phillips 1977a:99; Nielsen and Phillips 1977b; Phillips 1980:202–6; Phillips 1993:51, 54.

[36] Nielsen has also suggested that some of the ivory and bone objects found in the Lower Building and the Montagnola tumulus were made by the same workshop, which was perhaps located at Poggio Civitate. He has also noted parallels between a number of lotus-chain plaques found in the Lower Building and others discovered in the tumulus burial of Monte Calvario in Castellina in Chianti. Unfortunately, this tumulus contained no datable material (see Nielsen 1984a:340–43). For a discussion of the dating of the Montagnola tumulus, see Caputo 1962:60 and Strøm 1971:197.

[37] The ivory and bone objects were found in Poggione Tomb B; see Mangani 1990:10, 13–14, fig. 5, 1 and 2.

[38] Nielsen 1987:114–16, fig. 84, and 118, no. 39. It should be noted that the "canopic" antefix head, which was studied by Winter and used by Phillips to date the Lower Building, was not found in that structure. Instead, it was discovered 30 meters to the southeast in Trench 6A, located in a burned layer which Phillips associated with the destruction of the Lower Building (see Winter 1977:18–19, note 6, 21–23, 32). For additional discussion of the dating of these "canopic"-style antefix heads, see Nielsen 1984c:48–49.

III

Catalogue

Introduction to the Catalogue

In general, the material in the catalogue is presented according to vessel type. A typological discussion of each vessel shape precedes the catalogue entries for each identified vessel type. Within each type the examples are listed according to their current state of preservation. Fourteen distinct vessel shapes, as well as miscellaneous unidentifiable small sherds, some of them inscribed, were distinguished in the deposit:

I. Oinochoai
II. Alabastron
IIIa. Kantharoi
IIIb. Kantharoi Handle Fragments
IVa. Kyathoi
IVb. Kyathoi Handle Fragments
V. Cups
VI. Chalices
VII. Phiale
VIII. Jars
IX. Tripod Bowls
X. Footed Bowls
XI. Broad-Rimmed Shallow Bowls and Plates
XII. Lug Handled Bowls
XIII. Miscellaneous Plates
XIVa. Lids
XIVb. Miscellaneous Lid Finial Fragments
XV. Miscellaneous Fragments
XVI. Inscribed Fragments

The fourteen shapes have been divided into forty-five types or subtypes. The vessel shape-names utilized in the catalogue are based upon current and past scholarly convention, which initially had somewhat arbitrarily assigned Greek names to Etruscan shapes.[1] In the discussion of vessel typology, parallels for the shapes were sought first among the bucchero of northern Etruria before turning to that of the south. If no parallel was found for a shape in bucchero, the possibility of tracing its origin and development in impasto or metal was investigated.

Each entry is composed of twelve possible fields in addition to the catalogue number and title. The number preceding the title is the catalogue number established for this study and utilized to refer to the piece throughout the text. Blank fields indicate that the information was not applicable to the example. To avoid undue repetition, not all the field names appear in the catalogue entries. The following is a brief explanation of the remaining fields:

Fig.: Number of the line drawing that is provided for each vessel type discussed (located with plates at back of book). These drawings represent reconstructions showing the complete shape and do not always depict the vessel's actual state of preservation. Whenever possible, fragmentary examples have been reconstructed on the basis of the comparanda. The profile is depicted on the right side of the illustration. The scale of each drawing is noted on the illustrations.

---

[1] For a discussion of the known Etruscan names of vessel shapes, see G. Colonna, *ArchCl* 25–26 (1973–1974):132–50.

PL.: Photographs are provided for most of the pieces in the catalogue. The scale of each photograph is noted on the plates.

MURLO NO.: Poggio Civitate excavation inventory number.

FI: Number assigned by the Soprintendenza Archeologico per la Toscana if the piece has been consigned to the Italian state. Not all vessels from the Lower Building possess a Florence inventory number.

GRID: Grid designation for the piece as explained in Chapter 2 and illustrated in Figure 4. The grid number is preceded by an abbreviated trench designation, which indicates the location of the vessel in relation to the units of the Upper Building above. The following two abbreviations are used in the catalogue:

Rec. = Tesoro Rectangle

Tes. Ctd. = Tesoro Courtyard

STRATUM: Stratum/location in which the piece was found as determined by the excavation daybook.[2] The use of an asterisk indicates that the association of the vessel with the deposit is insecure. The strata are identified by the following numerical designations:[3]

1. In the mud-brick wall of the Lower Building.
2. In the burn stratum within the Lower Building.
3. Above the burn stratum and in the pavement of the Upper Building.[4]
4. In the stone foundation wall of the Upper Building.
5. Outside the Lower Building.

*I/O = Grid extends inside and outside Lower Building or stratum unknown.

I/O = Pieces joining inside and outside Lower Building.

DIMENSIONS: Major measurements of the piece given to the nearest thousandth of a meter.

CONDITION: State of preservation of the vessel.

DESCRIPTION: Thorough description of the vessel.

BIBLIOGRAPHY: All previous primary bibliography on the vessel.

OBSERVATIONS/COMPARANDA: Any important observations about the vessel, its technique of manufacture, or possible reconstruction are presented first, followed by a list of comparanda. Comparanda are listed as being either of the same or a similar type. A reference is provided for each published item of comparanda. Each reference includes a plate or an illustration number and, whenever possible, the provenience of the piece. If an item is unpublished, then its museum inventory number is provided. Any relevant comparanda from the site of Poggio Civitate are presented first.

ORNAMENT TYPE(S): If a vessel displays decoration, the appropriate ornament number(s) is (are) listed (See also Chapter 4.)

CATALOGUE

I. OINOCHOAI (**1–4**)

Two types of oinochoai are represented in the Lower Building.

TYPE 1: **1–3**.

This type of oinochoe is represented by a minimum of two and a maximum of three

[2] A detailed discussion of the stratigraphy of the Lower Building is presented above in Chapter 2.

[3] The appearance of two or more numbers separated by commas as a stratigraphic provenience indicates that a vessel was reconstructed from fragments originating from each numbered provenience. However, the use of a "/" between two numbers indicates that the precise stratigraphic provenience of the vessel is uncertain and that it may have originated from either numbered location. These latter fragments of insecure provenience either were found within the grid locations encompassed by the Lower Building walls but were not assigned to a stratum, or they possess a stratum designation but were assigned to multiple grids that extend across an area both inside and outside the Lower Building.

[4] Those vessels or vessel fragments reconstructed from sherds recovered from the pavement of the Upper Building that joined fragments found in the burn stratum within the Lower Building can, for the most part, be securely associated with the Lower Building. However, while the vessels or vessel fragments composed of sherds found solely within the pavement of the rooms of the Upper Building directly above the Lower most likely also originated from the earlier structure, their association with the Lower Building cannot be established with complete certainty.

examples.[5] It was previously identified as belonging to Type A in the series of "Chiusine" oinochoai classified by Batignani.[6] The oinochoai of Batignani's Type A have been grouped together according to their similar shape, molded decoration, and clay type (Batignani 1965:296, 306). The Type A oinochoai have an ovoid body with a rounded shoulder, a tall conical neck, and a trefoil spout. These oinochoai have a fairly restricted distribution, with the majority of examples concentrated in Chiusi, Orvieto, Vulci, and their respective territories (Batignani 1965:313). Although Batignani (1965:316) originally linked their production to Chiusi, it has more recently been suggested, on the basis of increasing find frequency, that they were also made in Orvieto (Camporeale 1970:79–80), and, perhaps, Vulci (Pellegrini 1989:85).

A closer analysis reveals that the oinochoai from Poggio Civitate, while possessing a decorative scheme like that of the oinochoai of Type A, find no close parallels for their shape among the oinochoai of this group (cf. Batignani 1965:296–304, pl. LXVI). By contrast, the examples from Poggio Civitate have a more pyriform than ovoid body, with a more angular shoulder and a much shorter, conical neck. The Poggio Civitate oinochoai, therefore, might be better classified as variants rather than examples of Batignani's Type A group. The unique appearance of the Poggio Civitate oinochoai may be attributed to their early date in the series,[7] and, as a result, their closer proximity to a metal prototype.

The oinochoai of Batignani's Type A have been linked to metal prototypes on the basis of their form and decoration, most specifically for the use of ridges, the molded decoration on the shoulder, and the rotelle (Batignani 1965:309; Camporeale 1970:78). It should be noted, however, that the bucchero oinochoai of Batignani's Type A, including the examples from Poggio Civitate, bear little resemblance to the metal examples with which they are most commonly compared (Camporeale 1970:1978 and note 2). As an alternative prototype, I would suggest the group of so-called Rhodian oinochoai.[8] These oinochoai were exported during the latter half of the seventh century to the major coastal centers of Etruria as well as to other parts of Italy, where they were later imitated. Not only do the Rhodian oinochoai bear a much closer resemblance to the bucchero type, especially including the examples from Poggio Civitate, but they also pose no chronological difficulties, since the production of the earliest Greek examples in this series is dated to the last third of the seventh century. In addition, the Rhodian oinochoai have already been identified as providing the inspiration for some Etruscan bucchero oinochoai, but the possibility of their relationship to the oinochoai classified by Batignani has not yet been considered.

Batignani originally assigned the appearance of her Type A oinochoai to the first half of the sixth century on the basis of their style (Batignani 1965:314–16). Camporeale, in a subsequent review of the evidence (1970:78), placed the beginning of their production specifically in the second quarter of the sixth century following the discovery in Vulci of several Type A oinochoai in tombs of that date. More recently, however, two Type A oinochoai were found in a tomb dated to the first decades

---

[5] **1** and **2** represent the same type of oinochoe, although **2** is slightly smaller. The handle **3** may belong to a third oinochoe or, alternatively, may form the lower portion of the handle of **2**.

[6] Batignani 1965:296–304. The attribution of the Poggio Civitate oinochoe (**1**) to the Batignani series was first made by Donati; see Donati and Michelucci 1981:57, no. 101; see also Pellegrini 1989:85, note 27; Rizzo 1990:142, no. 12.

[7] For a discussion of the chronology of the bucchero oinochoai, see Batignani 1965:316; Camporeale 1970:78 and note 4. The oinochoai from the Lower Building are among the earliest known examples of their type.

[8] For a discussion of the "Rhodian" oinochoai, including previous bibliography, see B. Shefton *Die "rhodischen" Bronzekannen* (Mainz, 1979), and especially pls. 6 and 8, and the review by G. Camporeale, in *ArchCl* 33 (1981):400–405. For a brief discussion of the influence of the "Rhodian" oinochoai on both bucchero and Etrusco-Corinthian pottery production, see Martelli 1978:169–70 and note 60; see also Gran-Aymerich 1995:54–55 and note 56.

of the sixth century at Chianciano, placing their chronology slightly earlier.[9]

1. Molded Oinochoe Fragment
Fig. 9; Pl. 1
MURLO NO.: 71-825
FI: 112482
GRID: Rec.7, B/4, E-F/2
STRATUM: 2
Max. Pres. Ht. 0.218; Diam. of body 0.175; Max. Pres. W. of mouth 0.90; Th. of wall 0.003; Diam. of rotella 0.038; Ht. of neck 0.034 m.

Mended from numerous pieces. Broken irregularly approximately at midbody. Missing entire lower section, large portions of upper section up to neck, lower half of handle, and much of rim. Missing portions of upper section of body, including petals, have been restored in plaster. Worn, but portions original shiny, burnished surface remain. Shiny black with brown undertone.

Molded oinochoe with pyriform body, conical neck, trefoil spout, and strap handle. Transition between short, conical neck and flaring rim set off with single round molding. Vertical strap handle attached to rim and shoulder. Eighteen outpressed petals (12 remaining) adorn shoulder, their rounded lower edges outlined with grooves. Below petals are three grooves, and above, two parallel ridges. Three incised parallel grooves run around exterior of preserved portion of trefoil spout. Molded rotella on each side of handle where it attaches at rim (one preserved, one scar). On outer face of preserved rotella is stamped design consisting of 4 groups of 5 outward-facing petals separated by 4 larger inward-facing petals. Three sets of parallel dotted lines define flattened surface above handle between rotelle. On preserved portion of molded handle is upper portion of seated figure, facing left and holding either a spear or a staff. Below base of handle is a scroll. For a complete description of the figure, see **3**.

The oinochoe is wheel-made in two pieces. The top portion was pressed into a mold while it was thrown on the wheel to produce the petalled decoration. The handle was pressed in a mold and then added separately. The lip was handmodelled. The body has been burnished in horizontal strokes, while the neck and handle were burnished vertically.

The drawing of the handle represents a composite derived from a complete example found on the site (Murlo no. 73-317) (Pl. 2).

BIBLIOGRAPHY: Nielsen and Phillips 1975: 359–60, ills. 4–6, pl. 62, figs. 5, 6; *Case e palazzi*:87–88, no. 129, pl. 3-129.

COMPARANDA: No exact parallels exist for this oinochoe. Variant of Batignani Type A (Batignani 1965:296–304). For similar examples, see Donati and Michelucci 1981:57, no. 101; Camporeale 1970:77–81, nos. 52, 53, pl. XIIa, b, from Orvieto; *Chianciano*:120–21, nos. C9, C10, pl. 6, from Chianciano. Three additional unpublished oinochoe handles recovered to the north of the Upper Building in Trench 18 display the same molded figural design: Murlo nos. 73-317, 73-318, and 73-319.

ORNAMENT TYPES: 13, 22.

2. Molded Oinochoe Fragment
Pl. 2
MURLO NO.: 71-546
GRID: Rec.7, D/3
STRATUM: 2
Max. Pres. Ht. 0.151; Max. Pres. Diam. 0.145; Diam. of rotella 0.037 m.

Mended from 24 pieces. Broken on both sides, across body and handle. Missing three-quarters of body, one rotella, and most of handle. Worn and chipped. Surface is black with brown undertone.

Same as **1** above, except that preserved rotella is decorated with molded rosette composed of 27 narrow elongated petals with

[9] Both oinochoai were found in a single deposition chamber tomb, whose date was determined by the presence of an Ionic cup of Villard and Villet Type B2; see *Chianciano*:120–21, nos. C9, C10. Pellegrini has also recently proposed a date in the first quarter of the 6th century B.C. for one of two oinochoai of Type A found in a chamber tomb at Poggio Buco. This date, however, is based more on the style than the context of the vessel, since the tomb contained several depositions covering a chronological span of 70 years beginning in the early 6th century; see Pellegrini 1989:85–86. On the basis of the available evidence, it would appear, therefore, that the first oinochoai of this type were produced during the first quarter of the 6th century B.C.

rounded outer edges arranged in a circle around a central dot.

The two fragments depicted in the photograph of the vessel actually join. However, the join is tenuous and could not be maintained for the photograph.

UNPUBLISHED.
COMPARANDA: Same as **1** above.
ORNAMENT TYPE: 21.

3. Oinochoe Handle Fragment
Fig. 10; Pl. 2
MURLO NO.: 71-558
FI: 114562
GRID: Rec.7, E/4
STRATUM: 2
Max. Pres. Ht. 0.068; Th. at top 0.027; Th. at base 0.037; W. at base 0.011 m.

Mended from 2 pieces. Broken at both ends. Worn and scratched. Surface is black with brown undertone.

Lower half of thick strap handle. Elliptical in section with wide flaring base. Outer surface displays molded decoration in low relief. Badly worn decoration preserves profile lower body of human figure seated on chair and facing left. Left arm of figure is bent at elbow and rests on his thigh. Preserved portion of the chair has straight back, square seat, and low armrest. Narrow rectangular legs of chair terminate in cones which may represent either equine hooves or feline paws. Beneath chair, griffin in left profile sits on its haunches, front legs straight and canted forward. Griffin displays rounded head with erect ears, prominent beak, and pommel on its crown. A molded scroll is attached to base of handle. Inner face of handle is smooth.

UNPUBLISHED.
COMPARANDA: This handle almost certainly originally belonged to an oinochoe of the same type as **1** and **2** above. Decoration same as **1** above.
ORNAMENT TYPE: 13.

TYPE 2: **4.**

This fragment represents a second type of oinochoe. Unfortunately, not enough of the vessel is preserved to permit secure identification of its complete shape. As a result, it must remain unclassified.

4. Fragmentary Oinochoe (3 fragments)
Fig. 10; Pl. 3
MURLO NO.: 71-821
FI: 114563
GRID: Rec.7, D/3
STRATUM: 2
Fragment A: Max. Pres. Ht. 0.099; Max. Pres. Diam. 0.078; Th. 0.004–0.006; Fragment B: Max. Pres. Ht. 0.064; Max. Pres. Diam. 0.148; Fragment C: Max. Pres. Ht. 0.072; Max. Pres. Diam. 0.107 m.

Three nonjoining fragments broken on all sides. Fragment A is mended from three pieces. Fragment B is mended from seven pieces. Fragment C is mended from five pieces. Surface worn, chipped, and burned. Missing spout, most of neck, and two-thirds of body. Mottled orange-brown in color. Biscuit is black.

Three fragments preserve portion of curving shoulder, upper body, and neck of an oinochoe. Two closely spaced, horizontal grooves appear near base of neck. A narrow rounded ridge defines junction between shoulder and neck below. Two additional pairs of closely spaced, horizontal grooves adorn lower portion of shoulder and body. Portions of two crudely incised feline(?) heads preserved on shoulder, above upper pair of grooves. Nearly identical, each head is composed of two concentric oval lines. Head on right is almost complete, missing only tip of right ear; that on left is broken along left edge of face. Each head displays a pair of pointed triangular ears, between which appear five individually incised, vertical tufts of hair. Faces of creatures display large, tangent almond-shaped eyes and elongated oval mouths. Head on left also has short triangular nose composed of two converging diagonal lines. Traces of additional incised decoration of unidentifiable type also appear on other preserved portions of vessel shoulder.

UNPUBLISHED.
COMPARANDA: Not enough of the oinochoe is preserved to determine its complete shape.
ORNAMENT TYPE: 25.

II. ALABASTRON (5)

One type of alabastron was found, represented by a single example.[10] It displays a flat circular base, a pyriform body that tapers to a narrow neck, and a flaring rim. Thin, flat-sided, vertical loop handle attached to rim and neck.

Alabastra of similar shape are common in Etrusco-Corinthian pottery during the late Orientalizing and early Archaic periods.[11] The shape, which is ultimately of Near Eastern origin, is generally linked to a Cypriot prototype. The bucchero alabastron from Poggio Civitate, however, lacks the molded ring around the neck, which is the distinctive feature of the Etrusco-Corinthian examples.

In addition to the example from Poggio Civitate, the only other published Etrusco-Corinthian type bucchero alabastron was recovered from Grotta di Castro near Bolsena (*CVA Gotha* 1:28, pl. 15.3). Although closer in conception to the Etrusco-Corinthian prototype than the alabastron from Poggio Civitate, this vessel also represents a variant. It possesses a second molded ring at the top of the neck and a trefoil spout. This alabastron has been stylistically dated on the basis of its stamped and incised decoration to the second half of the seventh century B.C.

The Etrusco-Corinthian alabastra provide a more secure *terminus post quem* for the bucchero example from the Lower Building. The beginning of their production is generally placed at the end of the seventh century and they continue to be made throughout the first half of the sixth century.[12]

5. Alabastron
Fig. 10; Pl. 3
MURLO NO.: 71-171
FI: 112474
GRID: Rec.7, D/3
STRATUM: 2
Ht. 0.073; Diam. of base 0.033–0.035; Diam. of preserved portion of rim 0.013. Decoration: Diam. of stamps: bottom 0.008; top 0.006 m.

Almost complete. Missing approximately one-half of rim. Surface chipped and worn. Burned mottled orange-gray. Biscuit is gray-black.

Small alabastron with flat circular base and pyriform body tapering to narrow neck with flaring rim. Thin, flat-sided, vertical loop handle attached to rim and neck. Alabastron decorated with two bands of irregularly spaced, stamped asterisk rosettes, one at base and one at midpoint of vessel. Each rosette composed of series of 8 impressed triangles arranged in circle with apices turned inward. Rosettes in lower band slightly larger in size.

Surface was first burnished, after which the two rows of rosettes were added.

BIBLIOGRAPHY: Nielsen and Phillips 1986:6, fig. 3a; *Case e palazzi*:88, no. 131, pl. 3-131.

COMPARANDA: Shape: no parallels noted. Decoration: rosettes of the same type as those on the upper register appear on the bowl **64**.

ORNAMENT TYPES: 4b, 4c.

IIIA. KANTHAROI (6–21)

Three types of kantharoi can be identified in the Lower Building.[13] The maximum number of

[10] Although the fabric of the alabastron was originally published as buccheroid, a reanalysis has revealed it to be bucchero; see Nielsen and Phillips 1986:6.

[11] For a discussion of the Etrusco-Corinthian alabastron, see G. Colonna, *ArchCl* 13 (1961):14; *ER* 4.2:512; Szilágyi 1981:40–41; Mangani 1986:36; Szilágyi 1992:87, note 21; Cherici 1988:127–29. Cherici, alternatively, citing the alabastron from the Lower Building as well as a morphologically similar, flat-based inkwell from Cerveteri as examples, has suggested that the Etrusco-Corinthian alabastron may actually have been inspired by bucchero examples; see Cherici 1988:129 and note 13. However, given the paucity of known bucchero examples, this appears unlikely.

[12] For a discussion of the chronology of the Etrusco-Corinthian alabastron, see *ER* 3:200 and note 6; Cristofani 1971: 81–82, note 60; Cherici 1988:127–28; see also Camporeale 1970:78.

[13] The origin and development of the kantharos has been a matter of debate. Opinions varied as to whether it was developed from an imported metal or local Villanovan ceramic prototype. Gras, however, has convincingly demonstrated its local origin, see M. Gras, *Opus* 3 (1984):325–339. For additional discussions of the evidence, see Camporeale 1970:66, note 1; Cristofani 1969:57; De Puma 1986:44; Ramage 1970:27–28; Rasmussen 1979:102–104; Gran-Aymerich 1995:57–58 and notes 73–76.

kantharoi found is 16, and the minimum possible number is 12.[14]

TYPE 1: **6**.

The first type, represented by **6**, belongs to Rasmussen Type 3a (Rasmussen 1979:102–3; Ramage Type 5a; see Ramage 1970:28) and is distinguished by a low ring foot and a shallow bowl. Specimens may have either strap handles, like the present example, or cylindrical handles. In addition, kantharoi of this type usually display no decoration.

The majority of kantharoi of Rasmussen Type 3a are from the major coastal centers of southern Etruria, including Cerveteri, Tarquinia, and Veii (Rasmussen 1979:102). A few examples have also been found in Latium (*Cerveteri* 1986:100 and note 18). This type is rare in northern Etruria: the only other published examples (besides **6**), also come from Poggio Civitate.[15] The type first appeared in the latter part of the third quarter of the seventh century and continued into the last quarter of the seventh century (Rasmussen 1979:102–3).

6. Kantharos
Fig. 10; Pl. 3
MURLO NO.: 71-801
GRID: Rec.7, A/3
STRATUM: 2
Ht. 0.11; Ht. to rim 0.061; Diam. of rim 0.133 m.

Mended from 18 pieces. Missing a small portion of tondo, some of cup wall, most of one handle, and upper exterior portion of other handle. Worn and chipped. Dull gray-black surface.

Kantharos with low ring-base, shallow convex bowl, and flaring wall with plain lip. Most of one handle and base of other preserved. Handle attached to body at carination and lip. Cup wall set off from floor at interior by shallow groove. Shallow groove also appears on exterior at base of wall just above carination.

UNPUBLISHED.

COMPARANDA: Kantharos of Rasmussen Type 3a (Rasmussen 1979: 102–3, pl. 30). Two additional kantharoi of this shape were also found at Poggio Civitate in Trench 17 (Murlo nos. 71-213 and 71-17); see *Case e palazzi*:80, nos. 60–61, pl. 3-61; Nielsen and Phillips 1976:145, figs. 37a, 38. For other examples of the same shape found outside Poggio Civitate, see Cristofani 1969:34, nos. 25, 26, fig. 15, pl. 16.1, from Veii; Palm 1952:54, no. 3, pl. I, from Veii and 59, no. 17, pl. VIII, from Veii; Gierow 1966:287, fig. 86.1, from Castel Gandolfo; *Cerveteri* 1980:225, no. 70, from Cerveteri; *Cerveteri* 1986:58–59, no. 34, from Cerveteri, and 66–67, no. 19, from Cerveteri.

TYPE 2A–E: **7–16**

7–16 represent either examples or variants of the Rasmussen Type 3e kantharos (Rasmussen 1979:104–6, pls. 31, 32). The examples from the Lower building have been subdivided into five subtypes (2A–E) on the basis of slight differences in their shapes. Kantharoi of Type 3e have a conical foot with a narrow stem and strap handles. The type displays a great deal of variation in the height of the foot and overall size. Examples are commonly decorated with diamond or arched notches on the carination, although hooked notches or hatched incisions may also appear. In addition, two or three incised horizontal lines may occur below the rim.

Type 3e is by far the most popular kantharos type; it was widely exported throughout Italy and the western Mediterranean (Rasmussen 1979:104–6; Villard 1962:1625–35). Kantharoi of Type 3e have a broad chronological span. They first appeared in the last quarter of the seventh century and continued into the last quarter of

[14] The maximum number, 16, represents all the entries in the catalogue and assumes that each entry would have represented an individual piece. I have determined that **6–17** must all represent individual examples, since none of these pieces can join. In addition, the four handle fragments, **18–21**, could be counted as each belonging to a separate kantharos or, alternatively, they could be counted as forming two sets. However, since no stratum was recorded for these handles, their position within the Lower Building is not secure. By removing them from the total, the maximum number of kantharoi becomes 12.

[15] Two additional examples have been found at Poggio Civitate in Trench 17: Murlo nos. 71-213 and 71-71; see *Case e palazzi*:80, nos. 60, 61, pl. 3-61.

the sixth (Rasmussen 1979:106). Since there is such wide variation among the kantharoi of Type 3e, as the examples from Poggio Civitate attest, I have listed only the most appropriate comparanda for each subtype distinguished in the catalogue.

TYPE 2A: **7** AND **8**.

Although fragmentary, **7** and **8** are clearly recognizable in shape and decoration as examples of the Type 3e.[16] Both pieces are to be restored with conical feet and probably had a low bowl.

7. Kantharos Fragment
Fig. 11; Pl. 3
MURLO NO.: 70-286
GRID: Rec.6
STRATUM: 2
Max. Pres. Ht. 0.058; Max. Pres. Diam. of rim 0.042 m.

Single fragment. Broken on 3 sides. Worn and chipped. Dull gray-black surface.

Fragment preserves small portion of rim and bowl of kantharos. Cup has strongly carinated bowl with sloping floor and straight sloping wall. Carination decorated with vertical notches. Three horizontal grooves encircle rim below lip.

BIBLIOGRAPHY: Phillips 1971:261, note 30, pl. 62, fig. 41.

COMPARANDA: Kantharos of Rasmussen Type 3e (Rasmussen 1979:104–6, pls. 31, 32). For other examples, see Cristofani 1969:40–41, nos. 8, 9, fig. 18, pl. 18.3, 18.4, from Veii and 44, no. 5, fig. 21, pl. 21.2, from Veii; Riccioni and Falconi Amorelli 1968:57, nos. 58–63, from Vulci; Micozzi 1989:60–62, nos. 76–78, pls. XXII, XXIII; Falconi Amorelli 1983:146, 157–59, fig. 64, from Vulci; Rizzo 1990:146, nos. 2, 3, fig. 312, from Vulci and 157, nos. 10, 11, fig. 342 g, h, from Vulci; *SG* 1.6, 4, no. 2, fig. 4, from San Giovenale and 10, no. 15, fig. 11, from San Giovenale; *SG* 1.7, 5, no. 2, fig. 5, from San Giovenale and 6, no. 30, fig. 5, from San Giovenale; Falconi Amorelli and Fabricotti 1971:204–5, nos. 36–39, pl. XLIVb, 36–39, from Vulci; Bartoloni 1972:91, no. 56, fig. 42, pl. LIA, from Poggio Buco; De Puma 1986:44–45, nos.VC 29, 31, pl. 13a, from Vulci; Camporeale 1972b:pl. XXXVIIIa, from Tarquinia; Palm 1952:54, no. 5, pl. II and 57, no. 11, pl. IV, from Veii; Donati and Michelucci 1981:83, no. 204, pl. 48.

8. Kantharos Fragment
Fig. 15; Pl. 12
MURLO NO.: 71-817
GRID: Rec.7, A-B/3
STRATUM: 2
Max. Pres. Diam. 0.054; Max. Pres. Ht. 0.070 m.

Single fragment. Broken on two sides. Worn, scratched, and chipped. Fragment has highly burnished surface. Black in color with brown undertone.

Fragment preserves approximately one-quarter of wall and tondo of kantharos. Cup has deep convex bowl with sharply sloping floor and thin flaring wall. Small ledge at carination decorated with series of notches. Three parallel grooves encircle rim below lip.

UNPUBLISHED.
COMPARANDA: Same as **7** above.

TYPE 2B: **9** AND **10**.

9 is the largest of the kantharoi found in the Lower Building. It is distinguished by its flaring wall and sharply sloping bowl. Kantharoi of this type generally have a deep carinated bowl and low foot. Although fragmentary, **10** also appears to be of this same subtype. It has the same kind of thick tall wall as **9**, and both examples are of the same fabric. Of the comparanda listed for **9** and **10**, the examples from Vulci are particularly close in shape and fabric.

9. Kantharos Fragment
Fig. 11; Pl. 4
MURLO NO.: 71-786

[16] It is possible that the two kantharos fragments **7** and **8** could instead be kantharoi of Rasmussen Type 3b, but since neither fragment preserves its foot, it is not possible to tell. Type 3b is distinguished from Type 3e by the presence of a broader, heavier flaring foot. Type 3b kantharoi, however, are generally much larger than **7** or **8** and more elaborately decorated; see Rasmussen 1979:103.

GRID: Rec.7, A/2
STRATUM: 2
Max. Pres. Ht. 0.133; Ht. of handle 0.109; Diam. of rim 0.154 m.

Mended from 5 pieces. Broken irregularly across wall and tondo. Chipped and worn. Shiny black surface.

Fragment preserves approximately one-third of wall and portion of tondo of kantharos. One strap handle preserved. Cup has deep convex bowl and tall, thick, flaring wall with plain lip. Strap handle attached to the top of rim and carination. The wall set off from bowl on interior at point of carination by shallow groove. Three finely incised parallel lines encircle rim (interrupted by handle) below lip. Small horizontal ledge at carination is hatched.

The kantharos is probably to be restored with a low conical foot.

UNPUBLISHED.

COMPARANDA: Kantharos of Rasmussen Type 3e (Rasmussen 1979:104–6, pls. 31, 32, esp. no. 169). For other examples, see *Vulci*:67, 70, nos. 42–51, fig. 24 and 14, 17, nos. 33–36, fig. 4, from Vulci; Rizzo 1990:108, nos. 14–19, fig. 207, from Vulci; Guzzo 1969:296, no. 29, pl. LXIII, from Cetona; Monaci 1965:438, no. 143, fig. 5d, from Pienza; Donati 1989:119, no. 17, fig. 42, pl. XL, from Saturnia; Palm 1952:55, Picazzano tomb XV, no. 10, pl. II and 57, Picazzano tomb XVII, no. 13, pl. IV, from Veii; Vulci, Museo Archeologico, inv. nos. 64253, 64156, 90128, 90113.

10. Kantharos Fragment
Pl. 4
MURLO NO.: 71-954
GRID: Rec.7Ext., X-Y/2
STRATUM: 2
Max. Pres. Ht. 0.096; Max. Pres. Diam. 0.085 m.

Mended from 4 fragments. Broken irregularly across both sides of handle. Missing foot, tondo, one handle, three-quarters of wall, and base of preserved handle. Chipped and worn. Shiny black surface.

Fragment preserves small portion of wall and upper portion of kantharos handle. Rim decorated with series of three parallel incised lines.

UNPUBLISHED.

COMPARANDA: Same as **9** above.

TYPE 2C: **11** AND **12**.

Similar to **7** and **8**, these are distinguished by a shallow bowl, with only a very slight curvature and a short stemmed foot. These kantharoi have a relatively low wall and narrow handles. Among the comparanda listed for these two pieces, those examples from the territory of Vulci are particularly close in shape and fabric.

11. Kantharos
Fig. 11; Pl. 4
MURLO NO.: 71-816
GRID: Rec.7, A/2; Rec.7Ext., X-Y/1-2; Tes. Ctd., A-B/0-1
STRATUM: 2
Ht. 0.119; Ht. to rim 0.072; Diam. of rim. 0.120 m.

Mended from 21 pieces. Portions of bowl and cup wall restored with plaster. Missing two-thirds of foot, small portion of tondo and cup wall, lower exterior portion of one handle, upper exterior portion of other handle, and several chips along carination. Pitted and worn, but still preserves original shiny surface in places.

Kantharos with shallow convex bowl and tall, straight, flaring wall with plain lip. Cup rests on low, hollow, conical foot with very short stem. Strap handles attached to body at carination and at lip. Tondo recessed from cup wall at point of carination. Small ledge on exterior at carination decorated with series of incised lines.

Surface burnished in horizontal strokes except for bottom of interior, which displays radiating pattern. Cup has very low foot.

UNPUBLISHED.

COMPARANDA: Kantharos of Rasmussen Type 3e (Rasmussen 1979:104–6, pls. 31, 32). For other examples of the same shape, see G. Camporeale, in *Aspetti* 65–68, nos. 39–44, fig. 18, pls. 14a–d, 16a, from Orvieto; Donati 1988:88–89, no. 111, fig. 12, from Roselle; Bartoloni 1972:120–21, nos. 51–53, 58, fig. 57, pls. LXIIg–l, LXIVd, from Poggio Buco and 175, 176, nos. 53–55, 56, pl. CXIXb–e, from Poggio Buco; Pellegrini 1989:90, nos. 284–289, pls. LXI, LXII, from Poggio Buco; *SG* 1.8, 41, no. 18, fig. 26, from San Giovenale and 44, nos. 36–38, fig. 27, from San Giovenale; Cristofani 1974:68, pl. XXVIa, from Massarosa; Matteucig 1951:43, no. 45, pl. XVII.14, from Poggio Buco; Museo Archeologico e d'Arte della Maremma, Grosseto, inv. nos. 1666, 1129, from Castro; Museo Archeologico e d'Arte della Maremma, inv. no. 3554, from Pitigliano; Paolucci 1988:93–94, figs. 94, 95, pl. L.1, 2, from Chianciano; A. Dani, *StEtr* 37 (1969):168, no. 1, pl. 2a, from Selvello (Vetulonia); A. Robert, in *Bucchero nero*:142, tomb 189, fig. 13, from Saint Julien de Pézenas.

12. Kantharos Fragment
Pl. 4
MURLO NO.: 71-803
GRID: Rec.7Ext., X-Y/1-2
STRATUM: 2
Max. Pres. Ht. 0.044; Max. Pres. Diam. of body 0.118; Max. Pres. Diam. of foot 0.051 m.

Mended from 6 fragments. Broken on all sides. Missing two-thirds of foot and tondo, all of wall, and both handles. Worn and chipped. Surface black in color with brown undertone.

Fragment preserves portion of foot and tondo of kantharos. Cup has slightly convex bowl with gently sloping floor and low, hollow, conical foot with short, cylindrical stem.

UNPUBLISHED.
COMPARANDA: Same as **11** above.

TYPE 2D–E: **13–16**

13–16 represent two unclassified variants of Rasmussen kantharos Type 3e. The lack of comparanda for both variants suggests that they may represent local or northern Etruscan types.

TYPE 2D: **13** AND **14**.

These are very similar in overall conception to Type 3e, except that they display a slightly convex wall, as distinguished from the customary straight, sloping wall. Another kantharos of this type was found at Poggio Civitate in Trench 18 (Murlo no. 73-212). Outside Poggio Civitate an example was discovered at Chiusi.

13. Kantharos
Fig. 12; Pl. 4
MURLO NO.: 71-568
FI: 112441
GRID: Rec.7, A/2
STRATUM: 2
Ht. 0.14; Ht. to rim 0.082; Diam. of rim 0.140; Diam. of foot 0.075 m.

Mended from numerous fragments. Missing one handle and large portion of cup wall and tondo, which have been restored in plaster. Large chip at side of preserved handle and at point of attachment for missing handle on cup wall. Worn and chipped. Wheel marks still visible on surface of foot, appearing as series of fine concentric circles. Shiny black surface with brown undertone.

Kantharos with convex body and flaring wall. Only one high, vertical strap handle preserved. Cup set on low, flaring, conical foot with short stem. Preserved handle attached at carination and lip. Two parallel grooves (interrupted by the handles) encircle rim below lip.

Surface of cup vigorously burnished in horizontal strokes except for bottom of interior, which displays radiating pattern.

BIBLIOGRAPHY: *Case e palazzi*:80, no. 65.
COMPARANDA: Unclassified variant of Rasmussen kantharos Type 3e (Rasmussen 1979:104–6, pls. 31, 32). A kantharos of this same shape was found at Poggio Civitate in Trench 18, Murlo no. 73-212; see Nielsen and Phillips 1975:364, ill. 11, pl. 66, figs. 24–26; *Case e palazzi*:80, no. 62, pl. 3-62. A kantharos with a similar shape was recovered from Castelluccio di Pienza. It is currently on display at Chiusi, Museo Archeologico.

14. Kantharos Fragment
MURLO NO.: 71-960
GRID: Rec.7, A/2; Rec.7, S.Wall, M1-3
STRATUM: 2,4(I/O)
Diam. of rim 0.144; Diam. at carination 0.122; Max. Pres. Ht. 0.095 m.

Mended from 9 fragments. Broken across tondo and on both sides. Missing both handles, bottom of foot, three-quarters of tondo, and two-thirds of cup wall. Chipped and worn, but still preserves much of original fine surface. Shiny black with brown undertone.

Fragment preserves one-third of kantharos with convex body, flaring wall, and conical foot. Only short, thick stem of foot preserved.

UNPUBLISHED.

COMPARANDA: Unclassified variant of Rasmussen kantharos Type 3e (Rasmussen 1979:104–6, pls. 31, 32). Same as **13** above.

TYPE 2E: **15** AND **16.**

Like **11**, these have a convex wall with a shallow bowl, with only a slight curvature. They also display a shallow groove on the exterior, just above the carination. Besides the examples from Poggio Civitate, the only other published example is from Artimino.

15. Kantharos
Fig. 12; Pl. 5
MURLO NO.: 71-739
GRID: Rec.7, E/4
STRATUM: 2
Ht. 0.143; Ht. to rim 0.079; Diam. of rim 0.125; Diam. of foot 0.070 m.

Mended from 9 pieces. Missing two-thirds of cup wall, portions of bowl, and one strap handle. Several chips along edge of rim and on foot. Worn and chipped.

Approximately two-thirds of small kantharos with high, vertical handles. Cup rests on hollow, flaring, conical foot with short, narrow, cylindrical stem. Cup has slightly convex, nearly flat, carinated bowl and convex wall with plain lip. Single preserved strap handle attached at carination and lip.

The handle has been irregularly made, and its interior and exterior portions are not aligned. The cup wall is set off from the cup floor on the interior by a shallow groove at the point of the carination. A deeper groove encircles the base of the cup wall on the exterior just above the carination.

UNPUBLISHED.
COMPARANDA: Unclassified variant of Rasmussen kantharos Type 3e (Rasmussen 1979:104–6, pls. 31, 32). Another cup of similar shape has been found at Artimino (*Artimino*:94, no. 46, fig. 69).

16. Kantharos Fragment
Pl. 5
MURLO NO.: 71-955
GRID: Rec.7, A-F/3
STRATUM: 2
Max. Pres. Ht. 0.107; Ht. of handle 0.093; Diam. of rim 0.128 m.

Mended from 9 pieces. Missing foot, one handle, most of bowl, and two-thirds of wall. Several large chips on handle. Surface is chipped, worn, and discolored.

Fragment preserves approximately one-third of short, slightly convex wall and one strap handle of bucchero kantharos. Handle attached to body at carination and lip.

UNPUBLISHED.
COMPARANDA: Appears to be same type as **15**, although not enough of the vessel is preserved to say with certainty.

TYPE 3: **17.**

This represents an unclassified kantharos type. It has a short wall, shallow sloping tondo, and a distinctive deep groove above the carination. Although this kantharos is similar in shape to Rasmussen's Kantharos Type 3e, its profile is so distinctive that it represents a new type. There are no known parallels for this kantharos type.

17. Kantharos Fragment
Fig. 12; Pl. 5
MURLO NO.: 71-802
GRID: Rec.7, A-F/1-4
STRATUM: 2
Max. Pres. Ht. 0.053; Diam. of rim 0.014 m.

Mended from 8 pieces. Broken irregularly across tondo, wall, and base of handle. Missing two-thirds of tondo, three-quarters of wall, entire foot, and both handles. Worn and chipped. Shiny black surface.

Fragment preserves approximately one-quarter of kantharos. Cup has shallow convex bowl and short flaring wall with plain lip. Base of one strap handle preserved. Cup wall offset from cup floor on interior by shallow groove at point of carination. Deeper groove encircles base of cup wall on exterior just above carination.

UNPUBLISHED.
COMPARANDA: No parallels noted.

IIIB. KANTHAROI HANDLE FRAGMENTS (18–21)

18 through **21** all represent kantharos handle fragments. Each fragment is described below.

18. Kantharos Handle Fragment
Pl. 6
MURLO NO.: 71-961
GRID: Rec.7, A/3
STRATUM: 2/3(*I/O)
Max. Pres. Ht. 0.076; W. at top 0.015; W. at base 0.023 m.

Mended from 3 pieces. Broken at base of interior section and below top of interior section. Missing lower, interior section. Scratched and worn, but still preserves portions of original shiny black surface.

Fragment preserves approximately two-thirds of kantharos strap handle.

UNPUBLISHED.

19. Kantharos Handle Fragment
Pl. 6
MURLO NO.: 71-962
GRID: Rec.7, A/3
STRATUM: 2/3(*I/O)
Max. Pres. Ht. 0.062; Max. Pres. W. 0.022 m.

Single fragment. Broken at base and below top of exterior section. Scratched and worn. Dull gray-black surface.

Fragment preserves lower exterior section of kantharos strap handle.

UNPUBLISHED.

20. Kantharos Handle Fragment
Pl. 6
MURLO NO.: 71-963
GRID: Rec.7, A/3
STRATUM: 2/3(*I/O)
Max. Pres. Ht. 0.096; W. at top 0.019; W. at base 0.025 m.

Mended from 2 pieces. Broken at base and top of exterior section. Missing portion of top and entire interior section. Scratched and worn. Dull gray-black surface.

Fragment preserves exterior section of kantharos strap handle.

UNPUBLISHED.

21. Kantharos Handle Fragment
Pl. 6
MURLO NO.: 71-964
GRID: Rec. 7, A/3
STRATUM: 2/3(*I/0)
Ht. 0.085; W. at top 0.016; W. at junction with lip 0.034; W. at base 0.024 m.

Mended from 2 pieces. Broken at point of attachment to rim and body. Scratched and worn. Dull gray-black surface.

Kantharos strap handle.

UNPUBLISHED.

IVA. KYATHOI (22–37)

A total of five kyathoi, representing four types, were found in the Lower Building. In addition, two body and nine handle fragments indicate the possible existence of eleven additional examples.

TYPE 1: 22–23

22 is an example of the first type of kyathos, which is generally mold-made and displays a deep bowl with an outward-curving wall between a carination at top and bottom, a tall rim, and a conical foot. In addition, this type invariably has handles decorated with a molded *potnia theron* on the interior, as in the case of the present example, classified by Valentini as Type A (Valentini 1969:417–21). The type includes cups of varying size and also often features molded and/or incised decoration. The kyathoi are also generally of a similar fine fabric. Of the comparanda cited for this vessel, only the example in Boston may have utilized a similar mold-type for the body as the cup from Poggio Civitate (Fairbanks 1928:219, no. 655).

Valentini, in her study of the *potnia theron*, lists 27 cups of this or similar type, as well as many other vessel types, the majority of which were found in the territory of Chiusi (Valentini 1969:417–24). She has therefore located the principal workshop for the production of the *potnia theron* of her Type A at Chiusi and, by extension, all of the vessels featuring this molded motif. The handle fragment **23** probably belonged to the same type of kyathos as **22**. It has the same shape as the handle of **22** and also displays a similar molded motif. There are no known examples of kyathoi of this type from a datable context besides the example from the Lower Building.

22. Kyathos Fragment
Fig. 13; Pl. 6
MURLO NO.: 71-569
GRID: Rec.7, A/2
STRATUM: 2
Max. Pres. Ht. 0.146; Diam. of rim 0.154 m.

Mended from 9 pieces. Broken across both sides and across wall. Small portion of cup wall restored in plaster. Missing foot and three-quarters of body. Slightly chipped and worn. Glossy surface. Black biscuit.

Fragment preserves portion of upper body and rim and complete handle of thin-walled, molded kyathos. Cup has convex, carinated body and very tall, nearly vertical rim. Preserved portion of cup wall articulated into series of narrow, outpressed scallops, of which only top rounded portions remain. Outpressed horizontal bulge above scallops encircles shoulder. Tall vertical rim broadly fluted and separated from body by thin rounded ridge. Similar rounded ridge also appears below base of handle. Handle is elliptical in profile and composed of curving exterior section with broad flaring base and nearly flat, tongue-shaped interior section. Tall crest projects midway down center of curving exterior portion of handle. Handle attached at lip and shoulder. Narrow rounded strut attached to rim below lip provides additional support for handle.

Face of handle preserves slightly worn molded decoration in low relief, which extends down onto top portion of rim. Decoration displays frontal *potnia theron* who stands holding a feline in each hand by its front paws. Two small birds are perched on goddess's shoulders, facing inward. Outlines of birds only faintly visible. Hair of goddess is flat on top, and on each side of her head, two long, coiled tresses fall onto her chest from behind her ears. Interior tress on right side is only partially represented. Face of goddess displays large oval eyes, short triangular nose, and small mouth set in U-shaped depression. Arms of goddess bend inward at elbows. She holds front paws of felines at hip level. Felines rendered in profile with frontal faces. They have pointed ears, large almond-shaped eyes, and long noses, and stand upright on hind legs with their bodies masking much of lower portion of goddess's body. Two tangent, curving lines between animals appear to indicate tails of felines. Eyes of both *potnia* and felines defined by oval incisions.

Since no wheel marks are visible on the body of the cup, it is possible that it was mold-made. The handle, which is mold-made in two pieces, was added separately. Since the molded relief on the inner face of the handle extends down onto the rim, either the handle and portion of the rim below it were molded together and added separately, or the molded decoration was applied after the handle was attached. The surface of the fragment has been vigorously burnished in horizontal strokes.

The cup is to be restored with a conical foot. The dimensions of the illustration are only approximate. They have been estimated on the basis of the proportions of similar kyathoi.

BIBLIOGRAPHY: Phillips 1972:252–53, pl. 49, fig. 4; Nielsen 1994b:65, 69, fig. 6.13.

COMPARANDA: For other examples of similar type, although with differing proportions, see Brijder 1976:93–95, pl. 90; Montelius 1904:1004, pl. 238, fig. 3, from Chiusi; B. Bouloumié, *StEtr* 52 (1984):102-3, no. 1, pl. xxxivc, d. Scalloped body and straight rim, see Fairbanks 1928:219, no. 655, pl. LXXXVIII, from Chiusi. Plain body and straight rim, see Pecchiai 1967:502, no. 45, pl. LXXXIVf, g, from Chiusi; *CVA Villa Giulia* 1:IV B 1, pl. 4.3, 4; *CVA Altenburg* 3:pl. 129.1–3; Chiusi, Museo Archeologico, inv. 205, from Chiusi; Siena, Museo Archeologico, inv. 320. Plain body and fluted rim, see G. M. A. Richter, *Handbook of the Etruscan Collection of the Metropolitan Museum of Art* (New York, 1940): fig. 35. Molded body with figural decoration and straight rim, see Valentini 1969:421–22, no. 19, fig. 5; *CVA British Museum* 7: IV B a, pl. 20.5. Molded body with figural decoration and fluted rim, see Hayes 1985:109–10; Donati 1968:325, no. 15, pl. LXIIg, from Chiusi. See also Valentini 1969:420–23.

ORNAMENT TYPE: 14.

23. Kyathos Handle Fragment
Fig. 13; Pl. 7
MURLO NO.: 71-561

FI: 112587
GRID: Rec.7, D-E/3
STRATUM: 2
Max. Pres. Ht. of front portion 0.081; Max. Pres. Width at base 0.033; Th. of front portion 0.008–0.009; Ht. of molded decoration 0.081 m.

Mended from 2 pieces. Broken at base of interior portion and just above middle of exterior portion. Missing lower half of exterior portion. Surface, especially of molded decoration, heavily worn. Burned. Gray-black in color. Black biscuit.

Fragment preserves upper, curving, exterior portion and almost entire flat, tongue-shaped interior portion of kyathos handle. Tall narrow crest projects from center of preserved exterior portion of handle. Face of handle preserves badly worn molded decoration in low relief of same type as found on handle of **22** above.

UNPUBLISHED.
COMPARANDA: This handle probably belonged to a kyathos. Same as **22** above.
ORNAMENT TYPE: 14.

TYPE 2: 24

24, an example of a second type of kyathos, is distinguished by a deep bowl with a convex wall. Other kyathoi of this type are known from Chiusi, Orvieto, and the territory of Vulci, although they all appear to be of coarser fabric than the example from Poggio Civitate. In addition, the majority of these cups all possess crested handles of the same type as **22** and **23**.

Two of the kyathoi listed in the comparanda section of the catalogue entry of **24** are from datable contexts. The kyathos from Heba (Magliano)[17] came from a chamber tomb that can be dated to the first half of the sixth century, and the example from Poggio Buco was found in a tomb of the same type dated from the end of the seventh to well into the second quarter of the sixth century (Matteucig 1951:51, no. 59, 62, Tomb G).

24. Kyathos
Fig. 13; Pl. 7
MURLO NO.: 71-572
GRID: Rec.7, D/3
STRATUM: 2
Max. Pres. Ht. 0.088; Diam. of rim 0.140; Diam. of foot 0.075 m.

Mended from 14 pieces. Broken irregularly across one side of foot and body. Several chips missing from bowl and rim. Small portion of body restored in plaster. Surface worn, chipped, and encrusted. Burned. Color varies from orange-brown to black. Black biscuit. Thin-walled fabric.

Fragment preserves approximately one-half of kyathos with deep, sharply carinated bowl and tall everted rim. Cup has convex wall with bulging shoulder. Bowl rests on hollow conical foot with narrow cylindrical stem and thin splaying base.

UNPUBLISHED.
COMPARANDA: The cup can be restored as a kyathos. For other examples of kyathoi of the same or similar shape, see Valentini 1969:418, no. 2, pl. CVIa, from Borghetto (Pienza); Matteucig 1951:51, no. 59, pl. XXI.9, from Poggio Buco; Cimino 1986:86, no. 213, pl. 51; Montelius 1910:1016, pl. 241, fig. 8, from Orvieto; Jucker 1991:192, no. 249. For examples of similar shape but with a molded body with figural decoration, see Minto 1935:53, Tomb 2a, pl. VI.1, from Heba (Magliano); L. Donati, *StEtr* 39 (1971):309, note 9, pl. LXIIIb, from Chiusi.

TYPE 3: 25–28

25 and **26**, these cups exemplify a third type of kyathos. Although they display slight differences in shape and decoration, they are of the same basic type: distinguished by a wide hemispherical bowl with a curving profile and a conical foot. In addition, both cups were made in a similar fashion, having been thrown in a mold. While **25** has a somewhat tauter profile with a straight shoulder and a short rim, **26** has a curving profile with a slightly bulging shoulder and a tall flaring rim. In addition, **25** has wide flat scallops and a central interior boss, while **26** displays a pattern of narrow protruding scallops. The two cups also display slight differences in technique, specifically in the attachment of their handles. On **26**, the scalloped decoration continues complete-

[17] Minto 1935:53, Tomb 2a. The date of the tomb is provided by the presence of an Etrusco-Corinthian alabastron.

ly around the cup, and the lower portion of the handle was attached directly over the scallops. As a result, the handle appears somewhat awkward and not organically fused with the cup. Although **25** is fragmentary, enough is preserved to show that the scallops were interrupted for the placement of the handle, as is seen on several of the other cups of this type from the site (Nielsen and Phillips 1986:10–14; see esp. Murlo nos. 73-287, figs. 5a, 6; 73-258, figs. 6, 7).

Both cups belong to a unique group of elaborate mold-made kyathoi found at Poggio Civitate, the majority of which were recovered in Trench 18 (fig. 6) (Nielsen and Phillips 1986:10–15). These kyathoi generally feature molded handles surmounted by finials and represent a hybrid type since their shape is essentially that of a phiale mesomphalos with an added foot and handle.[18] In addition, the scalloped cup fragments (**27** and **28**) and the handles (**31** and **34**), which preserve portions of scallops, most probably belonged to kyathoi of this type.[19]

The shape and decoration of the bowls of the kyathoi were ultimately inspired by Near Eastern bronze ribbed bowls that were first imported and later imitated in central Italy and Etruria during the eighth and seventh centuries B.C.[20] Examples of these bronze bowls are found at numerous sites in both northern and southern Etruria.[21] Near Poggio Civitate examples have been found at both Chiusi (Camporeale 1969:57 and note 4) and Vetulonia.[22] The bronze bowls inspired a number of ceramic imitations of varying degrees of faithfulness, first in impasto (Howes-Smith 1984:93 and notes 107, 108; see also Bartoloni 1972:162, no. 23, fig. 80, pl. CVIIId, from Poggio Buco) and later in buccheroid (see Camporeale 1967:65–71, pls. IX–XII, from Vetulonia; Reusser 1988:39, E41) and bucchero.[23] While none of these examples provides a direct parallel for the Poggio Civitate cups, several of the bucchero and buccheroid examples are of a broadly similar type.[24] In particular, the buccheroid kyathoi and kantharoi from Vetulonia clearly share a common origin with the examples from Poggio Civitate.[25] The Vetulonian kyathoi are dated to the middle of the seventh century. In contrast to these and the majority of other impasto and buccheroid types, however, the examples from Poggio Civitate represent more of an adaptation, rather than a direct imitation, of the original bronze prototype. They are better proportioned, of a finer fabric, and more refined in conception. They should, therefore, be considered a later generation of imitation. The addition of the conical foot to this type also may be the result of influence of earlier, Villanovan bronze kyathoi, as Rasmussen has noted in his discussion of his kyathos Type 4b.[26] On the other hand, the adoption of the flaring foot for the kyathos may have resulted from the influence of other bucchero shapes, such as cups and kantharoi (Rasmussen 1979:115).

---

[18] This distinctly Etruscan practice of transforming a bowl shape into a cup by the addition of a foot and handle is also seen in the kyathoi of Rasmussen Types 4a and 4b; see Rasmussen 1979:115–16.

[19] For a discussion of the shape of these handles, see the descriptions of kyathos handles Types 1 and 2 in this chapter.

[20] For the most recent and comprehensive discussion of the bronze ribbed bowls, see Howes-Smith 1984. See also Camporeale 1967:44–48. Howes-Smith has divided the bowls found in Italy into ten types, which cluster into three groups according to their chronology and style. The bowls have been dated between 750 and 650 B.C. It is not easy to distinguish between import and imitation, particularly in the case of the earliest examples.

[21] For a catalogue of the bowls, including proveniences, see Howes-Smith 1984:80–88.

[22] Camporeale 1967:44–48. In addition, Vetulonia has also been identified as a production center for the bronze ribbed bowls.

[23] Ramage believed that the ribbed bowls were not imitated in bucchero, since no bucchero examples had been identified previous to the publication of her study; see Ramage 1970:11. For bucchero imitations see (1) Pellegrini 1989:97, no. 318, pl. LXIII, from Poggio Buco; (2) Bartoloni 1972:96, no. 79, fig. 42, pl. LIIf, from Poggio Buco; (3) Edlund 1980:35, no. 45, pl. 17, provenience unknown; (4) *CVA Malibu, J. Paul Getty Museum* 6: pl. 326, attributed to Vulci.

[24] Of the bucchero examples listed in the previous note, nos. 1, 3, and 4 are clearly of the same general type as the bowls of the Poggio Civitate kyathoi. No. 3, in particular, has a very similar shape to that of **25** and even has the same type of decoration.

[25] Camporeale 1967:65–73, pls. IX–XI. In addition, a red impasto caryatid-supported bowl from Castelnuovo Berardenga also appears to be of a similar shape; see Bocci Pacini 1973:123, 126, figs. 2 and 3.

[26] Rasmussen 1979:115. In addition to the bronze examples cited by Rasmussen from Tarquinia, see also Camporeale 1969:57, pl. XV.2.

25. Scalloped Kyathos
Fig. 14; Pl. 7
MURLO NO.: 71-542
FI: 112465
GRID: Rec.7, D/2
STRATUM: 2
Max. Pres. Ht. of body 0.085; Ht. of foot 0.026; Diam. of rim 0.150; Diam. of foot 0.080 m.

Mended from 20 pieces. Missing handle, two-thirds of foot, and portions of body and rim. Missing portion of foot and some of missing portions of body restored with plaster. Large break in cup wall in area of missing handle. Foot heavily mended at point of attachment. Worn and chipped, but preserves much of original shiny surface.

Kyathos with deep, convex curving bowl, short vertical rim, and a tall conical foot with thick stem. Center of bowl decorated with low boss. Body of kyathos articulated into series of 15 broad outpressed scallops with rounded edges below rim. Each scallop enframed by narrow groove. Concave depressions of scallops visible in interior of cup. Two thin horizontal grooves encircle rim below lip. Molded scallops on body and, probably, incised lines on rim as well, interrupted by handle.

The cup was wheel-made in two sections. The bowl was thrown in a mold, after which the scallops were hand-tooled. The foot and missing handle were attached separately when the body was leather-hard. The presence of a handle is clearly indicated by the interruption of the scallop decoration visible below the large break in the cup wall.

BIBLIOGRAPHY: *Case e palazzi*:82, no. 80.

COMPARANDA: A kyathos fragment made from the same mold was found at Poggio Civitate in Trench 18, Murlo no. 73-286; see *Case e palazzi*:81, no. 76. For other examples of similar shape from Poggio Civitate, see Nielsen and Phillips 1986:10–15, figs. 5–9. No parallels noted outside Poggio Civitate.

26. Scalloped Kyathos
Fig. 14; Pl. 8
MURLO NO.: 71-555
FI: 112467
GRID: Rec.7, C/2
STRATUM: 2
Max. Pres. Ht. 0.094; Diam. of rim 0.170; Diam. of foot 0.085 m.

Body almost complete. Mended from numerous fragments. Missing handle. Portions of foot, body, and rim restored in plaster. Rim broken irregularly at point of attachment for handle. Surface chipped and heavily worn. Thin-walled fabric.

Scalloped kyathos with deep, curving, convex body and tall flaring rim. Cup sits on low conical foot with short thick stem. Thickened base of handle preserved at point of attachment to cup. Body of cup articulated into series of 18 narrow outpressed scallops. Elongated scallops bulge out below rim and gradually narrow toward base. Concave depressions of scallops visible in interior of cup.

The bowl was pressed into a mold while thrown on the wheel. The conical foot and strap handle were added separately when the body was leather-hard.

BIBLIOGRAPHY: Nielsen and Phillips 1977a: 95–96, ill. 15, figs. 28, 29; *Case e palazzi*:82, no. 81.

COMPARANDA: For kyathoi of similar shape from Poggio Civitate, see Nielsen and Phillips 1986:10–15, figs. 5–7. No parallels noted outside Poggio Civitate.

27. Scalloped Kyathos Fragment
Fig. 14; Pl. 28
MURLO NO.: 73-143
GRID: Rec.5, I-K/0-1
STRATUM: 2
Max. Pres. Ht. 0.035; Max. Pres. L. 0.073; Diam. of rim 0.160 m.

Mended from 2 pieces. Broken on 3 sides. Surface worn, chipped, and burned. Mottled orange-brown in color. Black biscuit.

Fragment preserves small portion of body and tall everted rim of kyathos. Rounded top portions of 3 outpressed scallops appear just below rim.

UNPUBLISHED.

COMPARANDA: Not enough of the fragment is preserved to determine its complete shape. It probably formed part of the bowl of a scalloped kyathos like **26** above.

28. Scalloped Kyathos Fragment
Pl. 8
MURLO NO.: 73-144
GRID: Rec.5, K/0
STRATUM: 2

Max. Pres. Ht. 0.032; Max. Pres. L. 0.067; Diam. of rim 0.145 m.

Mended from 2 pieces. Broken on 3 sides. Surface worn, chipped, and burned. Orange-brown in color. Black biscuit.

Fragment preserves small portion of body and tall everted rim of scalloped kyathos. Rounded outlines of top portions of 2 outpressed scallops appear on body, just below rim.

UNPUBLISHED.

COMPARANDA: Not enough of the fragment is preserved to determine its original shape. It probably formed part of the bowl of a scalloped kyathos like **26** above.

TYPE 4: **29**.

This specimen represents a fourth type of kyathos. Unfortunately, not enough of the cup is preserved to identify its complete shape with certainty. It appears, however, to be an early example of a small group of ring-footed kyathoi, examples of which have been found at Chiusi, Vulci, Heba (Magliano), Poggio Buco, Pescia Romana and, perhaps, Volterra.[27] In addition to a ring foot, these cups display a shallow carinated bowl with a convex wall and a tall everted rim. Like the kyathos from Poggio Civitate, they also have a tall crested handle, which often displays molded figural decoration on the interior or plastically applied human heads, and are crowned by conical finials. Of the examples listed in the comparanda section of the catalogue entry, the kyathos from Heba and those in the Louvre and Würzburg appear closest in shape to **29**. The other examples of this type are much more elaborate and probably later in date, displaying molded bodies and plastically applied decoration on their bodies and rims. The handle fragment **30**, which is of the same type as that of **29**, probably belonged to a similar kyathos.[28] Donati has located the workshop(s) for the production of some of the more elaborately decorated cups of this type in the territory of Vulci on the basis of their find frequency and the style of their decoration, particularly their plastically applied decorative heads.[29]

There are no examples of kyathoi of this type from a closely datable context. They are generally dated between the second and final quarters of the sixth century on the basis of the style of their decoration (Donati 1967:625–27; Pellegrini 1989:88; Camporeale 1991:132).

29. Kyathos Fragment
Fig. 14; Pl. 8
MURLO NO.: 71-553
GRID: Rec.7, F/3; B/2; Rec.7, W. Wall, F-C/7
STRATUM: 2,4 (I/0)
Max. Pres. Ht. 0.145; Diam. of rim 0.118 m.

Mended from 8 pieces. Missing foot, one-third of body, entire rim, and most of interior portion of handle. Worn and chipped. Black surface with brown undertone. Black biscuit.

Fragmentary kyathos with shallow carinated bowl and bulging convex wall. Two low rounded ridges mark carination on exterior. Additional low rounded ridge encircles top of cup wall below rim. Handle, elliptical in profile, consists of curving exterior section and straight, tongue-shaped interior section; only uppermost portion of interior section preserved. Tall thin crest runs along center of upper half of exterior section of handle; at top, finial consisting of round knob crowned by cone; top portion of the interior section displays molded gorgoneion in low relief. Creature has small, nearly square face with low forehead. Hair above forehead defined by series of short vertical incisions and falls in two tresses framing face. Eyebrows formed by two ridges curving up from top of nose. Creature displays large, almond-shaped eyes defined by fine ridges. Large nose with flaring nostrils domi-

[27] For examples of these kyathoi, see the comparanda listed in the catalogue entry. One of the cups of this type in the British Museum is listed as from Chiusi or Volterra. There also exists a similar type of kyathos, but with an uncarinated bowl, whose production has been ascribed to Vulci; see F. De Ruyt and T. Hackens, *Vases grecs, italiotes et étrusques de la collection Abbé Mignot* (Louvain, 1974):259–69, no. 59, figs. 134, 135.

[28] All examples of this handle type known to me occur on kyathoi of the same or similar type as **29**.

[29] Donati 1967:625–27. In addition, several of these kyathoi also display on their handles a molded potnia theron of a type which Valentini has ascribed to Vulci; see Valentini 1969:418, 423–24, nos. 27–35. It should be noted that the molded decoration on the handles of the examples from Poggio Civitate, **29** and **30**, appears unique among the known examples of cups of this type.

nates center of face. Wide, open, semicircular mouth has thick lips and protruding tongue with vertical groove down center. Left side of mouth is slightly misshapen, curling upward into cheek. Long vertical fang projects from both upper and lower jaw at each corner of mouth.

BIBLIOGRAPHY: Phillips 1972:253, pl. 52, figs. 9, 10.

COMPARANDA: For other examples of kyathoi of the same shape, see *CVA Würzburg* 3:pl. 11.11; Pottier 1897:33, C650, pl. 27; Minto 1935:46, pl. V, from Heba (Magliano). For examples of kyathoi of similar shape and with more elaborate molded and applied decorations, see *CVA Kassel* 2:pl. 66.4, 5; *CVA British Museum* 7:IV B a, pl. 19.1, from Chiusi or Volterra and pl. 19.3, from Vulci; *CVA Copenhagen* 5:IV B, pl. 214.6; *CVA Goluchów* 1:IV B, pl. 47, 2a, from Chiusi; Pellegrini 1989:88, no. 281, pl. LX, 281a, b, from Poggio Buco; Donati 1967:627, no. 30, pl. CXXVIIIb, from Pescia Romana; *CVA Compiègne* 1:IV B, pl. 21.6, from Chiusi; *Materiali* III:R.IV, no. 578, from Vulci; Reusser 1988:45–46, no. E56; Camporeale 1991:131, no. 127, pl. XCIXb, ascribed to Vulci. See also Valentini 1969:423–24, nos. 27–32.

ORNAMENT TYPE: 20.

IVB. KYATHOI HANDLE FRAGMENTS (30–37)

The handle fragments **30–37** are of types which generally belong to kyathoi. They can be divided into four types on the basis of their shapes.

TYPE 1: 30–33

This type consists of a strap handle with an added crest and conical finial, like that of **29**. The crests of these handles often vary in height and length. In addition, they commonly are adorned with plastically applied decoration, as is the case with **32**. Examples of handles of the same shape as those of Type 1 are found on kyathoi from Chiusi and Cortona. Related handles with shorter crests are also known from Poggio Buco and Vulci.

None of the examples listed in the comparanda as being the same shape as Type 1 were found in a datable context. Four of the related examples, however, can be dated. One kyathos with this handle type from Vulci[30] can be dated to the first quarter of the sixth century, and three additional examples, one from Vulci[31] and the other two from Poggio Buco (Matteucig 1951:51, nos. 57, 58, 62, Tomb G; Bartoloni 1972:91, no. 58, 107, Tomb VII), can be placed in the first half of the sixth century.

30. Kyathos Handle Fragment
Fig. 15; Pl. 9
MURLO NO.: 71-554
FI: 112588
GRID: Rec.7, C/3
STRATUM: 2
Max. Pres. Ht. 0.118; Ht. of relief, decorated side to top of finial 0.081 m.

Mended from 4 pieces. Broken above upper point of attachment to cup rim and at lower point of attachment to cup wall. Surface worn and burned, but still preserves much of original glossy finish. Top and exterior portion of handle burned mottled gray to orange-brown with orange-brown biscuit. Black interior portion with black biscuit.

Fragment preserves approximately three-quarters of molded handle crowned by rounded finial with small conical knob at top. Handle, elliptical in profile, consists of curving exterior section and flat, tongue-shaped interior section. Sides flare outward toward bottom and form wide base. Tall crest projects outward along spine of upper portion of handle. Outer surface of interior section preserves molded decoration executed in low relief. At top of handle appear two small inwardly inclined owls with profile bodies and frontal heads. Faces of owls feature large, incised circular eyes and long triangular beaks; bodies decorated with two sets of five diagonal lines which indicate feathers. Below owls appears a frontal, winged *potnia theron* who grasps a bird in each hand. Her hair is flat on top and hangs down on each side of head in small

[30] The tomb containing the kyathos has been dated between the end of the 7th century and 570 B.C.; see Rizzo 1990:104, 108, no. 26.

[31] *Materiali* III:16, no. 273. An Ionic cup of Villard and Vallet Type B2 provides a *terminus post quem* for this tomb group.

triangular wedge that reaches her shoulder; eyes rendered with large circular incisions, as are breasts. Neither mouth nor nose indicated. Two volute-shaped wings project upward from shoulders and curve inward toward her head. Surface area of wings decorated with series of incised lines which progress from horizontal at shoulder to vertical at tips of volutes. Goddess wears long garment and stands with arms held outward and bent inward at elbows. Two birds shown in profile with long curving necks and short pointed beaks. Wings rendered by series of diagonal lines, intersected by vertical line down center. Figural decoration is mold-made.

BIBLIOGRAPHY: Phillips 1972:252, pl. 49, fig. 3; *Case e palazzi*:84, no. 99, pl. 3-99; Phillips 1989b:99, fig. 22; Nielsen 1994b:65, 69, fig. 6.14.

COMPARANDA: The handle can be reconstructed as part of a kyathos. For parallels for the handle shape see **29** above.

ORNAMENT TYPE: 15.

31. Scalloped Kyathos Handle and Body Fragment
Fig. 15; Pl. 9
MURLO NO.: 71-544
GRID: Rec.7, D/3
STRATUM: 2
Max. Pres. Ht. 0.177; Max. Pres. Ht. of cup wall 0.056 m.

Mended from 4 pieces. Handle almost complete. Broken at point of attachment to rim and irregularly around all sides of cup wall. Two large chips on handle crest and smaller chip on lateral edge. Surface worn and burned, but still preserves some of original glossy finish. Color varies from orange-brown to dark mottled gray. Gray-black biscuit.

Kyathos strap handle and small portion of cup wall. Tall crest runs along center of upper half of handle. Crest crowned at apex by small knob-like finial with cone on top. Upper rounded portion of molded scallop preserved on cup wall next to base of handle.

UNPUBLISHED.

COMPARANDA: This fragment originally belonged to a scalloped kyathos like **26** above.

For other handles of similar shape, see *Cortona*:69, no. 35, from Cortona; Monaci 1965:436, no. 135, pl. XCIII; Guzzo 1969:297, no. 32, pl. LXIIIh, ascribed to Chiusi; L. Donati, *StEtr* 31 (1971):309 and note 9, pl. LXIIIb, from Chiusi. For examples of similar handles, but with shorter crests, see Falconi Amorelli and Fabricotti 1971:206, nos. 52, 53, pl. XLIIIb, from Vulci; Donati 1967:627, no. 20, pl. 128a, from Vulci; Mingazzini 1930:57, no. 211, pl. IV.11; *Materiali* III:16, no. 273, from Vulci; Matteucig 1951:51, nos. 57, 58, from Poggio Buco; Rizzo 1990:108, no. 26, fig. 209, from Vulci

32. Kyathos Handle Fragment
Fig. 15; Pl. 9
MURLO NO.: 71-564
FI: 112589
GRID: Rec.7, E/4; Rec.7Ext., X-Y/1-2
STRATUM: 2
Max. Pres. Ht. 0.160 m.

Mended from 9 pieces. Missing lower portion of exterior section of handle and most of hair of plastic head applied to outer face of interior section. Broken near base of exterior section of handle and below point of attachment to cup wall. Several large chips along edges. Chipped and worn, but still preserves original shiny black surface.

Molded strap handle fragment preserves entire exterior section, including small portion of cup wall and three-quarters of interior section of handle. Tall narrow crest runs along center of upper half of handle. Above crest, at top of handle, small cone crowns round finial. Sides of finial decorated with series of parallel, vertical stippled lines. Small, nearly identical, molded oval head in high relief appears on each side of crest, directly below finial. Hair is flat on top and falls in three vertical tresses on each side of head. Face displays low forehead, asymmetrical almond-shaped eyes, broad nose, and well-defined chin. Small thin mouth set within U-shaped depression. Two similar heads appear below ends of crest, one on each side of handle. Lower half of exterior section of handle bordered by two closely set, incised parallel lines. Two groups of lines are separated by large incised "X." Tall flat vertical ridge defines base of handle. Surface of ridge decorated with series of short diagonal stippled lines. Portions of three incised horizontal lines appear below handle on preserved fragment of cup wall. Attachment scars for small cross strut preserved on inner portion of handle.

BIBLIOGRAPHY: Phillips 1972:253, pl. 50, figs. 5–8; *Case e palazzi*:82, no. 82, pl. 3-82.

COMPARANDA: The handle originally belonged to a kyathos. For parallels for the handle shape, see **31** above.

ORNAMENT TYPE: 23.

33. Kyathos Handle Fragment
Fig. 16; Pl. 10
MURLO NO.: 71-545
GRID: Rec.7, E-F/4
STRATUM: 2
Max. Pres. Ht. 0.128 m.

Mended from 2 pieces. Missing lower half of exterior section. Chips missing along lateral edges. Surface worn.

Fragmentary strap handle. Tall crest runs along center of upper half of handle. Crest is crowned at apex by small, knob-like finial with cone on top.

UNPUBLISHED.

COMPARANDA: The handle originally belonged to a kyathos. For parallels for the handle shape, see **31** above.

TYPE 2: **34** AND **35**.

The shape of this type is essentially that of a strap handle, although the elaborate molded decoration causes some distortion to the profiles. Kyathos handles of this type also commonly have a supporting cross-strut, like that partially preserved on **34**. The closest parallels for both handles are found at Poggio Civitate. In addition, strap handles of similar type, the majority of which have a supporting cross-strut, are particularly common on kyathoi from Vulci and its territory.

Of examples cited in the comparanda section of the catalogue entry for **34**, only one, from Poggio Buco, comes from a datable context. It was found in a chamber tomb dated between the end of the seventh and the second quarter of the sixth century.[32] The remaining examples have been dated to the second and third quarters of the sixth century on the basis of their style.

34. Scalloped Kyathos Handle and Body Fragment
Fig. 31; Pls. 41–43
MURLO NO.: 71-563
FI: 112466
GRID: Rec.7, B-D/3
STRATUM: 2
Max. Pres. Ht. 0.146; Max. Pres. Ht. of rim 0.043; Max. Pres. Ht. of exterior section of handle 0.127; Max. Pres. Ht. of interior section of handle 0.063 m.

Mended from 6 pieces. Missing lower half of interior section of handle, small portion of wing of interior figure, both wings of exterior figure, and cross-strut. Large chip below point of attachment to body and along lower edge of preserved cup wall. Surface worn and scratched. Burned mottled orange-gray.

Fragment preserves a small portion of body and approximately three-quarters of molded handle of kyathos. Handle is elliptical in profile, composed of curving exterior section and straight interior section joined at top. Small, centrally positioned hole piercing rounded upper surface of handle may originally have served as point of attachment for finial. Outer face of each section molded in form of identical winged goddess. While figure on exterior section is almost completely preserved, missing only the wings, that on interior preserves only upper body with one complete and one partial wing. Goddess stands frontally with her elongated arms bent slightly inward at elbows and with hands resting flat on thighs. Outlines of hands and fingers are highlighted with incision. Narrow band of hair, defined by parallel vertical incisions, runs across forehead. Two similarly incised narrow bands, perhaps also meant to indicate hair, run along curving sides of top of handle, linking the women's heads. On each side of head, three long tresses, marked by diagonal incisions, fall down over shoulders and breasts. Oval head is in high relief. Face

[32] Matteucig 1951:51, nos. 59, 62, Tomb G. The example from Vulci was found in a chamber tomb which contained two depositions, the one dating before 560 B.C. and the other after the middle of the 6th century. De Puma placed the kyathos in the earlier group, citing the similarity of the vessel to examples found in the Lower Building at Murlo; see De Puma 1986:35, 46, VC 36.

displays incised almond-shaped eyes, long nose, wide mouth, and heavy chin. Two curling wings project outward from shoulders and curl inward on either side of head at eye level. Surface of wings decorated with incised diagonal lines. Triangular open area formed between wings and long locks of hair. Figure wears long garment, lower half of which is unarticulated, following simple rounded contours of handle. Garment terminates in double scallop. Partially preserved inset area below scallop on right decorated with series of incised vertical lines, which perhaps originally defined portions of undergarment. Three additional incised lines also visible farther to left, but surface here is badly worn. Interior side of curved section of handle preserves broken end of supporting strut. Small section of body preserved below exterior section of handle displays upper rounded portions of two outpressed scallops.

The handle is constructed from two molded sections. The bowl was thrown in a mold, after which the narrow scallops were hand-tooled.

BIBLIOGRAPHY: *Case e palazzi*:84, no. 100.

COMPARANDA: This handle probably belonged to a scalloped kyathos like **26** above. Another handle of the same shape was recently discovered at Poggio Civitate in Trench 26, but remains uncatalogued. For other handles of similar shape outside Poggio Civitate, see Guzzo 1969:296–97, no. 31, pl. LXIIIg, from Pescia Romana; Falconi Amorelli 1968:175, no. 20, pl. XXX.i, from Ischia di Castro; De Puma 1986:46, VC 36, pl. 13b, from Vulci; Matteucig 1951:51, nos. 59, 62, from Poggio Buco; Donati and Michelucci 1981:54, no. 92.

ORNAMENT TYPE: 17.

35. Kyathos Rim and Handle Fragment
Fig. 16; Pl. 11
MURLO NO.: 72-364
GRID: Rec.5, I /0
STRATUM: 2
Max. Pres. Ht. 0.071; Max. Pres. W. 0.051; Th. 0.012 m.

Single fragment. Handle broken at midpoint, and rim broken on each side and below point of attachment to handle. Missing top and exterior rear portion of handle. Surface is worn, scratched, and chipped.

Fragment preserves lower portion of interior section of molded handle and part of rim below. Preserved portion of handle has straight profile and displays molded figural decoration in low relief on its inner face. Decoration consists of frontal winged goddess shown from waist up and broken just below neck. Goddess originally had oval head and frontal wings that terminated in scrolls on either side of her head. Her arms bend in at elbows, and she clutches two long tresses in each hand. Tresses fall from below neck to level of waist and are separated by long incision down center. Two long narrow wings, partially covered by tresses, extend upward at an angle from waist and gradually widen toward neck. Back surface of handle only roughly finished. Long narrow flute appears on rim below handle.

The complete handle would have been mold-made in two sections and attached to the cup when its surface was leather-hard. To produce this handle, both sections were molded in the form of winged women and crowned by a finial in the form of a helmeted warrior's head. In the present example, the handle was not joined to the cup very cleanly. During the joining process some of the clay was pushed up irregularly over the base of the handle, obscuring some of the lower portion of the figured decoration.

UNPUBLISHED.

COMPARANDA: A number of other handles of the same or similar shape were recovered from Trench 18 at Poggio Civitate. See Nielsen and Phillips 1975:362–63, Murlo no. 72-289, ill. 9, pl. 65, figs. 15–17; Nielsen and Phillips 1986:10–15, Murlo nos. 73-265, 73-258, 72-279, figs. 5–9. See also *Case e palazzi*:81, nos. 74, 77–79, 95–98. There are also four additional unpublished examples (Murlo nos. 73-268, 73-269, 73-270, and 73-272), two of which are illustrated here (pl. 11). For a possible parallel for the vase shape, see Nielsen and Phillips 1977a:91–92, Murlo no. 73-239, ill. 13; fig. 14. For other handles of similar shape, see **34** above.

ORNAMENT TYPE: 16.

TYPE 3: **36**.

The handle, composed of a curving exterior section and a straight rectangular interior section, is crowned by a rounded biconical finial. The shape of this handle is basically a variant of the more common strap-handle type.

Another handle of the same shape, unfortunately not from a datable context, is found on a kyathos from Chiusi.

36. Kyathos Handle Fragment
Fig. 17; Pl. 11
MURLO NO.: 71-562
FI: 112581
GRID: Rec.7, E/2, C/1; Rec.8, A/1-4
STRATUM: 2
Max. Pres. Ht. 0.111 m.

Mended from 3 pieces. Broken irregularly at point of attachment to bowl and across interior portion. Missing top of finial and large chip from lower left side of exterior portion. Surface worn, chipped, and burned. Color varies from mottled gray to orange-brown. Gray-brown biscuit.

Fragment preserves approximately three-quarters of kyathos handle, elliptical in profile and composed of curving exterior section and straight rectangular interior section. Handle crowned by rounded biconical finial. Curved exterior portion of handle molded in form of winged goddess. She stands frontally, with arms bent inward at elbows, holding her wings, which originate at waist, curl up over her shoulders, and terminate toward back of her head. Narrow flange that terminates in semicircular projection (only one example since left one not preserved), probably representing a second, lower pair of wings, appears at each side of figure. Goddess wears long belted garment that extends almost to base of handle. Head in high relief. Facial features, now badly worn, include deeply set almond-shaped eyes, long thin nose, small mouth with thick lips, and prominent chin. Lower body of figure rendered as simple narrow tube. Molded decoration, in low relief on outer face of preserved interior section of handle, displays stylized floral motif composed of two superimposed lotus-palmette flowers. Complete upper flower and top portion of lower flower preserved. Each flower consists of three elements: base formed by two outwardly curving leaves, each with a pendant tear-shaped stolon; from center of first element rise two leaves curving inward to form heart-shaped volute; thin stalk originates from center of latter and terminates in lotus flower with 8 petals. Low rounded ridge frames outer edge of design.

The handle was mold-made in two sections. The figural decoration on the curving exterior section of the handle and the vegetal decoration on the interior section were mold-made. The finial was mold-made and added separately.

BIBLIOGRAPHY: Nielsen and Phillips 1977a:92–93, figs. 18–20; *Case e palazzi*:83, no. 90.

COMPARANDA: The handle can be reconstructed as part of a kyathos. A kyathos with a handle made from the same mold was found at Poggio Civitate in Trench 18 (see Nielsen and Phillips 1977a:91–92, Murlo no. 73-239, ill. 13, figs. 14–17. For other handles from Poggio Civitate of the same type, but made from different molds, see *Case e palazzi*:83, nos. 91–93. For a kyathos with a handle of the same shape, although with different decoration, from Chiusi, see Donati 1968:325, no. 15, pl. LXXIIIg.

ORNAMENT TYPES: 18, 19.

TYPE 4: **37**

This specimen can be restored as a type of tall broad strap handle generally found on kyathoi but also known in rare cases on kantharoi.[33] A buccheroid kyathos with a strap handle of the same type, displaying a very similar stamped decoration, was recovered from Poggio Aguzzo Tomb 8 (Murlo no. PA 72-32). These handles are especially characteristic of a small group of kyathoi with a tall conical foot, shallow hemispherical bowl, and broad tall handle, and correspond to Rasmussen's Type 3 (Rasmussen 1979:114). Examples of these kyathoi are known from a variety of sites in both northern and southern Etruria, including Cerveteri, Orvieto, Chiusi, Vetulonia, and Populonia.[34] Camporeale originally divided this type into two groups on the basis of form and decoration and assigned their production to Cerveteri and Populonia.[35] More recently Gregori (1991:76–78)

[33] I have found only one example of a kantharos, that from Populonia, which has this type of handle.

[34] Gregori, in her study of stamped bucchero and impasto from a workshop in Vetulonia, illustrates a number of kyathos or kantharos handle fragments which may also be of this type, but since they are broken, their shapes cannot be reconstructed with certainty; see Gregori 1991:66–75, nos. 10, 14, 27–29, 35–37.

[35] Camporeale 1967:115–20; Camporeale 1969:47-48. Bonamici, Cristofani, and Bagnasco Gianni have subsequently reassigned to a workshop in northern Etruria, perhaps at Populonia, some of the kyathoi originally assigned by Camporeale to Cerveteri; see Cristofani 1972:84–94; Bonamici 1972:106–14; Bagnasco Gianni 1993:207–16. See also Camporeale 1995: 77, note 15.

and Hayes (1985:63) have also suggested that examples of this type were produced at Vetulonia and possibly Orvieto, respectively. In addition, this type of kyathos—and in particular the handle—has been linked to a metal prototype (Camporeale 1967:117; Rasmussen 1979:114; Bagnasco Gianni 1993:209).

The tomb on Poggio Aguzzo containing the buccheroid kyathos with a handle of the same type as **37**, Type 4, has recently been dated by Tuck to the middle of the seventh century (Tuck 1996a:35–37 and 1996b). Kyathoi found outside Poggio Civitate with handles like Type 4 have been dated to the middle or third quarter of the seventh century on the basis of the tomb context of an example from the Tomba del Duce at Vetulonia.[36]

37. Kyathos Strap Handle Fragment
Fig. 17; Pl. 11
MURLO NO.: 72-419
GRID: Rec.5, F-H/0-1
STRATUM: 2/5(*I/O)
Max. Pres. Ht. 0.033; W. 0.044; Th. 0.004 m.

Mended from 4 fragments. Broken across top and bottom and chipped along sides. Surface worn.

Fragment preserves top curving portion of wide strap handle. Rounded ridge borders each side of handle. Cylinder-stamped animal frieze in low relief on surface of handle. Frieze, bordered on each side by four flat narrow ridges, consists of procession of fantastic animals, moving left. On far right a sphinx, of which only large head and portion of body, including recurving wing, are preserved. In front of sphinx, a winged feline of uncertain type. Creature displays small head with short neck, tall recurving wing and tail, and feline paws. Lower portion of hind leg of additional creature preserved at far left.

UNPUBLISHED.

COMPARANDA: The handle probably belonged to a kyathos. An unpublished kyathos with a handle of the same shape displaying a similar stamped design was recovered from Poggio Aguzzo Tomb 8, Murlo no. PA 72-232. In addition, a similar handle fragment was also recovered from Trench CA28 at Poggio Civitate, Murlo no. 69-92; see Cristofani and Phillips 1971:412, no. 3, fig. 2, pl. LXXXIVc. For other handles of the same shape recovered elsewhere, see Hayes 1985:63, C1; *CVA Heidelburg* 2:pl. 53.3, 4; Camporeale 1967:115–20, no. 85, pl. XXVa, b, from Vetulonia; Minto 1943:113, 152–53, fig. 57, pls. XXIII.5, XXXVIII.6, from Populonia; Bonamici 1972:95–97, nos. 4, 7, 12, pls. XVIc, XVIIa, b, XVIIIa, b, XIXd, e from Cerveteri, and 97, no. 21, pl. XXII, from Chiusi; Gregori 1991:78, no. 17, fig. 24, from Vetulonia. For a kantharos with handles of this shape, see Minto 1943:152, pl. XXXVIII.7, from Populonia.

ORNAMENT TYPE: 9.

V. CUPS (38–43)

Three types of cups are found in the Lower Building.

TYPE 1: 38

This is a previously unclassified type. It is distinguished by a deep spherical bowl and low conical foot with a short thick stem. The shape of the cup resembles Rasmussen cup Type 3a, although the vessel from Poggio Civitate has a deeper bowl (Rasmussen 1979:119, pl. 38, no. 20). A group of bucchero skyphoi with flat handles from Chiusi display a similar deep bowl, but they are more globular in shape and rest on a taller, flaring foot (Donati 1977:89, figs. 1a–d). The Poggio Civitate cup was probably ultimately inspired by Ionic cups of Villard and Vallet Type A, although the prototype has been freely adapted (Villard and Vallet 1955:14–31). In addition, certain impasto bowls may also have influenced the development of the shape.[37] A *terminus post quem* for this cup type is provided by the Ionic cups of Type A, which are dated to 640/630–600 B.C. (Villard and Vallet 1955:29).

---

[36] Bonamici 1972:110 and note 47; Bagnasco Gianni 1993:207; Rasmussen 1979:114–15, Type 3. For a discussion of the Tomba del Duce, see note 3 of the Introduction.

[37] Impasto cups and jars, which display spherical bodies reminiscent of that of the Poggio Civitate cup, are known from several sites. For examples of these impasto vessels, see Hayes 1985:14, A24, from Chiusi; Donati 1989:116, no. 21, fig. 41, pl. XXXIX, from Saturnia; Bartoloni 1972:132, no. 115, fig. 63, pl. LXXXIIIa, from Poggio Buco; Pellegrini 1989:31, no. 46, pl. X, from Poggio Buco.

38. Cup
Fig. 17; Pl. 11
MURLO NO.: 71-214
FI: 112460
GRID: Rec.7, A/2
STRATUM: 2
Ht. 0.102; Ht. of foot 0.019; Diam. of rim 0.135; Diam. of foot 0.061 m.

Mended from numerous fragments. Missing portions of bowl, rim, and handles as well as one-half of foot, which have all been restored in plaster. Chipped and worn, but some of finely burnished original surface remains.

Cup with deep spherical body, everted rim, and two horizontal loop handles rests on hollow conical foot with thin base and tall stem. Handles symmetrically placed, attached at shoulder, and tilt slightly upward. Single incised horizontal line runs around rim below lip. Incised horizontal zigzag bordered at top by horizontal line encircles interior of rim.

BIBLIOGRAPHY: *Case e palazzi*:80, no. 68.

COMPARANDA: No direct parallels noted, although the shape resembles that of Rasmussen cup Type 3a (see Rasmussen 1979:pl. 38, no. 217).

TYPE 2: **39** AND **40**.

41 and **42** probably also belong to this type, although not enough of their profiles are preserved to permit a reconstruction of their shapes with certainty. In total, these fragments represent either three or four cups.[38]

This second group constitutes a previously unclassified variant of Rasmussen cup Type 3b (Rasmussen 1979:119–20, pls. 38, 39). Though their shape is similar to that of the latter, they have a more rounded profile and possess a ring base instead of a conical foot. These cups can be classed among the numerous bucchero imitations of Ionic bowls of Villard and Vallet Type A2.[39] The closest parallel for these cups is provided by a cup found at Poggio Civitate in Trench 18 (Nielsen and Phillips 1986:10, Murlo no. 73-287, figs. 5a, 6). While no other close parallels exist in bucchero, certain Etrusco-Corinthian cups, particularly those of the Rosoni cycle, have a very similar shape.[40] The Ionic cups of Type A2, which are dated to 620–600 B.C., provide a *terminus post quem* for this cup type (Villard and Vallet 1955:29).

39. Cup
Fig. 18; Pl. 12
MURLO NO.: 71-557
GRID: Rec.7, C/3
STRATUM: 2
Max. Pres. Ht. 0.062; Diam. of rim 0.112; Diam. of base 0.039 m.

Mended from 18 pieces. Broken across one side. Missing approximately half of body and rim, a small portion of one handle, and almost all of other handle. Worn and chipped. Thin-walled fabric.

Fragmentary, thin-walled bucchero cup with shallow rounded bowl and short everted rim. Cup rests on low ring base. Loop handles attach at shoulder just below rim and tilt slightly upward.

UNPUBLISHED.

COMPARANDA: Unclassified variant of Rasmussen Type 3b (see Rasmussen 1979:119–20).

40. Cup Fragment
Fig. 18; Pl. 12
MURLO NO.: 71-953
GRID: Rec.7, D/3; D-F/3; E/4; C-D/2; Rec.7 S.Wall, M/4-5
STRATUM: 2,4(I/O)
Max. Pres. Ht. 0.050; Diam. 0.112 m.

[38] **41** and **42**, which are fragmentary, may either represent separate cups or, alternatively, may belong to the same cup.

[39] Villard and Vallet 1955:14–31, figs. 3A, B. For a discussion of the imitation of Ionic cups in bucchero, see M. Martelli, in *Archaeologica. Studi in onore di A. Neppi Modona* (Florence, 1975):209 and note 13. Martelli has also elsewhere suggested the possibility of metal prototypes for some of the bucchero cups; see Martelli 1978:166 and note 51. It should be noted that Ionic cups of Villard and Vallet Type A2 were found in the Lower Building; see Nielsen and Phillips 1974:268–70.

[40] For a discussion and presentation of these cups, see G. Colonna, *StEtr* 29 (1961):47–89. I do not mean to suggest that these Etrusco-Corinthian cups inspired the bucchero cups from Poggio Civitate. Rather, it would appear that they both share a common prototype.

Mended from 8 pieces. Broken irregularly across one side. Missing base, one complete handle, half of preserved handle, two-thirds of body and rim. Chipped and worn. Shiny black surface.

Same as **39** above, except that exterior surface of rim is decorated with incised horizontal line below lip and incised zigzag is bordered above by horizontal line on interior of rim.

UNPUBLISHED.
COMPARANDA: See **39** above.

41. Cup Fragment
Fig. 18; Pl. 12
MURLO NO.: 71-951
GRID: Rec.7, B/4
STRATUM: 2
Max. Pres. Ht. 0.033; Max. Pres. Diam. 0.064 m.

Mended from 8 pieces. Broken irregularly on 3 sides. Missing base, one handle, most of cup wall and rim. Chips missing from rim. Chipped and worn. Shiny black surface.

Fragment preserves small portion of curving shoulder and short everted rim of small thin-walled cup. One horizontal loop handle preserved. Handle tilts upward and attaches at shoulder.

UNPUBLISHED.
COMPARANDA: Not enough is preserved to determine its complete shape, although it appears to be similar to **39** and **40** above.

42. Cup Fragment
Fig. 18; Pl. 12
MURLO NO.: 70-287
GRID: Rec.6, G-J/1-4
STRATUM: 2
Max. Pres. Ht. 0.037; Max. Pres. Diam. 0.057 m.

Single fragment. Broken on all sides except along small portion of rim. Missing most of body, rim, foot, and one handle. Chips missing from rim. Worn and chipped. Shiny black surface.

Fragment preserves small portion of curving shoulder and short everted rim of small thin-walled bucchero cup. One horizontal loop handle preserved. Handle attaches at shoulder and tilts slightly upward.

UNPUBLISHED.
COMPARANDA: Not enough is preserved to determine its complete shape, although it appears to be similar to **39** and **40** above.

TYPE 3: **43.**

Not enough of this cup is preserved to permit secure identification of its complete shape. The preserved portions seem to indicate that the vessel is rather deep, like a skyphos, but there are no parallels in bucchero. Perhaps this cup represents a loose adaptation of Ionic cups of Type A, but with a deeper bowl and straighter profile (Villard and Vallet 1955:14–31).

43. Cup Fragment
Fig. 18; Pl. 12
MURLO NO.: 71-950
GRID: Rec.7, F/3; Rec.7, W.Wall, W/4; Rec.8, A/1-4
STRATUM: 2,4 (I/O)
Max. Pres. Ht. 0.066; Max. Pres. Diam. 0.101 m.

Mended from 6 pieces. Broken irregularly on 3 sides. Missing base and two-thirds of body and rim. Chipped and worn, but still preserves portion of original shiny surface.

Fragment preserves approximately one-third of cup with sharply sloping wall, high shoulder, and straight everted rim. Exterior surface of fragment decorated with series of parallel vertical grooves. Below grooves appear portions of three parallel horizontal lines.

UNPUBLISHED.
COMPARANDA: Not enough of the cup is preserved to reconstruct its shape with certainty. No parallels noted.

VI. CHALICES (44–46)

All three types of chalices found in the Lower Building are unclassified types.[41] Each is represented by a single example.

[41] For a discussion of the history and development of the chalice in Etruria, see Ramage 1970:25–27; Rasmussen 1979:96. While Ramage believes the chalice to be an imported type, inspired by the import of the Assyrian chalice, Rasmussen identifies it as a native Italic shape.

There are no known parallels for chalice Types 1 and 2. Other bucchero chalices have a taller flaring wall and a deeper, more convex bowl with a more sharply sloping floor (cf. Rasmussen 1979:pls. 27–29). Instead, closer parallels for both types, particularly **45**, are found among impasto chalices that were made throughout south Etruria and Latium during the seventh and early sixth centuries.[42] The closer proximity of both chalices to impasto rather than to bucchero examples suggests that they may represent early transitional types.

TYPE 1: **44**.

This chalice displays a shallow bowl with a nearly flat floor, a short, almost vertical wall, and a low conical foot.

44. Chalice
Fig. 18; Pl. 12
MURLO NO.: 74-12
GRID: Rec.5, I-J/0-1
STRATUM: 2
Ht. 0.067; Diam of rim 0.103; Diam. of foot 0.071 m.

Mended from 7 pieces. Broken irregularly across one side of wall and tondo. Missing approximately half of tondo and three-quarters of wall. Chip on side of foot. Worn and chipped. Shiny black.

Small chalice with slightly convex body and nearly vertical wall with sloping lip. Cup rests on hollow conical foot with wide base. Two parallel grooves decorate exterior cup wall.

UNPUBLISHED.

COMPARANDA: No parallels noted for this chalice in bucchero. Impasto examples noted in discussion above.

TYPE 2: **45**.

This example has a slightly convex body with a vertical wall and a sloping lip, and a short ledge at the carination. It is almost certainly to be restored with a low conical foot.

45. Chalice Fragment (2 fragments)
Fig. 18; Pl. 12
MURLO NOS.: 71-805; 71-806
GRID: Rec.8, A/3
STRATUM: 2
Diam. of rim 0.088; Max. Pres. Ht. 0.027 m.

Two nonjoining fragments. Fragment A: Mended from 4 pieces. Chip missing from rim. Fragment B: Mended from 7 pieces. Small piece of corroded bronze on underside. Both fragments broken irregularly across one side. Missing foot and one-third of body. Surface worn, scratched, and burned. Mottled orange-brown in color. Gray-black biscuit.

Fragment preserves approximately two-thirds of chalice with slightly convex body, vertical wall, and sloping lip. Short ledge appears at carination. Two parallel grooves encircle wall on exterior.

The chalice is to be restored with a conical foot.

UNPUBLISHED.

COMPARANDA: No parallels noted in bucchero. Impasto examples noted in discussion above.

TYPE 3: **46**.

This piece has a slightly convex bowl with an outcurving wall, a tall everted rim, and a low conical foot with a short stem. Not enough of the vessel is preserved to permit secure reconstruction of its complete shape. In addition, I know of no vessels which might aid in the identification of its

[42] Impasto chalices first appeared in the early 7th century and continued to be produced into the first half of the 6th century. They were generally of two types, either displaying a vertical or nearly vertical wall and a shallow bowl, like **44**, or a slightly convex wall and a more sharply carinated bowl with an sloping ledge at the carination, like **45**. For a discussion of the impasto types, including numerous citations of both examples, see *Cerveteri* 1986:91, no. 12; Pohl 1981:59–60. For an additional example of a shape similar to **44**, see *CVA Umbria* 1 (Terni):IV B k, pl. 8.6, from Fondo Altarocca. Impasto chalices have been found at Poggio Civitate, but they are later in date and much closer in shape to contemporary bucchero examples; see Bouloumié-Marique 1978:76, nos. 524, 525.

shape. Its relatively small size suggests that it is a chalice, although it might have had a handle(s).

A number of small kantharoi are known from Poggio Buco which display a somewhat similar shape, including an outcurving wall and flaring rim, but they have a more convex bowl with a sharply sloping floor.[43]

46. Chalice Fragment
Fig. 19; Pl. 46
MURLO NO.: 71-819
GRID: Rec.7, E/2-4
STRATUM: 2
Ht. 0.10; Diam. of rim 0.130; Diam. of foot 0.075 m.

Mended from 8 pieces. Broken irregularly across one side. Missing most of rim and three-quarters of body. Chip on foot. Chipped, worn, and burned, but still preserves much of original glossy surface. Color varies from orange-brown to black. Black biscuit.

One-third of chalice with slightly convex body, outcurving wall, and tall everted rim. Chalice rests on low conical foot with short stem. Two low flat ridges define carination between bowl and vessel wall. A third low flat ridge defines carination between wall and rim. Lower half of wall decorated with series of small, broad, outpressed scallops. Deep grooves outline top and sides of each scallop.

The body of this vessel was thrown in a mold.

UNPUBLISHED.
COMPARANDA: No parallels noted.

VII. PHIALE (47)

One fragmentary phiale was recovered from the Lower Building. As a shape, the phiale is rare in bucchero, although it is frequently represented in Etruscan art.[44] The Etruscan phiale is generally believed to be derived from Near Eastern, probably Assyrian, metal ribbed bowls, which were first imported and then later imitated in Etruria.[45] De Puma has suggested that the absence of ribbing on most bucchero phiale is to be attributed to the influence of Greek ceramic phialai which also omit this feature.[46]

The phiale from Poggio Civitate is small, with a deep convex bowl and a short conical boss. Similar phialai have been found at Roselle, Poggio Buco, Rome, and Accesa (Massa Marittima).[47] The other known examples of plain bucchero phialai are generally larger and have less convex bowls with conical or button-shaped bosses of greater dimensions.[48]

The phiale appeared relatively late in bucchero; no examples have been found in contexts

---

[43] For examples of these kantharoi, see Donati 1967:628, no. 36, pl. CXXVIIIc, from Poggio Buco; Bartoloni 1972:91, no. 57, fig. 41, pl. LIC, from Poggio Buco; Matteucig 1951:51, no. 56, pl. XXI.6, from Poggio Buco; Pellegrini 1989:no. 292, from Poggio Buco. These kantharoi, all of which feature elaborate molded and applied decorations, are usually dated to the first half of the 6th century B.C.

[44] The classic study of the phiale remains that of H. Luschey (*Die Phiale* [Bleicherade am Harz, 1939]). For a discussion of the bucchero phiale, see Rasmussen 1979:126–27. The phiale often appears in Etruscan art as a hand-held object, particularly in bronze statuettes and on funerary urns; see Edlund 1980:51; De Puma 1986:47–48 and note 58.

[45] Rasmussen 1979:127. For metal ribbed bowls see the discussion of the kyathos Type 3 above.

[46] De Puma 1986:48 and note 61. In his discussion, De Puma cites examples only of Attic phialai. However, it is equally possible that the bucchero shape could have been influenced by Corinthian examples. For a general discussion of Corinthian phialai, see Amyx 1988:464–65. In addition, the phiale appears among the earliest Etrusco-Corinthian shapes, and Rasmussen (1979:127) notes that two Etrusco-Corinthian phialai were found together with a bucchero example in the same tomb at San Giovenale. For a discussion of Etrusco-Corinthian phialai, see J. G. Szilágyi, *StEtr* 40 (1972):36–37, 40, pl. Vd. It should also be noted that there exist examples of nonribbed metal Etruscan phialai; see Donati 1989:128–30, no. 41, fig. 46, pl. XLVI; Montelius 1910:964, pl. 217, fig. 6.

[47] For these examples, see the comparanda cited in the catalogue entry.

[48] Cf. De Puma 1986:47–48, VC39, pl. 14a, b, from Vulci; von Mercklin 1936:390, no. 42, pl. XLI.10; *SG* I.5, 59, nos. 34, 35, pl. XXVII; 123, no. 22, pl. LIII, from San Giovenale; *Enea*:143, C47, C48, from Rome; A. Emiliozzi, *La collezione Rossi Danielli nel Museo Civico di Viterbo* (Rome, 1974):126, no. 118, pl. LXXIX; P. Villa D'Amelio, *NSc* 27 (1963): 20, nos. 6, 7, fig. 19.6–7, from San Giuliano; Falconi Amorelli 1968:172, no.13, pl. XXIX, c–d, from Ischia di Castro.

dated earlier than the last quarter of the seventh century (Rasmussen 1979:127). The phialai from Roselle (Donati 1988:88–89, 93, no. 124, fig. 12a,b) and Poggio Buco (Bartoloni 1972:96, nos. 79, 107, Tomb VII) come from contexts dated to the last quarter of the seventh and first half of the sixth centuries, but these are not likely to be among the earliest material in their deposits. Those from Rome are dated by their contexts to the second half of the sixth century.[49] The phiale from Accesa has been dated on the basis of its style to the first half of the sixth century (Camporeale 1997:168–169, no. 3).

47. Phiale Fragment
Fig. 19; Pl. 12
MURLO NO.: 71-947
GRID: Rec. 7Ext., X-Y/2
STRATUM: 2
Max. Pres. Ht. 0.031; Max. Pres. Diam 0.157 m.

Mended from 16 pieces. Missing rim, approximately two-thirds of body, and small portion of boss. Chipped and worn, but still preserves much of its original shiny surface.

Fragment preserves approximately one-third of small phiale with deep, curving, convex body and a large, central, hollow boss.

UNPUBLISHED.

COMPARANDA: For other examples of phialai of the same or similar shape, see: Donati 1988:88–89, no. 124, fig. 12a, b, from Roselle; Bartoloni 1972:96, no. 79, fig. 42, pl. LIIf, from Poggio Buco; Edlund 1980:35, 51, no. 45, pl. 17; *ER* 3:147, fig. 96, nos. 30–32; 192, fig. 124, nos. 2, 3, 6; 416, fig. 259, nos. 4–7; 437, fig. 275, nos. 1, 2, from Rome; Cimino 1986:93–94, 240–41, pl. 56; Camporeale 1997:168–169, no. 3, fig. 24, from Accesa (Massa Marittima).

VIII. JARS (48, 49)

Two types of jars have been identified, and both are previously unclassified types.

TYPE 1: 48.

This type is distinguished by an ovoid body with a tall sloping wall, an incurving shoulder, and a flat, slightly convex base. This shape is not common in bucchero. A group of bucchero jars with a very similar shape, although possessing a ring instead of a flat base and two handles in the form of bull's heads, is known from Chiusi and Cetona.[50] While the find circumstances of the examples from Chiusi are unknown, two of the examples from Cetona come from tombs dated by Cristofani to the last quarter of the seventh century (Cristofani 1971:80–81). In addition, impasto vessels of a related type are known from tombs of the eighth and seventh centuries in northern Italy, particularly in the area around Bologna[51] and Este.[52]

48. Fragmentary Jar (4 fragments)
Fig. 19; Pl. 13
MURLO NO.: 71-515
FI: 112995
GRID: Rec.7, F/3; Rec.7, S.Wall, M/3-4; Rec.8, A/1-4; B/1-4; C/1-4
STRATUM: 2,4,5(I/O)
Est. Diam. of jar at point of attachment to rim 0.100; Diam. of base 0.044. Fragment A: Max. Pres. Ht. 0.104; Max. Pres. W. 0.086; Diam. of stamped decoration 0.008. Fragment B: Max. Pres. Ht. 0.058; Max. Pres. W. 0.067. Fragment C: Max. Pres. Ht. 0.023; Max. Pres. W. 0.024. Fragment D: Max. Pres. Ht. 0.015; Max. Pres. W. 0.033 m.

---

[49] *ER* 3:201, 457, and note 5.

[50] For a discussion of these vessels, see Levi 1936:83–84, note 61 and Cristofani 1971:80–81.

[51] **48** displays a shape reminiscent of some of the jars and "situla-form" vases, which are found in both impasto and metal in the area of Bologna during the early Orientalizing period. Cf. R. L. Miller, in *Artefacts* 1986:270–71, figs. 1–6; *Castenaso* 1979:figs. 54, no. 4; 70, nos. 4, 5, 16; 71, nos. 7, 9; Montelius 1910:pls. 85.5, 93.3, 105.1. These examples come from tomb groups dated to the 8th and 7th centuries B.C.

[52] See F. R. Ridgway, in *Italy Before the Romans* (New York, 1979):431, figs. 6.7, 6.8; 439, fig. 12.9; 438, fig. 11.14; A. M. Chieco Bianchi and L. Calzavaro Capuis, *Este I*, vols. 1 and 2 (Rome, 1985):48, no. 3, pl. 5.3; 61, no. 3, pl. 12.3; 73, no. 31, pl. 23.31; 78, no. 13, pl. 126.13. The examples cited come from tomb groups of the Este II–III periods, which are dated to the 8th and 7th centuries B.C.

Four nonjoining fragments. Fragment A is mended from 7 pieces. Fragment B is mended from 4 pieces. Fragments C and D are single pieces. Each fragment is broken on all sides. Missing rim, half of base, and approximately two-thirds of body. Chipped and worn. Shiny surface. Black biscuit

Fragments preserve one-third of curving body and half of flat round base of small ovoid jar. Exterior surface preserves portions of three bands of individually stamped double volute palmettes set within recessed circles. Each palmette composed of two volutes with joined stems and incurving scrolls. Small round bud at base of palmette below the scrolls and three-petaled blossom in interior. Stamp set within circular field. Each band separated by two or three incised, irregularly spaced concentric lines.

BIBLIOGRAPHY: Phillips 1994:34, no. 16, fig. 4.23.

COMPARANDA: For vessels of a similar shape, see Giglioli 1935:13, pl. XLVIII.4, from Chiusi; L. A. Milani, *MonAnt* 9 (1899):Tomb 3, 160, b, fig. 22 and Tomb 5, 164–65, a, figs. 26, 28, from Cetona; Levi 1936:85, pl. 56, fig. 31, from Cetona and 83-84, pl. 59, figs. 37-38, from Chiusi. The same stamped decoration appears on the lid **114**.

ORNAMENT TYPE: 6a.

TYPE 2: **49**.

This jar displays an ovoid body with a short sloping wall and a bulging shoulder. No parallels for this shape are known in bucchero. Instead, possible comparanda for the shape are noted among early Iron Age impasto vessels from Latium[53] and southern Etruria (Hencken 1968:114, fig. 103f; 119, fig. 108e).

49. Fragmentary Jar (2 fragments)
Fig. 20; Pl. 13
MURLO NO.: 71-952 A, B
GRID: Rec.7 Ext., X-Y/2; Rec.7, C/3
STRATUM: 2,3
Est. diam. at point of attachment of rim 0.089; Est. Diam. of base 0.039. Fragment A: Max. Pres. Ht. 0.071; Max. Pres. W. 0.074. Fragment B: Max. Pres. Ht. 0.043 m; Max. Pres. W. 0.051 m.

Two nonjoining fragments. A: Mended from 10 pieces. Broken irregularly along all 4 sides. B: Mended from 3 pieces. Broken irregularly along all 4 sides. Missing most of base and wall and entire rim. Scratched and worn. Shiny, gray-black surface. Black biscuit.

Fragments preserve one-third of curving wall of small ovoid jar with flat base. Surface of bowl decorated with series of 13 grooves extending from just below shoulder to point just above base and increasing in width toward bottom. Resulting ridges between grooves divided by short, fine, vertical incisions. In addition, third through eighth ridges from top are further subdivided by horizontal as well as vertical incisions.

UNPUBLISHED.

COMPARANDA: No parallels noted.

IX. TRIPOD BOWLS (**50–52**)

One type of tripod bowl was found in the Lower Building.[54] It is represented by a minimum of two and a maximum of three examples.[55] The vessel displays a deep convex bowl with a vertical wall and a short, everted, thickened rim. The bowl rests on three molded supports that curve out at an oblique angle near the base and terminate in feline paws.

Although there are no exact parallels in either bucchero or impasto for these bowls, tripod pyxides of related shape are known from Rome and Narce. The pyxis from Rome was manufactured from buccheroid impasto and displays incised decoration (*CLP*:141, no. 5, pl. XXI, D5; see also *ER* 2:261–62, no. 5, fig. 232). Its con-

[53] In particular, the shape is reminiscent of many of the large impasto "dolia" and jars of smaller size found in burials of the Villanovan period. See G. Bartoloni, in *Artefacts*:236, fig. 4a; *CLP*:75, no. 2 (tomb VI), pl. IVa; 82, nos. 3, 4 (tomb X), pl. VII 3, 4; 88, no. 2 (tomb XXX), pl. XIB, 2; 112, no. 1 (tomb Y), pl. XIVA.

[54] Although the fabric of this vessel was originally published as impasto, an examination of the piece revealed it to be bucchero; see Nielsen and Phillips 1974:272.

[55] Not enough of the leg fragment **52** is preserved to determine whether it would have joined to the fragmentary bowl **51** or would have belonged to a third tripod bowl not preserved in the deposit.

vex carinated bowl has a sloping wall, and its convex lid is fitted with a spherical handle. The vessel rests on three supports that terminate in small, equine hooves. Narrow lateral flanges project from the sides of the supports. The pyxis was found in a tomb on the Esquiline hill that has been dated to the last third of the seventh century B.C.

The pyxis from Narce is painted and constitutes an adaptation of a Corinthian pyxis with added tripod supports (Dohan 1942:55, 60, no. 4, pl. XXX, no. 4). It displays a deep bowl with nearly straight sides and a convex lid. Two horizontal loop handles appear on the sides of the bowl. The vessel rests on three nearly vertical supports with wide, projecting lateral flanges that terminate in small humanoid feet. The vessel was recovered from a chamber tomb that can be dated to the middle of the seventh century B.C. Dohan (1942:60), in a discussion of these vessels from Narce and Rome, has suggested that the addition of feet to a pyxis was apparently an Italic idea.

Other tripod vessels of less closely related shapes are know from Narce,[56] Veii,[57] and Cerveteri.[58] All these vessels are made from impasto and display rounded bowls which rest on three supports. While the vessels from Narce and Cerveteri have short, slightly everted rims with flattened lips, the rim of the bowl from Veii is straight and possesses a rounded lip. The supports of the bowls are curvilinear in section and terminate in human feet. Projecting lateral flanges appear on the supports of the two vessels from Cerveteri and one of the vessels from Narce (Salskov Roberts 1974:69–70, no. 4151, fig. 35). This latter vessel from Narce is also painted with dark orange paint. The bowl from Veii comes from a tomb that has been dated to the first quarter of the seventh century B.C.[59] Only one of the vessels from Narce comes from a closely datable context; it was found in a tomb dated between the third quarter and end of the seventh century B.C. (Salskov Roberts 1974:72–74). The two tripod vessels from Cerveteri come from the Capanna tomb which has been dated to the first half of the seventh century B.C. (Prayon 1975:49).

A second type of tripod vessel has also been found at Veii (Cristofani 1969:50, no. 4, pl. 25, 5, fig. 25, 4). Like the other tripod bowls from Veii, Narce, and Cerveteri, it displays a rounded bowl and rests on three supports terminating in human feet. While the supports of the other bowl from Veii and of the two aforementioned tripod vessels from Narce are attached to the base of the vessel, the supports of this one are attached to the sides of the bowl. This vessel also features a short rim with a flattened lip. Two small holes spaced closely together have been drilled into the side of the vessel directly below the rim. The original context of this vessel is unknown.

Another type of bucchero tripod bowl is also known from Chiusi.[60] It has a very shallow bowl with a short convex wall and short but wide rectangular legs, each of which displays a molded female head. The leg bases, like the examples from Poggio Civitate, are molded in the form of feline paws, but the paws are much broader and have larger toes. None of these bowls has been recovered from a datable context.

A type of impasto tripod plate is also known from Veii (Palm 1952:66, no. 6, pl. 21; *CVA Roma, Museo Preistorico L. Pigorini* I:pl. 7, no. 7), Cerveteri (Ricci 1955:357, nos. 26, 27, fig. 77, nos. 6, 7; Mengarelli 1927:158–59, pl. 24), Capena,[61] and a private collection in Geneva (Camporeale 1991: 59, no. 54, pl. XXXVIII a, c). The vessel consists of a shallow plate with a horizontal rim. The bottom of the plate rests on three broad supports, which terminate in humanoid feet. The supports of the plates from Cerveteri and Veii are curvilinear in section and display projecting lateral flanges. The plates from Capena and the collection in Geneva rest on three nearly vertical, rectilinear supports.

---

[56] There are two examples from Narce; see Salskov Roberts 1974:69–70, no. 4151, fig. 35; *CVA Copenhagen* 5:IV B, 158, pl. 203, no. 1.

[57] There is one example from Veii; see Cristofani 1969:24, no. 21, fig. 5, pl. VII.2.

[58] There are two examples from Cerveteri; see Ricci 1955:356, no. 5, fig. 77, no. 16; 358, no. 38, fig. 77, no. 15; Mengarelli 1927:158–59, pl. 24.

[59] The bowl was recovered from Monte Michele Tomb B. For the dating of the tomb, see Cristofani 1969:70.

[60] *CVA British Museum* 7:IV B a, pl. 20, no. 14, from Chiusi; *Bildertafeln des Etruskischen Museums der Ny Carlsberg Glyptothek* (Copenhagen, 1928):pl. 40, no. H108.

[61] There are four examples from Capena; see R. Paribeni, *MonAnt* 16 (1906):301, no. 20; *CVA Roma, Museo Preistorico L. Pigorini* I:pl. 10, no. 6.

They also possess slightly broader rims. While the rims of the four vessels from Capena are decorated with stylized painted birds, the rim of the plate in Geneva displays a series of six, incised concentric circles. Camporeale has noted that plates like the example in Geneva, although more often lacking supports, are commonly found in the Falisco-Capenate region, where they appear to have been produced. He has dated the vessel in Geneva on the basis of the contexts of plates of similar type, including that of the plates from Capena, between the first and second quarters of the seventh century. The plates from Capena were found in a tomb that contained material that can be dated to the first half of the seventh century (Camporeale 1991:59). The two plates from Cerveteri were recovered from the Capanna tomb and can be dated to the first half of the seventh century (Prayon 1975:49). Finally, the plate from Veii comes from a tomb that can be dated to the first decades of the seventh century (Camporeale 1991:59, note 6).

Other parallels for the tripod bowls from Poggio Civitate can perhaps be found in bronze. A bronze tripod bowl very similar in conception to those from the Lower Building, although of larger proportions, was found in the "Isis-Tomb" at Vulci and dated to the first half of the sixth century.[62] Like the vessels from the Lower Building, it has a convex bowl with a vertical wall and a short, everted rim, and legs terminating in feline paws. The bronze bowl, however, has a much taller wall than those of the bucchero bowls, and broader, rectangular legs, which project outward from the base, then bend at a right angle, and continue straight down. In addition, a number of sixth-century bronze basin supports from Castel San Mariano have legs terminating in feline paws of a type similar to those found on the bowls from Poggio Civitate.[63]

50. Tripod Bowl
Fig. 20; Pl. 13
MURLO NO.: 72-281
FI: 112456
GRID: Rec.5, J/0
STRATUM: 2
Ht. 0.102; Ht. of bowl 0.037; Diam. of rim 0.121 m.

Almost complete. Mended from numerous fragments. Pieces missing from bowl, wall, and rim, which have been restored in plaster. Several small chips on rim. Small hole in base of bowl. Worn and burned, but original shiny surface remains in places. Mottled red-brown color with larger patches of black on underside of bowl and feet. Black biscuit.

Tripod bowl with deep convex body, vertical wall, and short, everted, thickened rim. Bowl rests on three molded supports, each semicircular in cross section and tapering toward base. In profile, support curves out at oblique angle near base and terminates in feline paw, articulated into four toes and with oval base. Short vertical striation appears above each digit, probably representing tendon. Two grooves encircle body of bowl. Between grooves, continuous pattern of squares with two diagonal lines intersecting in an "X." Carination decorated with notches.

The body of the bowl was thrown on a wheel. The legs were mold-made and then applied to the bowl when the clay had become leather-hard.

BIBLIOGRAPHY: Nielsen and Phillips 1974:272, ill. 9, pl. 58, fig. 15; *Case e palazzi*:86, no. 121, pl. 3-121; *Antiquarium*:30, fig. 25.

COMPARANDA: No exact parallels noted. For related vessels, see *CLP*:141, no.5, pl. XXI, D5, from Rome; Dohan 1942:55, 60, no. 4, 108, pl. XXX, no. 4, from Narce.

51. Tripod Bowl Fragment
Fig. 51; Pl. 13
MURLO NO.: 72-354
GRID: Rec.5, J/0-1; Tes. 26
STRATUM: 2, 5 (I/0)
Max. Pres. Ht. 0.80; Ht. of body 0.36; Diam. of rim 0.105 m.

Mended from numerous fragments. Missing two supports and base of third support as well

[62] S. Haynes, in *La civiltà arcaica di Vulci e la sua espansione*. Atti del X convegno nazionale di studi etruschi ed italici, Grosseto-Roselle-Vulci, 1975 (Florence, 1977):25–26, pl. VIIIf. Haynes notes that the tripod bowl from Vulci has been dated to the first half of the 6th century B.C. by Strøm.

[63] U. Höckmann, *Die Bronzen aus dem Fürstengrab von Castel San Mariano bei Perugia* (Munich, 1982):100–102, nos. 62, 63, fig. 66, pl. 58.2–7.

as small portions of bowl and wall. Several chips on rim. Surface worn, chipped, and burned. Mottled red-brown color with large patch of black on exterior wall and portion of base and smaller black patch on corresponding portion of interior wall. Black biscuit.

Same as **50** above, except that there is no decoration between the grooves on the body and the carination is plain. In addition, excavation along the northern flank of the Southeast Building in Trench 26 recently produced a leg fragment (Murlo no. 92-42) that joins this tripod bowl. This new fragment is not included in the illustration or photograph of the vessel contained in this volume.

UNPUBLISHED.
COMPARANDA: Same as **50** above.

52. Tripod Bowl Leg Fragment
Pl. 13
MURLO NO.: 71-91
GRID: Rec.7, C/2
STRATUM: 2
Max. Pres. Ht. 0.053; Max. Pres. W. 0.018 m.

Mended from 3 pieces. Worn, cracked, and chipped, but some of original surface remains.

Fragment preserves approximately three-quarters of molded support from tripod bowl. Support semicircular in cross section and tapering toward base. In profile, the support curves out at an oblique angle near base and terminates in feline paw, articulated into four toes and with an oval base. Short vertical striation appears above each digit, probably representing the tendon.

UNPUBLISHED.
COMPARANDA: Same as **50** above.

X. FOOTED BOWLS (53–55)

Two types of footed bowls were recovered.

TYPE 1: 53.

This type displays a low conical foot, a shallow bowl with a sharply carinated convex body and an inset, slightly inverted rim. The lid of the bowl has a convex carinated body and a short, slightly everted vertical rim. Footed bowls of similar shape are known from many sites in both northern and southern Etruria.[64] Generally, these footed bowls are not designed to be provided with lids. A notable exception is an example from Cetona, which, except for its taller foot, is very close in shape to the example from Poggio Civitate.[65] Covered bowls of a similar shape are also found in Etrusco-Corinthian pottery, although their occurrence is rare.[66]

Bowls of this type display a great deal of variation, particularly in the size and height of the foot and the sharpness of the carination, and, as a result, it is possible to identify several regional variants (Camporeale 1967:105). Camporeale has suggested that these bowls, especially the early examples, may be derived from metal prototypes (Camporeale 1970:106–7). In contrast to the majority of bucchero examples of this type, the bowl from Poggio Civitate displays a more sharply sloping profile and is more sharply carinated. In addition, the sloping ledge found at the point of the carination is broader than is commonly found, but this can be attributed to the need to accommodate a lid. Instead, with the exception of the examples from Cetona and Cortona, closer parallels for the Poggio Civitate bowl are to be found among the impasto examples.[67]

---

[64] For a discussion of these bowls, see Camporeale 1970:105–7. Footed bowls of this general shape are also found at Vulci, Veii, and Narce; see De Puma 1986:44, VC 27, pl. 12d, from Vulci; *Materiali* II, 9, tomb 122, nos. 139, 140, from Vulci; Camporeale 1969:20, no. 6, fig. 3.6, pl. IV.4, from Veii; Dohan 1942:69, no. 7, pl. XXXVII.9, from Narce.

[65] Of the examples cited in the comparanda section of the catalogue entry, only one bowl in addition to that from Cetona may have a lid, but the association of the lid with the bowl is not secure; see Hayes 1985:22, A52, A53. It should also be noted that the lid shown on impasto bowl Murlo no. 71-613, from Poggio Civitate, does not belong to the bowl since the bowl is impasto and the lid is bucchero; see *Case e Palazzi*:86, no. 120, pl. 3-120. In addition, Nielsen and Phillips have suggested that the impasto bowl Murlo no. 73-216 from Poggio Civitate may also have had a lid, although no lid has been found with it; see Nielsen and Phillips 1977a:89, ill. 5, figs. 7 and 8.

[66] I know of only one example of a covered bowl of this type in Etrusco-Corinthian pottery: see *CVA Firenze, Museo Archeologico* 1:III C e, pl. 2, no. 6, from Vetulonia.

[67] It should be noted that the impasto bowl from Poggio Civitate, Murlo no. 71-321 (cited in the comparanda section of the catalogue entry), was also found in the Lower Building. Unlike most of the bucchero examples, the majority of impasto bowls are strongly carinated, and most have a ledge at the carination.

Impasto and bucchero footed bowls of this general type were produced in Etruria during both the seventh and sixth centuries (Camporeale 1970:105). The two bucchero examples from Cetona, which are very close in shape to the example from the Lower Building, come from tombs dated to the last quarter of the seventh and the first years of the sixth century B.C.[68] The contexts of the three impasto examples most similar in shape to **53**, two of which are in Toronto (Hayes 1985:22, A52; 52–53, B42) and the third in Grosseto (Donati and Michelucci 1981:153, no. 358), are not known. They have been tentatively dated on the basis of their style from the middle of the seventh to the early sixth century B.C.

53. Covered Footed Bowl
Fig. 20; Pl. 13
MURLO NO.: 72-355; 72-356
FI: 112476; 112477
GRID: Rec.5, J-K/0
STRATUM: 2
Ht. of lid 0.067; Diam. of lid rim 0.140; Ht. of bowl 0.081; Diam. of bowl rim 0.130; Diam. of foot 0.070 m.

Lid: Missing one-quarter of body and rim. Handle chipped. Surface worn and burned. Exterior surface colored reddish-brown with black spots. Interior surface uniformly black. Black biscuit. Bowl: Almost complete. Mended from numerous fragments. Missing portions of rim, body, and foot. Missing portions of foot restored in plaster. Surface worn and burned. Exterior surface, including foot, colored reddish-brown with black spots. Interior of bowl, including rim, and interior of foot, uniformly black. Black biscuit.

Lid: Lid with convex carinated body and short, slightly everted vertical rim. Lid crowned by knob handle with thick, cylindrical concave stem. Small boss at top of handle. Three groups of narrow grooves encircle exterior surface of the lid: three at the base; two at the center; and two at the top, below the handle. Two additional grooves, heavily worn in places, encircle rim above edge.

Bowl: Shallow bowl with conical, sharply carinated body. Short sloping ledge at carination with short, inset, slightly inverted rim to accommodate lid. Low conical foot is hollow and has short flaring stem. Shallow circular depression at center of bowl.

BIBLIOGRAPHY: Nielsen and Phillips 1974:272–73, ill. 10, pl. 59, figs. 16, 17; *Case e palazzi*:86, no. 123.

COMPARANDA: Bowls of this type are generally not found with lids. For a covered bowl of the same shape, although with a taller pedestal foot, see *Etrusker*:283–84, no. 28, from Cetona. For other bucchero bowls of similar shape, see *Cortona*:73, no. 42, from Cortona; Levi 1936:fig. 40, from Cetona. For related bucchero bowls, see Camporeale 1970:105–8, nos. 76–86, fig. 34, pls. XXII, XXIII, from Orvieto; *Roselle*:52, no. 1, fig. 16, from Roselle; Bartoloni 1972:130, nos. 105–107, fig. 62, pl. LXXXIb–d, from Poggio Buco; Hayes 1985:112, C95, fig. 11; Museo Archeologico di Chiusi, Tomb A, Caditoia da Aducello (Sinalunga), no. 5.

For an impasto bowl of similar shape from Poggio Civitate, see Murlo no. 71-321; *Case e palazzi*:86, no. 120, pl. 3-120. For similar impasto bowls from outside Poggio Civitate, see Hayes 1985:22, A52; 52–53, B42; Donati and Michelucci 1981:153, no. 358. For related impasto bowls from Poggio Civitate and elsewhere, see Nielsen and Phillips 1977a:89, Murlo no. 73-216, ill. 5, figs. 7, 8, from Poggio Civitate; Bartoloni 1972:42, nos. 19–21, fig. 15, pl. XVIIIe–g, from Poggio Buco.

For examples of bucchero lids of similar shape, see Hayes 1985:125, C123, fig. 6, from Chiusi. For examples of impasto lids of similar shape, see Hayes 1985:19, A43; 40, B16.

TYPE 2: **54, 55.**

These bowls display a shallow, sloping, convex body with a shallow circular depression in the center of the body, a narrow, slightly everted rim, and a tall conical foot. There is a torus molding between the body and stem. A large quantity of bucchero, buccheroid, and impasto footed bowls of nearly identical shape, only lacking the torus molding between the stem and bowl, have been found at Poggio Civitate, the majority in Trench

[68] For the date of the covered example see A. Rastrelli, in *Etrusker*:283–84, no. 28 and 288. The other example from Cetona comes from a tomb group originally dated by Levi to the middle of the 6th century B.C. (Levi 1936:86). Levi's dates, however, are too low and should be raised by at least half a century; see M. Cristofani, *ArchCl* 23 (1971):12–25. The bowl from Cortona has been generically dated to the 6th century B.C.; see *Cortona*: 72, nos. 42–43.

18.[69] Due to the great number of these bowls (more than 150 are known), Bouloumié has postulated that they were produced on the site, constituting a local speciality (Bouloumié-Marique 1978:74 and note 14; B. Bouloumié, in *Case e palazzi*:139). Among these examples, the two bowls from the Lower Building are the only decorated examples; they are also distinguished by their fine fabric.

Outside Poggio Civitate, bucchero footed bowls of nearly identical shape, although lacking the torus molding between the stem of the foot and bowl, have been found at Cetona and Orvieto. The example from Cetona displays a figural cylinder stamped decoration of Chiusine type around its interior near the edge of the rim. This vessel comes from a chamber tomb dated between the last quarter of the seventh and the beginning of the sixth centuries (A. Rastrelli, in *Etrusker*:283, no. 27, and 288). The footed bowl from Orvieto was found in a chamber tomb containing at least two depositions. The bowl has been assigned to the later deposition, which dates to the first half of the sixth century (Camporeale 1994:35–36, fig. VII, f). In addition, a similar footed bowl has been recovered from Castelluccio in Pienza (Cimino 1986:100, no. 270, pl. 58). However, this vessel has a more curving profile than that of the footed bowls form Poggio Civitate, Cetona, and Orvieto. It also displays elaborate incised decoration on its interior. The bowl from Castelluccio in Pienza does not come from a datable context.

Other closely related examples, although with thicker, externally grooved rims and also lacking the torus molding between the stem of the foot and bowl, have been found at Orvieto (Montelius 1910:1017, pl. 242, fig. 11), and at Chiusi where they also are thought to have been produced.[70] One of the bowls from Chiusi was found in the Pania tomb, which has been dated by Cristofani to the years between 620 and 580 B.C.[71] In addition, bowls of a later type with bodies of a shape similar to those of the examples form Poggio Civitate, but with taller, thicker, grooved rims with applied decoration and lacking the torus molding between the bowl and stem, are also known from Chiusi (Donati 1968:pls. LXXVb, LXXVIIIf, g), Vulci (De Puma 1986:65–67, CA 13, fig. 18, pl. 22b, c), and Orvieto (see De Puma 1986:67, note 20).

54. Footed Bowl
Fig. 21; Pl. 14
MURLO NO.: 72-357;72-405
FI: 112453
GRID: Rec.5, J/0; I/1
STRATUM: 2
Max. Pres. Ht. of bowl 0.063; Diam. of rim 0.20; Max. Pres. Ht. of foot 0.050; Diam. of foot 0.105 m.

Two nonjoining fragments. Bowl: Mended from numerous pieces. Broken through stem. Missing several pieces of rim and body. Surface worn, cracked, and burned. Mottled orange-brown in color with small patch of black at edge of rim. Black biscuit. Foot: Mended from 6 pieces. Broken through stem and irregularly across one side of base. Chips missing from base and stem. Surface worn, scratched, and burned. Mottled orange-brown in color. Gray-black biscuit.

Footed bowl with shallow, sloping, convex body and short everted rim. Circular depression at center of bowl, which rests on tall conical foot. Base of foot slightly upturned. Torus molding between stem and bowl. Rim surface decorated with cylinder-stamped guilloche pattern. Ridge ornamented with diagonal notches encircles stem of foot.

[69] All these examples were found in Trench 18 in a sandy yellow layer above the burned stratum, which contained burned pottery of a type very similar to that found in the Lower Building. It is not clear whether the material in this sandy yellow layer, most of which is unburned, is to be associated with the material in the burn layer and the Orientalizing phase of the site, or whether it is later, from the Archaic period; see Nielsen and Phillips 1974:277; Nielsen and Phillips 1975:363; Nielsen and Phillips 1977a:86–87.

[70] A. Rastrelli, in *Etrusker*:283, no. 27. The footed bowls cited in the comparanda section of the catalogue entry for **54** in the Museum of Fine Arts, Boston, and in the British Museum have both been attributed to Chiusi on the basis of their cylinder-stamped decoration by Scalia (1968:364–66, no. 25 [MFA, Boston] and 368, no. 58 [British Museum]).

[71] Montelius 1910:987, pl. 224, no. 6b, c; Cristofani 1971:81–82. The other example from Chiusi comes from a tomb group which cannot be closely dated. The contents of the tomb, however, appear to be roughly contemporary with that of the Pania Tomb; see Montelius 1910:989, pl. 226, fig. 2a.

BIBLIOGRAPHY: *Case e palazzi*:85, no. 118.

COMPARANDA: A large number of bucchero, buccheroid, and impasto footed bowls of nearly identical shape, only lacking the torus molding between the stem and bowl, were found at Poggio Civitate in Trench 18; see Nielsen and Phillips 1974:277, Murlo no. 73-64, ill. 15, pl. 59, fig. 12; Nielsen and Phillips 1975:363, Murlo no. 73-33, ill. 10, pl. 64, figs. 18, 19; Nielsen and Phillips 1977a:86–87, Murlo no. 73-73, ill. 2, fig. 1; Bouloumié-Marique 1978:71-74, Forms F1 and F2, pls. IX, X, XII.

Footed bowls of nearly identical shape, although lacking the torus molding between the stem of the foot and bowl, have also been found at Cetona (Rastrelli, in *Etrusker*:283, no. 27) and Orvieto (Camporeale 1994:35–36, fig. VII, f). A similar footed bowl has also been recovered from Castelluccio in Pienza (Cimino 1986:100, no. 270, pl. 58). In addition, a number of footed bowls of similar shape, although with thicker, externally grooved rims and lacking the torus molding between the stem of the foot and bowl, have been found at Chiusi and Orvieto; see Montelius 1910:987, pl. 224, fig. 6c and 989, pl. 226, fig. 2a, both from Chiusi; Fairbanks 1928:212, no. 618, pl. LXXXI, attributed to Chiusi; *CVA British Museum* 7:IV B a, pl. 15, 5a, b, attributed to Chiusi; Montelius 1910:1017, pl. 242, fig. 11, from Orvieto.

ORNAMENT TYPE: 10b.

55. Footed Bowl
Fig. 21; Pl. 14
MURLO NO.: 78-219
GRID: Rec.5, J/0
STRATUM: 2
Max. Pres. Ht. 0.042; Diam. 0.185 m.

Restored from numerous fragments. Missing entire foot and portions of body and rim, much of which has been restored with plaster. Surface chipped, worn, and cracked. Base of bowl heavily restored, thus concealing attachment scar for foot.

Same as **54** above, except the bowl has a straighter profile and the cylinder-stamped pattern on the rim is of a slightly different type.

UNPUBLISHED.

COMPARANDA: For parallels see **54** above.

ORNAMENT TYPE: 10c.

XI. BROAD-RIMMED SHALLOW BOWLS AND PLATES (**56–101**)

Four types of shallow broad-rimmed bowls and plates were recovered from the Lower Building. None of these shapes are common in bucchero.[72]

Types 1, 2, and 3 are closely related in both shape and decoration, and can be discussed together as forming part of a single group. All the examples of these three types are small, have a low ring or disk base, and a broad horizontal or nearly horizontal rim, sometimes with a thickened outer edge. In addition, the surface of the rim of some of the examples is decorated with a low rounded ridge along the exterior edge.

TYPE 1: **56**, **57**.

This bowl type is distinguished by a tapering ring base and a slightly convex, sharply sloping body. There are a maximum of two and a minimum of one example(s) of bowls of Type 1, depending on whether or not **56** and **57** belong to the same vessel. Bowls of this type are unknown outside Poggio Civitate.

56. Bowl
Fig. 21; Pl. 14
MURLO NO.: 73-47
GRID: Rec.5, K/1
STRATUM: 2
Ht. 0.033; Diam. of rim 0.113; Diam. of base 0.045; W. of rim 0.019 m.

Mended from 8 pieces. Broken irregularly across one side of bowl and rim. Missing one-third of body and rim. Chips along side of rim and base. Worn and burned, but still preserves much of its original glossy surface. Bowl is fired black in interior and orange-brown to black on underside. Black biscuit.

[72] Rasmussen discusses material of this type under the category "bucchero as a domestic ware." Our knowledge of bucchero of this class, as he notes, is far from complete, but it is likely to increase as excavation focuses more on urban centers; see Rasmussen 1979:121.

Fragmentary small bowl with tapering ring base, shallow convex body, and wide horizontal rim. Low rounded ridge defines exterior edge of rim surface. Shallow groove runs along interior and exterior edges of rim. Surface of rim decorated with series of stamped double-volute palmettes. Two complete volute-palmettes and small portion of a third are preserved. Each palmette set within recessed triangle with rounded edges. Palmette composed of double volute with outcurving scrolls crowned by triangular bud. Long thickening stem curls outward from base of each volute. Two stems joined by short curving line. Triangular bud in intervening space.

BIBLIOGRAPHY: Rystedt 1983:140, fig. 106, note 192.
COMPARANDA: No parallels noted.
ORNAMENT TYPE: 7a.

57. Bowl Rim Fragment
Pl. 14
MURLO NO.: 73-126
GRID: Rec.5, K/1
STRATUM: 2
Max. Pres. Diam. 0.037; Max. Pres. W. 0.017; Th. 0.006–0.009 m.

Mended from 3 pieces. Broken on 3 sides. Missing bottom right side and lower portion of stamped decoration. Large chip on underside. Worn, but original glossy surface remains.

Same as **56** above.

UNPUBLISHED.
COMPARANDA: Same as **56** above.
ORMEMENT TYPE: 7a.

TYPE 2: **58–68**.

In contrast to bowls of Type 1, those of Type 2 have a fuller, more convex body with a curving profile. They may either have a ring or a disk base. In total, there are a maximum of 11 and a minimum of 9 bowls of this type which can be further subdivided according to their decoration. There are a maximum of 6 and a minimum of 4 bowls with ridges and stamped petal rosettes on their rims (**58–63**) and 5 examples with molded double-volute appliqués on their rims (**64–68**).

No exact parallels exist for these bowls outside Poggio Civitate. A group of related bucchero bowls are known from Chiusi, Cortona, and Roselle, but they have shorter rims and less curving profiles. The bowls from Chiusi and Cortona are generally found either in, or associated with, bucchero braziers, or "foculi," the production of which has been linked to Chiusi.[73] Since the "foculi" and their contents are generally dated to the second half of the sixth century, these bowls could not have served as prototypes for the examples from Poggio Civitate. Similarly, the bowls from Roselle have been recovered from contexts ranging in date from the middle of the sixth to the end of the fifth centuries B.C. (see Donati 1994:128, Plate type 1).

58. Bowl Fragment
Fig. 22; Pl. 15
MURLO NO.: 74-21
GRID: Rec.5, H/1-2; I-K/3; K/0-1; F-G/2; K/2-3
STRATUM: 2,3,5(I/O)
Diam. of rim 0.108; Max. Pres. Ht. 0.020; W. of rim 0.023 m.

Mended from 6 pieces. Missing base, most of body, and two-thirds of rim. Surface worn, chipped, and burned. Color of surface varies from light orange-brown to gray-black. Black biscuit.

Fragment preserves portion of small bowl with curving convex body and wide horizontal rim. Broad flat ridge encircles exterior edge of rim. Preserved on surface of rim are portions of decoration of three stamped flower-rosettes alternating with two sets of two incised concentric semicircles. Rosettes composed of series of six oval petals arranged in circle around central dot. Double incised semicircles placed with ends touching ridge along exterior edge of rim.

UNPUBLISHED.
COMPARANDA: For a complete example of a bowl of this type, see Plate 15 here and Phillips 1971:260, Murlo no. 70-100, pl. 61, figs. 27–29; Nielsen and Phillips 1974:262. This bowl was reconstructed from fragments recovered from Trench CA28 and Agger 4.

[73] For the "foculi" including bibliography, see *Civiltà*:293–94, no. 11.8; *Cortona*:82–84, no. 62.

For plain bowls of similar shape, but with slightly deeper profiles, see Hayes 1985:112–14, C96, C97, C99, fig. 11; *CVA British Museum* 7:IV B a, pl. 21, no. 11, from Chiusi; *CVA Brussels* 2:IV B, pl. 4, nos. 33–39; *CVA Sevrès* 1:IV B b, pl. 29, nos. 13, 14, from Chiusi; Cimino 1986:70–71, nos. 156–159, pl. 35; *Cortona*:86, no. 67, from Cortona; *Civiltà*:293–94, 11.8, no. 4, pl. 11.8; *CVA Altenburg* 3:pl. 128, no. 10; Donati 1994:128, Plate type 1, from Roselle.

ORNAMENT TYPE: 5.

59. Bowl Fragment
Fig. 22; Pl. 15
MURLO NO.: 72-385
GRID: Rec.5, J-K/0-1; I/2
STRATUM: 2,5(I/O)
Diam. of rim 0.103; Max. Pres. Ht. 0.026; W.of rim 0.021; Diam. of stamped decoration 0.010 m.

Mended from 3 pieces. Broken on all sides except along exterior edge of rim. Missing base, three-quarters of body, and two-thirds of rim. Several chips along edge of rim. Surface badly worn, encrusted, and burned. Surface color varies from gray-black to orange-brown. Black biscuit.

Same as **58** above, except the incised concentric semicircles on the rim face inward.

UNPUBLISHED.
COMPARANDA: Same as **58** above.

60. Bowl Fragment
Fig. 22; Pl. 15
MURLO NO.: 72-386
GRID: Rec.5, J/1
STRATUM: 2
Max. Pres. Dim. 0.061; Max. Pres. Ht. 0.025; Diam. of stamped decoration 0.010 m.

Mended from 2 pieces. Broken on all sides except along exterior edge of rim. Missing base, three-quarters of rim, and two-thirds of body. Surface heavily worn, chipped, and burned. While interior surface of fragment is gray-black in color, exterior is orange-brown. Black biscuit.

Same as **58** above.

UNPUBLISHED.
COMPARANDA: Same as **58** above.

61. Bowl Rim Fragment
Pl. 15
MURLO NO.: 74-19
GRID: Rec.5, I/1-2
STRATUM: 2
Diam. 0.125; Max. Pres. W. 0.018; Th. 0.004–0.005 m.

Broken on 3 sides. Large chip missing from rim surface along interior side. Most of stamped decoration missing. Chipped, worn, and burned. Color of surface varies from orange to gray-brown. Gray-black biscuit.

Same as **58** above.

UNPUBLISHED.
COMPARANDA: Same as **58** above.

62. Bowl Rim Fragment
Pl. 15
MURLO NO.: 72-387
GRID: Rec.5, I-J/0-1
STRATUM: 3(*I/O)
Max. Pres. Diam. 0.029; Max. Pres. W. 0.018; Th. 0.045–0.060; Diam. of stamped rosette 0.009 m.

Broken on 3 sides. Chipped, worn, and burned. Upper surface of fragment gray-black, underside orange-brown. Black biscuit.

Same as **58** above.

UNPUBLISHED.
COMPARANDA: Same as **58** above.

63. Bowl Rim Fragment
Pl. 15
MURLO NO.: 73-110
GRID: Rec.5, K/1
STRATUM: 2/3 (*I/O)
Max. Pres. L. 0.032; Max. Pres. W. 0.017; Th. 0.004–0.005 m.

Broken on 3 sides. Chipped, worn, and burned. Color of surface varies orange-brown to dull gray. Gray-black biscuit.

Same as **58** above.

UNPUBLISHED.
COMPARANDA: Same as **58** above.

64. Bowl
Fig. 22; Pl. 15
MURLO NO.: 72-329
FI: 112451
GRID: Rec.5, J/0
STRATUM: 2
Ht. 0.033; Diam. of rim 0.140; Diam. of base 0.049; Diam. of stamped decoration 0.008 m.

Almost entire. Mended from numerous fragments. Small portions of body restored with plaster. Missing one molded palmette appliqué. Surface slightly worn.

Low bowl with short disk base; shallow, curving, convex body; and wide horizontal rim. Rim surface decorated with series of three evenly spaced, molded appliqués representing stylized palmettes. Each appliqué composed of two volutes with joined stems and inward-curving tangent scrolls crowned by small lotus bud. Appliqués separated by series of individually stamped asterisk-rosettes which encircle interior edge of rim. Each rosette composed of 8 impressed triangles with their apices turned inward and arranged in a circle.

BIBLIOGRAPHY: Nielsen and Phillips 1974:271–72, ill. 7, pl. 58, figs. 10, 11; *Case e palazzi*:85, no. 114, pl. 3-114.

COMPARANDA: Same as **58** above. A similar appliqué decorates the rim of a large, unpublished impasto plate fragment (Murlo no. 78-40) recovered from the Lower Building and currently on display in the Murlo Antiquarium.

ORNAMENT TYPES: 4b, 24.

65. Bowl
Fig. 22; Pl. 15
MURLO NO.: 73-6
FI: 112452
GRID: Rec.5, J/1
STRATUM: 2
Ht. 0.024; Diam. 0.120; Diam. of base 0.050; L. of applied decoration 0.019; W. of applied decoration 0.018–0.019 m.

Complete. Chips along edge of rim where one appliqué is missing.

Low bowl with short ring base, shallow, curving, convex body, and wide horizontal rim. Surface of rim preserves decoration of 2 unevenly spaced molded appliqués representing stylized palmettes. Each appliqué composed of two volutes with joined stems and inward-curving tangent scrolls crowned by small lotus bud.

BIBLIOGRAPHY: Nielsen and Phillips 1974:272, ill. 8, pl. 57, figs. 12–14; *Case e palazzi*:85, no. 110, pl. 3-110.

COMPARANDA: Same as **58** above.

ORNAMENT TYPE: 24.

66. Bowl Fragment
Fig. 23; Pl. 16
MURLO NO.: 72-394
GRID: Rec.5, I/1
STRATUM: 2
Ht. 0.029; Diam. 0.105; Diam. of base 0.047 m.

Mended from 6 pieces. Missing three-quarters of rim and applied decoration on preserved rim surface. Chipped, worn, and burned, but still preserves traces of original shiny burnished surface. Color of upper surface varies from tan to black, underside completely black. Black biscuit.

Same as **64** above, except the rim has a slightly thickened outer edge, and a low rounded ridge defines the exterior edge of the rim surface.

UNPUBLISHED.

COMPARANDA: Same as **58** above.

67. Bowl Fragment
Fig. 23; Pl. 16
MURLO NO.: 74-16
GRID: Rec.5, I/2; I-J/2-3
STRATUM: 2,5(I/O)
Ht. 0.029; Diam. 0.120; Diam. of base 0.052 m.

Mended from 4 pieces. Missing half of base, three-quarters of body, and applied decoration on rim. Badly worn, chipped, and burned. Surface varies in color from gray to black. Gray-black biscuit.

Same as **64** above. Attachment scar for molded appliqué preserved on rim surface.

UNPUBLISHED.

COMPARANDA: Same as **58** above.

68. Bowl Fragment
Fig. 23; Pl. 16
MURLO NO.: 71-551
GRID: Rec.7Ext., X-Y/1-2
STRATUM: 2

Max. Pres. Ht. 0.025; Max. Pres. Diam. of rim 0.035; L. of applied decoration 0.023; W. of applied decoration 0.016 m.

Mended from 4 fragments. Broken on 3 sides. Worn and burned, but still preserves some of original glossy surface. While upper surface of fragment is black, exterior edge of rim and underside are mottled orange-brown. Black biscuit.

Same as **64** above. A single appliqué is preserved on the rim.

UNPUBLISHED.
COMPARANDA: Same as **58** above.
ORNAMENT TYPE: 24.

TYPE 3A: 69–78

These plates all display shallow sloping bodies with straight profiles. Some examples (**70–72**) are decorated with a low conical boss in the center.[74] In all other respects, they are similar to the bowls of Types 1 and 2. They are represented by a maximum of ten and a minimum of four examples.

Plates of a similar shape, unfortunately without provenience, are known from private collections and museums. Other plates with similar profiles, but with thickened and/or grooved rims have been found at Chiusi, Cortona, and Perugia.[75] Like the Type 2 bowls, plates of this type are also associated with the bucchero "foculi" and, therefore, cannot have served as prototypes for the Poggio Civitate examples.[76] Type 3A is also similar in shape to Rasmussen's Plate Type 2 from Cerveteri, although the plates of Type 3A have broader rims. Rasmussen has dated his Plate Type 2 to the fifth century (Rasmussen 1979:124, Plate Type 2, pl. 40, figs. 243 and 244).

69. Plate
Fig. 23; Pl. 16
MURLO NO.: 73-44
FI: 112449
GRID: Rec.5, K/1
STRATUM: 2
Ht. 0.20; Diam. of rim 0.123; Diam. of base 0.050; L. of applied decoration 0.022; W. of applied decoration 0.014 m.

Almost complete. Mended from 21 pieces. Missing portions of rim, body, and base, and part of one appliqué. Worn and burned. Color varies from tan to black. Black biscuit.

Small plate with short disk base; shallow, sloping, convex body; and wide, slightly everted rim with thickened outer edge. Surface of rim decorated with series of 4 evenly spaced, molded appliqués representing stylized palmettes. Each appliqué composed of 2 volutes with joined stems and inward-curving tangent scrolls crowned by small lotus bud.

BIBLIOGRAPHY: *Case e palazzi*:85, no. 111.

COMPARANDA: No exact parallels noted. For examples of plates of similar shape, see Hayes 1985:113–14, nos. C101–103, fig. 11; *CVA Brussels* 2:IV B, pl. 4, no. 29; Cimino 1986:96, no. 252, pl. 57, from Castelluccio in Pienza. Similar profile, but with externally thickened and/or grooved rim, see *Cortona*:85, no. 66; *CVA Sèvres* 1:IV B b, pl. 29, nos. 11, 12, 15, 16, from Chiusi; Cimino 1986:94–95, nos. 243, 244, pl. 56; *Civiltà*:294, 11.8, nos. 5, 6, pl. 11.8; Hayes 1985:113–14, C104.

ORNAMENT TYPE: 24.

70. Plate Fragment
Fig. 23; Pl. 16
MURLO NO.: 72-342
FI: 112448
GRID: Rec.7, A-F/1-4
STRATUM: 2
Ht. 0.019; Diam. of rim 0.130; Diam. of base 0.050; L. of applied decoration 0.022; W. of applied decoration 0.014 m.

---

[74] Conical bosses appear on the kyathos **25**, the phiale **47**, the plates **70–72**, **79**, and **112**, and the bowl or plate fragment **136**. Bagnasco Gianni has noted that in both Greece and the Near East the boss or "ombelicus" is a characteristic of vessels utilized for ritual, see Bagnasco Gianni 1994:19 and note 66. Of the vessel shapes with bosses from the Lower Building, the phiale is the only vessel type commonly associated with ritual. It therefore is unclear whether the bosses on the other bucchero vessels in the deposit implied a ritual use for these vessels as well or if the bosses were merely decorative.

[75] More examples of these plates, in addition to those already cited in the catalogue entry, are on display in the museums at Perugia and Chiusi. I was also able to see numerous examples in the storerooms of the Chiusi Museum.

[76] For the "foculi," see above note 73.

Mended from 5 pieces. Broken irregularly across one side. Missing approximately one-half of plate. Base has slight chip on side of break. Slightly worn. Shiny black surface.

Same as **69** above, except for a narrow rounded ridge around the exterior edge of the rim surface and a low boss in the center of the plate. Only two appliqués are preserved on the rim.

BIBLIOGRAPHY: *Case e palazzi*:85, no. 112.
COMPARANDA: Same as **69** above.

71. Plate Fragment
Pl. 16
MURLO NO.: 74-17
GRID: Rec.5, K/1
STRATUM: 2
Ht. 0.041; Diam. of rim 0.106; Diam. of base 0.060; L. of applied decoration 0.021; W. of applied decoration 0.021 m.

Mended from 9 pieces. Broken irregularly across 3 sides. Missing two-thirds of rim and approximately one-quarter of body. Worn and chipped. Shiny black surface.

Same as **69** above, except for the low boss that decorates the center of the plate. Only one molded appliqué is preserved on the rim.

UNPUBLISHED.
COMPARANDA: Same as **69** above.

72. Plate Fragment
Fig. 24; Pl. 16
MURLO NO.: 72-411
GRID: Rec.5, I-J/0-1
STRATUM: 2
Ht. 0.031; Diam. of rim 0.180; Diam. of base 0.070; W. of rim 0.020 m.

Mended from numerous pieces. Broken irregularly on 3 sides. Most of rim and half of body missing. Worn, chipped, and burned. While preserved portion of rim and small area below it are black, remaining surface of plate is mottled orange-brown. Black biscuit.

Same as **69** above, except for the low boss decorating the center of the plate.

UNPUBLISHED.
COMPARANDA: Same as **69** above.

73. Plate Fragment
Pl. 16
MURLO NO.: 72-360
GRID: Tes. Ctd., B/0
STRATUM: 2
Diam. of rim 0.130; L. of applied decoration 0.021; W. of applied decoration 0.019 m.

Single fragment. Broken on 3 sides. Missing base and three-quarters of rim and body. Worn and burned. While most of upper surface of the fragment is black, underside is mottled orange-brown. Black biscuit.

Same as **69** above. One molded appliqué preserved on rim.

UNPUBLISHED.
COMPARANDA: Same as **69** above.

74. Plate Fragment
Pl. 17
MURLO NO.: 72-396
GRID: Rec.5, I-J/1-2
STRATUM: 2
Diam. of rim 0.150; L. of applied decoration 0.027; W. of applied decoration 0.021 m.

Mended from 3 pieces. Broken on 3 sides. Missing base and approximately three-quarters of rim and body. Worn, chipped, and burned. Surface varies in color from gray-brown to black. Black biscuit.

Same as **69** above. One molded appliqué and portion of attachment scar for a second are preserved on rim.

UNPUBLISHED.
COMPARANDA: Same as **69** above.

75. Plate Fragment
Pl. 17
MURLO NO.: 72-362
GRID: Rec.7, B/3; C/5
STRATUM: 2
Diam. of rim 0.175; L. of applied decoration 0.024; W. of applied decoration 0.024 m.

Mended from 4 fragments. Broken on 3 sides. Missing foot and approximately three-quarters of body and rim. Small portion of body restored in plaster. Applied decoration cracked and missing top portion. Worn and burned.

Surface color varies from black to orange-brown. Black biscuit.

Same as **69** above. Only one molded appliqué is preserved on surface of rim. Two of holes in appliqué are incompletely perforated, still retaining portions of their centers.

The unfinished state of oval appliqué provides useful information regarding the technique of its manufacture. The clay cylinders remaining in the centers of two of the three holes indicate that the holes were produced by perforating the appliqué with a hollow cylindrical tube. In this case, apparently, the two holes were not completely excised before withdrawing the tube and, as a result, portions of their interiors remained.

UNPUBLISHED.
COMPARANDA: Same as **69** above.

76. Plate Fragment
Pl. 17
MURLO NO.: 72-397
GRID: Rec.5, I/1
STRATUM: 2
Diam. of rim 0.130 m.

Mended from 3 pieces. Broken on 3 sides. Missing base, approximately three-quarters of body and rim, and half of applied decoration. Chipped, worn, and burned. Color of surface varies from orange-brown to black. Black biscuit.

Same as **69** above. Only one-half of a molded appliqué is preserved on rim.

UNPUBLISHED.
COMPARANDA: Same as **69** above.

77. Plate Fragment
Pl. 17
MURLO NO.: 71-533
GRID: Rec.7Ext., X/2
STRATUM: 2
Diam. of rim 0.150; L. of applied decoration 0.021; W. of applied decoration 0.021 m.

Single fragment. Broken on 3 sides. Small chip missing on right edge of applied decoration. Worn and burned. Mottled orange-brown in color. Black biscuit.

Same as **69** above. Only one appliqué is preserved on rim.

UNPUBLISHED.
COMPARANDA: Same as **69** above.

78. Plate Fragment
Pl. 17
MURLO NO.: 71-534
GRID: Rec.7Ext., X/2
STRATUM: 2
Diam. of rim 0.130; L. of applied decoration 0.022; W. of applied decoration 0.019 m.

Mended from 2 pieces. Broken on 3 sides. Missing base, three-quarters of rim, and most of body. Worn and burned, but still preserves some of original glossy surface. While upper surface and sides of fragment are black, underside varies in color from black to orange-brown. Black biscuit.

Same as **69** above. Only one molded appliqué is preserved on rim.

UNPUBLISHED.
COMPARANDA: Same as **69** above.

TYPE 3B: **79**

This plate, unlike those of Type 3A, has a carinated body. In all other respects it is identical to plates of Type 3A. Like plates **70–72**, it has a low conical boss in the center. Although plates of a similar type exist in museums and collections, all of them are without known provenience.

79. Plate Fragment
Fig. 24; Pl. 17
MURLO NO.: 72-393
GRID: Rec.5, I-J/1-2
STRATUM: 2
Max. Pres. Ht. 0.019; Diam. 0.139; Diam. of base 0.055 m.

Mended from 4 pieces. Missing approximately one-quarter of body and three-quarters of rim. Worn, chipped, and burned. Color of surface varies from tan to black. Black biscuit.

Fragmentary plate with low disk base; shallow, sloping, carinated body; and horizontal rim with thickened outer edge. Center of plate decorated with low boss.

UNPUBLISHED.
COMPARANDA: For examples of plates of

similar shape, see Beazley and Magi 1939:149–50, nos. 84, 85, figs. 37, 38, pl. 45; *CVA Copenhagen* 5:IV, pl. 203, no. 10; Donati and Michelucci 1981:96–98, nos. 253–262.

Miscellaneous Rim and Appliqué Fragments: **80–89**. Not enough of each fragment is preserved to assign them to a definite bowl or plate type. Since appliqués of this type commonly adorn the rims of bowls and plates Types 1–3, they are presented here.

80. Rim Fragment with Applied Decoration
Pl. 17
MURLO NO.: 74-15
GRID: Rec.5, I-J/0-1; I/1-2; F-H/0-1
STRATUM: 2,3,5(I/O)
Diam. 0.144; Th. of rim 0.007; Max. Pres. W. 0.021 m.

Mended from 8 pieces. Broken on 3 sides. Missing base, body, and one-half of rim. Worn and chipped. Shiny black surface.

Fragment preserves approximately one-half of externally thickened, wide horizontal rim from small plate or bowl. Short, narrow, rounded ridge defines exterior edge of rim surface. Rim decorated with two molded appliqués, representing stylized palmettes. Each appliqué composed of two volutes with joined stems and inward-curving tangent scrolls crowned by small lotus bud.

UNPUBLISHED.
ORNAMENT TYPE: 24.

81. Rim Fragment with Applied Decoration
Pl. 17
MURLO NO.: 71-552
GRID: Rec.7 Ext., X-Y/1-2
STRATUM: 2
Diam. 0.125; Th. of rim 0.006; L. of applied decoration 0.024; W. of applied decoration 0.019 m.

Mended from 2 fragments. Broken on 3 sides. Large chip on outer edge. Worn and burned. While upper surface and edge of rim are orange-brown, underside varies in color from orange-tan to black. Black biscuit.

Same as **80** above, except lacking ridge along outer edge of rim surface. Only one molded appliqué is preserved on rim.

UNPUBLISHED.
ORNAMENT TYPE: 24.

82. Rim Fragment with Applied Decoration
Pl. 17
MURLO NO.: 70-280
GRID: Rec.6, I/1
STRATUM: 2
Diam. 0.120; Th. of rim 0.006; L. of applied decoration 0.023; W. of applied decoration 0.019 m.

Single fragment. Broken on 3 sides. Worn and burned. Mottled orange-brown in color. Orange-brown to black biscuit.

Same as **80** above. Only one appliqué is preserved on rim.

UNPUBLISHED.
ORNAMENT TYPE: 24.

83. Rim Fragment with Applied Decoration
Pl. 17
MURLO NO.: 72-391
GRID: Rec.5, I-J/1
STRATUM: 2
Diam. 0.140; Th. of rim 0.007; L. of applied decoration 0.023; W. of applied decoration 0.019 m.

Mended from 2 fragments. Broken irregularly across one side and diagonally from point of attachment to body along interior to exterior edge. Large chip along exterior edge. Chipped and worn. Burned. Mottled tan-orange in color.

Same as **80** above, except lacking ridge along outer edge of rim surface. Only one molded appliqué is preserved on rim.

UNPUBLISHED.
ORNAMENT TYPE: 24.

84. Rim Fragment with Applied Decoration
Pl. 17
MURLO NO.: 74-29
GRID: Rec.6/7 Doorway, A
STRATUM: 2
Max. Pres. Diam. 0.028; Max. Pres. W. 0.019; Th. of rim 0.007; L. of applied decoration 0.019; W. of applied decoration 0.018 m.

Single fragment. Broken on 3 sides. Worn and burned. Mottled orange-brown in color. Black biscuit.

Same as **80** above, except lacking ridge along exterior edge of rim surface. Only one molded appliqué is preserved on rim.

UNPUBLISHED.
ORNAMENT TYPE: 24.

85. Rim Fragment with Applied Decoration
Pl. 17
MURLO NO.: 71-535
GRID: Rec.7, E/2
STRATUM: 2
Max. Pres. Diam. 0.032; Max Pres. W. 0.014; Th. of rim 0.006; L. of applied decoration 0.023; Max. Pres. W. of applied decoration 0.016 m.

Single fragment. Broken on 3 sides. Missing top portion of applied decoration. Large chip on exterior edge. Chipped, worn, and burned. While top of rim is orange-brown in color, its exterior edge and underside are black. Black biscuit.

Same as **80** above. Only one molded appliqué is preserved on rim.

UNPUBLISHED.
ORNAMENT TYPE: 24.

86. Rim Fragment with Applied Decoration
Pl. 17
MURLO NO.: 71-736
GRID: Rec.7, C/2
STRATUM: 2
Max. Pres. Diam. 0.025; Th. of rim 0.004 m.

Single fragment. Broken on 3 sides. Lower half of applied decoration missing. Surface worn.

Same as **80** above, except lacking ridge along exterior edge of rim surface. Upper half of molded appliqué representing stylized palmette is preserved on rim. Only tops of two volute scrolls and crowing lotus bud remain.

UNPUBLISHED.
ORNAMENT TYPE: 24.

87. Rim Fragment with Applied Decoration
Pl. 17
MURLO NO.: 71-536
GRID: Rec.7, F/3
STRATUM: 2
Max. Pres. Diam. 0.024; Th. of rim 0.003–0.004; W. 0.013 m.

Single fragment. Broken on 3 sides. Missing right half of applied decoration. Surface worn, but still preserves much of original glossy finish.

Same as **80** above. Left half of molded appliqué is preserved on rim. One inward-curving volute and half of crowning lotus bud remain.

UNPUBLISHED.
ORNAMENT TYPE: 24.

88. Molded Appliqué Fragment
Pl. 17
MURLO NO.: 71-537
GRID: Rec.7, C/2
STRATUM: 2
Max. Pres. L. 0.024; Max. Pres. W. 0.017; Th. 0.005 m.

Single fragment. Broken irregularly along top and across back. Chipped on top. Missing crowning lotus bud. Surface extremely worn. Back of appliqué preserves traces of attachment scar to rim.

Same as molded appliqué on **80** above.

UNPUBLISHED.
ORNAMENT TYPE: 24.

89. Molded Appliqué Fragment
Pl. 17
MURLO NO.: 71-538
GRID: Rec.7, A-F/1
STRATUM: 2
Max. Pres. L. 0.013; Max. Pres. W. 0.011; Th. 0.004 m.

Single fragment. Broken through center and along exterior edge. Slightly worn. Shiny black surface.

Same as molded appliqué on **80** above.

UNPUBLISHED.
ORNAMENT TYPE: 24.

TYPE 4: **90–101**.

Type 4 plates have a straighter profile than do plates of Type 3, and all have externally thickened rims. In addition, Type 4 plates appear to be larger than both the plates and bowls of Types 1, 2, and 3, and display a different decorative treatment on their rims. Instead of stylized palmette appliqués or stamped rosettes, they are decorated with a cylinder-stamped double guilloche. Although none of the fragments has a base preserved, it is likely that the base would have been a ring or disk, like those of Types 1 and 3. There are a maximum of 12 and a minimum of 7 examples of plates of this type. No close comparanda exist for these plates.[77]

90. Plate Fragment
Fig. 25; Pl. 18
MURLO NO.: 74-18;72-371
GRID: Rec.5, I-J/1-2
STRATUM: 2
Max. Pres. Ht. 0.039; Diam. of rim 0.260; Th. of rim 0.007–0.009; W. of stamped decoration 0.010 m.

Mended from 10 pieces. Broken on 3 sides. Missing base and approximately three-quarters of body and rim. Chipped, worn, and burned. Color of surface varies from orange-brown to black. Black biscuit.

Fragment preserves portion of plate with shallow sloping body and wide horizontal rim with thickened exterior edge. Surface of rim defined on interior by shallow groove and on exterior by low rounded ridge. Rim decorated with continuous, cylinder-stamped, double-guilloche band, consisting of two concentric guilloche bands with dotted centers linked by vertical bars and separated by dots.

UNPUBLISHED.
COMPARANDA: No parallels noted.
ORNAMENT TYPE: 11.

91. Plate Fragment
Pl. 18
MURLO NO.: 72-372
GRID: Rec.5, I/1
STRATUM: 2
Diam. of rim 0.260; Th. of rim 0.007–0.009; W. of stamped decoration 0.010 m.

Single fragment. Broken irregularly on 3 sides. Missing foot and three-quarters of wall and rim. Chipped, worn, and burned. Mottled orange-brown in color. Black biscuit.

Same as **90** above.

UNPUBLISHED.
COMPARANDA: Same as **90** above.

92. Plate Fragment
Pl. 18
MURLO NO.: 72-374
GRID: Rec.5, F-G/1; J/0; G/4
STRATUM: 2,5(I/0)
Diam. 0.260; Th. of rim 0.005–0.008; W. of stamped decoration 0.011 m.

Mended from 3 pieces. Broken on 3 sides. Missing base, most of body, and three-quarters of rim. Chips missing along exterior edge of rim. Worn and scratched. Shiny black surface.

Same as **90** above.

UNPUBLISHED.
COMPARANDA: Same as **90** above.

93. Plate Fragment
Fig. 25; Pl. 18
MURLO NO.: 70-276
GRID: Rec.6, I/1
STRATUM: 2
Diam. 0.260; Max. Th. of rim 0.006–0.009; W. of stamped decoration 0.011 m.

Single fragment. Broken on 3 sides. Missing

[77] The nearest possible parallel is a group of redware broad-rimmed plates found at a number of sites in southern and central Etruria, Latium, and Campania. These plates, however, which are sometimes referred to by the Etruscan name *spanti*, have more curving profiles, generally are carinated, and have convex rims. For a discussion of these plates, including bibliography, see *Cerveteri* 1986:92–93, no. 9; Bagnasco Gianni 1994.

base, most of body and rim. Slightly worn. Shiny black surface.

Same as **90** above.

UNPUBLISHED.

COMPARANDA: Same as **90** above.

94. Plate Fragment
Pl. 18
MURLO NO.: 74-14
GRID: Rec.5, J/2; I/2; J-K/0
STRATUM: 2,5(I/0)
Diam. 0.260; Th. of rim 0.006–0.008; W. of stamped decoration 0.011 m.

Mended from 5 pieces. Broken on 3 sides. Missing base and most of body and rim. Several chips missing along underside of rim. Worn and burned. Color varies from orange-brown to black. Gray-black biscuit.

Same as **90** above.

UNPUBLISHED.

COMPARANDA: Same as **90** above.

95. Cylinder-Stamped Rim Fragment
Pl. 18
MURLO NO.: 72-373
GRID: Rec.5, J/0
STRATUM: 2
Diam. 0.261; W. 0.021–0.022; Th. 0.006–0.009; W. of stamped decoration 0.011 m.

Mended from 3 pieces. Broken on 3 sides. Worn and burned. Color of surface varies from orange-brown to black. Black biscuit.

Same as **90** above.

UNPUBLISHED.

COMPARANDA: Same as **90** above.

96. Cylinder-Stamped Rim Fragment
Pl. 18
MURLO NO.: 72-377
GRID: Rec. 5, J/1
STRATUM: 2
Diam. 0.230; W. of rim 0.023; Th. 0.006–0.009; W. of stamped decoration 0.010 m.

Single fragment. Broken irregularly on 3 sides. Chipped, worn, and burned. Mottled tan to orange in color. Black biscuit.

Same as **90** above.

UNPUBLISHED.

COMPARANDA: Same as **90** above.

97. Cylinder-Stamped Rim Fragment
Pl. 18
MURLO NO.: 72-376
GRID: Rec.5, J/0
STRATUM: 2
Diam. 0.270; Max. Pres. W. 0.018; Th. 0.006–0.008; W. of stamped decoration 0.010 m.

Single fragment. Broken irregularly on 3 sides. Worn and burned. Mottled tan-brown in color. Black biscuit.

Same as **90** above.

UNPUBLISHED.

COMPARANDA: Same as **90** above.

98. Cylinder-Stamped Rim Fragment
Pl. 18
MURLO NO.: 73-90
GRID: Rec.5, K/O
STRATUM: 3(*I/O)
Diam. 0.260; Max. Pres. W. 0.022; Th. 0.0055–0.009; W. of stamped decoration 0.011 m.

Single fragment. Broken on 3 sides. Worn and chipped.

Same as **90** above.

UNPUBLISHED.

COMPARANDA: Same as **90** above.

99. Cylinder-Stamped Rim Fragment
Pl. 18
MURLO NO.: 73-89
GRID: Rec.5, H/1
STRATUM: 2
Max. Pres. Diam. 0.030; Max. Pres. W. 0.19; Th. 0.005–0.009; W. of stamped decoration 0.011 m.

Single fragment. Broken on 3 sides. Worn surface.

Same as **90** above.

UNPUBLISHED.
COMPARANDA: Same as **90** above.

100. Cylinder-Stamped Rim Fragment
Pl. 18
MURLO NO.: 71-58
GRID: Rec.7, A/2
STRATUM: 2
Max. Pres. Diam. 0.049; Max. Pres. W. 0.025; Th. 0.0055–0.0085; W. of stamped decoration 0.011 m.

Single fragment. Broken on 3 sides. Shiny black surface.

Same as **90** above.

UNPUBLISHED.
COMPARANDA: Same as **90** above.

101. Cylinder-Stamped Rim Fragment
Pl. 18
MURLO NO.: 72-379
GRID: Rec. 5, F-H/0-1
STRATUM: 2/5 (I/O*)
Max. Pres. Diam. 0.024; Max. Pres. W. 0.019; Th. 0.007–0.009; W. of stamped decoration 0.011 m.

Single fragment. Broken on 3 sides. Worn and chipped.

Same as **90** above.

UNPUBLISHED.
COMPARANDA: Same as **90** above.

XII. LUG HANDLED BOWLS (102–110)

These fragments all consist of portions of triangular lug handles and broad rims. Not enough of any one of these fragments is preserved to permit a secure reconstruction of their shape. A more complete buccheroid footed bowl, recovered from Trench 18, with similarly shaped handles that display the same type of stamped decoration as **102–109** and a similar broad rim provides a probable reconstruction for these fragments (Murlo no. 73-230; Nielsen and Phillips 1977a:90–91, ills. 10, 11, fig. 11). This bowl, whose exact reconstruction is uncertain since no complete example exists, has a shallow carinated body and a tall conical foot, and can be restored with either three or four handles.

A raised ridge along the interior edge of **103** appears to indicate the point of attachment for the curving wall of a shallow bowl. Further support for the reconstruction of **102–110** as bowls is provided by a rim and handle fragment nearly identical to **110**, which was found two meters outside the west wall of the Lower Building below Rectangle 7 (pl. 19). This fragment (Murlo no. 72-427) also retains a portion of sloping wall that identifies its shape as a bowl. Therefore, it is likely that **102–110** were portions of similar bowls. Thus, they constitute a maximum of 9 bowls if each of the handle fragments represents a single example; 3 bowls, if each is reconstructed with four handles; or 4 bowls, if reconstructed with three handles.

There are no exact parallels for this bowl type outside Poggio Civitate. A bucchero footed bowl with a broad rim and handles of the same shape as the bowls of this type, but with a deeper, uncarinated body, has been found at Orvieto (Montelius 1904:1019, pl. 244, figs. 2a, b). Notably, the handles of this vessel are also decorated with palmette designs. Unfortunately, this bowl is not from a closely datable context.

102. Rim and Handle Fragment
Fig. 25; Pl. 19
MURLO NO.: 72-413
GRID: Rec.5, J/0
STRATUM: 2
Diam. 0.210; Max. Pres. W. at handle 0.035; Max. Pres. W. of rim 0.014–0.015; Th. 0.007 m.

Mended from 2 pieces. Broken on 3 sides. Large chip on surface of rim near handle. Worn, scratched, and burned. Mottled reddish brown in color. Black biscuit.

Fragment preserves triangular lug handle and portion of broad rim of bowl. Surface of handle decorated with stamped, stylized, double-volute palmette. Palmette consists of 2 long-stemmed volutes with outcurving scrolls joined by narrow horizontal band and crowned by lotus bud. Short vertical striations fill area below stems.

UNPUBLISHED.
COMPARANDA: Not enough of the fragment is preserved to permit secure identification of its shape. A footed buccheroid bowl with similar handles and rim found in Trench 18 provides a likely reconstruction for the vessel; see Nielsen

and Phillips 1977a: 90–91, Murlo no. 73-230, ills. 10, 11, fig. 11.

A bowl of related shape has been found at Orvieto; see Montelius 1904:1019, pl. 244, figs. 2a, b.

ORNAMENT TYPE: 7b.

103. Rim and Handle Fragment
Fig. 25; Pl. 19
MURLO NO.: 73-140
GRID: Rec.5, K/0
STRATUM: 2
Diam. 0.230; Max. Pres. W. 0.0375; Max. Pres. W. 0.005–0.007 m.

Mended from 2 fragments. Worn, scratched, and possibly burned. Reddish-brown in color. Black biscuit.

Same as **102** above.

UNPUBLISHED.

COMPARANDA: Same as **102** above. A raised ridge along the interior edge of the fragment appears to indicate the point of attachment for the curving wall of a shallow bowl.

104. Rim and Handle Fragment
Fig. 25; Pl. 19
MURLO NO.: 73-141
GRID: Rec.5, K/0
STRATUM: 2
Max. Pres. Diam. 0.098; Max. Pres. W. 0.038; Th. 0.005–0.0065 m.

Mended from 2 pieces. Broken on 3 sides. Worn, chipped, and burned. Reddish-brown in color. Black biscuit.

Same as **102** above.

UNPUBLISHED.

COMPARANDA: Same as **102** above.

105. Rim and Handle Fragment
Fig. 25; Pl. 19
MURLO NO.: 73-142
GRID: Rec.5, K/0-1
STRATUM: 2
Max. Pres. Diam. 0.095; Max. Pres. W. 0.040; Th. 0.005–0.0075 m.

Mended from 3 pieces. Broken on 3 sides. Worn, scratched, and burned. Reddish-brown in color. Black biscuit.

Same as **102** above.

UNPUBLISHED.

COMPARANDA: Same as **102** above.

106. Rim and Handle Fragment
Fig. 25; Pl. 19
MURLO NO.: 73-139
GRID: Rec.5, K/0-1
STRATUM: 2
Max. Pres. Diam. 0.071; Max. Pres. W. 0.032; Th. 0.005–0.006 m.

Mended from 2 pieces. Broken on 3 sides. Badly worn, scratched, and burned. Reddish-brown to black in color. Black biscuit.

Same as **102** above.

UNPUBLISHED.

COMPARANDA: Same as **102** above.

107. Rim and Handle Fragment
Pl. 19
MURLO NO.: 73-138
GRID: Rec.5, K/1
STRATUM: 2
Max. Pres. Diam. 0.068; Max. Pres. W. 0.034; Th. 0.005–0.007 m.

Mended from 2 pieces. Broken on 3 sides. Worn, chipped and burned. Reddish-brown in color. Black biscuit.

Same as **102** above.

UNPUBLISHED.

COMPARANDA: Same as **102** above.

108. Rim and Handle Fragment
Fig. 25; Pl. 19
MURLO NO.: 72-414
GRID: Rec.5, J/0
STRATUM: 2
Max. Pres. Diam. 0.051; Max. Pres. W. 0.034; Th. 0.006–0.0075 m.

Single fragment. Broken on 3 sides. Worn, chipped, and burned. Reddish-brown in color. Black biscuit.

Same as **102** above.

UNPUBLISHED.
COMPARANDA: Same as **102** above.

109. Rim and Handle Fragment
Pl. 19
MURLO NO.: 74-13
GRID: Rec.5, K/1
STRATUM: 2
Max. Pres. Diam. 0.064; Max. Pres. W. 0.033; Th. 0.007 m.

Single fragment. Broken on 3 sides. Worn, chipped, and burned. Reddish-brown in color. Black biscuit.

Same as **102** above.

UNPUBLISHED.
COMPARANDA: Same as **102** above.

110. Rim and Handle Fragment
Fig. 25; Pl. 19
MURLO NO.: 72-428
GRID: Rec.7, C/5
STRATUM: 1
Max. Pres. Diam 0.046; Max. Pres. W. 0.037; Th. 0.007 m.

Single fragment. Broken on 3 sides. Worn and chipped. Shiny black surface.

Fragment preserves a portion of the rim and triangular lug handle of small bowl. Exterior edge of handle molded in form of double palmette consisting of incurving double volute crowned by lotus bud; below this, a second incised incurving double volute. In addition, surface of rim preserves portion of cylinder-stamped, stylized double guilloche composed of 2 individual bands of S-shapes. Each pair of opposing S-shapes linked by vertical bar with a dot on each side; another dot in intervening space between each pair of bars.

UNPUBLISHED.

COMPARANDA: A nearly identical rim and handle fragment (Murlo no. 72-427, pl. 19), unpublished, was found outside the western wall of the Lower Building below Rectangle 7. See also **102** above. The double palmette molded on the edge of this handle is very similar in conception to the Ornament Type 24, the molded volute palmette appliqué.

ORNAMENT TYPES: 12, 26.

XIII. MISCELLANEOUS PLATES (**111, 112**)

Two additional plates were recovered from the Lower Building. Both are previously unclassified types.

TYPE 1: **111**

This plate is distinguished by a shallow sloping body, a short, slightly everted rim, and a low, externally thickened ring base. Plates of a related type are known from tombs at Vulci (De Puma 1986:35, 46, Tomb C, VC 38; Rizzo 1990:93, 99, Tomb XIII, nos. 46–49) and Poggio Buco (Bartoloni 1972:Tomb VIII, 118, nos. 42–47, 135) dated to the end of the seventh and the first half of the sixth century. These plates, however, have a more sharply sloping body and short inverted rims.

111. Plate
Fig. 26; Pl. 20
MURLO NO.: 72-358
GRID: Rec.5, J/1
STRATUM: 2
Max. Pres. Ht. 0.033; Diam. of rim 0.180; Diam. of base 0.068 m.

Mended from numerous pieces. Missing three-quarters of rim and portions of body. Badly worn and cracked.

Fragmentary plate with a low, externally thickened ring base, shallow, sloping, convex body and short, everted rim with a rounded edge.

UNPUBLISHED.

COMPARANDA: No exact parallels noted. For other bucchero plates of similar shape, see DePuma 1986:46, VC 38, pl. 13e, from Vulci; Bartoloni 1972:118, nos. 42–47, pl. LXXIIa–f, from Poggio Buco; Rizzo 1990:99, nos. 46–49, fig. 180, from Vulci.

For a similar example in impasto from Poggio Civitate, but with a flanged rim, see Bouloumié-Marique 1978:pl. 13, Form 1d.

TYPE 2: **112**

This plate has a thick, shallow, sloping body with a large conical boss at the center and an externally thickened ring base. Not enough of the plate is preserved to determine the orientation or exact position of its rim. Although no other identical examples of this type of plate are known, two plates, one now in Hamburg and the other in Toronto, may represent later versions of the type. Both plates have a broadly similar shape and decoration, including a conical boss and a cylinder-stamped frieze. However, while the Hamburg plate, like that from Poggio Civitate, displays a frieze around the interior, the plate in Toronto has a frieze around the rim. Although the two plates are without provenience, the cylinder-stamped friezes on both the Hamburg[78] and Toronto (Hayes 1985:111–12, C94) plates have been identified as Chiusine types. In addition, the use of cylinder-stamped friezes on the interior of a plate is also seen on other plates from Chiusi (cf. Montelius 1910:pl. 224, figs. 6a, b; *CVA British Museum* 7:IV B a, pl. 15, 5a, b; Fairbanks 1928:212, no. 618, pl. LXXXI).

112. Plate Fragment (2 fragments)
Fig. 26; Pl. 20
MURLO NO.: 71-83
GRID: Rec.7, A-F/3
STRATUM: 2
Fragment A: Max. Pres. Ht. 0.043; Max. Pres. Diam. 0.164; Max. Pres. Diam. of base 0.052; Th. 0.007–0.009; Max. Pres. W. of stamped decoration 0.024 m. Fragment B: Max. Pres. W. 0.032; Max. Pres. Ht. 0.019; Th. 0.005–0.008 m.

A: Mended from 18 pieces. Missing portions of body and most of rim. Chipped all around outer edge of base. Chipped and cracked. Underside preserves original shiny black surface.

B: Single fragment. Broken on all sides. Worn and cracked.

Fragment A: Fragment preserves most of externally thickened ring base and approximately two-thirds of shallow sloping body of plate. Center of plate decorated with low boss encircled by wide groove. Portions of continuous cylinder-stamped frieze preserved in two areas along edge of plate wall. Frieze framed at top by two wide bands and one thin band and at bottom by one thin and one wide band. Largest preserved portion of frieze displays procession of four fantastic and real animals moving to right. Procession led by large stag, of which most of antlers, one foreleg, and two rear legs, and rear portion of the body are preserved. Griffin, behind stag, displays small oval head with triangular beak, long neck, tall central recurving wing and curling tail. Winged quadruped, perhaps a sphinx, follows griffin. Only lower body and bottom portion of wing of creature preserved. At far left, grazing stag, of which only bent head, lower portion of antlers, and forepart of body, including forelegs, are preserved. Stylized plants appear beneath two stags and sphinx. Farther to left a segment of frieze repeats, preserving lower portions of four animal legs and stylized plant.

Fragment B: Single fragment preserving on its surface portions of figured frieze, moving to right. At center of fragment, horse and rider, both missing their heads. Rider sits with right arm held forward and bent upward at elbow and with left arm bent downward and held behind him. In front, at far right, another horse, of which only rear portion of body, including hind legs and tail, is preserved. Small portion of additional, unidentifiable figure appears at far left. Shallow narrow groove runs along base of frieze.

The association of fragment B with the plate is not secure. It is slightly thicker than the cylinder-stamped portion of fragment A. In addition, the inclusion of the fragment with the cylinder-stamped scene depicted on fragment A would produce an unusually long frieze.

UNPUBLISHED.

COMPARANDA: No exact parallels noted. For plates of similar shape, see von Mercklin 1936:391–92, no. 44, fig. 3, pl. XLII.1; Hayes 1985:111–12, C94, fig. 11.

ORNAMENT TYPE: 8.

XIVA. LIDS (113–131)

Seven types of lids can be identified, comprising a maximum number of 19 examples.[79] In general, lids were utilized with a wide variety of bucchero vessels, including kantharoi (Cimino

[78] Scalia 1968:374–75 and note 39, no. 116, motif XIII, fig. 5b. Scalia expressed doubts about the authenticity of this plate because of its uncommon shape. The discovery of a similar plate at Poggio Civitate should help to dispel this uncertainty.

[79] The maximum number of 19 represents the total number of lids and lid fragments and assumes that each catalogue entry would have represented one example.

1986:no. 206a, pl. 49), chalices (Fairbanks 1928:219, no. 654, pl. LXXXVIII), pyxides (Monaci 1965:pl. XCIVa, b), amphoras (*CVA Brussels* 2:IV B, pl. 2.1a, b, 2a, b; Donati 1968:pl. LXXVIIb, c), kyathoi (Montelius 1910:pl. 227, fig. 11), ollas (*Cortona*:85, no. 64) and bowls (*Case e palazzi*:86, no. 122, pl. 3-122). Although lids were certainly produced at a number of Etruscan sites, the manufacture of lidded vessels is particularly characteristic of the bucchero production of Chiusi.

It is notable that with only two exceptions none of the lids recovered from the Lower Building can be securely matched to the vessels they covered.[80] The lid of the footed bowl **53** presents a secure fit and was found together with the bowl it covered. It is also probable that the fragmentary lid **114** covered the fragmentary jar **48**. The two fragments, while not found together, were discovered in the same general area. Both are of the same fabric and are decorated with the same stamped motif. In addition, their estimated diameters would allow them to fit together.

The remaining lids are most likely to be associated with the broad-rimmed bowls and plates, but none of the examples whose diameter can be measured or estimated produces a secure fit on these or any other vessels from the deposit. It is possible that the lids were manufactured independently, to be used interchangeably on different vessel types without concern for a secure fit. Such a practice, although undocumented elsewhere, is possible. The presence of flanges on most of the lids, though, appears to indicate that they were constructed to cover specific vessels.[81] It is possible that some of these vessels have been lost, but the disappearance of all of them is unlikely. It is also possible that in some cases an exact fit between lid and vessel was not necessary. The circumstances at Poggio Civitate might best be explained by a combination of these two factors.

TYPE 1: **113**

This lid is distinguished by a shallow convex body with a short vertical rim and short flange on the underside at the junction between rim and body. Examples of this type are also known from Chiusi, but not from datable contexts.

113. Lid
Fig. 27; Pl. 21
MURLO NO.: 71-394
GRID: Rec.7, A/3
STRATUM: 2
Diam. 0.175; Diam. of flange 0.135; Max. Pres. Ht. 0.042 m.

Mended from 16 fragments. Missing approximately one-third of rim and portions of body, most of which have been restored in plaster. Finial from handle also missing. Surface badly worn.

Fragmentary lid with sloping convex body and narrow rim with thickened outer edge. Preserved portion of handle cylindrical in section and tapers toward top. Short, slightly inverted flange encircles underside of lid at juncture between rim and body. Upper half of body articulated into series of molded outpressed scallops, which radiate around a low molded ridge. Four scallops with rounded ends turned inward; set at cardinal points of lid, they separate 4 groups of 4 scallops with rounded ends turned outward. Concave impressions of scallops visible on underside of the lid. Group of three concentric grooves runs around lower half of body, below petals. Three rounded horizontal ridges encircle base of handle.

UNPUBLISHED.

COMPARANDA: It is uncertain what type of vessel this lid covered. For examples of other lids of the same shape with similar decoration, see Cimino 1986:84, no. 206a, pl. 49; G. Camporeale, in *Etruria Mineraria*:396, pl. LXXXVIc; *CVA Copenhagen* 5:IV B, pl. 215.10; *CVA Sèvres* 1:IV B c, pl. 29.7, from Chiusi; *CVA Villa Giulia* 2:IV B 1, pl. 5, 4–6. Similar shape and different decoration, see Donati 1968:330, no. 64, pl. LXXVd, from Chiusi; Camporeale 1972a:90, no. 2, pl. XXXIIb, from Orvieto.

TYPE 2: **114–118**

These lids have a sloping convex body, a narrow horizontal rim, and a short vertical or nearly vertical flange on the underside at the

[80] This takes into consideration not only the size of lids and vessels, but also their fabric and decoration.

[81] It is also possible that the flange was utilized not only to ensure a perfect fit with a matching vessel, but also to help prevent the lid from sliding off whatever vessel it was placed upon.

junction between the rim and body. While the closest parallels for these lids are found at Poggio Civitate,[82] lids of a similar shape are also known from Chiusi and Cortona, but unfortunately not from closely datable contexts.

114. Fragmentary Lid (5 fragments)
Fig. 27; Pl. 21
MURLO NO.: 71-513 A-E
FI: 112446
GRID: Rec.7, E-F/4; C/4; C/1
STRATUM: 2
Est. Diam. of lid 0.105. Fragment A: Max. Pres. L. 0.058; Max. Pres. W. 0.045; Th. 0.005; Diam. of stamped design 0.009. Fragment B: Max. Pres. L. 0.033; Max. Pres. W. 0.043; Th. 0.005; Diam. of stamped design 0.009. Fragment C: Max. Pres. L. 0.021; Max. Pres. W. 0.023; Th. 0.006; Diam. of stamped design 0.009. Fragment D: Max. Pres. L. 0.022; Max. Pres. W. 0.016; Th. 0.006; Diam. of stamped design 0.009. Fragment E: Max. Pres. L. 0.012; Max. Pres. W. 0.016; Th. 0.006; Diam. of stamped design 0.009 m.

Five nonjoining fragments. Fragments A and B broken on 3 sides. Fragments C, D, and E broken on all sides. Worn, but fragments A–D still preserve much of original glossy finish.

Five fragments of lid with sloping convex body and narrow horizontal rim with rounded edge. Rim set off from body by shallow groove. Short vertical flange encircles underside of lid at juncture between rim and body. Surface of lid preserves portions of three concentric bands of individually stamped palmette designs. Each palmette composed of two volutes with joined stems and incurving scrolls. Small round bud at base of palmette below scrolls and three-petalled blossom in interior. Stamp set within circular field. The three bands are separated by two shallow grooves.

BIBLIOGRAPHY: Phillips 1972:252, pl. 49, figs. 1, 2; Phillips 1994:34, no. 17, fig. 4.24.

COMPARANDA: This lid may have covered the jar **48**. Both the lid and the jar have the same stamped decoration. For examples of other lids of the same shape from Poggio Civitate, see Phillips 1971:259, Murlo no. 70-40, pl. 58, figs. 6, 7 and 261, Murlo no. 70-153A, B, pl. 62, figs. 38, 39; Nielsen and Phillips 1975:359, Murlo no. 72-369, ill. 2, pl. 63, fig. 3; and the unpublished fragments Murlo nos. 72-368, 72-412.

For other lids of similar shape, see Hayes 1985:93, C54, fig. 6; *Cortona*:85, no. 64, from Cortona; Cimino 1986:100–101, no. 272, pl. 58; Monaci 1965:440, nos. 157, 158, pl. XCIVa, b; De Puma 1986:64, CA 3-7, fig. 16, nos. 3–5, from Chiusi; *CVA Budapest* 1:IV B, pl. 4.5, 6, ascribed to Chiusi; *CVA Heidelberg* 2:pl. 49, 5; *CVA Brussels* 2:IV B, pl. 4.4.

ORNAMENT TYPE: 6a.

115. Fragmentary Lid (4 fragments)
Fig. 27; Pl. 21
MURLO NO.: 71-518
GRID: Rec.7, B/3; D/4
STRATUM: 2
Est. Diam. of lid 0.121. Fragment A: Max. Pres. L. 0.061; Max. Pres. W. 0.035; Th. 0.004; Diam. of stamped decoration 0.007. Fragment B: Max. Pres. L. 0.056; Max. Pres. W. 0.051; Th. 0.004–0.005; Diam. of stamped decoration 0.007. Fragment C: Max. Pres. L. 0.028; Max. Pres. W. 0.029; Th. 0.005; Diam. of stamped decoration 0.007. Fragment E: Max. Pres. L. 0.021; Max. Pres. W. 0.019; Th. 0.004; Diam. of stamped decoration 0.007 m.

Four nonjoining fragments. Missing finial and approximately one-half of body and rim. Fragments A and C mended from 2 pieces. Fragments B and D are single fragments. Fragments A and B broken on 3 sides. Fragments C and D broken on all sides. Worn and chipped, but still preserve much of original glossy surface.

Four fragments preserve portions of lid with convex body and narrow horizontal rim with rounded edge. Rim set off from body by low rounded ridge and shallow groove. Short flange with rounded edge projects obliquely from underside of lid at juncture between body and rim. Portions of 3 bands of individually stamped asterisk-rosettes circle upper surface of lid, each

[82] It is important to note that all the lids from Poggio Civitate cited as comparanda for lid Type 2 were found either in the destruction debris surrounding the Lower Building or in the walls of the Upper Building in the area immediately above the Lower Building. It is, therefore, probable that these lid fragments were originally part of the Lower Building deposit and were displaced during the construction of the Upper Building.

separated by 3 or 4 thinly incised concentric lines. Each rosette is composed of 16 small impressed triangles arranged around circle with their apices turned inward.

UNPUBLISHED.

COMPARANDA: It is not certain what type of vessel this lid would have covered. For parallels for the shape, see **114** above. The same stamped decoration appears on the lid fragment **117**.

ORNAMENT TYPE: 4a.

116. Lid Fragment
Fig. 28; Pl. 21
MURLO NO.: 71-946
GRID: Rec.7, F/4
STRATUM: 2
Diam. 0.128; Max. Pres. Ht. 0.024 m.

Mended from 7 pieces. Broken irregularly across one side. Missing finial and one-third of body and rim. Large chip missing from outer edge of rim. Chipped and worn, but still preserves much of original shiny surface.

Same as **114** above, except surface is undecorated.

UNPUBLISHED.

COMPARANDA: It is not certain what type of vessel this lid would have covered. For parallels for the shape, see **114** above.

117. Lid Fragment
Fig. 28; Pl. 21
MURLO NO.: 71-524
GRID: Rec.8, A/1-4
STRATUM: 2
Est. Diam. 0.120; Max. Pres. L. 0.047; Max. Pres. W. 0.030 m.

Mended from 2 pieces. Broken on 3 sides. Worn and chipped. Shiny black surface.

Fragment preserves small portion of sloping convex body and horizontal rim of lid. Rim has rounded edge and is set off from body by shallow groove. Short rounded flange runs along underside of fragment at junction between rim and body. Surface of fragment decorated with two flat concentric ridges, which encircle body just above rim. Ridges separated by shallow groove. Preserved above ridges are portions of three stamped asterisk-rosettes. Each rosette composed of series of 16 impressed triangles arranged in circle with their apices turned inward.

UNPUBLISHED.

COMPARANDA: It is not certain what type of vessel this lid would have covered. For parallels for the shape, see **114** above. The same stamped decoration appears on the fragmentary lid **115**.

ORNAMENT TYPE: 4a.

118. Fragmentary Lid (2 fragments)
Fig. 28; Pl. 21
MURLO NO.: 71-527A, B
GRID: Rec.7, E/3
STRATUM: 2
Fragment A: Max. Pres. L. 0.039; Max. Pres. W. 0.027; Th. 0.004; Diam. of stamped palmettes 0.006; L. of stamped S 0.010. Fragment B: Max Pres. L. 0.0190; Max. Pres. W. 0.018; Diam. of stamped palmettes 0.006 m.

Two nonjoining fragments, both broken on all sides. Worn and chipped. Shiny black surface.

Fragment A: Shallowly curved lid fragment. Upper surface decorated with two groups of finely incised horizontal lines. Group of two lines at top of fragment and three near center. Portions of decorative band of individually stamped double-volute palmettes set within recessed circles preserved between the two groups of lines. Each palmette composed of two incurving volutes joined at stem. Two complete palmettes and portions of a third preserved. At base of fragment, below second group of lines, portions of a second stamped decorative band consisting of individually stamped chain of oblique "S" designs. One complete and portions of 6 additional "S" designs preserved.

Fragment B: Shallowly curved lid fragment. Upper surface decorated with 2 groups of finely incised horizontal lines. Group of 2 lines at top of fragment and three at base. Between the two groups of lines, portions of decorative band of individually stamped double-volute palmettes set within recessed circles. Each palmette composed of two incurving volutes joined at stem. Two complete palmettes and portions of third are preserved.

UNPUBLISHED.

COMPARANDA: Not enough of the lid is preserved to determine its complete shape with certainty. It appears, however, to be similar in shape to **114–117** above. For parallels for the shape see **114**.

ORNAMENT TYPES: 3, 6b.

TYPE 3: **119**

This lid has a shallow sloping body with an everted lip and a short vertical flange on the underside at the junction between the rim and body. There are no parallels noted for this lid type.

119. Fragmentary Lid (2 fragments)
Fig. 28; Pl. 22
MURLO NO.: 71-949A, B
GRID: Rec.7Ext., X-Y/2; E/2
STRATUM: 2/3 (*I/O)
Est. Diam. of lid 0.116. Fragment A: Max. Pres. L. 0.110; Max. Pres. W. 0.056; Ht. 0.015. Fragment B: Max. Pres. L. 0.047 m.

Two nonjoining fragments. Fragment A: Mended from 5 pieces. Broken irregularly on 3 sides. Fragment B: Mended from 2 pieces. Broken irregularly on three sides. Missing finial and two-thirds of body. Chipped and worn. Shiny black surface with brown undertone.

Fragmentary lid with shallow, slightly convex body and short sloping rim. Short flange encircles underside of lid. Surface of lid decorated with 2 sets of 4 irregularly incised concentric lines.

UNPUBLISHED.

COMPARANDA: It is not certain what type of vessel this lid would have covered. No parallels noted.

TYPE 4: **120–122**

These lids are all relatively small in size and display a shallow convex body with a narrow horizontal rim and a short vertical flange on the underside at the junction between rim and body.

A lid of identical shape was found at Poggio Civitate in Trench 18 (Murlo no. 73-208). Two lids of a very similar shape, both unfortunately without provenience, are now in Toronto.

120. Lid
Fig. 28; Pl. 22
MURLO NO.: 72-432
GRID: Rec.5, J/0
STRATUM: 2
Diam. 0.103; Max. Pres. Ht. 0.042; Diam. of flange 0.093 m.

Mended from numerous fragments. Missing small portion of body and approximately one-third of rim. Large chip on side of handle. Worn and badly cracked, but much of original glossy surface remains. Black biscuit.

Small lid with shallow convex body and narrow horizontal rim with thin rounded edge. Lid crowned by thick conical handle with short cylindrical stem. Short flange encircles underside of lid at junction between rim and body. Series of five narrow incised lines run around upper surface of lid.

UNPUBLISHED.

COMPARANDA: It is not certain what type of vessel this lid would have covered. For an example of a lid of the same shape, see Nielsen and Phillips 1977a:91, Murlo no. 73-208, ill. 12, figs. 12, 13, from Poggio Civitate. For lids of similar shape, see Hayes 1985:91, C50, fig. 6; 126, C124, fig. 6.

121. Lid
Fig. 28; Pl. 22
MURLO NO.: 72-404
GRID: Rec.5, J/0
STRATUM: 2
Ht. 0.038; Diam of rim 0.085; Diam. of flange 0.075 m.

Almost complete. Mended from 7 fragments. Handle broken on 3 sides. Several chips missing along edge of rim. Worn, encrusted, and burned. While most of upper surface of lid is orange-brown in color, underside is black. Black biscuit.

Small lid with shallow convex body and disk handle. Lid has narrow horizontal rim with rounded edge. Rim set off from body by low rounded ridge. Two incised shallow grooves define sides of ridge. Disk handle rests on short cylindrical stem and is crowned by conical boss. Short rounded flange encircles underside of lid at junction between body and rim.

UNPUBLISHED.

COMPARANDA: For parallels for the shape see **120** above.

122. Lid Fragment
Fig. 28; Pl. 22
MURLO NO.: 71-804
GRID: Rec.7Ext., X-Y/2
STRATUM: 2
Ht. 0.032; Diam. of rim 0.102; Diam. of flange 0.090 m.

Mended from 7 pieces. Missing approximately one-half of body. Several chips along edge and large chip on top of handle. Worn, scratched, and burned. While upper surface is orange-tan in color, underside is black. Black biscuit.

Fragmentary lid with shallow convex body and narrow, slightly everted rim with rounded edge. Lid has flattened conical handle with short cylindrical stem. Rim set off from body by low flat ridge defined by 2 shallow grooves. Short flange with rounded edge encircles underside of lid at junction between rim and body.

UNPUBLISHED.

COMPARANDA: It is uncertain what type of vessel this lid would have covered. For parallels for the shape see **120** above.

TYPE 5: **123**

This type, which is represented by only one example, has a shallow, sloping, convex body, a broad tapering rim, and a slightly inverted tall flange on the underside at the junction between rim and body. No parallels were noted.

123. Lid
Fig. 29; Pl. 123
MURLO NO.: 71-820
GRID: Rec.7, D-F/3-4
STRATUM: 2
Diam. of rim 0.165; Diam. of flange 0.135 m.

Restored from 8 pieces. Broken irregularly along 2 sides. Large fragment missing from body, a small section of which has been restored in plaster. Surface worn, chipped, and burned. Color varies from mottled orange to gray to black. Gray-black biscuit.

Fragmentary lid with loop handle; shallow, sloping, convex body; and broad horizontal rim with rounded edge. Tall, slightly inverted flange with rounded edge encircles underside of lid at junction between rim and body. Three groups of irregularly incised concentric lines decorate lid surface: 3 around handle, 4 at center, and 3 near edge.

UNPUBLISHED.

COMPARANDA: It is not certain what type of vessel this lid would have covered. No parallels noted.

TYPE 6: **124–126**

These lids all display convex bodies that vary in depth and short rounded rims. Lids of this type are also attested in impasto at Poggio Civitate; a similar example is known from Chiusi, but its context is unknown.

124. Lid
Fig. 29; Pl. 22
MURLO NO.: 71-784
GRID: Rec.7; Rec.7, S. Wall, M/3
STRATUM: 2,4(I/0)
Diam. 0.108; Max. Pres. Ht. 0.053 m.

Almost complete. Mended from 7 fragments. Missing three-quarters of handle. Worn and chipped.

Lid with curving convex body and rounded rim. Approximately one-quarter of small loop handle preserved on top of lid.

UNPUBLISHED.

COMPARANDA: It is not certain what type of vessel this lid would have covered. For examples of bucchero lids of similar shape, see *CVA Brussels* 2:IV B, pls. 3.16, 4.36; *CVA Sèvres* 1:IV B c, pl. 29.3, from Chiusi. For examples of impasto lids of similar shape from Poggio Civitate, see Bouloumié-Marique 1978:86, Form K, nos. 435, 436, pl. XIV.

125. Lid Fragment
Pl. 23
MURLO NO.: 71-957
GRID: Rec.7Ext., X-Y/2; Rec.7, A-D/6
STRATUM: 2,3,5 (*I/0)
Diam. 0.099; Max. Pres. Ht. 0.039 m.

Mended from 3 pieces. Broken across one side. Missing handle and approximately one-half of body. Scratched and worn. Shiny black surface.

Lid with curving convex body and rounded

rim. Approximately one-half of small loop handle preserved on top of lid.

UNPUBLISHED.
COMPARANDA: Same as **124** above.

126. Lid Fragment
Pl. 23
MURLO NO.: 71-956
GRID: Rec.7Ext., X-Y/2
STRATUM: 2
Max. Pres. Diam. 0.087 m.

Mended from 2 pieces. Broken irregularly along 2 sides. Missing two-thirds of body and one-half of handle. Scratched and worn. Shiny black surface.

Same as **124** above, except the body is less convex.

UNPUBLISHED.
COMPARANDA: Same as **124** above.

TYPE 7: 127 AND 128

Lids of Type 6 have a shallow convex body and rounded rim. No parallels with a known provenience were noted for this type.

127. Lid Fragment
Fig. 29; Pl. 23
MURLO NO.: 71-948
GRID: Rec.7, E/2
STRATUM: 2
Max. Pres. Ht. 0.019; Diam. 0.15 m.

Mended from 4 pieces. Broken irregularly across one side. Missing finial and approximately two-thirds of body. Large chip on body. Chipped, worn, and slightly discolored, but still preserves much of original shiny surface. Black with strong brown undertone.

Fragment preserves approximately one-third of lid with shallow, curving, convex body and rounded rim. Surface of lid decorated with series of 5 irregularly incised concentric lines.

UNPUBLISHED.
COMPARANDA: It is not certain what type of vessel this lid would have covered. For another lid of similar shape, see Fairbanks 1928:226, no. 687, pl. XCIV.

128. Lid Fragment
Fig. 30; Pl. 24
MURLO NO.: 72-418
GRID: Rec.5, F-H/0-1
STRATUM: 2/5 (*I/O)
Max. Pres. L. 0.020; Max. Pres. W. 0.021; Th. 0.004; W. of stamped decoration 0.009 m.

Single fragment. Broken on all sides except along a short portion of rim. Surface worn and scratched.

Fragment preserves small portion of lid with slightly curving, thin-walled body and narrow rounded rim. Surface displays two and one-third units of a cylinder-stamped guilloche band bordered by incised lines.

UNPUBLISHED.
COMPARANDA: Not enough of the lid is preserved to determine its complete shape with certainty. It appears, however, to be of the same shape as **127** above.
ORNAMENT TYPE: 10a.

XIVB. MISCELLANEOUS LID FINIAL FRAGMENTS (129–131)

129 through **131** represent miscellaneous lid finial fragments. Not enough of these fragments is preserved to assign them to a specific lid type.

129. Lid Finial
Fig. 30; Pl. 24
MURLO NO.: 71-541
GRID: Rec.7, F/3
STRATUM: 2
Max. Pres. Ht. 0.029; Max. Pres. Diam. 0.023 m.

Single fragment. Broken irregularly at point of attachment to lid. Slightly chipped and worn. Shiny black surface.

Finial consisting of broad flaring cone set on short and narrow cylindrical stem.

UNPUBLISHED.
COMPARANDA: For other examples of lids with conical finials of a similar shape from Poggio Civitate, see **120** above, and the lid Murlo

no. 73-208, recovered from Trench 18; see Nielsen and Phillips 1977a:91, ill. 12, figs. 12, 13. See also *CVA Brussels* 2:IV B, pl. 4, no. 41; *CVA Villa Giulia* 2:IV B 1, pl. 5, nos. 3, 5.

130. Lid Finial
Pl. 24
MURLO NO.: 71-965
GRID: Rec.7, E/4
STRATUM: 2
Max. Pres. Ht. 0.029; Max. Pres. Diam. of top 0.021 m.

Single fragment. Broken around circumference of attachment to lid. Chipped and slightly worn. Shiny black surface.

Lid finial with tapering cylindrical shaft surmounted by flat convex knob. Base of finial preserves small portion of lid.

UNPUBLISHED.

COMPARANDA: For examples of lids with finials of similar shape, see Hayes 1985:91, C50, fig 6; 93, C54, fig. 6; 126, C124, fig. 6; *Cortona*:85, no. 64, from Cortona; Montelius 1910:pl. 227, fig. 11, from Chiusi; Cimino 1986:81, no. 198, pl. 46.

131. Lid Finial
Fig. 30; Pl. 24
MURLO NO.: 72-426
GRID: Tes. Ctd, B/1
STRATUM: 2/3(*I/0)
Max. Pres. Ht. 0.028; Diam. of top 0.059 m.

Mended from 5 pieces. Broken at point of attachment to lid. Missing portion of disk. Several chips along edge of disk. Surface chipped and worn.

Finial composed of large disk with concave surface and rounded edge set upon short, broad, cylindrical stem. Low boss at center of disk.

UNPUBLISHED.

COMPARANDA: For lids with finials of similar shape, see **53** above and Hayes 1985:40, B16.

XV. MISCELLANEOUS FRAGMENTS (132–136)

132 through **136** represent miscellaneous fragments that are too small to assign to a vessel shape.

132. Stamped Fragment
Fig. 30; Pl. 24
MURLO NO.: 72-288
GRID: Tes. Ctd, D-F/0-1
STRATUM: 2
Max. Pres. L. 0.013; Max. Pres. W. 0.0165; Th. 0.0035 m.

Single fragment. Broken on all 4 sides. Slightly worn.

Small, slightly curving body fragment. Surface preserves portions of three stamped quadrupeds set within recessed squares. Central stamp, almost entirely preserved, displays right-facing, striding quadruped with large triangular head and recurving tail. Short crescent-shaped projection, possibly a wing, springs from center of creature's back. Horizontal groove below stamps.

UNPUBLISHED.

COMPARANDA: The fragment is too small to assign to a particular vessel type.

ORNAMENT TYPE: 1.

133. Stamped Fragment
Fig. 30; Pl. 24
MURLO NO.: 72-417
GRID: Rec.5, J/0
STRATUM: 2
Max. Pres. L. 0.014; Max. Pres. W. 0.020; Th. 0.003–0.005 m.

Single fragment. Broken on all sides. Missing portions of stamped decoration. Small chip on one edge.

Small, slightly curving, triangular fragment with smooth underside. Surface of fragment preserves portions of 2 stamped asterisk-rosettes, composed of series of impressed triangles with their apices turned inward and arranged in circle. Low flat ridge runs along one edge.

UNPUBLISHED.

COMPARANDA: This fragment is too small to assign to a particular vessel type.

ORNAMENT TYPE: 4d.

134. Strap Handle Fragment
Fig. 30; Pl. 24
MURLO NO.: 72-415
GRID: Rec.5, I/0

Stratum: 2
Max. Pres. L. 0.026; Max. Pres. W. 0.029; Th. 0.007 m.

Single fragment. Broken at both ends and along part of one lateral edge. Worn and burned. Mottled orange-brown in color with black spots. Orange-brown biscuit.

Fragment preserves portion of curving strap handle with tapering sides. Exterior surface of handle preserves decoration of 3 complete rows and tops of fourth row of 3 stamped concentric circles.

Unpublished.

Comparanda: This fragment is too small to assign to a particular vessel type.

Ornament Type: 2.

135. Incised Cup or Bowl Fragment
Fig. 30; Pl. 24
Murlo no.: 71-548
Grid: Rec.7, A/1
Stratum: 3(*I/O)
Max. Pres. Diam. 0.025; Th. 0.005 m.

Single fragment. Broken on all sides. Large chip on exterior surface. Worn, chipped, and burned. While upper surface of fragment is black, underside is gray-brown. Black biscuit.

Fragment preserves small portion of wall and transition to rim of a cup or bowl. Outer surface preserves upper portions of 3 incised, intersecting double circles.

Unpublished.

Comparanda: Not enough of the fragment is preserved to assign it to a particular vessel type.

136. Bowl or Plate Fragment
Pl. 25
Murlo no.: 72-513
Grid: Rec.5, H/0
Stratum: 2
Max. Pres. L. 0.025; Max. Pres. W. 0.078 m.

Single fragment. Chipped and worn, but still preserves portions of original glossy surface.

Fragment preserves portions of thick ring base and tondo of plate or bowl. Center of tondo decorated with tall rounded boss.

Unpublished.

Comparanda: Not enough of the fragment is preserved to assign it to a particular vessel type. An unpublished fragment of similar shape was found at Poggio Civitate in Trench 18, Murlo no. 70-229.

XVI. Inscribed Fragments (137–139)

137 through **139** all display inscriptions. Unfortunately, none of these fragments can be assigned to a specific vessel shape. The individual inscriptions will be discussed below in Chapter 4.

137. Inscribed Rim Fragment
Fig. 30; Pl. 25
Murlo no.: 71-344
FI: 110953
Grid: Rec.7, D/1
Stratum: 2
Max. Pres. L. 0.026; Max. Pres. W. 0.021; Th. 0.002 m.

Single fragment. Broken on 3 sides. Surface is slightly worn, but still preserves much of original glossy finish.

Fragment preserves small portion of thin-walled, curving body and narrow rounded rim of small bucchero bowl or cup. Surface of fragment decorated with 3 groups of incised horizontal lines. Four lines appear just below rim, 3 at middle of fragment, and 2 lines at base. Between the groups of lines at middle and base are preserved traces of 3 inscribed Etruscan letters. At right edge is preserved only an unidentifiable, small, curving stroke, at center a *rho*, and along left edge the semicircular, curving, right side of a *theta*, or possibly, a *phi*.

Unpublished.

Comparanda: The fragment comes from the rim area of a thin-walled cup or bowl. However, not enough of the fragment is preserved to assign it to a particular vessel type.

138. Inscribed Fragment
Fig. 99; Pl. 25
Murlo no.: 75-15
FI: 107746
Grid: Rec.9, D/1
Stratum: 2
Max. Pres. L. 0.049; Max. Pres. W. 0.027; Th. 0.004 m.

Mended from 2 pieces. Broken on all sides. Worn and chipped.

Slightly curving body fragment. Surface of fragment preserves portions of 3 incised Etruscan letters. Along right edge appears an unidentifiable curve, perhaps part of a *beta*, at center is a *lambda*, and along left edge an *alpha*.

UNPUBLISHED.

COMPARANDA: Not enough of the fragment is preserved to determine its orientation or vessel type. The piece has been drawn to facilitate the reading of the inscription.

139. Inscribed Fragment
Fig. 30; Pl. 25
MURLO NO.: 72-353
FI: 107741
GRID: Rec.5, F-H/0-1
STRATUM: 2/5 (*I/O)
Max. Pres. L. 0.033; Max. Pres. W. 0.035; Th. 0.006–007 m.

Single fragment. Broken on all sides. Surface worn and scratched.

Slightly curving body fragment from cup or bowl. Portion of inscription preserved on surface of fragment. Inscription consists of 5 letters, separated by a dot into two partial words. Letters of inscription, from right to left, are: *pi* or "c" (?), *iota*, the dot, *nu*, *alpha*, and *pi*.

UNPUBLISHED.

COMPARANDA: Not enough of the fragment is preserved to determine its orientation or the vessel type. The piece has been drawn to facilitate the reading of the inscription.

IV

Decoration

This chapter presents a detailed analysis of decorative motifs that appear on the bucchero vessels recovered from the Lower Building. The discussion of decorative schemes is separated from that of vessel typology on account of the complexity and diversity of the former and the recurrence of the same motifs on different vessel types.

The discussion of decoration is organized by decorative technique. A total of four techniques, comprising thirty-three decorative motif types and subtypes, as well as three inscriptions, can be distinguished. These techniques, in order of descending frequency, are: individual stamped decoration, cylinder-stamped decoration, molded decoration, and incised decoration. For each category a general discussion of the technique appears first, followed by an analysis of the motifs represented in the technical group. Each motif is described individually. Each entry includes references to figures and plates as well as to the vessel types on which the motif is displayed and their catalogue numbers. A detailed analysis of the motif, including relevant comparanda, follows.

Stamped Decoration

Stamped decoration is obtained by impressing a design into leather-hard clay (for the technique of stamped decoration, see Camerini 1985:18, pl. III, no. 5; also De Puma 1986:9). Since no actual stamps have been found to date, it is assumed that they were made either of a perishable material, such as wood or bone, or a reusable one, such as metal.[1] In general, the use of stamped decoration on ceramic vessels may have been inspired by the desire to emulate the effect of embossed decoration in metalworking.[2] This explanation seems particularly likely for early Etruscan ceramics, in which the relationship between metalworking and ceramics was especially close (Gran-Aymerich 1995). There is also a great deal of overlap in the iconography of the decoration, and the same motifs appear in both media. Finally, the tendency of some of the early ceramic workshops utilizing stamps to cover completely the surface of a vessel with stamped designs is particularly reminiscent of embossed metalwork.[3]

---

[1] Phillips has speculated that a small bronze disk, found at the site, decorated with a small rosette (Murlo no. 78-218), may have been utilized as a die for making a stamped decoration. He notes that the shape, size, and decoration on the disk are close to the rosette stamps on several *rocchetti* from Poggio Civitate. Phillips has used the evidence of the bronze die to suggest that all the dies utilized to produce the stamps on the pottery and clay objects from Poggio Civitate were made locally (see Phillips 1994:37, 44, figs. 4.30, 4.31, and 4.38). In addition, the rosette design on the bronze disk is also similar to that displayed on the rotelle of the oinochoai (**1** and **2**). Alternatively, Warden has postulated that the bronze disk was manufactured to decorate furniture or perhaps a chariot (see Warden 1985:117, no. 224, and fig. 37).

[2] Gregori 1991:80, note 5; Pieraccini 1996:101, note 23. In addition, the influences of both woodworking and textiles should probably also be considered. I thank Dr. Nielsen for making this suggestion.

[3] This tendency is particularly evident among many early stamped vessels from Bologna and Vetulonia. For examples from Bologna, see *Castenaso* 1979:106, fig. 70, nos. 2, 9, 11, 42. For Vetulonia, see Gregori 1991:figs. 30, 38.

The use of stamped decoration on pottery in Etruria can be traced back to the beginning of the Villanovan period. The practice is documented at Villanovan Tarquinia (Hencken 1968:32–33), Vetulonia (*CVA Firenze, Museo Archeologico* 1:IV B k, fig. 1), Bologna (*Castenaso* 1979:figs. 9.1, 17.1, 69.7–9; Miller 1986:267–68), and to a lesser extent also at Veii (*NSc* 17 [1963]:fig. 31). An interest in the textured surface treatment of ceramic vessels is already apparent in the Apennine Bronze Age, particularly in the use of the punching technique (Puglisi 1959:63–64, figs. 22–24). During the early seventh century, stamped decoration was utilized on both the earliest bucchero and contemporary impasto, but the repertoire of designs was limited (Rasmussen 1979:138). From the beginning, stamps were generally arranged in bands or zones and were repeated a number of times on the same vessel.

The technique became extremely popular during the second half of the seventh century and early decades of the sixth. Although stamped decoration was used in southern Etruria, notably at Cerveteri,[4] the practice was much more common in the north, particularly at late Villanovan Bologna (Montelius 1910:pls. 84, 85; 87, figs. 18, 19; 88, figs. 8, 9; 92; *Castenaso* 1979:103, fig. 70, nos. 2, 9, 11; Miller 1986:267–69). Workshops of stamped bucchero and impasto have been identified at Vetulonia, Roselle, and probably Populonia,[5] as well as at many other smaller, northern Etruscan sites in the territories of Chiusi and Florence during the later Orientalizing period (F. Nicosia, in *Aspetti e problemi*:55–56, pls. XIX–XXIV; L. Donati, in *Artimino*:82–83; Mangani 1990:12, note 22). The practice continued, although on a more limited basis, into the first half of the sixth century.

At Poggio Civitate stamped decoration appears very frequently on bucchero and impasto pottery associated with the Orientalizing phase of habitation (for a selection of stamped pottery from the site, see Phillips 1994:29–46). It is the most commonly occurring type of decoration on the bucchero from the Lower Building: twelve different stamps representing seven motif types and subtypes have been identified on the bucchero in the deposit. The figured stamps will be discussed first, followed by the nonfigured examples.

FIGURED STAMPS

1. Winged Quadruped (**132**; Figs. 30, 31, Pl. 24) Stamp displays right-facing, striding quadruped with large triangular head and recurving tail. Short crescent-shaped projection, possibly a wing or a head, springs from center of creature's back. Rear leg of figure truncated by edge of stamp. Dimensions .008 × .006 m. Stamp appears on small bucchero fragment.

Both the extremely small size and consequent lack of detail render the identification of this figure difficult. It can be identified as a sphinx, a winged lion, or perhaps a chimaera—all creatures known among the repertoire of bucchero stamps and commonly occurring in Etruscan Orientalizing art.[6]

The same stamp appears on a small impasto jar fragment found in Trench CA24[7] and on a bucchero plate recovered from Trench 23 (Murlo no. 80-177; see *Case e palazzi*:132, no. 492, pl. 3-492; Phillips 1994:32, "Quadruped V," no. 10, fig. 4.16). A nearly identical stamp on which the rear leg of the creature is complete was found on a bucchero fragment recovered from Trench 21 (Murlo no. 77-133; Rystedt 1983:127, fig. 92). In addition, the just-mentioned impasto jar fragment from Trench CA24 also features a stamp of similar type and the same dimensions, except that the quadruped is facing left rather than right (stamp appears on the lower register of decoration on the fragment; Phillips 1994:32, no. 9, "Quadruped IV").

---

[4] Stamped decoration was utilized on bucchero at Cerveteri, but the practice was limited (see Gran-Aymerich 1995:49, note 29). It was much more commonly used on Caeretan redware pithoi and braziers, the production of which began in the last quarter of the 7th century B.C. (see Serra Ridgway 1986:285–86; Pieraccini 1996:101–102).

[5] Vetulonia: Gregori 1991:64–81. Roselle: Bocci 1970:157; Donati 1991:82–99. Stamped designs are found on bucchero from Populonia, but the technique does not seem to have been as popular there as at Vetulonia and Roselle; see Minto 1943:136, fig. 46; *Etrusker* 1987:253, no. 55.

[6] For a discussion of the lion in Orientalizing art, see W. L. Brown, *The Etruscan Lion* (Oxford, 1960):1–45; for the sphinx, see M. Fullerton, *RömMitt* 89.1 (1982):15–20; for the chimaera, see O. Terrosi Zanco, *StEtr* 32 (1964):29–72; see also Johansen 1971:78–79, 86–90.

[7] This stamp appears on the upper register of decoration on the fragment. See Phillips 1971:260, Murlo no. 70-

Outside Poggio Civitate, small winged stamped creatures of a similar type appear on the handles of a buccheroid kantharos dated to the middle of the seventh century from Vetulonia[8] and on the handle of a buccheroid cup found in a stratum dated 630–580 B.C. at Massarossa.[9] Related Orientalizing stamped creatures, although not always winged, have also been found at Roselle (on a bucchero fragment dated to ca. 600 B.C.; see L. Donati, in *Roselle*:47, no. 12, pl. VIIa), Vetulonia,[10] and Massarossa (*Versilia*:87, no. 33, fig. 35).

NONFIGURED STAMPS

2. Concentric Circles (**134**; Figs. 30, 31, Pl. 24)
   Stamp composed of 2 concentric circles. Diameter 0.004 m. Stamp appears on small strap-handle fragment.

Concentric circles are among the earliest and most widespread of stamp types. They first appeared on impasto vessels at the beginning of the Villanovan period.[11] Concentric circles then appeared on the earliest bucchero and contemporary impasto, and were commonly used throughout Etruria during the Orientalizing period.[12] Impressions made by the same stamp are also found on an unpublished impasto handle fragment from the Lower Building (Murlo no. 77-223).

3. Circumscribed Oblique "S" (**118**; Figs. 28, 31, Pl. 21)
   Stamp composed of circumscribed, flattened, oblique "S"-design. Length 0.011 m. Stamp appears on fragmentary lid.

Oblique "S"-designs first appeared in Etruria in the first quarter of the seventh century on Orientalizing painted vases (as, e.g., on an amphora from the Bottega dei pesci Stoccolma; see Martelli 1987:85, no. 31; 86, no. 33). During the Orientalizing period they are represented in a number of media, including ivory, and are especially common on metalwork.[13] Similar oblique "S"-designs, although generally later in date, are also found outside Etruria on East Greek painted vases (Walter-Karydi 1973:90, 94, pl. 131, no. 1064a; pl. 134, no. 1057). The motif is probably derived from the guilloche chain.[14]

The oblique "S" is not a common stamped motif. At Poggio Civitate additional examples of this stamp occur on two bucchero lid fragments found outside the west wall of the Lower Building below Rectangle 6 of the Upper Building.[15] Similar oblique "S"-stamps were also discovered on bucchero lid fragments discovered in the west wall of Rectangle 7 of the Upper Building (Murlo no. 70-40; see Phillips 1971:259, pl. 58, figs. 6, 7).

Outside Poggio Civitate, similar, although slightly more curved, "S"-stamps have been

[8] The stamp appears on the handles of a kantharos found in the Group 4 of the Tomba del Duce. Camporeale has identified the figure as a winged lion (1967:120–22, no. 86, fig. 16b, pl. XXVIa–c). For the dating of the Tomba del Duce, see this volume, Introduction, note 3.

[9] The stamp appears on the handle of a buccheroid impasto cup found in a mixed stratum dated to 630–580 B.C.; see M. Cristofani, in *Archeologica: scritti in onore di Aldo Neppi Modona* (Florence, 1975):194, 199, fig. 9.

[10] This stamp appears on a number of bucchero and buccheroid vessels from Vetulonia, which have been dated to the third quarter of the 7th century B.C.: see Talocchini 1963:440, fig.3; Gregori 1991:76, Stamp 1, figs. 1–15. The figure has been identified as a lion by Camporeale (1967:68–69).

[11] Hencken 1968:32–33, fig. 21, no. 158, from Tarquinia; G. Berganzi, *StEtr* 41 (1973):7, fig. 2, nos. 4–6, fig. 4, from Roselle; *Castenaso* 1979:figs. 9.1, 15.2, 19.1, from Bologna; Falchi 1965:pl. III, nos. 4, 26, from Vetulonia. Concentric circles are also a common motif on metalwork during the Villanovan and Orientalizing periods; see Hencken 1968:fig. 33, no. 73b; fig. 39, no. 97b; fig. 66, 196b; also Strøm 1971:figs. 24, 38, 53, 63.

[12] Rasmussen 1979:137, no. 5; Camporeale 1967:pl. XXXIX, c–g, from Vetulonia; Nicosia 1974:pls. XIX, XX, XXIIa, from Artimino.

[13] Ivory: *Etrusker* 1987:158–59 (from Marsigliana d'Albegna). Metalwork: Strøm 1971:70, no. S40, fig. 49 (from Tarquinia); Pareti 1947: pl. XIII, no. 134; pl. XV, no. 51; pl. XXXVI, nos. 251–54 (from Cerveteri); Curtis 1925:23–24, no. 21, pl. 8 (from Palestrina).

[14] This is particularly evident in examples where the "S"-designs are arranged very closely together; see Pareti 1947:pls. XV, no. 151, LXI, no. 525. Phillips, citing a suggestion by Nielsen, has also proposed that the motif may be related to the stylized ducks on late Villanovan pottery from the area of Bologna; see Phillips 1971:259, note 14.

[15] Murlo no. 70-153 A, B; see Phillips 1971:261, pl. 62, figs. 38, 39. These fragments, which were found outside of the Lower Building in Rec. 6, D-E/6, may form part of the same lid as **118**.

found on Orientalizing bucchero and impasto vessels ranging in date from the second to the final quarter of the seventh century B.C. from Cerveteri, Veii, and perhaps Tarquinia.[16]

4a. Asterisk Rosette Type 1 (**115**, **117**; Figs. 27, 28, 31, Pl. 21)

Rosette composed of 16 small impressed triangles arranged around a circle with their apices turned inward. Diameter of stamp 0.007 m. Stamp appears on 2 fragmentary lids.

4b. Asterisk Rosette Type 2 (**5**, **64**; Figs. 10, 22, 31, Pls. 3, 15)

Stamp composed of 8 small impressed triangles arranged around a circle with their apices turned inward. Diameter of stamp 0.008 m. Stamp appears on alabastron and broad-rimmed bowl.

4c. Asterisk Rosette Type 3 (**5**; Figs. 10, 31, Pl. 3)

Rosette composed of 8 small impressed triangles arranged around a circle with their apices turned inward. Diameter of stamp 0.006 m. Stamp appears on alabastron.

4d. Asterisk Rosette Type 4 (**133**; Figs. 30, 31, Pl. 24)

Rosette composed of twelve small impressed triangles arranged around a circle with their apices turned inward. Diameter of stamp 0.006 m. Stamp appears on small fragment of unidentified vessel type.

Rosettes are among the most widespread and ancient of stamped ornaments (Gregori 1991:80, note 5). In Etruria, they first appeared, often arranged in bands, on impasto urns at the beginning of the Villanovan period (Hencken 1968:32–33, fig. 33). During the Orientalizing period they were also commonly used as embossed decoration on metalwork (Strøm 1971: figs. 27, 30, 31, 33, 62; Montelius 1910:pl. 224, figs. 2–4). Stamped rosettes appear on the earliest bucchero and contemporary impasto in both southern and northern Etruria (Rasmussen 1979:138; Ramage 1970:16–17).

Although they differ in size and number of petals, the asterisk rosettes ornaments 4a–d, Types 1–4, are similar in design. They all consist of small, impressed triangles arranged around a circle with their apices turned inward, a particularly common stamp type at Poggio Civitate. Additional examples of Type 1 stamped asterisk rosettes have been found on a lid fragment recovered from the west wall of Rectangle 7 of the Upper Building.[17] Sixteen-petalled rosettes similar to asterisk rosette Type 1, although smaller in size and with longer rays, appear on a bucchero lid fragment recovered from this same location[18] and on a bucchero lid reconstructed from fragments found outside the north wall of the Lower Building and in Trench 17.[19] No additional examples of asterisk rosette Types 2–4 have been recovered from the site.

Outside Poggio Civitate, rosettes composed of eight impressed triangles similar to asterisk rosette Types 2 and 3, although with different dimensions, have been found on Orientalizing bucchero and buccheroid vessels dated to the seventh and early sixth centuries B.C. from Vetulonia, Chiusi, and Castelnuovo Berardenga.[20] No parallels for the asterisk rosette Types 1 and 4 were noted. Other, related rosettes with differing numbers of triangular petals are also known on bucchero and buccheroid vessels dated to the middle of the seventh century B.C. from Poggio

[16] Cerveteri: Pareti 1947:369, no. 403, pl. LV; 421–22, no. 525, pl. LXVI; Rasmussen 1979:93–94, no. 2, pl. 25, fig. 120; 138, no. 10; *Cerveteri* 1986:58–59, nos. 29, 33. Veii: Palm 1952: Picazzano Tomb 19, pl. VII, no. 5; Cristofani 1969:Monte Michele Tomb D, 29, no. 2, fig. 11, pl. XII.2; Rasmussen 1979:pl. 23, fig. 99. Tarquinia: Hencken 1968:380–81, fig. 371f. It is possible that the caryatid chalice strut on which the stamp appears, although found at Tarquinia, was manufactured at or in the territory of Cerveteri; see Capecchi and Gunnella 1975:46–50, fig. 3.

[17] Murlo no. 72-369: see Nielsen and Phillips 1975:359, ill. 2, pl. 63, fig. 3. The fragment was found in meters 4 and 5 of the west wall of Rectangle 7.

[18] Murlo no. 72-370; see Nielsen and Phillips 1975:358–59, ill. 3, pl. 3, fig. 4. The fragment was found in meters 4 and 5 of the west wall of Rectangle 7.

[19] Murlo no. 71-613; Nielsen and Phillips 1975:358–59, ill. 1, pl. 62, figs. 1, 2. A reexamination of excavation records has revealed that contrary to what was published in the excavation report, no fragments of this lid were found inside the Lower Building.

[20] Vetulonia: Stamped asterisk rosettes appear on buccheroid vessels dated between the second and third quarters of the 7th century B.C.; see Gregori 1991:76, Stamp II; 77, Stamp VII; figs. 12, 13, 16, 18, 25–27, 29. See also Camporeale 1967:126–27, figs. 19, 20, 21b, pls. XXVIIb, c, XXVIIIa, XXIXb, c. Chiusi: von Mercklin

Buco (M. Cristofani-Martelli, *StEtr* 40 [1972]:82–83, pl. XIIa) and Roselle (Naumann and Hiller 1959:22, pl. 9, nos. 2, 9).

5. Petal Rosettes (**58–63**; Figs. 22, 31, Pl. 15)
Rosettes composed of 6 small oval petals surrounding incised circle. Diameter of stamp 0.010 m. All appear on rims of broad-rimmed bowls.

Petal rosettes commonly appeared as embossed and applied decoration on metalwork, particularly in southern Etruria, during the Orientalizing period.[21] Later, they were also found on incised bucchero (Bonamici 1974:35–36, no. 38, pl. XIXa–c), although they were not a common stamp ornament on bucchero.

At Poggio Civitate the stamped petal rosettes are all found decorating the rims of a series of small broad-rimmed bowls, almost all of which have been found in the Lower Building.[22] These rosettes are all the same size and appear to be from the same stamp. This particular petal rosette stamp is unknown outside Poggio Civitate. Related stamped rosettes, although with longer and more numerous petals, have been found on bucchero vessels at Roselle (Donati 1991:82–99; Bocci 1965:183–84, inv. no. 2072, fig. 37) and Massarossa (*Versilia*:84, no. 26, fig. 35).

6a. Double-Volute Palmette Type 1 (**48**, **114**; Figs. 19, 27, 31, Pls. 13, 21)
Double-volute palmette composed of 2 volutes with joined stems and incurving scrolls. Small round bud at base of palmette below scrolls and three-petalled blossom in interior. Stamp set within circular field. Diameter of stamp 0.007 m. Stamp appears on jar and lid.

6b. Double-Volute Palmette Type 2 (**118**; Figs. 28, 31, Pl. 21)
Blossomless double-volute palmette composed of 2 volutes with joined stems and incurving scrolls. Stamp set within circular field. Diameter of stamp 0.007 m. Stamp appears on fragmentary lid.

Double-volute palmettes of this type are commonly found in Etruscan art of the Orientalizing and Archaic periods (for a brief discussion of the palmette in early Etruscan art, see Johansen 1971:108; also Rystedt 1983:142). They first appeared in Etruria at the beginning of the Orientalizing period when the motif was borrowed from Phoenician art. The motif is represented on a wide variety of media, particularly during the seventh century, including metalwork,[23] worked bone and ivory,[24] painted pottery,[25] incised (Bonamici 1974:15, no. 1, pl. 1; 20, no. 11, pl. VIc; 32–33, no. 34, pl. XVIb) and stamped bucchero.[26] A palmette may appear alone, as in the present examples, or as part of a lotus and palmette chain, or they may be grouped together to form more complex floral ornaments.[27]

Note 20 continued
no. 44, pl. XLII.1. This plate can be dated to the first half of the 6th century B.C. on the basis of its cylinder-stamped decoration; see the discussion of the Miscellaneous Plate Type 2 in the catalogue (Chapter 3 above). Castelnuovo Berardenga: The stamped rosettes appear on a fragmentary bucchero cup from Poggione Tomb B, which has been dated to the end of the 7th and the first decades of the 6th century B.C.; see Mangani 1990:12, fig. 2.1.

[21] Strøm 1971:figs. 37, 38, 42, 53, no. 58; for later examples, see also G. C. Cianferoni, in *Studi e Materiali* 6 (1991):109, figs. 18, 19.

[22] A nearly complete bowl stamped with flower rosettes of this type was put together from fragments found in Trench CA28 and Agger 4 (Murlo no. 70-100; pl. 15). It should be noted, however, that in the published illustration of this vessel the rosettes are incorrectly drawn with 5 petals instead of 6; see Phillips 1971:260, pl. 61, figs. 27–29.

[23] Strøm 1971:figs, 25, 51, 52, 56, 67; Johansen 1971:pls. XXII–XXIII; Minto 1943:123, fig. 40a; Camporeale 1967:pl. D, nos. 1c, d; *Cento preziosi:* 22, no. 28, 29, nos. 37-38.

[24] Caputo 1974:pls. VII, XIIb. See also *Restauri archeologici* (Florence, 1969):26–27, cat. nos. 14, 15, pl. XI, figs. 1, 2; *Cento preziosi:* 56, no. 73, 79, no. 106, 98, no. 143.

[25] The palmette is a particularly common motif of the workshop of the Painter of the Calabrese Urn at Cerveteri; see F. Buranelli, *L'urna Calabresi di Cerveteri* (Rome, 1976):figs. 2, 4, 5, 8, 10.

[26] Rystedt has suggested that the motif, which appears in northern Etruria on late Orientalizing bucchero pottery, was adopted from examples on metalwork from the south; see Rystedt 1983:142 and note 201.

[27] The palmette is used as a component part of the "tree of life" and related floral motifs; see Johansen 1971:pls. XXXII, nos. 37, 38; XXXIII, nos. 39, 40. For the "tree of life," see the discussion of ornament 19 below.

No additional examples of stamped double-volute palmette Type 1 are known from Poggio Civitate.[28] Stamped palmettes similar to those of Type 1, although of larger dimensions and with different arrangements of blossoms, are found on an impasto handle fragment from Trench 6A[29] and on two impasto *rocchetti*, one from Trench CA24[30] and the other from Trench 17.[31] Other examples of stamped double-volute palmette Type 2 were found on two lid fragments recovered outside the west wall of the Lower Building below Rectangle 6 (Rec. 6,D–E/6) of the Upper Building (Murlo no. 70-153 A, B; see Phillips 1971:261, pl. 62, figs. 38, 39).

Outside Poggio Civitate, stamped double-volute palmettes nearly identical to those of Type 1 were found on two buccheroid kantharos handle fragments recovered from a tomb at Vetulonia dated to the third quarter of the seventh century.[32] Stamped double-volute palmettes very similar to double-volute palmette Type 1, although differing in both the number and arrangement of their blossom petals, have also been found elsewhere on bucchero, buccheroid, and impasto vessels and fragments. These examples, dated from the mid-seventh to the second half of the sixth century, were discovered at a number of sites in both southern and northern Etruria and Latium, including Rome,[33] Cerveteri,[34] Vulci,[35] Roselle,[36] Vetulonia,[37] Massarossa,[38] Pisa,[39] Fiesole,[40] and Accesa.[41] Blossomless double-volute palmettes similar to stamped double-volute palmette Type 2, but of larger dimensions, have also been discovered at Roselle.[42]

---

[28] For a discussion of this stamp type, see Phillips 1994:102–5, Palmette Type I, nos. 16, 17, figs. 4.23, 4.24.

[29] Murlo no. 68-442; see Phillips 1994:34–35, Palmette II, no. 18, fig. 4.25. Phillips notes that the handle fragment comes from a stratum associated with the Orientalizing occupation of Piano del Tesoro.

[30] Murlo no. 70-207; see Phillips 1994:35, Palmette III, no. 19, figs. 4.26–4.28. Trench CA24 represents a *fossa* filled with mixed debris from both the Orientalizing and Archaic phases of the site.

[31] Murlo no. 71-84; see Phillips 1994:35, Palmette III, no. 20, fig. 4.29. Trench 17 contains material of mixed context from both the Orientalizing and Archaic phases of the site.

[32] The two kantharos handle fragments were found in a tomb in the Poggio Valli necropolis. The tomb was originally dated to the end of the 7th or beginning of the 6th century by Talocchini on the basis of the similarity of several bucchero vessel fragments from the tomb to bucchero vessels found in Groups 2 and 4 of the Tomba del Duce (see Talocchini 1963:440–44, figs. 1, 2). As a result of the subsequent redating of the depositions in the Tomba del Duce, this kantharos type is now dated to the middle of the 7th century; see this volume, Introduction, note 3. Since no measurements are provided, it is not possible to determine whether these stamps are of the same diameter as those from Poggio Civitate.

[33] A stamped double-volute palmette appears on an impasto cup fragment found during excavation of the Temple of Caesar. The fragment was found in a stratum containing material from the 6th and 5th centuries (see *ER* 3:281, 293–94, fig. 184.4).

[34] Stamped double-volute palmettes appear on a redware pithos and on an impasto olla from Cerveteri. The pithos, which is from an unknown context, is now in the Louvre; see Pottier 1897:pl. 36, D251. Serra Ridgway (1986:286) has dated redware pithoi of this type with stamped decoration to the last quarter of the 7th century. The olla has been dated typologically by Pallottino between the final decades of the 7th and the first half of the 6th century (M. Pallottino, *StEtr* 21 [1950]:399, figs. 1–5).

[35] The stamps appear on a bucchero bowl from Vulci. De Puma has suggested a date shortly before 600 B.C. for the bowl on the basis of the similarity of its stamped decoration to the stamped double-volute palmette Types 1 and 2 from the Lower Building (De Puma 1986:44, VC 27, pl. 12e).

[36] The stamps appear on a bucchero body fragment found in a stratum containing material from the 6th century (see Naumann and Hiller 1959:pl. 9, no. 15) and on a buccheroid foot fragment recovered in a mixed stratum containing material from the 6th through 5th centuries (see Bocci 1965:190, inv. no. 3005, pl. LV).

[37] The stamps appear on a buccheroid lid fragment found in deposition IIa of the Circolo dei Leoncini d'Argento, which has been dated to the third quarter of the 7th century (see S. Bruni, *I lastroni a scala* [Rome, 1986]:121–22, pl. XLIVa).

[38] The stamp appears on an undated bucchero lid fragment (see *Versilia*:84–86, no. 27, fig. 35).

[39] The stamp appears on a bucchero bowl fragment, which has been dated to the first half of the 6th century (see Bonamici 1989:1143, fig. 4, no. 4).

[40] The stamps appear on several bucchero fragments of unknown date (see Bonamici 1989:1143, note 22).

[41] The stamps appear on the handles of a buccheroid kantharos which has been dated to the second half of the 7th century (see Camporeale 1997:152–53, no. 35, Type 1, no. 1, fig. 22.4, pl. XXX, 1 and 3).

[42] The stamps appear on 2 bucchero bowl fragments dated between the end of the 7th and the first half of the 6th century (see *Roselle*:47, no. 12, pl. VIIa; Donati 1991:figs. 24, 27c).

7a. Double-Volute Palmette Type 3 (**56**, **57**; Figs. 21, 31, Pl. 14)

Palmette composed of double volute with outcurving scrolls crowned by triangular bud. Long thickening stem curls outward from base of each volute. Both stems joined by short, curving line. Triangular bud appears in intervening space. Stamp set within triangular field 0.018 m high and 0.027 m wide. Stamp appears on bowl rim and bowl rim fragment.

7b. Double-Volute Palmette Type 4 (**102–109**; Fig. 25, Pl. 19)

Stylized palmette composed of long-stemmed double volute with outcurving scrolls. Scrolls joined by narrow horizontal band and crowned by triangular bud. Second triangular bud appears below junction of volutes. Area below stems and bud decorated with short vertical striations. Preserved stamped impressions are too worn to permit accurate measurement. Stamp appears on rim and handle fragments.

These examples have been designated as a separate type because they are both more elaborate than and stylistically distinct from the double-volute palmette Types 1 and 2. Like Types 1 and 2 above, the double-volute palmette Types 3 and 4 are ultimately derived from Near Eastern, probably Phoenician, art.[43] Motifs of similar type are also commonly found on East Greek, especially "Rhodian," painted vases dated to the late seventh and early sixth centuries (Walter-Karydi 1973:figs. 28, 59, 95–105, 157). While isolated double-volute palmettes are often found in Etruscan Orientalizing art, this particular variant, with long, outwardly curving stems, is not common. No other examples of stamped double-volute palmettes of Type 3 are known from Poggio Civitate. But a similar stamped double-volute motif, without the long curving stems, is found on a bucchero sherd recovered from Trench 17,[44] and Rystedt has noted the similarity in shape of this stamped motif to that of some of the akroteria from the Lower Building.[45]

It is possible that all eight of the stamped impressions of the double-volute palmette Type 4 appearing on the lug handle fragments **102–109** were made from the same stamp. However, the examples are too worn to permit accurate measurement. Two additional double-volute stamped palmettes very similar to Type 4 appear on the handles of a buccheroid bowl recovered from Trench 18 (Murlo no. 73-230; Nielsen and Phillips 1977a:90–91, ills. 10, 11, fig. 11). These stamps are, however, smaller than the Type 4 stamps. No examples of stamped double-volute palmettes of either Type 3 or 4 have been found elsewhere. A similar motif is represented on the openwork handles of a number of bucchero cups dated to the last quarter of the seventh and the first decades of the sixth century, examples of which have been found at several sites in the Arno and Ombrone valleys and at Cerveteri.[46]

CYLINDER-STAMPS

To produce cylinder-stamped decoration it is necessary to first incise on a cylinder the desired motif or design as a negative image (on the technique see Camporeale 1972a:11–13; Camerini 1985:23; De Puma 1986:9). Then the cylinder is rolled across the wet clay leaving the positive image as relief decoration. To date, only one cylinder-stamp has been found in Etruria (at Roselle).[47] It is made of terracotta and is provided with holes on its short sides for insertion into a handle.[48] In general, the application of cylinder-stamped decoration on pottery, particularly bucchero, is thought to be derived from embossed decoration on metalware (Camporeale 1972a:11–12).

The date of first use of cylinder-stamped decoration on ceramic vessels in Etruria has not

[43] The motif is derived from the Near Eastern "tree of life" compositions; see Rystedt 1983:138–39, note 187. For Near Eastern examples, see Herrmann 1986:pls. 37–41 (from Nimrud).

[44] Murlo no. 77-201 (see Rystedt 1983:140, fig. 105).

[45] Rystedt (1983:140, fig. 106) has compared this stamped motif to variant D of her PC1 akroterial group.

[46] For a discussion of these cups, see Nicosia 1974:60; Rystedt 1983:140–41; figs. 107, 108; Mangani 1990:12–13, fig. 3, 1–3.

[47] C. Curri, in *Studi di antichità in onore di Guglielmo Maetzke*, vol. 2 (Rome, 1984):243–49, pls. 1–4.

[48] It is also possible that the stamps could have been made of other materials in addition to terracotta, including bone, stone, or wood; see Camporeale 1972a:12–13.

yet been definitively established due to the paucity of vessels displaying this decorative technique from well-dated contexts. Cylinder-stamped decoration, perhaps inspired by Corinth, is utilized on Caeretan redware, as well as bucchero by the last quarter of the seventh century.[49] The cylinder-stamped decoration appearing on the handle of a buccheroid kyathos (Murlo no. PA 72-32) from Tomb 8 from Poggio Aguzzo may represent one of the earliest datable examples of this decorative technique. Tuck recently dated this tomb to the middle of the seventh century (Tuck 1996a:35–37, 175, no. 66; 1996b: 399–400). The use of cylinder-stamped decoration on bucchero reached its greatest popularity during the first quarter of the sixth century and continued on a more limited basis for the remainder of that century (Camporeale 1962:142; Camporeale 1964; Camporeale 1972a:11). Workshops of cylinder-stamped bucchero have so far been identified at Tarquinia (Camporeale 1972b), Orvieto (Camporeale 1972a:107–22), and Chiusi (Scalia 1968:357–401), although, as the discovery of a cylinder-stamp at Roselle attests, the technique was also utilized at other Etruscan centers.

Cylinder-stamped decoration is used only on a limited basis on bucchero from Poggio Civitate. Five different stamp types have been identified on bucchero from the Lower Building. The figured cylinder-stamped impressions will be discussed first, followed by the nonfigured examples.

FIGURED MOTIFS

8. Figured Frieze Type 1 (**112**; Fig. 26, Pl. 20)
Frieze bordered at top by 2 wide bands and one thin, and at bottom by one thin and one wide band. Largest preserved portion of frieze displays procession of 4 fantastic and real animals moving left to right. Procession led by large stag, of which most of antlers, one foreleg, 2 rear legs, and rear portion of body are preserved. Griffin behind stag. Griffin displays small oval head with long neck, prominent breast, tall recurving wing, and curling tail. Winged quadruped, perhaps sphinx, follows griffin. Only lower body and bottom portion of wing of creature preserved. At far left, grazing stag, of which bent head, lower portion of antlers and forepart of body, including forelegs, are preserved. Stylized plants appear beneath stags and sphinx. Farther to left is another portion of frieze, presumably repeat of figures already described, which preserves lower portions of 4 animal legs and stylized plant. Stamp appears on fragmentary plate.

Additional nonjoining fragment preserves portions of a frieze, although it does not appear to represent the same stamped impression.[50] At center of fragment, a horse and rider, both missing their head. Rider sits with right arm held forward and bent upward at elbow, and with left arm bent downward and held behind him. In front, at far right, another horse, of which rear portion of body is preserved. Small portion of additional, unidentifiable figure at far left. Not enough of stamped impression preserved to determine its length.

There are no published stamps with this combination of figures. Both the style and iconography of the individual figures find close parallels among the cylinder-stamped friezes from Chiusi.[51] As in the Chiusine examples, the figures on the Poggio Civitate frieze are in very low relief and their contours are not clearly defined. In addition, all the identifiable figures on the frieze, including the griffin (Scalia 1968:figs. 12a–d), grazing stag (ibid., fig. 10a), and horse

[49] For discussions of the origin and use of cylinder-stamping on Caeretan redware, see Weinberg 1954:122, 137; S. P. Boriskovskaya, in *Wissenschaflicke Zeitschrift der Universtät Rostock* 19 (1970):567; Serra Ridgway 1986:285–86; Pieraccini 1996:101, 105. For the use of this technique on bucchero, see Camporeale 1962; Camporeale 1964; Scalia 1968; Camporeale 1972a; Camporeale 1972b; Cristofani 1971:80–81; Rasmussen 1979:141; L. Venuti, *StEtr* 44 (1988):47–50.

[50] The association of this fragment with **112** is not secure. If the fragment did belong to the plate, then it must have been decorated with 2 concentric cylinder-stamped friezes, since it is unlikely that the animal figures and horse and rider could have all fit together on a single stamp.

[51] For a discussion and catalogue of the cylinder-stamps from Chiusi and its territory, see Scalia 1968. Scalia's study is not comprehensive and deals only with friezes featuring human and animal figures.

and rider (ibid., pl. LXXXIVe), find close counterparts among the scenes on Chiusine stamps. Finally, the shape of the vessel on which the stamp appears has also been linked to Chiusi (see the discussion of this plate above, in Chapter 3, Miscellaneous Plates Type 2).

9. Figured Frieze Type 2 (**37**; Fig. 17, Pl. 11)
Frieze, bordered on each side by 4 flat narrow ridges, consists of procession of fantastic animals, moving left. On far right a sphinx, of which large head and portion of body, including recurving wing, are preserved. In front of sphinx, winged feline of uncertain type.[52] Creature displays small head with short neck, tall recurving wing and tail, and feline paws. Lower portion of hind leg of additional creature preserved at far left. Not enough of stamp preserved to determine length of cylinder. Stamp appears on kyathos handle fragment.

A buccheroid kyathos recovered from Tomb 8 on Poggio Aguzzo displays a very similar stamp on its handle.[53] Unfortunately, the handle from the Lower Building is too fragmentary to determine whether it depicts the same stamped design. In a recent study, Anthony Tuck has dated the tombs on Poggio Aguzzo to the middle of the seventh century (Tuck 1996a:35–37; 1996b:399–400).

There are no known parallels for this stamp elsewhere. While the style of the stamp, including the low relief and poorly defined contours of the figures, is characteristic of Chiusi, there are no other known examples of this combination of figures among published Chiusine stamps. On the other hand, the use of an elaborate border on the stamp is a typical feature of stamps from Orvieto, although there is no counterpart for this particular border among the stamps classified from that city (Camporeale 1972a:108). It should be noted that the application of a figured cylinder-stamp to a strap handle is uncommon.[54]

NONFIGURED MOTIFS

10a. Guilloche Type 1 (**128**; Fig. 30, Pl. 24)
Stylized guilloche consisting of series of oblique "S"-designs separated by dots. Not enough of stamped design preserved to determine length of cylinder. Stamp appears on lid fragment.

10b. Guilloche Type 2 (**54**; Fig. 21, Pl. 14)
Stylized guilloche consisting of series of oblique "S"-designs separated by dots. Footed bowl too heavily restored to determine length of cylinder. Stamp found on rim of footed bowl.

10c. Guilloche Type 3 (**55**; Fig. 21, Pl. 14)
Stylized guilloche consisting of series of oblique "S"-designs separated by dots. Footed bowl too heavily restored to determine length of cylinder. Stamp appears on rim of footed bowl.

Originally of Near Eastern derivation, the guilloche is a common motif in Etruscan Orientalizing and Archaic art.[55] It may be rendered either as a continuous chain, which may be dotted or undotted, or, as in the present examples, as a series of individual oblique "S"-designs separated by dots. These three stamped guilloches are all of similar type. They are differentiated only by their size and the rendering of the "S"-designs. Thus, while the "S"-designs of the guilloche Types 1 and 2 are elongated and somewhat flattened, those of guilloche Type 3 are more curving and wrap more strongly around the dots.

---

[52] The figure could represent a griffin, a winged lion, or even a second sphinx—all creatures found on stamped bucchero. A chimaera with a long narrow body like that of the creature on the frieze appears on a stamp from Chiusi (Scalia 1968:pl. LXXXV.C).

[53] Murlo no. PA 72-32. Anthony Tuck has suggested that the kyathos from Tomb 8 was produced locally (Tuck 1996a:58–59, 175, no. 66; Tuck 1996b:399–400).

[54] Among the examples listed among the comparanda for **37**, only the kyathoi from Tomb 8 at Poggio Aguzzo and Orvieto display figural stamped friezes on their handles. The arrangement of the frieze on the handle from Orvieto, however, which consists of superimposed pairs of heraldically posed figures, is completely different from that of the Poggio Civitate frieze (see Hayes 1985:63, C1).

[55] Camporeale 1972a:83. For Near Eastern examples, see Barnett 1975:pls. 27, 29, 32, 33 (from Nimrud); Crowfoot and Crowfoot 1938:41, no. 7, fig. 12, pl. XXI.7 (from Samaria); Thureau-Dangin et al. 1931:134, nos. 108–11, pl. XLVII (from Arlsan-Tash).

These stamps find no exact parallels at Poggio Civitate or elsewhere in Etruria. A similar stamped guilloche also composed of a series of oblique "S"-designs is found on a bucchero kantharos fragment from Artimino dated to the third quarter of the seventh century (Nicosia 1974:60–61, no. 10, pl. XXIV). Related cylinder-stamped guilloche designs, although composed of a continuous pattern, appear on late-seventh- and sixth-century bucchero vessels from Cerveteri[56] and Orvieto,[57] and on a seventh-century red-ware pithos from Cerveteri.[58]

11. Stylized Double Guilloche Type 1 (**90–101**; Fig. 25, Pl. 18)

Stylized guilloche consisting of 2 concentric guilloche bands with dotted centers. Bands linked by vertical bars and separated by dots. Length of the cylinder could not be determined. Stamp appears on rims of plate fragments.

12. Stylized Double Guilloche Type 2 (**110**; Fig. 25, Pl. 19)

Stylized double guilloche composed of 2 individual bands of "S"-shapes. Each pair of opposing "S"-shapes linked by vertical bar with dot on each side; another dot in intervening space between each pair of bars. Fragment too small to determine length of cylinder. Stamp found on bowl rim and handle fragment.

Both of these motifs, stylized double guilloche Types 1 and 2, are probably derived from the vertical heart-shaped volute palmette ornaments like the "tree of life," originally found in Near Eastern art and later popular in both Greece and Etruria during the Orientalizing period.[59] Related motifs are also found on a number of late-seventh- and early-sixth-century East Greek painted vases (Walter-Karydi 1973:pls. 98, no. 697; 101, nos. 862, 863).

While additional examples of both stamped impressions are known from Poggio Civitate, no examples of either type have been found elsewhere. Another example of stylized double guilloche Type 1 appears on the shoulder of an impasto oinochoe found in the Lower Building below Rectangle 7 (Murlo no. 71-232; see *Case e palazzi*:87, no. 127, pl. 3-127); and stamps of this same pattern, but made from cylinders of different sizes, appear on the rims of a number of footed bowls recovered in Trench 18 (Murlo nos. 73-223, 73-224, 73-230; see Nielsen and Phillips 1977a:89–91, ills. 7–11; figs. 9–11; *Case e palazzi* 85, nos. 115–118). An unpublished handle fragment recovered outside the west wall of the Lower Building below Rectangle 7 preserves a small portion of a stamped impression very similar to stylized double guilloche Type 2 but with a slightly different design (Murlo no. 72-427; pl. 19).

A stamped guilloche similar to stylized double guilloche Type 1, although consisting of only a single band of dotted "eyes," appears on a number of bucchero vessels from Orvieto (Camporeale 1972a:90–91, Frieze 31, pl. XXIIa, b) and on a bucchero chalice from Chiusi (Camporeale 1972a:120–22, Frieze 1, pl. XLIa, b), both dated to the first half of the sixth century on stylistic grounds. Stylized guilloche patterns very similar to stylized double guilloche Type 2 appear on a series of painted revetment plaques from Acquarossa dated to the first quarter of the sixth century.[60] In addition, an openwork bone inlay

[56] The guilloche appears on a bucchero chalice dated to the last quarter of the 7th century B.C.; see Pareti 1947:pl. LXVIII, no. 529; Rasmussen 1979:Type 2d, 98–99, no. 51, pl. 60, no. 11.

[57] Cylinder-stamped guilloche patterns appear on a number of bucchero vessels from Orvieto, which have been dated to the second quarter of the 6th century B.C.; see Camporeale 1972a:83–92, Friezes 27–31, pls. XXVII–XXXI.

[58] Pareti 1947:439, pl. LXX, no. 654. The pithos, which in addition to the guilloche design displays stamped metope-like decoration, can be dated to the last quarter of the 7th century B.C., according to the chronology proposed by Serra Ridgway (1986:286).

[59] The derivation of the motif is particularly clear in the case of the stylized double guilloche Type 2. Here the top and interior portions of the scrolls of the double volutes have been omitted, but their crowning buds have been retained in the central row of dots. In addition, the vertical dotted bars probably represent a schematized version of the bands often seen linking the double volutes, as in the stamped double volute palmette Type 4. The stylized double guilloche Type 1 probably represents an even more schematized version of this pattern. Wikander, in her study of the painted decoration found on revetment plaques from Acquarossa, has illustrated the evolution of similar stylized guilloche patterns from vertical volute palmette ornaments (see Wikander 1988:104–5, fig. 33, A–C).

[60] Wikander 1981:figs. 52–55, 87. For a discussion of the chronology of these terracottas, see Wikander 1988:126.

from the Montagnola tomb, composed of a series of interwoven volute palmette designs and dated to the last quarter of the seventh century, also displays a pattern very much like that of the stylized double guilloche Type 2 (Caputo 1974:46, pl. XVc).

MOLDED DECORATION

Molded decoration is obtained by impressing soft clay into a mold that has been made in the negative image of the desired decoration (for the technique, see Camerini 1985:20–21, pl. IV; Nijboer 1998:96–97, 104). Three techniques of molded decoration are attested among the bucchero from the Lower Building.

In the first, known as the jigger technique (see Richter 1936:61–65; Wisseman 1978:45; Camerini 1985:20, pl. IV.5; De Puma 1986:9–10), either all or a portion of the body of a vase is thrown in a mold on the wheel. The use of the jigger is attested in the seventh century among the earliest bucchero and contemporary impasto, and continued well into the sixth century.[61] Richter has suggested that the molds, none of which have yet been recovered, were made of terracotta (Richter 1936:63). The technique was probably developed to imitate ribbed decoration in metalwork (Rasmussen 1979:129; Camerini 1985:20).

In the second, only a portion of the vase, usually the handle or the supporting struts, is made with a mold. The molds may have been made from metal, terracotta, or perhaps wood. As yet, no molds have been found. It has not been determined when this type of decoration began to be used on bucchero. Among the earliest examples of the technique may be the molded caryatid figures on bucchero chalices[62] and the bucchero statuettes recovered most notably from the Regolini Galassi tomb, but also found elsewhere.[63]

For molded appliqués, the third technique, the clay is pressed into a small mold to form relief decorations, which are attached to the vase at the leather-hard stage before firing.[64] It is possible that a wet solution of the clay may have been used as a bonding agent. The use of molded appliqués on bucchero vessels began some time in the late seventh or early sixth century and enjoyed its greatest period of popularity, particularly in northern and central Etruria, during the latter half of the sixth century.[65]

MOLDED VESSELS

Eleven vessels with molded bodies thrown in a jigger were found in the Lower Building. They include two oinochoai (**1** and **2**), seven kyathoi (**22**, **25-28**, **31**, and **34**), a chalice (**46**), and a lid (**113**). Each piece was thrown in a different jigger. While the kyathoi, chalice, and lid were all thrown in a jigger as one piece, the oinochoai, as is customary in the case of closed shapes, were made in individual sections. In addition, with the exception of one kyathos (**22**), the contours of the molded scallops on the exterior of the vessels produced by the jigger were hand-tooled before firing.

MOLDED VESSEL BODY PARTS

HANDLES

13. Enthroned Figure (**1**, **3**; Figs. 9, 10, Pl. 2)
Design consists of human figure, probably male, in left profile, seated on throne.

---

[61] Rasmussen 1979:129. The jigger was used at a number of Etruscan sites during the 7th century B.C. for the manufacture of buccheroid vessels, especially kantharoi and kyathoi; see Camporeale 1967:65–71, pls. IXa, b–XII.

[62] The production of the earliest bucchero chalices with caryatid supports is generally placed in the last quarter of the 7th century B.C. These chalices have been assigned to a workshop in Cerveteri; see Capecchi and Gunnella 1975:Group I, 51; Rasmussen 1979:96; Salskov Roberts 1988:72.

[63] In his publication of the Regolini Galassi tomb, Pareti originally assigned a group of 33 bucchero statuettes to the right niche of the tomb, which he dated to 675 B.C., see Pareti 1947:272–81, 511, N. 233, pl. XXVIII. However, Strøm, in a subsequent reanalysis of the tomb, convincingly reassigned the statuettes to the ante-chamber of the tomb. Strøm has dated the ante-chamber to 625 B.C., see Strøm 1971:164, 168. See also Capecchi and Gunella 1975:99, note 1.

[64] For a discussion of the technique, see Richter 1936:62 and note 1; Wisseman, 1978:46; Camerini 1985:23–25; De Puma 1986:9. The application of molded decoration to ceramic vessels in Etruria may have been inspired by Corinth where the practice is documented from the early 7th century B.C.; see Weinberg 1954:133–36.

[65] The use of molded decoration, including plastically applied heads and finials, is especially characteristic of 6th century B.C. bucchero from Chiusi, Vulci, and Orvieto; see Donati 1967; Donati 1968; Donati 1969.

Figure wears long diagonal mantle and holds scepter or staff in outstretched right arm. Scepter terminates at top in double lotus. Left arm is bent at elbow and lies flat on thigh. Hair, bound tightly across top of head, falls down on side of head covering ear. Figure has large almond-shaped eye, prominent nose, and small mouth. Square-seated chair with low arm rest and tall back terminating at top in scroll. Crescent-shaped projection above scroll, which may constitute lower portion of bird. Narrow rectangular legs of chair terminate in what appear to be either equine hooves or feline paws. Beneath chair, griffin in left profile seated on haunches with straight front legs. Griffin displays rounded head with erect ears, prominent beak, and pommel on brow. Beginning of wing is evident curving up from back. Chair provided with low foot rest. Motif appears on oinochoe handle and on oinochoe handle fragment.

In addition to the two examples of this molded design known from the Lower Building, three examples, all unpublished, have been found to the north of the Upper Building in Trench 18 (Murlo nos. 73-317; 73-318; 73-319). All five of these examples appear on oinochoe strap handles, and only one is complete (Murlo no. 73-317; pl. 2). No examples of this same molded design have been found elsewhere.

A very similar molded design appears on two bucchero oinochoai and on the struts of three bucchero caryatid chalices, none of which has a known provenience.[66] The iconography of this design is similar to that from Poggio Civitate in all respects, except that its chair is shorter and a bird instead of a griffin lies below it. Capecchi and Gunnella, in their study of bucchero caryatid chalices, have assigned this molded design, as well as the one with which it is commonly paired on the chalices, to a workshop in or near Chiusi on the basis of the close similarity of the molded figures to those found on Chiusine cylinder-stamped friezes; and they have dated the chalices to the end of the second quarter of the sixth century on the basis of these iconographic parallels.[67] Cristofani and Zevi have proposed a slightly earlier date for the chalices with this molded design, placing them in the first third of the sixth century (Cristofani and Zevi 1965:26–27). They have noted, moreover, that the chalices with molded rather than openwork designs on their supports, as is the case for the examples with the seated figures, are stylistically later and should be assigned to the latter half of this period. It should be emphasized that these dates are not secure, since they are based solely on stylistic analysis and not on archaeological context. In addition, as Gunnella has noted, there is no indication of how long the molds from which the figures were made remained in use (Capecchi and Gunnella 1975:66).

The determination of the gender and, consequently, the identity of the figure represented on the molded design remains problematic.[68] In the case of the molded design attributed to Chiusi, the figure is usually identified as male, although Salskov Roberts, citing examples of similar seated figures in Near Eastern art, has recently suggested that the figure may instead be a female (Salskov Roberts 1988:76–77). Very similar seated figures, generally with birds below them, appear in cylinder-stamped friezes on bucchero from Chiusi, although here too both the gender and identity of the figures, as well as the meaning of the scenes themselves, are not readily apparent (Capecchi and Gunnella 1975:62 and notes 3, 4). Seated figures holding staffs, likewise of uncertain identity, also appear on terracotta frieze plaques from Poggio Civitate and Velletri and on stone *cippi* from Chiusi.[69] The motif is repeated in

[66] For the oinochoai, see (1) *CVA Altenburg* 3:pl. 124.4. (2) Giglioli 1935:14, pl. L, no. 3. For the caryatid chalices, see (1) *CVA Villa Giulia* 1:IV B 1, pl. 2, 2–4. (2) Capecchi and Gunnella 1975:63, no. 2, pl. IVa. (3) Paris, Louvre, inv. no. C685. For a discussion of the motif, see Capecchi and Gunnella 1975:59, IIIC, 62, 64–66; Cristofani and Zevi 1965:26–27, Type E; Salskov Roberts 1988: 76–77.

[67] Capecchi and Gunnella 1975:65–66. In addition, the two oinochoai on which the molded design appears are types generally associated with Chiusi (see Giglioli 1935:14, pl. L, no. 3; *CVA Altenburg* 3: commentary to pl. 124, 1, 2, 4, 5). In his discussion of the oinochoe in Altenburg, E. Bielefeld notes, however, that the handle on which the molded designs appear is not securely associated with the oinochoe.

[68] For a general discussion of the evolution and possible meanings of the seated figure in Villanovan and Etruscan art, see J. M. Gran-Aymerich, "À propos des vases 'à tenons perforés' et du thème des personnages assis," *MEFRA* 88.2 (1976):427–54.

[69] T. N. Gantz, *StEtr* 39 (1971):pls. I, Va, b, VIb, c. These seated figures have been identified by various scholars as either divine or human.

the well-known seated akroterial statues from Poggio Civitate.[70]

14. *Potnia Theron* Type 1 (**22**, **23**; Fig. 13, Pls. 6, 7) Decoration displays frontal *potnia theron* who stands holding a feline in each hand by its front paws. Two small birds perch on goddess's shoulders, facing inward. (Outlines of birds are now only faintly visible.) Hair of goddess flat on top, and on each side of her head, 2 long coiled tresses fall onto chest from behind ears. Interior tress on right side only partially represented. Face of goddess displays large oval eyes, short triangular nose, and small mouth set in U-shaped depression. Arms bent inward at elbows. She holds front paws of felines at hip level. Felines in profile with frontal faces, pointed ears, large almond-shaped eyes, and long noses; they stand upright on hind legs with their bodies masking much of lower portion of goddess's body. Two tangent, curving lines between animals appear to indicate tails of felines. Eyes of both *potnia* and felines defined by oval incisions. Design appears on kyathos and kyathos handle fragment.

15. *Potnia Theron* Type 2 (**30**; Fig. 15, Pl. 9) At top, molded design displays 2 small owls, inclined inward, with profile bodies and frontal heads. Faces of owls feature large, incised circular eyes and long triangular beaks; bodies decorated with 2 sets of 5 incised diagonal lines which indicate feathers. Below owls a frontal winged *potnia theron* grasps a bird in each hand. Her hair, flat on top, hangs down on each side of head in small triangular wedge that reaches shoulder. Eyes of goddess rendered with large circular incisions, as are breasts. Neither mouth nor nose indicated. Two volute-shaped wings project upward from shoulders and curve inward toward her head. Surface area of wings decorated with series of incised lines that progress from horizontal at shoulder to vertical at tips of volutes. Goddess wears long garment and stands with arms held outward, bent inward at elbows. Two birds in profile with long curving necks and short pointed beaks. Wings rendered with one vertical line down center and series of diagonal lines on each side. Design appears on kyathos handle fragment.

16. Winged Goddess Type 1 (**35**; Fig. 16, Pl. 11) Decoration consists of frontal winged female. Type illustrated by single fragmentary example, preserved from waist up and broken just below neck. Goddess originally had oval head and frontal wings that terminated in scrolls on either side of head. Arms bent in at elbow, she clutches 2 long tresses in each hand. These tresses fall from below neck to waist level and are separated by long incision down center. Two long narrow wings, partially covered by tresses, extend upward at an angle from waist and widen gradually toward neck. Design found on kyathos handle fragment.

17. Winged Goddess Type 2 (**34**; Fig. 16, Pl. 10) Each side of molded kyathos handle displays winged goddess standing frontally, with elongated arms bent slightly inward at elbows and with hands resting flat on thighs. Outlines of hands and fingers highlighted with incision. Narrow band of hair, defined by parallel vertical incisions, runs across forehead. Two similarly incised narrow bands, perhaps also meant to indicate hair, run along curving sides of top of handle, linking goddesses' heads. On each side of head, 3 long tresses, marked by diagonal incisions, fall down over shoulders and breasts. Oval head in high relief. Face displays incised almond-shaped eyes, long nose, wide mouth, and heavy chin. Two curling wings project outward from shoulders and curl inward on either side of head at eye level. Wing area decorated by incised diagonal lines. Triangular open area formed between wings and long locks of hair. Figure wears long garment, lower half of which is unarticulated, following simple rounded contours of handle. Garment terminates in double scallop. Partially preserved inset area below scallop on right decorated with series of incised vertical lines, which perhaps originally defined

[70] Edlund-Berry, in her study of the akroterial statues, identified them as divinities (I. E. M. Edlund Gantz, *DialArch* 6 (1972):194–212; Edlund-Berry 1992:181–207).

portion of an undergarment. Three additional incised lines also visible farther to left, but surface here is badly worn.

18. Winged Goddess Type 3 (**36**; Fig. 17, Pl. 11) Exterior section of kyathos handle fragment molded in form of winged goddess standing frontally, arms bent straight inward at elbows. She holds what are either wings or long tresses of hair, which originate at waist, curl up over shoulders, and terminate toward back of head. On each side of figure, narrow flange terminates in semicircular projection (only one example since left one not preserved) and probably represents a second, lower pair of wings originating from shoulders. She wears long, belted garment extending almost to base of handle. Head in high relief; features of face, now badly worn, include deeply set, almond-shaped eyes, long thin nose, small mouth with thick lips, and prominent chin. Lower body of figure rendered as simple narrow tube.

Originally of Near Eastern origin, the winged goddess first appeared in Etruscan art in the middle of the seventh century B.C.[71] She is represented in a number of variants and may appear alone, together with animals in her role as mistress of the beasts, or *potnia theron*, and may be shown with multiple wings or sometimes even wingless. The representation of the goddess on the handles of vases, especially kyathoi, seems to be largely an Etruscan phenomenon and was particularly characteristic of the bucchero production of Chiusi.[72] The goddess was also often represented on the figured supports of caryatid chalices in bronze, ivory, and, more commonly, in bucchero.[73]

Of the four representations of the goddess on bucchero from the Lower Building only one, *potnia theron* Type 1, is a previously identified type. It belongs to Type A in Valentini's classification of *potnia theron* representations (1969:417–30). Although she appears on a number of vessel shapes, the *potnia theron* of Type A was represented most frequently on kyathos handles. Valentini has identified the principal workshop(s) for the production of *potnia* representations of this type in or near Chiusi on the basis of their find frequency.[74] She tentatively dated the earliest examples of her Type A, on the basis of style, to the end of the seventh century, and it is clear that the motif continued to be used throughout the greater part of the sixth century as well (Valentini 1969:415, note 2, 417).

Potnia theron Type 2 is represented by a single example from Poggio Civitate. There are no known parallels for this design. The *potnia theron* holding birds is not a common motif in Etruscan art; she is more commonly depicted with quadrupeds.[75] A similar molded *potnia* has been

[71] For a discussion of the *potnia theron* in Etruria, see Damgaard Andersen 1992/1993; Krauskopf 1984:774–92; Johansen 1971:61–70.

[72] Damgaard Andersen 1992/1993:85, 98–102; Valentini 1969:416. The origin and significance of the placement of representations of the goddess on the handles of bucchero cups have not been discussed. A possible precedent, however, may be provided by a small group of early Orientalizing *a jour* bronze kyathos handles with representations of a female figure, perhaps the *potnia theron*, flanked by stylized ducks, the production of which Camporeale has tentatively assigned to Vetulonia (Camporeale 1969:59–60; see also G. Proietti, *Il Museo Nazionale Etrusco di Villa Giulia* [Rome, 1980]:76, nos. 81, 82). On the basis of these handles as well as a number of additional iconographic representations on other objects, Damgaard Andersen has suggested that a local, *potnia theron* type goddess may have existed in the Iron Age in central Italy. The iconography of this goddess would have been subsequently transformed during the later Orientalizing period as a result of the influence of imported Near Eastern representations of a similar deity.

[73] For a comprehensive discussion and typology of bucchero caryatid chalices, including a classification of their figured supports and a presentation of the bronze and ivory examples, see Capecchi and Gunnella 1975:35–116. See also Cristofani and Zevi 1965:23–27; Salskov Roberts 1988; Gran-Aymerich 1995:56–57.

[74] Valentini 1969:416–17. Valentini also notes that a smaller workshop, producing a limited number of *potnia theron* representations of Type A, may also have been located at Vulci.

[75] Damgaard Andersen 1992/1993:85. In her catalogue of representations of "Artumes" as the *potnia theron*, Krauskopf lists only three examples of the goddess holding birds (Krauskopf 1984:nos. 5, 7, 8). For an additional example, see also F. Canciani and F. W. von Hase, *La tomba Bernardini di Palestrina* (Rome, 1979):pl. 24.5. It should be noted that among the known representations of the *potnia theron* holding birds, the molded design on the Poggio Civitate handle is the only example in which the goddess holds the birds with her arms bent inward, toward herself. In all other cases the goddess grasps the birds by their necks with her arms bent outward. This difference in the pose of the *potnia theron* on the handle from Poggio Civitate probably bears no difference in meaning, but rather was dictated by the limited amount of space available on the handle surface for the design.

catalogued by Valentini as her Type C (Valentini 1969:432–34, fig. 9). In contrast to the example from Poggio Civitate, this *potnia* has a frontal body and a profile (rather than frontal) head and arms bent outward holding the birds. Valentini has attributed this design, which appears on the handles of a number of skyphoi, to a workshop based in or near Chiusi.[76] In a study of these skyphoi, Donati has dated the examples with the potnia theron of Type C, on the basis of their style, to the second quarter of the sixth century (Donati 1977:94). In addition, the *potnia* with arms bent outward holding birds is also represented on cylinder-stamped bucchero friezes of uncertain date from Chiusi (Valentini 1969:435–42, Schemes I–X, fig. 11; also Donati 1977:93, note 36).

Outside Etruria, the *potnia theron* holding birds was a relatively common motif in Orientalizing and Archaic Greek art and, in particular, was especially popular at Corinth, appearing frequently on Early and Middle Corinthian painted vases.[77] Phillips has suggested a possible derivation of the iconography of the molded design on this handle from Dorian sources (Phillips 1972:252).

The molded design *potnia theron* Type 2 is notable, in addition, for the inclusion of owls over the head of the *potnia theron*, since owls are not commonly depicted with the goddess.[78] The closest parallel for the design is found at Poggio Civitate itself, suggesting that the pairing of the *potnia theron* with owls may represent a local motif. Similar pairs of molded owls, although both facing right, appear on two bucchero handles, probably from a large crater, found in Trench 17.[79] A third fragment, which has now been joined to one of the two handles, is decorated with a large molded *potnia theron* (Murlo no. 70-347; see *Case e palazzi*:133, no. 503; see also Phillips 1989b:99 and note 39). The goddess is represented in left profile and holds two large lotus flowers in her hands.

Twelve additional handles with the same molded design as winged goddess Type 1, although made from different molds (several of which are complete and attached to kyathoi), were found in Trench 18 .[80] Two examples are illustrated here (pl. 11). The majority of complete examples are molded in the form of winged goddesses on both the interior and exterior of the handle, but others have a flat exterior surface bordered by ridges terminating in circles with dots in the center.[81] The complete examples reveal the goddess to have an oval head in high relief and show that her wings terminate in inward-curling scrolls on either side of her head. In addition, in several examples the head of the goddess is crowned by a finial in the form of a helmeted warrior's head or a rounded biconical knob (*Case e palazzi*:81, pl. 3-74; 84, pl. 3-95). Phillips has speculated that the biconical knob finial may have been a hat (Phillips 1993:64).

Images of female figures, both winged and wingless, with arms bent and holding their braids are relatively frequent in Etruscan Orientalizing art, although no exact parallels exist for the design of the winged goddess Type 1.[82] But a

---

[76] Valentini 1969:434. For a discussion of these skyphoi, see also Donati 1977:92–94.

[77] For a discussion of representations of the *potnia theron* with birds in Greece, see C. Christou, *Potnia Theron* (Thessaloniki, 1968):61–77; Damgaard Andersen 1992/1993:94-98. For the *potnia theron* in Corinthian vase painting, see Amyx 1988:618–19. See also Donati 1977:92 and note 34.

[78] The small birds perched on the shoulders of the *potnia theron* representations classified by Valentini as her Type A may represent owls, as Phillips has suggested for an example of this type from Poggio Civitate. In the majority of examples, however, the design is not clear enough to discern the type of birds with certainty. See Phillips 1989b:99, fig. 24; Valentini 1969:pls. CVa, b, CVIb, c, CVIIa–c, CVIIIb.

[79] The two handles have been published separately; see Phillips 1968:122, Murlo no. 67-87, pl. 52, fig. 4; Phillips 1971:259, Murlo no. 70-269, fig. 13.

[80] *Case e palazzi*:81–84, nos. 74, 77–79, 95–98, Murlo nos. 72-280, 73-258, 73-265, 73-285, 72-279, 72-320, 72-319, 73-313; Nielsen and Phillips 1986:12–15, figs. 5b–d, 6–9. There are also four additional unpublished examples: Murlo nos. 73-268, 73-269, 73-270, 73-272.

[81] For examples of handles in which both sides are molded in the form of the winged goddess, see *Case e palazzi*:84, pl. 3-95. For examples in which only one side is molded in the form of the goddess, while the other is flat, see *Case e palazzi*:81, pl. 3-74.

[82] Bonfante (1976:17) has suggested that the gesture in Etruscan art of a female figure holding her tresses, or, alternatively, her wings represents a transformation of the original Near Eastern image of the naked goddess holding her breasts. According to Bonfante, since the female figures in Etruscan art typically were clothed, the gesture of holding the breasts lost its meaning and subsequently was changed into the more "realistic" gesture of holding the tresses or wings. For additional discussion, including bibliography, of the possible derivation and meaning of the gesture as well as a list of additional Etruscan examples, see Capecchi and Gunnella 1975:44–45 and note 1.

similar iconography is displayed by several of the molded caryatid figures on the supports of bucchero chalices dated from the end of the seventh through the first half of the sixth centuries and produced at Chiusi (Capecchi and Gunnella 1975:Group IIIC, 59, 65, 66, pl. IIIB), Vulci (Capecchi and Gunnella 1975:Group IIA, 51–55, pl. II), and an additional workshop located somewhere in southern Etruria (Capecchi and Gunnella 1975:Group IVD, 71–94, pl. VIA).

An uncatalogued handle fragment displaying the same type of molded decoration as winged goddess Type 2 was found in Trench 26 in the area of the Southeast Building. No examples of this molded design are known elsewhere. The iconography of the design is unusual. While in most examples the goddess is depicted either holding animals or birds in her guise as the *potnia theron* or, alternatively, grasping her tresses or wings, in this case she is simply depicted with her arms hanging straight down, hands open and palms resting on her thighs. Bronze figures in a similar pose, although with wings emanating from their waists, appear on the corners of a basin frame from Castel San Mariano dated to the first half of the sixth century.[83] Several female-shaped chalice supports, also dated within the first half of the sixth century, from Castelnuovo Berardenga, have their arms and hands in the same position as winged goddess Type 2 but lack wings.[84] A number of molded bucchero caryatid figures from Cerveteri display a related design, except they too are wingless and hold their arms at the sides of their bodies (Capecchi and Gunnella 1975:99–102, Types 1 and 2, pl. XIIIa, b; Camporeale 1991:126, no. 19, pl XCVI.c). These figures have been dated to the end of the seventh and first quarter of the sixth centuries.

Four additional examples of the winged goddess Type 3, at least one of which was certainly made from the same mold, were found in Trench 18.[85] No examples of molded designs of this type are known elsewhere. The iconography of this representation is unclear. It is not readily apparent whether the curling projections on the front of the goddesses represent tresses of hair or frontal wings. Equally uncertain is the meaning of the two flanges terminating in semicircular projections placed at the sides of the goddess, which may indicate wings or perhaps the tips of a mantle.

Gunnella has noted a similar confusion in the representation of some of the goddesses depicted on the figured supports of bucchero caryatid chalices from Cerveteri and Tarquinia, dated to the last quarter of the seventh century, and those from Chiusi, dated to the second quarter of the sixth century.[86] These figures display an iconography very similar to that of the goddess molded on the Poggio Civitate handles. In the case of the figures from Cerveteri and Tarquinia, Gunnella has identified the curling projections on the front of the goddesses as hair, since no additional hair is represented and the projections seem to emanate from the sides of the figures' heads (Capecchi and Gunnella 1975:43–44, Group IA). By contrast, she has interpreted similar projections on the figure from Chiusi as wings, since tresses of hair are clearly indicated, and the tops of the wings curl in but do not touch the head.[87] Considering the size and configuration of these projections, however, it would appear that in all cases they originally represented wings. Most probably the artist has confused the frontal wings with tresses and thus has omitted the standard representation of straight shoulder-length locks.[88]

---

[83] U. Höckmann, *Bronzen aus dem Fürstengrab von Castel San Mariano bei Perugia* (Munich, 1982):72, pl. 40, nos. 1–3. See also Giglioli 1935:19, pl. LXXXV, nos. 1, 6. These bronze figures have been dated on the basis of their style to the first half of the 6th century B.C.

[84] Bocci Pacini 1973:124–25, 131, figs. 2, 3, pls. XLIVd, XLVd, XLVIc. These figures were found in a stratum dated to the first half of the 6th century B.C. See also *Case e palazzi*:160–61, pl. 4-30, 35.

[85] Murlo nos. 73-239, 72-321, 73-282, 72-325; see *Case e palazzi*:83, nos. 89, 91–93. Nielsen and Phillips originally noted that the handle Murlo no. 71-562 (**36**), which displays the molded design of the winged goddess type 3, was made from the same mold as Murlo no. 73-239 (Nielsen and Phillips 1977a:91–93).

[86] Capecchi and Gunnella 1975:Group IA, 44–47, 50–61, fig. 2, pl. Ia, from Cerveteri and Tarquinia; and Group IIIC, 59, 65, 66, pl. IIIb, from Chiusi. The examples from Tarquinia may actually have been made at Cerveteri.

[87] Gunnella has noted that volute wings of this type, which emanate from the waist, also appear on winged goddesses represented on cylinder-stamped bucchero friezes from Chiusi and may represent an iconographic convention of that city (see Capecchi and Gunnella 1975:58–61, esp. note 3, p. 60, Group IIIB).

[88] This opinion has also been expressed by Gunnella, who notes how the curling tresses on the caryatid figures from Tarquinia and Cerveteri clearly suggest wings (Capecchi and Gunnella 1975:45). For a discussion of the derivation and evolution of the iconography of these figures, see Bonfante 1976:17.

Conversely, the artist of the winged goddess Type 1 has clearly understood the distinction between the frontal locks and the tresses and has modeled the figure grasping the hair with the wings at the side.

In addition, while Capecchi and Gunnella (1975:Group IA, 44 and note 1; Group IVD, 71 and note 2) have identified the lateral projections on caryatid figures as wings, Cristofani and Zevi (1965:25, Type BI [α] and [β]) have suggested they may represent a mantle. In support of the identification of these projections as wings, it should be noted that while bucchero supports with representations of goddesses do exist with two pairs of wings, in no case is the presence of a mantle unequivocally indicated (see Capecchi and Gunnella 1975:pls. XIIIc, XVb). It would appear that in the case of both the molded figures on the handle from Poggio Civitate, as well as many of the figured supports of the chalices, the iconography of the goddess has either been misunderstood or has become sufficiently schematized to prevent ready interpretation.

The close similarity between the winged goddess Type 3 and the figured struts, especially those from Cerveteri and Tarquinia, suggests that they may be derived from a common prototype. The iconographic link between these figures is further strengthened by their coupling with a "tree of life" design which appears on the back of the handle and alternates with the figures as a support decoration on the chalices.[89]

19. Tree of Life (**36**; Fig. 17, Pl. 11)

Molded decoration displays stylized "tree of life" composed of 2 superimposed lotus-palmette flowers. Each flower consists of 3 elements. Base is formed by 2 outwardly curving leaves, each with tear-shaped stolon. From center of first element rise 2 leaves curving inward to form heart-shaped volute. Thin stalk originates from center of latter and terminates in lotus flower with 8 petals. Low rounded ridge frames outer edge of stamp. Estimated length of design 0.075 m; width 0.035 m. Decoration appears on kyathos handle fragment.

Originally a Near Eastern motif, the "tree of life" first appeared in southern Etruria during the second quarter of the seventh century.[90] Representations of the motif are known in a variety of media, including metalwork, ivory, and incised bucchero.[91]

A number of additional examples of this motif, one of which was made from the same mold as Ornament 19, have been found at Poggio Civitate, and all appear on the interior portion of molded *potnia theron* handles like the present example.[92] The closest parallels for the Poggio Civitate design are provided by the mold-made and stamped supports from a number of bucchero caryatid chalices from southern Etruria and Cerveteri, the former dated to the last quarter of the seventh century and the latter to the end of the seventh and the first quarter of the sixth century.[93]

[89] Gunnella notes, however, that the association of the winged female figures with the "tree of life" design, although likely, is not certain with respect to the examples from Tarquinia, since the molded supports were found without the chalice (Capecchi and Gunnella 1975:Group IA, a, 43–44, 47, figs. 2, 3, pl. Ia, b). For the "tree of life" see the discussion for ornament Type 19 below.

[90] For a discussion of the origin and development of the motif in Etruria, including citations of additional examples, see W. von Bissing, *StEtr* 2 (1927):19–38; Johansen 1971:107; Capecchi and Gunnella 1975:44 and notes 2, 3.; R. Stucky, in *Archéologie au Levant. Recueil à la mémoire de Roger SAIDAH* (Lyon, 1982):215–20. For additional Near Eastern examples, see Herrmann 1986:pls. 37–41 (from Nimrud); Crowfoot and Crowfoot 1938:40, fig. 10, pl. XXI, 1–5 (from Samaria); Thureau-Dangin et al. 1931: 131–32, nos. 97–98, fig. 48, pl. XLV (from Arlsan Tash).

[91] Metalwork: F. Canciani and F. W. von Hase, *La tomba Bernardini di Palestrina* (Rome, 1979):42–43, nos. 34, 35, pl. 21, fig. 3, pl. 23, fig. 3; Curtis 1925:20, no. 14, pl. 5, figs. 2, 3. Ivory: Curtis 1925:25–26, no. 14, figs. 2, 3. Incised bucchero: Bonamici 1974:21–22, no. 13, pl. VIIIb; 35–36, no. 38, pl. XIXa–c; Johansen 1971:pl. LIVa.

[92] The same molded decoration has been found on the handle of a kyathos from Trench 18: Murlo no. 73-239; see Nielsen and Phillips 1977a:91–92, fig. 14 and *Case e palazzi*:83, no. 89, pl. 3-89. For other examples of nearly identical type, also found in Trench 18, see Murlo nos. 72-321, 73-282, and 72-325: *Case e palazzi*:83, nos. 91–93.

[93] For a discussion of these chalices, see Capecchi and Gunnella 1975:44, 42–51, Group Ia, fig. 3, pl. 1b; 76, 87–94, Group IVe, e', e'', pl. 10a–c. The chalices of Group I have been assigned to a workshop at Cerveteri. The precise place of manufacture of chalices of Group IV, which on the basis of find frequency appears to have been in southern Etruria, has not been determined.

In fact, a fragment from Poggio Civitate, mistakenly identified as a chalice support, was previously believed to have been produced in Cerveteri,[94] but following the discovery of a number of handles with molded decoration of the same type at Poggio Civitate, the fragment was subsequently identified as part of the interior portion of a kyathos handle. The existence of these handles indicates that this stamped motif and those found on the chalices from Cerveteri were derived from a common prototype rather than having been produced at the same workshop. Related Orientalizing motifs, both dated to the last quarter of the seventh century, are also found on an embossed bronze handle from Quinto Fiorentino (Caputo 1974:42–43, pl. XIe, f) and on a bronze relief, probably from southern Etruria, now in Copenhagen (Johansen 1971:107, no. 38, pl. XXXII).

20. Molded Gorgoneion (**29**; Fig. 14, Pl. 8) Creature displays small, almost square face with low forehead. Hair above forehead, defined by series of short vertical incisions, falls in 2 tresses framing face. Eyebrows formed by 2 ridges curving up from top of nose. Eyes are large, almond-shaped, and defined by fine ridges. Large nose with flaring nostrils dominates center of face. Wide-open semicircular mouth has thick lips and protruding tongue with vertical groove down center. Left side of mouth slightly misshapen (perhaps as a result of a flaw of molding), curling upward into cheek. One long vertical fang projects from both upper and lower jaw at each corner of mouth. Gorgoneion appears on handle of kyathos fragment.

No other gorgoneia of this type have been found at Poggio Civitate or elsewhere. A closely related gorgoneion with a similar facial structure appears on a small carved ivory plaque recovered from the Lower Building (Pl. 8).[95] Other molded bucchero gorgoneia of a similar type have been found at Poggio Civitate, but they have broader faces and their hair has a central part.[96] The latter examples, which are close in style to the faces of the gorgoneia on the antefixes from the Upper Building, appear to be slightly later in date and can probably be associated with the Archaic phase of the site (Nielsen and Phillips 1975:361–62).

A gorgoneion with a face very similar to that of the example from the Lower Building, but with triangular wedges of hair framing its head, appears on the crest of a handle of a kyathos now in Florence (L. Donati, *StEtr* 39 [1971]:309, pl. LXIII). The use of small molded or stamped gorgoneia on bucchero vessels was common during the sixth century and was especially characteristic of vessels, often oinochoai, made in Chiusi.[97] The motif also occurs on a more limited basis at other Etruscan sites, including Orvieto, Vulci, and Tarquinia.[98] Like the Archaic gorgoneia from Poggio Civitate, the examples from these sites differ from

[94] Murlo no. 67-338. This fragment, which was found to the north of the Upper Building in Trench 1AB–1AE, was originally published as a possible chalice support by Phillips (1968:122, pl. 52, fig. 5; Cristofani and Phillips 1971:412–13, no. 4). Capecchi, accepting Phillips's identification of the fragment, attributed it to a workshop in Cerveteri on the basis of the close similarity of its molded decoration to that found on the struts of several caryatid chalices. She dated the fragment to the first years of the 6th century B.C., placing it at a point between the earlier and later representations on the chalices, those of her Groups I and IV (Capecchi and Gunnella 1975:104–5, type X, fig. 10).

[95] Murlo no. 71-102. The similarity of the gorgoneion appearing on the carved ivory to that of the molded bucchero gorgoneion was first noted by Phillips (1972:253, pl. 52, figs. 9, 10). I would suggest, however, that the correspondence between the 2 designs is not as close as Phillips suggested. In contrast to the bucchero gorgoneion, the ivory example has a less monstrous, more human face: it has less prominent cheeks, a smaller nose with less flaring nostrils, and it displays an upper row of teeth in addition to the fangs.

[96] For examples of these molded gorgoneia, see Phillips 1972: 254–55, pl. 52, figs. 26–28; Nielsen and Phillips 1975:361–62, ill. 7, pl. 65, figs. 11, 12; ill. 8, pl. 62, figs. 13, 14. See also *Case e palazzi*:135, nos. 519–22

[97] For examples of bucchero vessels decorated with molded gorgoneia and associated with Chiusi and its territory, see Giglioli 1935:pl. XLIII.8; V. Tusa, *ArchCl* 8 (1956):pls. XXXVI–XXVIII; Valentini 1969:pl. CX, c; Pecchiai 1967:fig. 19, pl. LXXXVIIIc.

[98] Orvieto: Giglioli 1935:pl. LIV; Hayes 1985:84, C35. Vulci: Falconi-Amorelli 1968: 175, no. 21, pl. XXXIc; Beazley and Magi 1939:134–36, no. 46, pl. 41; *CVA British Museum* 7:IV B a, pl. 19, no. 2. Tarquinia: Giglioli 1935:pl. LII.

Ornament 20 because they too are dated to the Archaic period after the motif had been transformed by Greek influence.[99] This is the only example of a gorgoneion appearing on the handle of this particular type of kyathos. On all the other published examples (see the comparanda section for **29**), the handle is decorated by a female head, a male figure, or a *potnia theron*.

OINOCHOAI ROTELLE

21. Flower Rosette (**2**; Pl. 2)
Design composed of 27 narrow, elongated petals with rounded outer edges arranged in a circle around central dot. Design appears on rotella of oinochoe.

No other examples of this molded design are known from Poggio Civitate or elsewhere. Flower rosettes commonly appear on the rotelle of oinochoai, first in bronze (Minto 1943:147–48, figs. 53a–d; Shefton 1979:pls. 6.1, 9.1) and later in bucchero (Hayes 1985:86, C39 and 124, C120). These rosettes, however, are generally composed of fewer and thicker petals. Rosettes of a similar type, although stamped rather than molded and of smaller size, are found on bucchero from Roselle dated from the end of the seventh through the middle of the sixth century (Donati 1991:87, figs. 10–14). Outside Etruria, similar long-petalled rosettes are found on painted vases from East Greece and Corinth, and on Rhodian metalwork.[100] The motif was undoubtedly inspired by the rosettes found on the rotelle of bronze "Rhodian" oinochoai.

22. Stylized Lotus and Palmette (**1**; Fig. 9, Pl. 1)
Design composed of 4 groups of 5 outward-facing petals separated by 4 larger inward-facing petals arranged in a circle. Design appears on rotella of oinochoe.

No additional examples of this molded design are known on bucchero from Poggio Civitate or elsewhere in Etruria. The design represents a schematized lotus and palmette chain in which the rear curving portions of the palmettes have been omitted. A very similar motif appears on a pair of gilded Orientalizing silver plaques with repoussé decoration from the Montagnola tomb at Quinto Fiorentino dated to the last quarter of the seventh century.[101] Other, related designs are also found as granulated decoration on Etruscan gold earrings "*a bauletto*" from Chiusi, Cerveteri, and Populonia,[102] and as painted motifs on Caeretan hydriai,[103] all of which are dated to the second half of the sixth century. Outside Etruria, the motif, originally of Assyrian origin, appears on Orientalizing painted vases from East Greece,[104] especially Rhodes, and Corinth (Payne 1931: 146–48, fig. 54).

MOLDED APPLIQUÉS

23. Daedalic Female Head (**32**; Fig. 15, Pl. 9)
Hair is flat on top and falls in 3 tresses on either side of head. Face displays low forehead, asymmetrical almond-shaped eyes, broad nose, and heavy chin. Small thin mouth set within U-shaped depression. Four examples of this appliqué adorn kyathos handle fragment.

---

[99] Krauskopf has noted that while Etruscan representations of gorgons and gorgoneia during the Orientalizing period follow their own stylistic development independent of those from Greece, Etruscan examples of the Archaic period conform much more strongly to Greek prototypes; see I. Krauskopf, s.v. "Gorgones (In Etruria)," in *LIMC* IV.I:340, 344–45.

[100] East Greece: Walter-Karydi 1973:fig. 79, pl. 73, nos. 563, 564, 567; pl. 74, nos. 566, 568, 570, 572. Corinth: for examples, see Payne 1931:fig. 124. Rhodian metalwork: F. Villard, *MonPiot* 49.2 (1956):26, fig. 1, pl. 3, Vb.

[101] Caputo 1974:49–50, pl. XVIIIb. Both Nicosia and Cristofani have identified these plaques as Rhodian on the basis of their decoration. It should be noted, however, that the parallels on Rhodian metalwork cited by both authors consist not of similar lotus and palmette designs, but of rosettes. It is equally possible, therefore, that the plaques were of Etruscan and not Rhodian manufacture. See F. Nicosia, in *Restauri archeologici* (Florence, 1969):49, nos. 38, 39; Cristofani 1971:86 and note 87.

[102] For the earrings from Chiusi and Cerveteri, see M. Cristofani and M. Martelli, *L'oro degli Etruschi* (Novara, 1983): 166, 167, figs. 143, 144. For those from Populonia, see Minto 1943:pl. XXX, no. 9.

[103] J. P. Hemelrijk, *Caeretan Hydriae* (Mainz, 1984):102, fig. 58a and f.

[104] W. Schiering, *Werkstätten orientalisierender Keramik auf Rhodos* (Berlin, 1957):pl. 11; Walter-Karydi 1973:45, figs. 65–69.

The use of human heads, especially female, as applied decoration on bucchero vessels is known from Vulci (Donati 1967:619–32), Chiusi (Donati 1968:319–56), and Orvieto (Donati 1969:441–62). The practice began sometime in the early sixth century and enjoyed its greatest popularity during the second half of that century.[105] These heads find a close parallel in an example from Chiusi, which Donati places in his Group A (1968:328, no. 44, pl. 80d). The placement of the heads on the handle, however, as Phillips has noted, is particularly elaborate and finds closer parallels in kyathoi from the zone of Vulci (Phillips 1972:253 and note 24; also Donati and Michelucci 1981:62, no. 107). In addition, the application of human heads to kyathos handles, while rare at Chiusi, is common at Vulci (see Donati 1969:460, fig. 5). On the other hand, the type of stippled decoration found on the finial and base of the handle commonly appears on bucchero from Chiusi.[106] This handle, therefore, as noted by Phillips, may fall within the sphere of influence of both Chiusi and Vulci (Phillips 1972:253).

24. Molded Double-Volute Palmette Appliqué (**64**, **65**, **68–71**, **73–78**, **80–89**; Figs 22, 23, Pls. 15, 16, 17)

Design consists of 2 volutes with joined stems and inward-curving, tangent scrolls crowned by small lotus bud.

All these appliqués appear on the rims of a series of small bowls and plates from the Lower Building (**64–89**). The examples have the same dimensions, although they vary in the quality of their execution. A similar molded design adorns a rim and handle fragment, **110** (Pl. 19). In addition, a similar appliqué, though much larger in size than those occurring on the rims of the bucchero bowls from the Lower Building, decorates the rim of a large, unpublished impasto plate fragment (Murlo no. 78-40) recovered from the Lower Building and currently on display in the Murlo Antiquarium. No parallels exist for these appliqués outside Poggio Civitate. The motif is iconographically very similar to that of the stamped double-volute palmette Type 2. A similar molded motif appears on an impasto handle fragment from Artimino, which Nicosia has dated to the middle of the seventh century.[107] The placement of molded decorations on the rims of bowls is uncommon.

INCISED DECORATION

The incised decoration on the Lower Building bucchero is of two types, determined by the tool used to create the design. Fine incision, done with a sharp-pointed implement, created narrow and deep lines, while grooved incision, done with an instrument that has a wide round or pointed tip, produced broad and shallow lines.

Incised decoration appeared on the earliest bucchero in the seventh century and continued throughout the sixth century (Rasmussen 1979: 131–32; Camerini 1985:25–27, pl. VII). The technique is generally believed to be derived from engraved metalwork (Rasmussen 1979:134). While the majority of incised decoration on bucchero consists of simple horizontal lines or linear motifs, more complex ornaments, including animal and floral decoration, also appear (Bonamici 1974; Rasmussen 1979:132–36). The use of incised animal and floral decoration, however, is rather limited and uncommon in northern Etruria;[108] it is much more characteristic of bucchero production of the south, particularly around Cerveteri and Veii.

LINEAR MOTIFS

The majority of incised decoration on the bucchero from the Lower Building consists of

[105] Donati 1967:625; Donati 1969:460–61. Molded heads appear on both Corinthian and East Greek pottery during the 7th and 6th centuries B.C.; see Weinberg 1954:134–35; Amyx 1988:451–52. It is unclear, however, whether Greek vessels featuring molded heads provided the inspiration to Etruscan potters for the use of this decoration on bucchero.

[106] This has also been pointed out by J. G. Szilágyi (1981:28, nos. 5, 6). See also Donati 1968:pls. LXXIIa, LXXIVe, LXXXd, LXXXIIe.

[107] The handle was found in tumulus D of the necropolis of Prato di Roselle at Artimino; see F. Nicosia, in *Etruria mineraria*: 356, pl. LXIIc.

[108] A few animal friezes are also known on bucchero from Vulci and Tarquinia. The examples from Tarquinia may be imports from Cerveteri; see Rasmussen 1979:136.

simple horizontal lines and grooves. In a few cases, more complex linear ornaments do occur. Incised zigzags appear on the rims of two cups (**38**, **40**; Figs. 17, 18). The surface of cup fragment, **43** (Fig. 18, Pl. 12), is covered with vertical striations, perhaps in an attempt to imitate ribbing. In addition, a tripod bowl (**50**; Fig. 20, Pl. 13 is decorated with a pattern of cross-hatched squares.

A more complex design appears on a jar whose surface is decorated with a series of thirteen incised grooves (**49**; Fig. 20, Pl. 13). The resulting ridges between the grooves are divided by short fine, notched, vertical incisions. The third through eighth ridges from the top are further subdivided by horizontal and vertical incisions.

No parallels exist for this design. The reticulated design produced by the combination of wide grooves and fine incisions is suggestive of either carved decoration on wooden vessels or the woven patterns of basketry.

FIGURED MOTIFS

25. Incised Felines (**4**; Fig. 10, Pl. 3)
Design consists of 2 crudely incised feline heads, nearly identical. Each composed of 2 irregularly incised, concentric oval lines. Head on right almost complete, missing only tip of right ear; head on left broken along left edge of face. Each head displays pair of triangular pointed ears, between which appear 5 individually incised vertical tufts of hair. Faces have large, tangent almond-shaped eyes and elongated oval mouths. Head on left also has short triangular nose composed of 2 converging diagonal lines. Design appears on shoulder of oinochoe fragment.

No parallels exist for this design. The presence of the pointed ears would seem to identify the heads as felines, perhaps lions, but the design is so haphazardly drawn that it is impossible to determine the identity of the creatures with certainty. The use of incised decoration of this type is extremely rare not only at Poggio Civitate, but in northern Etruria in general. Not enough of the oinochoe on which the design appears is preserved to determine its complete shape and possible place of manufacture.

FLORAL MOTIFS

26. Double-Volute Palmette (**110**; Fig. 25, Pl. 19)
Stylized palmette composed of double volute with joined stems and incurving scrolls. Motif appears on rim and handle fragment.

The motif is a variant of the common Orientalizing double-volute palmette design. It is iconographically similar to that of both the stamped double-volute palmette Type 2, Ornament 6b, and the double-volute palmette appliqué, Ornament 24.

INSCRIPTIONS

Three fragments recovered from the Lower Building display inscriptions (**137–139**; Fig. 30, Pl. 25). While the inscription on a cup fragment (**137**) was added before firing, those on the 2 body fragments (**138**, **139**) were incised later. All three are fragmentary, and with the possible exception of **139**, not enough letters are preserved for interpretation. Paleographically, all the letter forms conform to those known from other Archaic inscriptions from Chiusi and its territory.[110]

139 preserves the letters "nap," which, since they are preceded by a period, form the first three letters of a word (Fig. 30, Pl. 25). Two words are known in the Etruscan language which begin with these three letters. The first *nap*, which is known from four inscriptions, has been interpreted from its context as a unit of linear measurement, perhaps a boundary (*TLE*[2] 203, 381, 569, 570). There is only on known example of the second, *naplan*. It appears in a painted inscription in the medallion of a red-figured kylix, the so-called Cup of Avle Vipinas, from Veii, dated to the middle of the fifth century (*TLE*[2] 942; ill. in Martelli 1987:210, no. 160). Heurgon had originally proposed that *naplan* was the name of the vase itself, whose owner would have been Avle Vipinas.[111]

[109] As will be discussed in the conclusions, the presence of these inscriptions may have important implications for determining the function of the Lower Building.

[110] The letter forms of these inscriptions correlate well with those appearing in a group of inscriptions from Chiusi which Cristofani noted in a study of a number of other inscriptions found at Poggio Civitate; see Cristofani and Phillips 1971:426–27.

[111] J. Heurgon, in *Mélanges J. Carcopino* (Paris, 1966):521.

Colonna, however, has rejected this interpretation, suggesting instead that the word was part of a didascolon referring to the painted scene on the vase, which depicts two satyrs, one carrying a wineskin on his back (*ArchCl* 25 [1973–1974]:25–26). Colonna suggested that *naplan* in reference to the wineskin, means goatskin.[112]

[112] In a letter dated 4 May 1993, Professor Colonna offered these comments about the inscription: "Il frammento di iscrizione etrusco che ha sottoposto alla mia attenzione *potrebbe*, ma solo come una possibilità tra molte, contenere il nome *naplan*, che in tal caso sarebbe molto esteso, se la mia proposta del 1974 è giusta, dall'otre al vaso per bere. Ma si tratta solo di una possibilità. Nella fotocopia inviatami non risulta sicuro il punto prima di *nap*[.] e d'altra parte il punto singolo in una iscrizione del VII–VI sec. è molto sospetto. Non mi pare sicuro nemmeno lo *p*. Tutto è molto incerto. Il che non toglie importanza alla sua scoperta, che incrementa l'enigmatico corpus di Murlo!" I thank Professor Colonna for his observations.

V

Conclusions

The Nature of the Deposit

An analysis of the stratigraphy and distribution of the bucchero in the Lower Building reveals that its contents were disturbed during both its destruction and the construction of the Upper Building. Displacement of material clearly occurred during the digging of the foundation trenches for the Upper Building, as joins made between pottery fragments found in the Lower Building and others in the walls and pavement of the Upper Building attest. Additional joins, although limited in number, were made between fragments of pottery found inside the building proper with others found outside its walls. This material could have been deposited during the collapse of the Lower Building, during cleanup activities, or during the construction of the Upper Building. Although fragments were clearly displaced, no evidence was found of the existence of intrusive material in the deposit. All of the bucchero was homogeneous in style and clearly belonged to the same general period. It would appear, therefore, that all of the pottery found in the building belonged there.

An analysis of the distribution of vessels in the building has revealed some patterns in their deposition. It appears that the bucchero vessels, possibly along with the imported pottery, were being stored by shape and class in two principal areas in the northern half of the building, one below Rectangle 5 and the other below Rectangle 7 of the Upper Building. There is no indication that the vessels were in use at the time of the building's destruction. Although the excavators have suggested that much of the material found in the building, including the bucchero, fell from an upper storey, it seems equally likely that the pottery was being stored, possibly on shelves, on the ground floor.

The examination has also revealed that the closest parallels for both the shapes and the decoration of the bucchero in the Lower Building were found at Poggio Civitate itself, in the bucchero vessels and fragments in Trench 18. Although no definitive stratigraphic evidence or joins were found to link the two deposits, these parallels establish the contemporaneity of the two deposits and suggest that the material found in Trench 18 came from an area proximate to, if not actually from, the Lower Building.

Although the recoverable distribution pattern of the bucchero suggests that material was found for the most part in its original place of deposition, some movement and disturbance of material clearly occurred during the digging of the foundation trenches for the Upper Building. It is not certain to what extent the deposit of bucchero found in the Lower Building represents what was actually inside the building at the time of its destruction.

Limitations to the Study

It must be emphasized that the study of the bucchero from the Lower Building is severely limited by a number of factors. Foremost among them is the general lack of comparable contemporary deposits from northern Etruria or, for that matter, southern Etruria. Potentially useful evidence exists from the excavation of a number of settlements in the north, including Castelnuovo Berardenga, Artimino, Massarossa, and Massa Marittima.[1] Much of this evidence is unpublished or is in the process of publication. The few known contemporary tombs in the north either contained little bucchero or bucchero of a different character from that found in the Lower Building. In addition, much potentially useful information regarding the excavation of both the necropoleis and the habitations of the major cities of northern Etruria remains unpublished. There are few available and even fewer recent publications of bucchero from Chiusi, Populonia, Roselle, and Vetulonia.[2] In addition, many of the published studies are limited to analysis of specific vessel types and decorative motifs. As yet, no comprehensive treatment of the development and typology of northern Etruscan bucchero has been attempted. Until this evidence becomes available, many of the conclusions regarding the style, place of manufacture, and chronology of the bucchero from the Lower Building must remain tentative.

VESSEL TYPOLOGY AND DECORATION

In discussing both vessel typology and decoration, the terms *previously identified type*, *variant type*, and *unique type* will be employed. The term *previously identified type* is self explanatory. In this study, the term *variant type* is used for Lower Building bucchero vessels or decorative motifs that are generally similar to a type classified by previous scholars in shape or design. The term *unique type* is utilized for Lower Building vessels and decorative motifs for which no known parallels exist. Vessel typology will be examined first, followed by decoration, in order to determine both the media and the sources of inspiration for the shape and ornamentation. The results of these two investigations will then be combined to separate imported from locally produced vessels, and to place the bucchero from the Lower Building within the overall context of contemporary Etruscan bucchero production.

VESSEL TYPOLOGY

In general, the closest parallels for the shapes of the bucchero vessels from the Lower Building outside Poggio Civitate occur in vessels found at Chiusi and Vulci and smaller sites within their respective territories. A few parallels were also found at other sites, including Orvieto, Vetulonia, Populonia, Artimino, Massa Marittima, Cortona, and cities in southern Etruria. These were limited, however, to only a few vessel types. In addition the jar Type 2 (**49**), chalice Type 1 (**44**) and Type 2 (**45**), and the tripod bowl (**50–52**) find their closest parallels in vessels from southern Etruria, Latium, and Narce. Only eleven types or subtypes precisely represent previously identified vessel types and forms (Table 3),[3] and nineteen types or subtypes represent previously unclassified variants of recognized types (Table 4). There are also thirteen vessel types that have unique bucchero shapes (Table 5). Finally, two vessel types, the oinochoe Type 2 and the cup Type 3, are too fragmentary to properly classify.

The evidence presented in Tables 3 and 4 demonstrates that the primary influence for the shapes of certain bucchero vessels found in the Lower Building came from central coastal and northern interior Etruria. There are very few close comparanda from the major coastal cities of

[1] Castelnuovo Berardenga: P. Bocci Pacini, *StEtr* 41 (1973):121–41; E. Mangani, in *Case e palazzi*:161–62; E. Mangani, in *Etrusker*:334–37; Mangani 1990; Mangani 1992. Artimino: Nicosia 1974:55–66; L. Donati, in *Artimino*:82–97. Massarossa: M. Cristofani, in *Archeologica: Scritti in onore di Aldo Neppi Modona* (Florence, 1975):194–99; *Versilia*:84–86; Massa Marittima: Camporeale 1995; Camporeale 1997:157–72.

[2] Chiusi: No substantial presentations of chronologically secure deposits of bucchero have appeared since the publications of R. Bianchi-Bandinelli (*MonAnt* 30 [1925]:209–578) and Montelius (1904:pls. 213–231). See also D. Levi, *NSc* 7 (1931): 215–16, fig. 14; A. Minto *NSc* 14 (1938): 121–23, figs. 2 and 3. Populonia: Minto 1943 is the only substantial publication of material that includes a presentation of bucchero. See also A. Minto *NSc* 1 (1925):350, 361, figs. 5, 19, and 20; A. Minto *MonAnt* 34 (1931):309, 352–53, fig. 22, pl. XIV, 2–8. Roselle: Naumann and Hiller 1959; Bocci 1965; Bocci 1970:157–60, pl. 16, fig. a; *Roselle*; Donati 1988; Donati 1991; Donati 1994:122-33. Vetulonia: For publications of bucchero from Vetulonia, see D. Levi *NSc* 2 (1926):184–85, fig. 8; *CVA Firenze, Museo Archeologico* I:IV B k, l, pls. 14–17; Talocchini 1963:440–44; Falchi 1965; Camporeale 1967; Gregori 1991.

[3] For a discussion of the chronology and context of the comparanda listed in Table 3, see the discussions of the corresponding vessel types in Chapter 3.

TABLE 3: BUCCHERO VESSELS OR VESSEL FRAGMENTS REPRESENTING PREVIOUSLY IDENTIFIED TYPES

Shape	Type	Catalogue Number	Location of Parallel(s)
Kantharos	Type 1	6	Cerveteri, Veii, Vulci, and Tarquinia
	Type 2A	7, 8	Vulci and Veii
	Type 2B	9, 10	Vulci and its territory
	Type 2C	11, 12	Vulci and its territory
Kyathos	Type 1	22, 23	Chiusi
	Type 2	24	Chiusi, Vulci, Orvieto
Kyathos Handle	Type 1	30–33	Chiusi and its territory
	Type 2	34, 35	Vulci and its territory
	Type 3	36	Chiusi
	Type 4	37	Chiusi, Orvieto, Vetulonia, Populonia, and Cerveteri
Lid	Type 1	113	Chiusi

the north—Vetulonia, Populonia, and Roselle—except for the case of the kyathos handle Type 4 and the phiale, and the broad rimmed shallow bowl Type 2. While the kyathos handle Type 4 finds parallels in vessels from Populonia and Vetulonia, comparanda for the phiale and broad rimmed shallow bowl Type 2 exist at Roselle. All three of these types, however, also have additional comparanda to the south, either at Chiusi or in the territory of Vulci. A few parallels occur in bucchero vessels found in southern Etruria, but they are limited to kantharoi, which are the most commonly occurring and widely distributed bucchero types, and the kyathos handle Type 4, of which there are also examples in northern Etruria.

It is particularly notable that thirty-two of the forty-five vessel types and subtypes represented in the deposit are either variant or unique types. Most of these vessels were probably locally produced. The majority of the variant types find their closest parallels in vessels known from Chiusi and its territory, and a few can be linked to Vulci and its territory, and Orvieto. In addition, several of the variant types, including the oinochoe Type 1, the kyathos Type 4, the broad-rimmed shallow bowls and plates Types 2, 3A, and 3B, and the miscellaneous plate Type 2, are either among the earliest, or are the earliest, datable examples of their types.

The antecedents of the unique types can be traced to a variety of sources: the Type 3 kyathos can be linked to a metal prototype; chalices Types 1 and 2 and jar Type 2 appear to have their origins in impasto; the alabastron has an Etrusco-Corinthian prototype; and the tripod bowl finds its closest parallels in ceramic vessels from southern Etruria, Rome, and Narce, as well as in a metallic vessel from Vulci. But the origins of chalice Type 3, the broad-rimmed shallow bowls and plates Types 1 and 4, the lug handled bowl, and lids Types 3, 5, and 7 are still unclear.

DECORATION

The bucchero from the Lower Building is richly decorated. Of the 139 catalogued vessels and fragments from the deposit, only fifteen are undecorated. There are thirty-three individual decorative motif types and subtypes and three inscriptions, along with a wide variety of decorative techniques. Individual stamped decoration is the most common, followed by molded decoration, cylinder-stamping, and incision. Although the use of incised figural decoration appears in only oinochoe **4**, it is noteworthy since it is usually found only on bucchero from the south. While the majority of decorated vessels display only one form of decoration, twenty-one vessels feature two forms of decoration, and one vessel has three. Eleven vessels are stamped and incised (**48**, **58–63**, **114**, **115**, **118**, **132**), nine are molded and incised (**1**, **2**, **25**, **30**, **32**, **34**, **50**, **51**, **113**), one is stamped and adorned with molded appliqués (**64**), and one is molded, cylinder-stamped, and incised (**110**).

The zone of influence for the decoration is much broader than that for the shapes; it encompasses sites in both northern and southern Etruria. In contrast to the vessel shapes, it is not possible to isolate one or two primary centers of influence. In addition, many of the motifs cannot be linked to a single site, since they often appear contemporaneously at a number of places.

TABLE 4: VESSELS REPRESENTING VARIANTS OF RECOGNIZED TYPES

Shape	Type	Catalogue Number	Location of Recognized Parallel(s) and/or Citation for Type
Oinochoe	Type 1	1, 2	Similar examples at Chiusi and Orvieto
Kantharos	Type 2D	13, 14	Variant of Rasmussen Type 3e; Chiusi
	Type 2E	15, 16	Variant of Rasmussen Type 3e; Artimino
	Type 3	17	Variant of Rasmussen Type 3e
Kyathos	Type 4	29	Similar, but later, examples at Heba (Magliano), Vulci, and Chiusi
Cup	Type 1	38	Variant of Rasmussen Type 3a (see Rasmussen 1979:119)
	Type 2	39–42	Variant of Rasmussen Type 3b (see Rasmussen 1979:119–20)
Phiale	Type 1	47	Similar examples at Roselle, Poggio Buco, Rome, and Accessa (Massa Marittima)
Jar	Type 1	48	Similar examples at Chiusi and its territory
Footed Bowl	Type 1	53	Similar examples at Chiusi and its territory
	Type 2	54, 55	Similar examples at Chiusi and its territory, and Orvieto
Broad-Rimmed Shallow Bowls and Plates	Type 2	58–68	Similar, but later, examples at Chiusi, Cortona, and Roselle
	Type 3A	69-78	Similar, but later, examples at Chiusi
	Type 3B	79	Similar, unprovenienced examples in museums and collections
Misc. Plates	Type 1	111	Similar examples at Vulci
	Type 2	112	Similar, but later, examples at Chiusi
Lids	Type 2	114–118	Similar examples at Chiusi and its territory
	Type 4	120-122	Similar, unprovenienced examples in museums
	Type 6	124–126	Similar example at Chiusi

Instead, the influences appear to have been multiple, and they varied according to the decorative technique employed.

The closest parallels for the stamps were found in the north on bucchero and buccheroid vessels from Vetulonia, Massarossa, Roselle, Massa Marittima, and the territory of Chiusi, and to a much more limited extent, also in the south at Cerveteri and Veii. Parallels for the cylinder-stamps were principally discovered on vases at Chiusi, Orvieto, and Artimino. Parallels for the molded decoration occurred on vessels found at Chiusi and its territory, and at Cerveteri.

Only one exact parallel was found for the decorative motifs on the bucchero from the Lower Building (Table 6): the molded *potnia theron* Type 1, Ornament 14, appears on vessels from Chiusi.[4]

[4] Since I was not able to measure the molded decorations on the vessels from Chiusi, I cannot state with certainty that the examples from the Lower Building were made from the same mold.

TABLE 5: UNIQUE VESSEL SHAPES

Shape	Type	Catalogue Number
Alabastron	Type 1	5
Kyathos	Type 3	25, 26
Chalice	Type 1	44
	Type 2	45
	Type 3	46
Jar	Type 2	49
Tripod Bowl	Type 1	50–52
Broad-Rimmed, Shallow Bowls and Plates	Type 1	56, 57
	Type 4	90–101
Lug Handled Bowl	Type 1	102–110
Lids	Type 3	119
	Type 5	123
	Type 7	127, 128

The majority of the decorations represent variations of previously known types. Most of these variations, particularly in the case of the stamps, are rather simple, involving only minor differences in details and dimensions. For example, the stamped asterisk rosettes, Types 1–4, Ornaments 4a–d, differ in dimensions and sometimes in the number of petals from other known examples. The circumscribed oblique "S," Ornament 3, varies in its size and orientation, and the guilloches, Types 1–3, Ornaments 10a–c, in their design. Some of the variations, however, are more complex, especially in the case of the molded representations of the *potnia theron* and the winged goddesses.

Eight of the decorative motifs are unique on bucchero (Table 7). The majority of decorative motifs are Orientalizing in character and have direct antecedents in the Near East. Most of the patterns first appeared on objects in the minor arts in southern Etruria during the first half of the seventh century, and only later, toward the latter half of the seventh century, were they found in the north. Many of the ornaments, especially the stamped examples, appeared first on metalware. Outside Etruria, in several cases ornaments similar to those found on the bucchero from the Lower Building also appear on contemporary painted vases, especially East Greek examples.

TABLE 6: DECORATIVE MOTIFS WITH EXACT PARALLELS

Ornament Type	Description
14	Molded *Potnia Theron;* Paralleled at Chiusi

These similarities, however, are probably to be attributed to a common source of inspiration in the Near East rather than to direct influence. It is notable that while many of the ornaments on the bucchero from the Lower Building have antecedents in the seventh century, the parallels for the majority of the vessel shapes are more commonly dated to the last quarter of the seventh and first half of the sixth centuries B.C.

SHAPE AND DECORATION

It is notable that only four of the eleven vessel types or subtypes representing previously identified types, listed in Table 3, which are decorated, have exact parallels for both their shape and decoration. The kantharoi Types 2A–C all have parallels at Vulci and its territory, and examples of the Type 1 kyathoi are known at Chiusi. The remaining examples are undecorated or have either variant or unique ornaments.

Of the thirteen unique vessel shapes, three have unique ornaments (Table 8) and one,

TABLE 7: UNIQUE DECORATIVE MOTIFS

Ornament Type	Description
5	Stamped Petal Rosette
7a	Stamped Double-Volute Palmette Type 3
7b	Stamped Double-Volute Palmette Type 4
11	Cylinder-Stamped Stylized Double Guilloche Type 1
12	Cylinder-Stamped Stylized Double Guilloche Type 2
22	Molded Lotus and Palmette
24	Molded Double-Volute Palmette Appliqué
25	Incised Felines

TABLE 8: UNIQUE VESSEL TYPES WITH UNIQUE DECORATIONS

Shape	Type	Catalogue Number	Ornament Type
Jar	Type 2	49	Patterned Incision
Broad-Rimmed Shallow Bowls and Plates	Type 1	56, 57	7a
	Type 4	90–101	11
Lug Handled Bowl	Type 1	102–110	7b, 12, 24

alabastron **5**, is decorated with Ornaments 4b and 4c, which are variant types. The remaining eight unique types are either unadorned or decorated simply with grooves or incised lines.

Of the nineteen variant vessel types or subtypes, three have variant decorations (Table 9), two are adorned with unique motifs (Table 10), and the remaining eleven are either plain or decorated with simple grooves or incised lines.

There appear to be some general relationships between decorative techniques and shapes. Simple incised decoration or grooves are found on nearly all vessel shapes and frequently occur with other decorative techniques. Next to incision, stamps appear on the greatest variety of vessel types. They are most commonly found on lids and on the rims of bowls and plates, but they also appear on the alabastron, and a jar. Cylinder-stamps, with the exception of one example on a handle, adorn plates and bowls. Molded decoration appears on handles and on the rims of bowls and plates. While the application of molded decoration to handles has antecedents in Chiusi, most notably in the case of the representations of the *potnia theron* and winged goddesses, the application of molded decoration to rims, particularly molded appliqués, appears to be a local development.

DISTRIBUTION OF PARALLELS FOUND AT POGGIO CIVITATE

At Poggio Civitate, the greatest number of parallels for both shape and decoration of the bucchero from the Lower Building were found in Trench 18: exact or nearly exact parallels for eight vessel and seven ornament types were found there (Fig. 6). In particular, a kyathos and kyathos handle recovered from the Lower Building were produced from the same two molds as a kyathos and kyathos handle from Trench 18. These correspondences between the bucchero from the Lower Building and that found in Trench 18 further establish the contemporaneity of the two deposits and reinforce the likelihood that the burned bucchero in Trench 18 originally formed part of the contents of the Lower Building. Limited parallels for the shape and decoration of the bucchero from the Lower Building, i.e., products of the same workshop, were also found in a few additional areas on the site. These finds are

TABLE 9: VARIANT VESSEL TYPES WITH VARIANT DECORATIONS

Shape	Type	Catalogue Number	Ornament Type
Oinochoe	Type 1	1	13, 22
		2	21
Kyathos	Type 4	29	20
Jar	Type 1	48	6a
Footed Bowl	Type 2	54, 55	10b, 10c
Miscellaneous Plate	Type 2	112	8
Lid	Type 2	114, 115, 117, 118	3, 4a, 6a, 6b

TABLE 10: VARIANT VESSEL TYPES WITH UNIQUE DECORATIONS

Shape: Broad-Rimmed Shallow Bowls and Plates

Type	**Catalogue Number**	**Ornament Type**
Type 2	58–68	5, 24
Type 3a	69-78	24

randomly dispersed and display no recognizable pattern of distribution. Additional examples of one vessel and two ornament types were found on fragments recovered from the south and west walls of the Upper Building. It is probable that these fragments were removed from the ruins of the Lower Building when the foundation trenches of the Upper Building were dug. Later they came to be deposited in the foundations of the Upper Building walls. This same explanation also accounts for the joins between fragments found in the Lower Building and others discovered in walls of the Upper Building. Elsewhere on the site, smaller numbers of parallels for either shape or decoration were found, often in mixed contexts, in Tesoro Trenches 1, 6a, 17, 21, 23, 26, Agger 4, Civitate Trenches CA24, CA28, and in Poggio Aguzzo Tomb 8.

CONCLUSIONS: VESSEL TYPOLOGY AND DECORATION

The sources of inspiration or influence for the bucchero from the Lower Building seem to have somewhat different geographical distributions for the vessel shapes, on the one hand, and the decorative motifs, on the other. While the largest number of parallels for the shapes occurred in vessels found at sites in central coastal and northern interior Etruria, the parallels for the decoration comprised a much wider and somewhat more diverse area; this included some of the same locations as the shapes, most notably Chiusi, as well as other sites in northern coastal and southern Etruria. Very few exact parallels, however, for either shapes or decorations were found outside the site. Instead, the majority of vessel shapes and decorations of the bucchero in the Lower Building were variant or unique types. In addition, many of the variant and unique shapes also displayed variant or unique decorative motifs. The closest comparanda at Poggio Civitate itself for both vessel shape and decoration of the Lower Building bucchero come from Trench 18.

IMPORTS

Only five bucchero vessel types or subtypes from the Lower Building, comprising a total of nine examples, can be securely identified as imports (Table 11). The primary criterion for their identification is the combination of their paucity at Poggio Civitate and the presence of a number of exact parallels at other sites.

The kantharos Type 1, which is represented by a single example, is an extremely rare shape in northern Etruria; the only other known examples have been found at Poggio Civitate. Instead, kantharoi of this type are commonly found at sites in southern Etruria and Latium. Prior to the discovery of the examples from Poggio Civitate, no kantharoi of this type had been published from sites north of Vulci. The Type 1 kantharos, therefore, is likely to be an import from southern Etruria, although its precise place of manufacture is uncertain, since kantharoi of this type are found at too many sites to localize their place or places of production. The kantharoi Types 2A–C also represent imports, almost certainly from Vulci or its territory. A large number of exact and nearly exact parallels have been found for these types at Vulci, many of which appear to be of the same fabric as the examples from the Lower Building.[5] Finally, the Type 1 kyathos, which is represented by at least one, and possibly two, fragmentary examples, is most probably an import from Chiusi or its territory. There are abundant parallels for both the shape and the molded decoration found on the handles of these cups both at and in the area of Chiusi.[6] In addition, the kyathos Type 2 and the lid Type 1

[5] After handling a number of kantharoi from Vulci and Castro during a visit to the Grosseto Museum, I was able to determine that they were of the same shape and fabric as kantharoi Types 2A–C from the Lower Building.

[6] After handling a number of kyathoi from Chiusi during visits to the Museo Civico in Chiusi and the Museum of Fine Arts in Boston, I was able to determine that they were of the same fabric and shape as the kyathos Type 1 from the Lower Building.

TABLE 11: IMPORTED VESSELS

Shape	Type	Catalogue Number	Place of Manufacture
Kantharos	Type 1	6	Southern Etruria
	Type 2A	7, 8	Vulci or its territory
	Type 2B	9, 10	Vulci or its territory
	Type 2C	11, 12	Vulci or its territory
Kyathos	Type 1	22, 23	Chiusi

can be listed as potential imports. While they both have exact or nearly exact parallels at other sites, their parallels do not exist in sufficient quantity to justify the identification of these pieces as definite imports. Their status, therefore, must remain uncertain.

The place of production of the nineteen variant and thirteen unique vessel types or subtypes is uncertain. The unique vessel types, particularly those also having unique decorative motifs, are most likely to have been locally produced, since no parallels exist for them outside the site.

LOCAL PRODUCTION

No direct evidence for pottery production has yet been found at Poggio Civitate. A program of neutron activation analysis was conducted on a sample of ceramics from the site, including bucchero, but the results were inconclusive.[7] The tests revealed that many of the fabrics shared a similar elemental composition, suggesting that they were all manufactured from the same raw clay. Samples tested from a local clay bed, however, did not match that of the ceramics. Although local production of the vessels with similar elemental composition remains a strong possibility, it cannot be proven until their clay source is identified. In the absence of such positive identification, petrographic analysis could aid in identifying the clay source. The source is likely, however, to be in the Poggio Civitate region, since the transportation and preparation of such a large amount of material would otherwise have presented severe logistical problems.

Thus, the strongest evidence for the production of bucchero on the site is the lack of close comparanda elsewhere for the majority of the vessel shapes and decorations. The probability of local production is much greater for vessel types of which numerous examples are known either in the deposit or on the site. These include kyathos Type 3, kyathos handles Types 1–3, footed bowl Type 2, and broad-rimmed plates and bowls Types 1–4. In addition, the large proportion of variant and unique shapes and ornaments found in the deposit also argues in favor of local production. Finally, the fact that the sources of inspiration for the vessel shapes are different from those for their decorations further suggests the presence of an eclectic local workshop. It is probable, therefore, that all, or at least the majority, of variant and unique types and subtypes found in the Lower Building were produced on the site. Given that objects of bone, antler, ivory, and metal, as well as architectural terracottas,[8] were manufactured at Poggio Civitate, it would not be surprising to find local production of pottery.[9]

---

[7] It is not clear whether any samples of bucchero found in the Lower Building were included in this study, since the article does not state site locations from which the ceramic samples were taken; see Tobey, Nielsen, and Rowe 1986.

[8] Bone, antler, and ivory: Nielsen 1984a:333–48; Nielsen, in *Case e palazzi*:94–98; Nielsen 1995; also see above, Chapter 2, Ivory, Antler, and Bone Objects. Metalwork: Warden et al. 1982:26–35; Warden 1985:123–25; Warden et al. 1991:151–56; Warden 1993; Nielsen 1993, 1998; also see above, Chapter 2, Metal Artifacts. Architectural Terracottas: Winter 1977:28, pl. 11, figs. 2–4; Nielsen 1987:92, 116; 1993:29–30; Edlund-Berry 1989, esp. pp. 22, 29–30 and notes 6–8; Nielsen 1998:98–102.

[9] While Donati (*Case e palazzi*:132) has speculated that the bucchero recovered from the site was locally manufactured, Phillips (1994:44) has previously suggested that both the stamped impasto and bucchero vessels found on Poggio Civitate were locally made. It should also be noted that both Bouloumié-Marique (1978:112, note 29) and Bouloumié (in *Case e Palazzi*:139) have speculated that the utility and coarseware pottery found on the site was locally produced. For a review of the evidence for the production of ceramics at the site, see Nijboer 1998:168–70.

TABLE 12: LOWER BUILDING BUCCHERO VESSEL TYPES CORRESPONDING TO RASMUSSEN'S SOUTHERN ETRUSCAN TYPES

Shape	Type	Catalogue Number	Rasmussen Type
Kantharos	Type 1	6	Type 3a
	Type 2A	7, 8	Type 3e
	Type 2B	9, 10	Type 3e
	Type 2C	11, 12	Type 3e
	Type 2D	13, 14	Variant of Type 3e
	Type 2E	15, 16	Variant of Type 3e
Kyathos Handle	Type 4	37	Type 3
Cup	Type 1	38	Variant of Type 3a
	Type 2	39–42	Variant of Type 3b

RELATIONSHIP OF THE BUCCHERO FROM THE LOWER BUILDING TO THE TYPOLOGY OF BUCCHERO FROM SOUTHERN ETRURIA

The examination of the bucchero from the Lower Building has revealed that very few of the types or subtypes found in the deposit, only nine of a total of forty-five, overlap with Rasmussen's typology of bucchero (Rasmussen 1979) from southern Etruria (Table 12). Of these nine types or subtypes, four (kantharos Types 1, 2A, 2B, and 2C) are exact parallels for Rasmussen's types; one (kyathos handle Type 4), a potentially exact parallel; and four (kantharos Types 2D and 2E and cup Types 1 and 2) are variants of his types. The kantharos Types 1 and 2A–C, as noted above, are almost certainly imports, the former type from an unknown location in southern Etruria and the latter from Vulci. The kyathos handle Type 4, which is fragmentary, is most likely reconstructed as a kyathos similar to Rasmussen Type 3 (Rasmussen 1979: 114). Examples of these kyathoi are known from sites in both northern and southern Etruria, and it now appears that they were produced in both areas (Cristofani 1972:84–94; Bonamici 1972: 106–14; Bagnasco Gianni 1993:207–16). The places of production of kantharos Types 2D and 2E and cup Types 1 and 2 are uncertain. It should be noted that Rasmussen's Type 3e kantharos (Rasmussen 1979:104–6) and Type 3a and 3b cups (Rasmussen 1979:119–20) are among the most common bucchero shapes in both northern and southern Etruria, and therefore, it is not surprising that variants of them were found in the Lower Building.

The bucchero from the Lower Building, like all bucchero from northern Etruria, is much more richly decorated than bucchero of the same period found in the south. While the bucchero of southern Etruria utilizes many of the same decorative techniques, including stamped, cylinder-stamped, and mold-made decorations, the repertoire of ornament types is fairly limited, and different decorative techniques are rarely combined on the same vessel.

THE LOWER BUILDING BUCCHERO WITHIN THE CONTEXT OF BUCCHERO PRODUCTION DURING THE ORIENTALIZING PERIOD IN NORTHERN ETRURIA

The lack of overlap between Rasmussen's southern typology and the bucchero from Poggio Civitate establishes that the bucchero from the Lower Building belongs to a regional style distinct from the typology of the south. The "Lower Building typology" includes material from the coastal and inland sites of northern Etruria and extends as far south as Vulci. At present it seems more correct to refer to regional styles for the northern bucchero, rather than to a typology, because the known northern bucchero displays greater variation from site to site and is not standardized in terms of shape and decoration like much of the contemporary bucchero from southern Etruria. During the late Orientalizing period, northern Etruscan potters tended to develop their own unique and variant shapes and decorative motifs. This phenomenon can be observed not only within the

Orientalizing bucchero from Poggio Civitate, but also within the bucchero from such sites as Artimino[10] and Castelnuovo Berardenga.[11] The lack of standardization in the north suggests that bucchero production was less of an "industry" at this point than in the south and that there were more independent local workshops involved.[12] This pattern of individual production was undoubtedly tied to the contemporary political situation in the north where numerous autonomous settlements flourished (Nicosia 1972:389; Mangani 1990:12; Stoddart 1995:97–98). The changed consumption patterns and need for status objects among the elites in these centers fostered the development of craft specialization and the consequent appearance of local workshops.[13] The workshops in these settlements appear to have produced fine bucchero and other status items for much more limited markets, perhaps only for local consumption, and to suit individual taste, as some of the more exotic vessels from northern sites attest.[14] It is not until toward the middle of the sixth century, when larger cities began consolidating their territories, that a more standard typology developed for the north.[15]

CHRONOLOGY

EXTERNAL EVIDENCE

Little external evidence exists for the dating of the individual vessel types found in the Lower Building. Unfortunately, the majority of known bucchero vessels from northern Etruria were discovered during unsystematic excavations, and little, if any, attention, was given to their provenience and context. Even in the case of excavations in which the finds were properly recorded, little importance was placed on local Etruscan ceramics, especially bucchero. Instead, the emphasis was placed on the recovery of imported pottery and precious materials. In addition, although numerous studies have been conducted on the various decorative techniques of northern Etruscan bucchero, the issues of their advent and duration have not been addressed. As a result, the majority of bucchero from northern Etruria has been dated solely on the basis of the stylistic judgments of individual scholars, and no firm chronology exists for the majority of vessel types.

Only ten of the forty-five vessel types or subtypes identified in the building find parallels in

[10] For a discussion and presentation of the bucchero finds from Artimino, see Nicosia 1974:55–66; Nicosia 1972:375–90; L. Donati, in *Artimino*:82–96.

[11] For a discussion and presentation of the bucchero from Castelnuovo Berardenga, see Bocci Pacini 1973:121–41; E. Mangani, in *Case e palazzi*:161–62 and in *Etrusker*:334–38; Mangani 1990:12–20, figs. 2, 3; Mangani 1992.

[12] Phillips (1994:44) has speculated that the Orientalizing period of northern Etruria was one of intensive local production but limited importation. Nijboer (1998:51-53) has noted that in general the inter-regional distribution of locally produced fine ceramic wares in Etruria was limited. This seems to be particularly true among the smaller settlements of the north as the relative infrequency of imports during the Orientalizing period attests. Certainly, in the case of Poggio Civitate the amount of imported pottery is minimal in comparison to the quantities of locally produced wares.

[13] Nijboer (1998:190) has recognized this general pattern of development elsewhere in Etruria during the Orientalizing period as well.

[14] This point has been emphasized by both Nicosia (1972:389–90) and Mangani (1990:14–18) in their respective discussions of the bucchero from Artimino and Castelnuovo Berardenga. Mangani has also suggested a similar situation regarding the production of carved objects in ivory, antler, and bone in the area. In addition, Stoddart (1995:97) has noted that during the late Orientalizing period, the political authority of centers such as Murlo and Acquarossa appears to have been accompanied by the development of distinctive styles in art. Notably, Edlund Berry (1989) has distinguished a distinctive style in the decorative architectural terracottas from Poggio Civitate, which she has designated "the Murlo style." Finally, as Nijboer (1998:83, 106, 191) and Gran-Aymerich (1993:22–23, 35) have noted, the production of bucchero gradually evolved from prestige ceramics for banquets to semi-luxury vessels and eventually to common table wares. The rate of this development differed between the north and south of Etruria as a result of both the different political situation in the north and the initiation of bucchero production approximately a half century later in northern sites (see note 3 of the Introduction). Thus, while many of the bucchero vessels produced in the north during the latter half of the seventh and early sixth centuries represent "highly crafted, individually made artifacts" (Nijboer 1998:104)—e.g., the kyathoi with elaborately molded handles from Poggio Civitate—much of the contemporary bucchero in the south was already being produced in a series. For additional discussion of this process, see Nijboer 1998:103–106.

[15] Mangani (1990:19) notes that in the case of the settlements in the Ombrone Valley, including Poggio Civitate, the products of Chiusi gradually became predominant during the course of the 6th century B.C.

vessels found in securely datable contexts,[16] and an additional four vessels in the deposit can be linked to well-dated prototypes.[17] The contexts of the parallels recovered from securely datable contexts, however, are all funerary and generally do not provide a chronological range any narrower than that of the Lower Building itself, since the majority of these tombs contained multiple depositions that often spanned considerable amounts of time. In fact, the Lower Building constitutes one of the few narrowly datable contexts for bucchero in northern Etruria and has already been used to provide the *terminus post quem* for several vessel types.[18]

Five vessel types from the Lower Building have parallels or prototypes dated before the end of the seventh century. Their dates range from the middle through the final quarter of the seventh century. Kantharos Type 1 (**6**), which corresponds to Rasmussen's kantharos Type 3a, has been dated to the latter half of the third and the fourth quarter of the seventh century on the basis of tomb contexts in southern Etruria (Rasmussen 1979:102–103). Kyathoi with handles like kyathos handle Type 4 (**37**), which correspond to Rasmussen's kyathos Type 3, have been dated to the middle or third quarter of the seventh century (Rasmussen 1979:114; Bonamici 1972:110; Bagnasco Gianni 1993:207). Cup Types 1 and 2 (**38–42**) were inspired by East Greek prototypes of Villard and Vallet cup Types A and A2, respectively. While the Villard and Villet cup Type A is dated to 640/630–600 B.C., their cup Type A2 is dated to 620–600 B.C. (for the chronology of these cups see above, Chapter 3). Finally, jar Type 1 (**48**) has close parallels in two jars found in a tomb group at Cetona dated to the last quarter of the seventh century (Cristofani 1971:80–81; see also above, Chapter 3).

Five additional vessel types, while lacking direct parallels in datable contexts, may be placed in the seventh century on the basis of either their similarity to earlier vessel types in ceramic or bronze or their style and/or decoration. Kyathos Type 3 (**25, 26**) has been shown to constitute a later adaptation of the Near Eastern bronze ribbed bowls that were first imported and later imitated in central Etruria and Italy during the eighth and seventh centuries (see above, Chapter 3). While clearly not as early in style as the buccheroid kantharoi and kyathoi of similar type known from Vetulonia, which are dated to the middle of the seventh century, their shape and decoration, nevertheless, still suggest a seventh-century date, most likely in the last quarter. This date is also supported by the parallels for the molded decoration which commonly appear on the handles of the kyathoi of this type found at Poggio Civitate.[19] A date in the last quarter of the seventh century is probable for chalice Types 1 and 2 (**44** and **45**), and jar Type 2 (**49**). While the two chalice types find their closest parallels in impasto chalices dated to the seventh and early sixth centuries, the jar finds parallels in related impasto vessels dated to the eighth and seventh centuries (see above, Chapter 3). In addition, although the oinochoai of Type 1 (**1–3**) are generally dated in the first half of the sixth century, if my suggestion that they were inspired by seventh-century Rhodian bronze prototypes should prove correct, this could indicate a late-seventh-century date for this type as well (see above, Chapter 3). Finally, the tripod bowl (**50–52**) may also be of seventh-century date. However, although its shape finds parallels in ceramic vessels dated to the second half of the seventh century, it also shares some similarities with metal vessels dated to the first half of the sixth century (see above, Chapter 3). Consequently, it could date to either the seventh or sixth century.

Six vessel types find parallels or prototypes in vessels dated between the last quarter of the seventh and the first half of the sixth century B.C.

---

[16] (1) Kantharos Type 1, **6**; (2) Kantharoi Types 2A–E, **7–16**; (3) Kyathos Type 2, **24**; (4) Kyathos Handle Type 1, **30–33**; (5) Kyathos Handle Type 2, **34**, **35**; (6)Kyathos Handle Type 4, **37**; (7) Phiale, **47**; (8) Jar Type 1, **48**; (9) Footed Bowl Type 1, **53**; (10) Footed Bowl Type 2, **54**, **55**.

[17] (1) Oinochoe Type 1, **1–3**; (2) Alabastron, **5**; (3) Cup Type 1, **38**; (4) Cup Type 2, **39–42**.

[18] The dates of the Lower Building have been cited to provide a *terminus post quem* for the production of oinochoai of Batignani's Type B and for crested kyathoi handles decorated with applied human heads. For the oinochoai, see Donati and Michelucci 1981:57, no. 101; Pellegrini 1989:85–86. For the handles, see Donati and Michelucci 1981:62, no. 107.

[19] The other scalloped kyathoi of this type known from Poggio Civitate all have handles with molded figural decoration like that of kyathos handle Type 2, **34** and **35**, and Type 3, **36**, from the Lower Building (see above, Chapter 3). For a discussion of the style and chronology of the decoration on these handles, see the discussion of ornament Types 16–19 in Chapter 4.

The alabastron **5** was inspired by an Etrusco-Corinthian prototype whose production began at the end of the seventh century and continued into the first half of the sixth (see above, Chapter 3). Kantharos Types 2A–E (**7–16**), which are either examples or variants of Rasmussen's Type 3e, have been dated between the last quarter of the seventh and the third quarter of the sixth century on the basis of tomb contexts in southern Etruria (Rasmussen 1979:106). A kyathos with a handle similar to kyathos handle Type 2 (**34**, **35**) was found in a chamber tomb at Poggio Buco dated between the end of the seventh and the second quarter of the sixth centuries (Matteucig 1951:51, no. 59, 62 Tomb G; see above, Chapter 3). Two close parallels for footed bowl Type 1 (**53**) come from tombs in Cetona dated to the last quarter of the seventh and the first years of the sixth centuries (see above, Chapter 3). Finally, footed bowl Type 2 (**54**, **55**) finds close parallels in vessels from Cetona, Chiusi, and Orvieto which have been dated between the last quarter of the seventh and the first half of the sixth centuries (see above, Chapter 3). The remaining three vessel types with datable parallels or prototypes are placed in the first half of the sixth century.[20]

The dating of the comparanda for the ornaments found on the bucchero has only limited chronological value since many of the motifs, particularly the stamped examples, persisted for long periods of time. For example, close parallels for the stamped, winged quadruped, Ornament 1, were found on buccheroid vessels from Vetulonia dated to the middle of the seventh century and on a bucchero cup from Massarossa dated between the last quarter of the seventh and the early sixth century (see above, Chapter 4). In general, while the antecedents for the majority of the ornaments were found on objects of the early Orientalizing period and dated in the first half of the seventh century, the closest parallels for the ornaments appeared on objects dated to the last quarter of the seventh and the early sixth century. Unfortunately, only a single exact parallel was found for the ornaments on the bucchero, and it was not datable (see above, Decoration, and Table 6). The investigation of the motifs, like that of the vessel shapes, places the date of the majority of the bucchero between the last quarter of the seventh and the first quarter of the sixth century.

INTERNAL EVIDENCE

The internal evidence for the dating of the Lower Building is provided by the imported pottery, carved objects in ivory, antler, and bone, and gold jewelry found in the deposit (for a complete review of the evidence for the dating of the Lower Building, see above, Chapter 2, Chronology, and Table 2). The analysis of these objects supports a *terminus post quem* for the building of 620–580 B.C. On the basis of this evidence, the excavators proposed a median date of 600 B.C for the destruction of the building.

This study has revealed that most of the bucchero in the Lower Building falls well within the range of dates of the imported pottery in the deposit. While a few vessels may date as early as the third quarter of the seventh century, the majority of the bucchero vessels cannot be dated any earlier than the last quarter of the seventh century, and several of the vessel types fall into the first quarter of the sixth century. Thus, the new chronological evidence afforded by the examination of the bucchero indicates that the building was destroyed sometime during the first quarter of the sixth century.

Conversely, the determination of the date of the construction of the building still remains problematic. It must be emphasized that all the material recovered from the Lower Building, including the bucchero pottery, represents only the contents of the structure at the time of its destruction. Consequently, depending on the length of the life span of the building, its final contents may not preserve clear evidence for the date of its construction. Although the evidence is not abundant, there does exist material datable to around the middle of the seventh century on Piano del Tesoro, which may have originally been associated with the Lower Building. A number of unpublished bucchero fragments recovered elsewhere on Piano del Tesoro find close parallels in vessels dated toward the middle of the seventh century B.C.[21] In addition, as I have noted, a few of the bucchero vessels recovered from within the Lower Building could conceivably date to that period as well. Furthermore, Anthony Tuck has recently dated nine tombs excavated on Poggio Aguzzo to the middle of the seventh century (Tuck 1996a:35–37

[20] These include: (1) Kyathos Type 2, **24**; (2) Kyathos Handle Type 1, **30–33**; (3) Phiale, **47**.

[21] I thank Dr. Anthony Tuck for pointing out this material to me; see Tuck 1996a:33–35.

and 1996b:399–400). As noted above, one of these tombs, Poggio Aguzzo Tomb 8, contained a buccheroid kyathos (Murlo no. PA 72-32) whose handle is stamped with a cylinder-stamped motif almost identical to that on a handle fragment of similar type (**37**) recovered from the Lower Building.[22] The presence of this handle fragment within the area of the Lower Building, as well as of a small number of additional ceramic vessel fragments recovered elsewhere on Poggio Civitate that are directly comparable to vessels found in the Poggio Aguzzo tombs, suggests that the Orientalizing period occupation of Piano del Tesoro, and possibly the Lower Building, may date back to about the middle of the seventh century.

THE BANQUET

In addition to furnishing important information regarding bucchero chronology and vessel typology, the bucchero and other materials found in the Lower Building provide invaluable data on Etruscan daily life. The Lower Building contains one of the few known sealed deposits of bucchero found within a structure. This material provides us with a rare glimpse of what we might expect to find in a nonfunerary assemblage of bucchero at the turn of the seventh century in terms of both number and variety of shapes. Analysis of the ceramic finds in the building has revealed that they constitute the remains of an elaborate banquet service, the only one known in Etruria from a nonfunerary context.[23] This discovery, along with the one made at Ficana in Latium (Rathje 1983), allows us to establish, for the first time, the components of a banquet service in Etruria in a nonfunerary context.

In a series of illuminating articles, Rathje has discussed banqueting in the context of the innovations that occurred in the society and culture of central Italy as a result of contacts with the Greeks and Phoenicians during the Orientalizing period (Rathje 1983; 1988; 1990; 1994). Foremost among these developments was the introduction of Greek- and Near Eastern-style banqueting and the increased emphasis on the drinking of wine.[24] The primary evidence for these innovations, as attested by the funerary record, is the change in the vase repertoire that occurred at this time, particularly the appearance of new shapes, many of them Greek and Near Eastern in origin, as well as the mass importation of objects commonly used in banqueting services (Rathje 1983:21 and 1990:280; Bouloumié 1986:72; Cristofani 1987b:124–25). That the banquet and the consumption of wine also had important ideological implications as a status activity of the elite is demonstrated by the numerous finds of elaborate banqueting sets in many of the wealthy Orientalizing tombs.[25] Later, begin-

[22] It should be noted that it is not absolutely certain that this handle was found within the walls of the Lower Building, since the grids assigned to the piece by its excavator (Rec. 5, F-H/0-1) encompass an area inside, and extending for a distance of approximately 2 m outside, the Lower Building. It is possible that the handle was reconstructed from fragments recovered both inside and outside the building within the limits of the area designated by these grid coordinates, but the excavation daybook is not specific in this regard. However, the documentation does clearly indicate that the handle was recovered from the burn stratum below the pavement of the Upper Building. Therefore, the handle can be securely associated with the Orientalizing occupation of the site. Moreover, considering the close proximity of the Lower Building to the grid coordinates assigned to the piece, even if the handle was not actually found in the building, it almost certainly originated from this structure.

[23] J. Berkin, "An Etruscan Banquet Service from Poggio Civitate (Murlo)," *AJA* 98 (1994):299.

[24] Although the date of the initial cultivation of wine in Italy is a matter of some debate, it appears likely that wine was present in Italy before the Orientalizing period. For a discussion of the evidence see Rathje 1983:21; Gras 1985:255–67; F. Delpino, "L'Ellenizzazione dell'Etruria villanoviana: sui rapporti tra Grecia ed Etruria fra IX e VIII secolo A. C.," *Secondo Congresso Internazionale Etrusco, Atti*, vol. 1 (Rome, 1989):105–16; Bouloumié 1986:72; Cristofani 1987a:37–40. I would also like to thank Amy Bogaard for providing me with a copy of her unpublished paper "Wine and Banqueting in Orientalizing and Archaic Etruria." What appears to have taken place during the Orientalizing period, therefore, was not the introduction of wine, but rather the introduction of wine drinking and related customs as a status activity. See also Nijboer 1998:3, 188.

[25] Rathje also notes that, in addition to banquet equipment, wine itself was also imported, as the discovery of Phoenician wine amphoras in a number of wealthy tombs in Latium attests; see Rathje 1988:83; Cristofani 1987a:38; see also A. Rathje, "I *keimelia* orientali," *Opus* 3.2 (1982):341–54; Rathje 1990:281–82; B. Bouloumié, "Le symposion greco-étrusque et l'aristocracie celtique," in *Les princes celtes et la Méditerranée* (Paris, 1988):343–83.

ning in the sixth century, the banquet became a common theme in Etruscan art.[26] Notably, one of its earliest depictions is at Poggio Civitate itself, on a group of terracotta frieze plaques from the Upper Building.[27]

Unfortunately, no direct evidence for the presence of wine was found in the Lower Building. But the discoveries within the building of abundant quantities of Etruscan bucchero and imported Greek drinking cups, fashioned in shapes generally associated with wine drinking, and two large bronze cauldrons,[28] which presumably functioned as mixing bowls, strongly argue for its presence. Elsewhere on the site, the discovery of an Early Corinthian and a Samian amphora in Trench 18,[29] a deposit of material which is contemporary with the Lower Building, may offer additional indirect evidence for wine. While the Samian amphora has been identified as a type generally associated with the transport of oil, the Corinthian amphora could have contained wine or oil.

A number of difficulties limit the extent to which the banquet service in the Lower Building can be reconstructed. As noted above in the discussion of the finds, the deposit was subjected to a number of disturbances and, as a result, it is not certain to what extent the material recovered from the building is representative of its contents at the time of its destruction. In addition, we are not yet certain what constituted a complete Etruscan banquet service or, for that matter, if indeed there was a "standard" service. Although it is generally assumed that the burial equipment found in Etruscan tombs represents a service for a funerary banquet to be held either at the tomb or in the afterlife, no general attempt has yet been made to determine the essential components of such a service.[30] In addition, the extent to which the funerary record is reflective of "real-life" activities remains a matter of debate (see Rathje 1994:96). It is distinctly possible that both the quantities and types of equipment chosen for the tomb were determined by specific funerary rituals and eschatological beliefs. It is also conceivable that regional variations existed in mortuary rituals and practices which intimately affected the selection of tomb furniture. Similar problems arise in an attempt to assess the iconographic record for the banquet, since it is not at all certain whether the representations, the majority of which are funerary in nature, were idealized or whether they reflected specific events. In this context, it is interesting to note that very few depictions of the banquet in Etruscan art show the participants both eating and drinking.[31] The overwhelming majority of the scenes involve only drinking.

Despite these limitations, however, the funerary and iconographic records still remain the only sources of evidence in Etruria for recon-

[26] For a discussion of the banquet in Etruscan art, see S. De Marinis, *La tipologia del banchetto nell'arte Etrusca arcaica* (Rome, 1961); see also Cristofani 1987b:126–31. In addition, A. Tuck (1994), in an illuminating article, has demonstrated that the representation of the seated banquet in the Orientalizing period had conceptual roots in the burial practices of the Villanovan period. According to Tuck, "the widespread thematic expression of the dead at meal in Villanovan contexts helps to explain the pervasive use of the iconography of the funerary banquet in tombs throughout Etruria from the Archaic period onward."

[27] The original publication of these friezes was by Small (1971: 25–61, fig. 1). Rathje notes that the banquet depicted on the frieze plaques of the Upper Building represents the earliest known scene of the reclining banquet in Etruria (see Rathje 1983: 24; Rathje, in *Case e Palazzi*:122–23; Rathje 1994; also Cristofani 1987b:126). Rathje, in a recent reanalysis of the frieze, has conclusively identified one of the participants in the banquet as a woman (Rathje 1989:78–79; Rathje 1994:96). See also J. P. Small, "Eat, Drink, and Be Merry. Etruscan Banquets," in De Puma and Small 1994:87.

[28] These two cauldrons are unpublished. Both were found on the floor of the Lower Building below Rectangle 7; see Warden 1985:86.

[29] Early Corinthian amphora: Murlo no. 72-430; see *Case e palazzi*:77, no. 46; Phillips 1989a:30, figs. 4–6. Samian amphora: Murlo no. 73-202; see Nielsen and Phillips 1977a:93–94, figs. 21–23; *Case e palazzi*:77, no. 47; Phillips 1989a:32, figs. 14–18. A small dipper found with the amphora suggests oil rather than wine as its contents.

[30] An important step in this direction has been made by Bouloumié (1986:72–73), who has identified the components of an Etruscan wine service.

[31] For some examples of artistic representations depicting banqueters both eating and drinking, see F. Nicosia, *StEtr* 37 (1962):369–401, pls. XCIIIc, XCIVa and b, and XCVII; Steingräber 1985:pls. 35, 146–47, 166, 271; Small 1971:28, fig. 1; A. Andrén, *OpRom* 8 (1974):pls. III, fig. 7, VII, figs. 17, 18, XXIV, fig. 53.

structing banqueting practices. According to the evidence of the funerary record, it would appear that vessels of different fabrics and materials were commonly utilized together in the banquet service. Therefore, in presenting the evidence for a banqueting service from the Lower Building, it will be necessary to take into account not only the bucchero, but all the other vessels found in the building: the imported pottery, the impasto, and the metalware. Since only a portion of the impasto pottery from the building has been published, as noted in Chapter 2, it will not be possible at this time to a make a full accounting of these vessels.[32] Besides the two bronze cauldrons already mentioned, no additional metal vessels of securely identifiable type were found.[33] The available information is presented in Table 13.[34]

Given our lack of knowledge regarding the specific details and logistics of Etruscan banqueting, an attempted analysis of this material raises more questions than it answers.[35] Since we do not know what constitutes an individual banquet setting, if such a concept existed at all, it is not possible to determine the distribution of the vessels among the participants or how many banqueters the service would have accommodated. On the basis of the number of chalices present in the deposit, Rathje estimated that the banquet service discovered at Ficana would have served thirty people.[36] Rathje was able to make this estimate since the chalice was essentially the only cup type present, and presumably each banqueter needed a cup. In the case of the material in the Lower Building, there is no single requisite type present in sufficient number to allow such an estimate.

Our limited knowledge of the function of different vessel types in the banquet ritual also prevents us from determining the capacity of the service. For example, there are a maximum number of seventeen kantharoi and kyathoi respectively and twenty-one cups. If we knew that each banqueter was provided with one cup of each type, then we could estimate that the pottery from the Lower Building represented a service for approximately twenty people. It is also possible, however, that there was no difference in function among these cup types and that each could equally be used at any moment in the banquet, or that the criterion for the assignment of cup types was not function, but status or gender.[37] Thus, for example, while those of greater status may have utilized the imported Greek cups, others drank from either their imitations in bucchero or vessels of a different shape. In this case, on the basis of the maximum total number of cups, the material could have provided service for fifty-nine. That one of these possibilities might actually be the case is indicated by some of the representations of banqueting in Etruscan art. On the frieze plaques from the Upper Building at Poggio Civitate, the banqueters are shown with three kinds of cups: hemispherical bowls, skyphoi, and kylikes (Fig. 7). On the frieze plaques from Velletri one ban-

[32] A total of 27 impasto vessels recovered from the Lower Building, consisting of 4 fineware and 23 coarseware vessels, have been published. For a discussion of this material see above, Chapter 2.

[33] Warden notes that two body fragments and handles from bronze vessels were found in the Lower Building. He conjectures that one of the handles may have belonged to a bucket or pail and the other to a large open vessel, possibly a cauldron (1985:86, 88, nos. 139, 140, 146, 147). In addition, two bronze figurines found in the building, representing a wrestler and a trainer, served as vessel attachments; see K. M. Phillips Jr., *OpRom* 9 (1973):177–82; P. G. Warden, *AJA* 86 (1982):233–38; Warden 1985:89.

[34] It must be emphasized that the assignment of the various vessel types to categories and the categories themselves are admittedly somewhat arbitrary. The goal is to provide some type of general reconstruction of the banqueting service. I have omitted the two large impasto pithoi and two impasto cooking lids from this tabulation, since it is unlikely that they would have been used in a banquet service.

[35] Some potentially useful information on banqueting and drinking parties, including the composition of the *kylikeia*, is provided by some of the painted scenes depicted in Etruscan tombs. These paintings, however, are much later in date than the service from the Lower Building. In addition, the applicability of iconographic evidence to the current study, particularly in the case of representations from funerary contexts, is limited, as has been discussed above. For other scenes from painted tombs, which, in contrast to those representations already mentioned (above, note 31), depict the participants only drinking, see Steingräber 1985:pls. 41, 72, 116–119, 132, 174, 196.

[36] Rathje 1983:18.

[37] Rathje (1983:7–29) has argued in reference to the Ficana banquet service that differences in banqueting equipment may signify some internal hierarchical distinction.

TABLE 13: VESSELS IN THE BANQUETING SERVICE[a]

Category	Fabric/ Material	Minimum	Maximum	Max. Total of Type	Max. Total of Category
Drinking Cups					59
Kantharos				17	
	Bucchero	12	16		
	Impasto	1	1		
Kyathos				17	
	Bucchero	16	16		
	Impasto	1	1		
Cup				21	
	Bucchero	5	6		
	Ionic[b]	5	5		
	Laconian	8	8		
	Corinthian	1	1		
	Impasto	1	1		
Chalice				3	
	Bucchero	3	3		
Phiale				1	
	Bucchero	1	1		
Serving or Setting Vessels					94
Jar				2	
	Bucchero	2	2		
Tripod Bowl				3	
	Bucchero	2	3		
Footed Bowl				4	
	Bucchero	3	3		
	Impasto	1	1		
Broad-Rimmed Shallow Bowl				13	
	Bucchero	10	13		
Lug Handled Bowl				9	
	Bucchero	3	9		
Deep Bowl				6	
	Impasto	6	6		
Shallow Carinated Bowl				1	
	Impasto	1	1		
Broad-Rimmed Shallow Plate				23	
	Bucchero	12	23		
Miscellaneous Plate				5	
	Bucchero	2	2		
	Etrusco-Corinthian	3	3		

[a] For explanation of the tabulations of the numbers of bucchero vessel types, see Ch. 3. For the impasto and imported Greek and Etrusco-Corinthian pottery, see these types in Ch. 2.

[b] Phillips notes that the total number of Ionic bowls in the Lower Building could have been 20 or more. At present, I have listed only the published examples (see Phillips 1989a:32).

TABLE 13: VESSELS IN THE BANQUETING SERVICE—*Continued*

Category	Fabric/ Material	Minimum	Maximum	Max. Total of Type	Max. Total of Category
Broad-Rimmed Shallow Plate or Bowl Rim Fragment				10	
	Bucchero	6/7	10		
Lid				18	
	Bucchero	18	18		
Containers					14
Aryballos				1	
	Etrusco-Corinthian	1	1		
Alabastron				1	
	Bucchero	1	1		
Olla				10	
	Impasto	10	10		
Cauldron				2	
	Bronze	2	2		
Pouring Vessel					6
Oinochoe				6	
	Bucchero	3	4		
	Impasto	2	2		

queter is shown with a rhyton and the others with skyphoi (A. Andrén, *OpRom* 8 [1974]:pl. III, fig. 7). Similarly, while some of the banqueters in the painted scenes in the Golini tomb at Orvieto hold kylikes, others have phialai (*Alimentazione*:168).

By the same token, we also do not know if sets of plates and bowls were assigned to individual banqueters or used communally. Many of the broad-rimmed shallow bowls and plates from the deposit have similar dimensions, indicating that they might have been produced as single elements of individual place settings. On the frieze plaques from the Upper Building a table is placed before each pair of reclining banqueters (Fig. 7). On each table appear two low and two tall bowls, not unlike those recovered from the Lower Building, in an alternating arrangement. It appears there that each banqueter was provided with his/her own setting. Finally, the composition of the individual settings may also have been determined by the purpose and type of banquet. It would appear that both seated and reclining banquets took place in Etruria, and it is conceivable that each required a different type of banquet service.[38]

The vessels in the service can be broken down into four different categories: drinking cups, serving or setting vessels, including plates and bowls, containers for either liquids or food, and pouring vessels (Table 13).[39] Serving and setting vessels form the largest category, comprising a maximum number of ninety-four examples. This category includes all the bowls, plates, jars, and lids. While many of the small broad-rimmed shallow bowls and plates, lug handled bowls, footed bowls, Etrusco-Corinthian plates, and jars could have been used equally for serving or individual place settings, the larger plates, and tripod and impasto bowls seem better adapted to a serving function. In addition, some of the impasto bowls may have been used for the preparation of food. The presence of so many plates and bowls renders it clear that this is not a service for drinking only (*symposion*), but, like the service discovered at Ficana, for banqueting (*syndeipnon*; Rathje 1983:18). Drinking cups form the second largest

[38] Rathje has suggested that the reclining banquet may not have been introduced into Italy until the advent of Corinthian and Ionian influence in the early Archaic period. Before this time, presumably, the seated banquet would have been the predominant form (see Rathje 1983:23–26 and 1990:284–86; see also Tuck 1994).

[39] I have included the bucchero lids in the category "serving and setting vessels" based on the assumption that they covered bowls or plates.

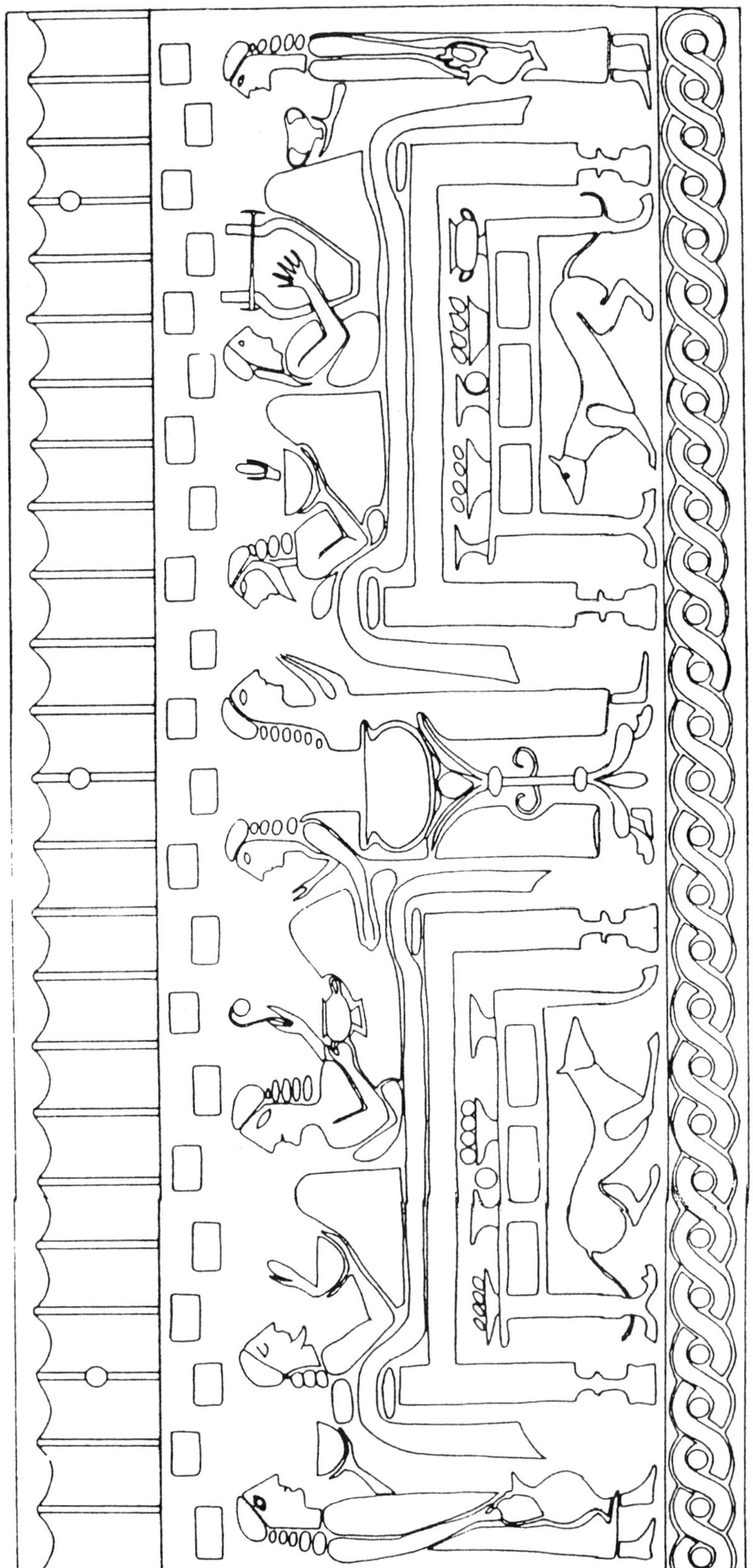

Figure 7. Reconstruction of the Poggio Civitate banquet frieze (J. P. Small, StEtr 39 [1971]; drawn by M. G. Butterworth, S. Ferranti, and H. Linden)

and most varied category. There are a total of fifty-nine cups of six different types, including kantharoi, kyathoi, chalices, "Ionic"-type cups, a skyphos, a kotyle, and a phiale. The presence of a phiale is particularly notable since it represents one of the few examples found in a habitational context; the majority of other known examples were found in funerary of votive contexts.[40] Containers form the next category with a total of fourteen examples. They include the two bronze cauldrons and the ten impasto ollas. While the bronze cauldrons undoubtedly served as containers for liquids, presumably water or wine, and functioned as kraters or mixing bowls, the impasto ollas could have functioned as containers for water or wine or held foodstuffs. Finally, the bucchero alabastron and Etrusco-Corinthian aryballos could also have had a function in the banquet service, serving as receptacles for oil or perfume.

Although no comprehensive study has yet been undertaken to determine the components of an entire banquet service, Bouloumié has identified the composition of an Etruscan wine service on the basis of a comparative study of Etruscan tomb groups (Bouloumié 1986:72–73). While his study was limited to bronze vessels, it is likely that the same equipment would have been utilized in a ceramic service as well. Bouloumié has postulated that an Etruscan wine service has six essential elements: these include vessels for wine and water, a mixing bowl, a dipper or ladle, a filter, and a serving vessel. In addition, there may also be a container or tray on which to hold the service. Of the six elements, the deposit from the Lower Building lacks a filter and a dipper and, perhaps, containers for both wine and water. It is possible that the dipper or ladle and the filter, like the bronze cauldrons, were made of metal. The absence of such metal vessels is not surprising, since, being objects of value, they may have been salvaged from the remains of the building by the inhabitants of the site. While the impasto ollas may have served as containers for wine and water instead of the more common amphoras and hydriai, there is still nothing that may have served as a jug.[41] It is possible that the oinochoai were used for this function or that the hydriai, like the dipper or ladle and filter, were made of metal. Considering the Etruscan predilection for metal vessels, it would not be surprising if some of the elements of the service were represented only in metal and others, like the drinking cups, had metal counterparts.

A comparison of the banquet service from the Lower Building with that found at the Latin city of Ficana (Rathje 1983) reveals a number of similarities as well as some notable differences. Although Ficana was a Latin, not an Etruscan, city, it is likely that the banqueting customs of the two cultures were similar. The Ficana banquet service was found in two rubbish pits located in a courtyard near the foundations of a monumental building (Rathje 1983:10–11, figs. 3, 4). This structure, like the Lower Building, had a tiled roof and is assumed to have been a habitation, probably the house of a high-ranking family. The building has been dated on the basis of its contents, which included both local and imported ceramic material, to the second half of the seventh century (Rathje 1983:9–10). Although there is no secure stratigraphic evidence linking the house to the rubbish pits that contained the banquet service, their association seems likely since pottery fragments of the same type were found in both places (Rathje 1983:25).

As in the case of the deposit from the Lower Building, it is not certain whether the Ficana material represents a complete banquet service. The service is composed of a large quantity of both redware and red impasto ceramic vessels. Like the banquet service from the Lower Building, it formed a table service for eating as well as drinking (Fig. 8). The service itself consists of: four *holmoi*, or cauldron stands, several fragmentary cauldrons with griffin protomes, about thirty chalice-type drinking cups, a kotyle, a large number of plates (with ring or high foot), at least four types of ollas, several one-handled cups and "*tazze cratere*," at least nine pyxides, numerous fragments of smaller bowls and ollas, and a few possible fragments of oinochoai and hydriai (Rathje 1983:11–18). While the specific

[40] Of the examples cited as comparanda for the phiale from the Lower Building, only the phiale from Accesa was recovered from a habitational context. All the other examples with known proveniences are from either funerary or votive contexts. Funerary: San Giovenale, San Giuliano, Poggio Buco. Votive: Roselle, Rome. For references for these vessels, see the discussion of the phiale in Chapter 3.

[41] Alternatively, it is possible that the wine, and perhaps the water as well, were contained in skins.

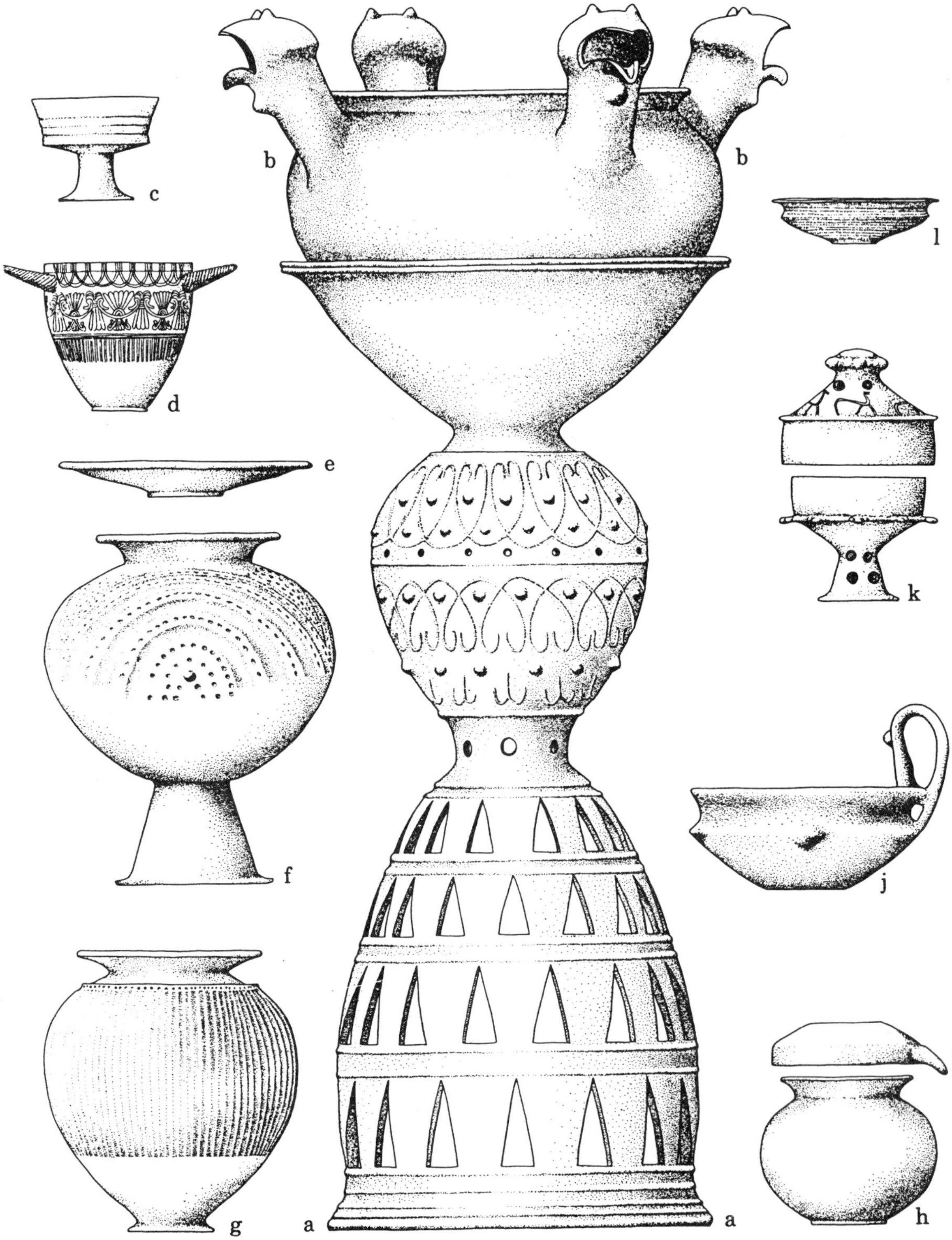

Figure 8. Typology of vases belonging to the banquet service found at Ficana (Rathje 1983; drawn by T. Fisker)

shapes of the vessels found in the two banquet services show little correspondence, their functions would appear to overlap substantially. Since the exact quantities for many of these vessel types have not been published, it is not possible to compare closely the relative percentages of vessel types in the two services. It is clear, however, that the principal category of vessels from Ficana was containers for liquids, followed by cups, and then by plates and bowls, while the principal category from the Lower Building was plates and bowls, followed by drinking cups, containers, and then pouring vessels. The Lower Building banquet service also has a greater variety of shapes. For example, there is only one principal cup type at Ficana, the chalice, while at Poggio Civitate there are three: kantharoi, kyathoi, and "Ionic"-type cups. Another difference between the two services is that there are no pyxides in the Lower Building material, while at least nine were found at Ficana. It is possible, however, that the covered bowl or tripod bowls from the Lower Building functioned as containers like a pyxis.

There are also similarities between the two deposits. Few oinochoai were found in either deposit: only a maximum of six at Poggio Civitate and perhaps one or two at Ficana. Neither site produced any dippers, strainers, or jugs although it is possible that they were made of metal. Finally, both deposits appear to have included objects of special value, the kotyle from Ficana and the Greek pottery from Poggio Civitate, which may have been status objects.

DOMESTIC VERSUS FUNERARY DEPOSITS OF BUCCHERO

Rathje noted in her study of the Ficana material that almost all the shapes found in the deposit have parallels in contemporary tombs (Rathje 1983:19–20). From this observation she deduced that the assemblages from the tombs reflected those used in daily life. Although there are fewer contemporary tombs available for comparison with the Lower Building material, it appears that many of the Lower Building pieces have general parallels in tomb contexts.[42] The only types missing from the Lower Building deposit which appear frequently in tombs are amphoras and jugs. There are more plates and bowls in the Lower Building than from funerary deposits, but this seems logical since the Lower Building deposit was functional and not just a representation of requisite types.[43] It is also possible that the funerary ritual required different quantities of the various vessels and did not emphasize eating. While there is no secure evidence concerning banquet and funerary ideologies, it appears that the repertoire of vase shapes utilized was essentially the same.

THE ORIENTALIZING BUCCHERO AND THE FUNCTION OF THE LOWER BUILDING

The Lower Building at Poggio Civitate contains one of the few known chronologically secure deposits of bucchero pottery from a nonfunerary context in Etruria. An analysis of the find spots of the vessels within the structure suggests that the bucchero, as well as the imported ceramic wares, was being stored by shape and class at the time of the destruction of the building. While a few vessels may date as early as the third quarter of the seventh century, the majority of the bucchero dates from the last quarter of the seventh and the first quarter of the sixth centuries B.C. It would appear, therefore, that the Lower Building was destroyed sometime during the first quarter of the sixth century B.C. The determination of the date of the construction of the building is more problematic. The currently available evidence, although scant, suggests that the structure could date back to around the middle of the seventh century B.C.

This study also has revealed that, for the most part, the bucchero from the Lower Building is typologically different from that of southern Etruria. The shapes of the vessels are somewhat similar to those of Chiusi and Vulci. Their decorations are comparable to those found on bucchero from Chiusi, Vetulonia, and Roselle, as well as a number of sites in southern Etruria, most notably Cerveteri. Nevertheless, most of the ves-

[42] The 9 tombs excavated on Poggio Aguzzo, the hill adjacent to Poggio Civitate, are now being prepared for publication by Anthony Tuck. Once they are published, it will be interesting to compare their contents to the material recovered from the Lower Building.

[43] It is also possible that if funerary meals were *al fresco*, they might have omitted ceramic plates and used slabs of bread instead. I thank Dr. Jean Turfa for this suggestion.

sel shapes and decorations are not identical to the ones from these other sites and represent either variant or unique types. The closest parallels for the shapes and decorations of the Lower Building bucchero were found at the site of Poggio Civitate itself, particularly among the deposit of burned bucchero recovered from Trench 18. This material almost certainly was burned in the same conflagration that destroyed the Lower Building and originally may even have been contained in this structure.

Only a few imported bucchero vessels were identified in the deposit; these imports were attributed to Chiusi, Vulci, and an indeterminate site in southern Etruria. The lack of close comparanda for the bucchero vessels elsewhere, in combination with the fact that the majority of shapes and decorations represent variant or unique types, suggests that the bucchero was locally produced. Unfortunately, a program of neutron activation analysis conducted on the bucchero and samples of local clay produced an inconclusive result. The diverse and often unusual shapes and decorations that are represented by the vessels in the deposit attest to the ingenuity of the local potters, and add further support to Gran Aymerich's (1995) thesis regarding the complex relationship between bucchero and vessels in other materials. Finally, the variety and sophistication of the bucchero vessels in the deposit suggest that they may not represent the earliest products of the local workshop. Their antecedents, however, currently remain unknown.

A review of bucchero production both at Poggio Civitate and other sites within northern Etruria indicates that during the latter half of the Orientalizing period the production of bucchero in the north of Etruria was less of an "industry" than in the south. There were more local workshops involved and, consequently, a much greater stylistic diversity. This in turn may reflect the political situation within northern Etruria at this time, suggesting the existence of numerous autonomous settlements with their own ceramic production facilities and artistic styles.

In most discussions concerning the site of Poggio Civitate, continuity of function between the Upper and Lower Buildings has been assumed. While some scholars proposed that the site constituted the home of a small northern Etruscan league, with the Upper—and presumably the Lower—Building functioning as a meeting hall and residence,[44] others have suggested that both structures served as aristocratic residences, which may also have incorporated administrative or religious activities.[45]

While there is nothing in the plan of the Lower Building that clearly indicates its purpose or function, both its monumental size and its elaborate architectural decoration suggest that it was a structure of some importance. The large amounts of locally made as well as imported luxury goods, many of them of a personal nature, attest to the great wealth of the inhabitants. Many of the finds were domestic in character, and the presence of a storage area, apparently for foodstuffs, as well as cooking vessels, suggests that the building served, at least in part, as a habitation.

The analysis of the bucchero pottery and, more specifically, the identification of an elaborate banquet service, further reinforce the notion of the high status of the occupants already apparent in the archaeological record. The majority of the bucchero pottery was extremely ornate, and many of the vessels certainly were prestige objects. The determination that most of the bucchero appears to have been produced at the site also expands our understanding of the already considerable scope of local craft production. Furthermore, the presence of inscriptions on three bucchero fragments in the deposit is particularly notable. While inscriptions commonly occur on material dedicated in sanctuaries or on vases placed in tombs, their presence on vessels in a purely residential site would be unusual.[46]

---

[44] Nielsen and Phillips, in *Case e palazzi*:64–68; Phillips 1993:79–83. This interpretation has also been accepted by Edlund-Berry, although she says that the site may have been a type of sanctuary (see Edlund 1987:87–92; Edlund-Berry 1989:30 and note 37; 1992:196–215; 1994:26). See also Chapter 1, note 14.

[45] Cristofani 1975:9–17; Rystedt 1983:87 and 1984:367–75; M. Torelli, in *Case e palazzi*:26–30; Warden 1985:147–50; Damgaard Andersen 1990:79; Rathje 1989:75–76; Jannot 1988:95–96; Nijboer 1998:171.

[46] It is possible that these inscribed bucchero vessels represented gifts rather than dedications; see M. Cristofani, "Il dono in Etruria," *Parola del Passato* 30 (1975):132–52; see also G. Bonfante and L. Bonfante, *Lingua e cultura degli Etruschi* (Rome, 1985):65; E. Richardson, "An Archaeological Introduction to the Etruscan Language," in *Etruscan Life and Afterlife: A Handbook of Etruscan Studies*, ed. L. Bonfante (Detroit, 1986):216–26.

Although the number of people accommodated by the banquet service identified in the Lower Building cannot be determined, the remains indicate that it would have been a fairly large group. If the ceramic material from other Orientalizing deposits on the site, most specifically, that found in Trench 18, were added to that from the Lower Building, it is clear that the size of this banquet service, already considerable, would be more than doubled. The presence of such a large amount of banqueting equipment on the site indicates that the facilities were capable of accommodating large groups of people. In what context these banquets would have been held, whether religious, political, or simply social, unfortunately cannot yet be determined.

Concordance I: Catalogue Number to Murlo Number

Cat. No.	Murlo No.	Florence No.[1]	Cat. No.	Murlo No.	Florence No.
1.	71-825	Fi 112482	32.	71-564	Fi 112589
2.	71-546		33.	71-545	
3.	71-558	Fi 114562	34.	71-563	Fi 112466
4.	71-821	Fi 114563	35.	72-364	
5.	71-171	Fi 112474	36.	71-562	Fi 112581
6.	71-801		37.	72-419	
7.	70-286		38.	71-214	Fi 112460
8.	71-817		39.	71-557	
9.	71-786		40.	71-953	
10.	71-954		41.	71-951	
11.	71-816		42.	70-287	
12.	71-803		43.	71-950	
13.	71-568	Fi 112441	44.	74-12	
14.	71-960		45.	71-805/806	
15.	71-739		46.	71-819	
16.	71-955		47.	71-947	
17.	71-802		48.	71-515	Fi 112995
18.	71-961		49.	71-952A, B	
19.	71-962		50.	72-281	Fi 112456
20.	71-963		51.	72-354	
21.	71-964		52.	71-91	
22.	71-569		53.	72-355/356	Fi 112476/477
23.	71-561	Fi 112587	54.	72-357/405	Fi 112453
24.	71-572		55.	78-219	
25.	71-542	Fi 112465	56.	73-47	
26.	71-555	Fi 112467	57.	73-126	
27.	73-143		58.	74-21	
28.	73-144		59.	72-385	
29.	71-553		60.	72-386	
30.	71-554	Fi 112588	61.	74-19	
31.	71-544		62.	72-387	

[1] Vessels lacking a Florence Archaeological Superintendency inventory number have not yet been consigned to the Italian state.

Cat. No.	Murlo No.	Florence No.
63.	73-110	
64.	72-329	Fi 112451
65.	73-6	Fi 112452
66.	72-394	
67.	74-16	
68.	71-551	
69.	73-44	Fi 112449
70.	72-342	Fi 112448
71.	74-17	
72.	72-411	
73.	72-360	
74.	72-396	
75.	72-362	
76.	72-397	
77.	71-533	
78.	71-534	
79.	72-393	
80.	74-15	
81.	71-552	
82.	70-280	
83.	72-391	
84.	74-29	
85.	71-535	
86.	71-736	
87.	71-536	
88.	71-537	
89.	71-538	
90.	74-118;72-371	
91.	72-372	
92.	72-374	
93.	70-276	
94.	74-14	
95.	72-373	
96.	72-377	
97.	72-376	
98.	73-90	
99.	73-89	
100.	71-58	
101.	72-379	

Cat. No.	Murlo No.	Florence No.
102.	72-413	
103.	73-140	
104.	73-141	
105.	73-142	
106.	73-139	
107.	73-138	
108.	72-414	
109.	74-13	
110.	72-428	
111.	72-358	
112.	71-83	
113.	71-394	
114.	71-513A–E	Fi 112446
115.	71-518	
116.	71-946	
117.	71-524	
118.	71-527A, B	
119.	71-949A, B	
120.	72-432	
121.	72-404	
122.	71-804	
123.	71-820	
124.	71-784	
125.	71-957	
126.	71-956	
127.	71-948	
128.	72-418	
129.	71-541	
130.	71-965	
131.	72-426	
132.	72-288	
133.	72-417	
134.	72-415	
135.	71-548	
136.	72-513	
137.	71-344	Fi 110953
138.	75-15	Fi 107746
139.	72-353	Fi 107741

CONCORDANCE II: MURLO NUMBER TO CATALOGUE NUMBER

Murlo No.	Florence No.[1]	Cat. No.
70-276		93
70-280		82
70-286		7
70-287		42
71-58		100
71-83		112
71-91		52
71-171	Fi 112474	5
71-214	Fi 112460	38
71-344	Fi 110953	137
71-394		113
71-513A-E	Fi 112446	114
71-515	Fi 112995	48
71-518		115
71-524		117
71-527A,B		118
71-533		77
71-534		78
71-535		85
71-536		87
71-537		88
71-538		89
71-541		129
71-542	Fi 112465	25
71-544		31
71-545		33
71-546		2
71-548		135
71-551		68

Murlo No.	Florence No.	Cat. No.
71-552		81
71-553		29
71-554	Fi 112588	30
71-555	Fi 112467	26
71-557		39
71-558	Fi 114562	3
71-561	Fi 112587	23
71-562	Fi 112581	36
71-563	Fi 112466	34
71-564	Fi 112589	32
71-568	Fi 112441	13
71-569		22
71-572		24
71-736		86
71-739		15
71-784		124
71-786		9
71-801		6
71-802		17
71-803		12
71-804		122
71-805;806		45
71-816		11
71-817		8
71-819		46
71-820		123
71-821	Fi 114563	4
71-825	Fi 112482	1
71-946		116
71-947		47

Murlo No.	Florence No.	Cat. No.
71-948		127
71-949A, B		119
71-950		43
71-951		41
71-952A, B		49
71-953		40
71-954		10
71-955		16
71-956		126
71-957		125
71-960		14
71-961		18
71-962		19
71-963		20
71-964		21
71-965		130
72-281	Fi 112456	50
72-288		132
72-329	Fi 112451	64
72-342	Fi 112448	70
72-353	Fi 107741	139
72-354		51
72-355/356	Fi 112476/477	53
72-357/405	Fi 112453	54
72-358		111
72-360		73
72-362		75
72-364		35
72-372		91
72-373		95
72-374		92
72-376		97
72-377		96
72-379		101
72-385		59
72-386		60
72-387		62
72-391		83
72-393		79
72-394		66
2-396		74
72-397		76
72-404		121
72-411		72
72-413		102
72-414		108
72-415		134
72-417		133
72-418		128
72-419		37
72-426		131
72-428		110
72-432		120
72-513		136
73-6	Fi 112452	65
73-44	Fi 112449	69
73-47		56
73-89		99
73-90		98
73-110		63
73-126		57
73-138		107
73-139		106
73-140		103
73-141		104
73-142		105
73-143		27
73-144		28
74-12		44
74-13		109
74-14		94
74-15		80
74-16		67
74-17		71
74-19		61
74-21		58
74-29		84
74-118; 72-371		90
75-15	Fi 107746	138
78-219		55

Abbreviations and Works Cited

Ancient Italy
1984 *Ancient Italy: Crossroads of the Mediterranean.* Ed. T. Hackens, N. D. Holloway, and R. Ross Holloway. Louvain and Providence.

Alimentazione
1987 *L'alimentazione nel mondo antico.* Ed. G. Barbieri. Rome.

Antiche officine
1993 *Antiche officine del bronzo.* Ed. E. Formigli. Siena.

Antiquarium
1988 *Antiquarium di Poggio Civitate.* Florence.

Amyx, D.
1988 *Corinthian Vase Painting of the Archaic Period.* Vol. 2. Berkeley.

Artefacts
1986 *Italian Iron Age Artefacts in the British Museum.* Ed. J. Swaddling. London.

Artimino
1987 *Artimino (Firenze) Scavi 1974.* Ed. G. Capecchi. Florence.

Aspetti e problemi
1974 *Aspetti e problemi dell'Etruria interna. Atti dell'VIII convegno nazionale di studi etruschi ed italici, Orvieto, 27–30 giugno 1972.* Florence.

Bagnasco Gianni, G.
1993 "A proposito di tre kyathoi in bucchero a rilievo." In *Bonghi Jovino* 1993:207–16.
1994 "Circolazioni culturali nel mondo antico. Un esempio in Etruria: Il piatto Spanti." *Studi etruschi* 59:3-21.

Barnett, R. D.
1975 *A Catalogue of the Nimrud Ivories.* London.

Bartoloni, G.
1972 *Le tombe di Poggio Buco nel Museo Archeologico di Firenze.* Florence.
1981 Review of T. B. Rasmussen, *Bucchero Pottery from Southern Etruria* (1979). In Archeologia classica 33:386–91.

Batignani, G.
1965 "Le oinochoai di bucchero pesante di tipo 'chiusino.'" *Studi etruschi* 33:295–316.

Beazley, J. D., and F. Magi
1939 *La raccolta Benedetto Guglielmi nel Museo Gregoriano Etrusco.* Vol. 1. Vatican City.

Bocci, P.
1965 "Catalogo della ceramica di Roselle." *Studi etruschi* 33:109–90.
1970 "Correnti di commercio ed influssi culturali a Roselle." In *Studi sulla cittá antica. Atti del convegno di studi sulla città etrusca e italica preromana,* 157–60. Bologna.

Bocci Pacini, P.
1973 "Un ritrovamento arcaico presso Castelnuovo Berardenga." *Studi etruschi* 41:121–41.

Bonamici, M.
1972 "Contributi alla classificazione del più antico bucchero decorato a rilievo. III. Il bucchero di produzione ceretana." *Studi etruschi* 40:95–114.
1974 *I buccheri con figurazione graffite*. Florence.
1989 "Contributo a Pisa aracaica." In *Secondo Congresso Internazionale Etrusco, Firenze, 26 maggio–2 giugno 1985, Atti*, vol. 2 (Rome, 1989):1135–47.

Bonfante, L.
1976 "The Orientalizing Context of the Etruscan Back Braid." In *In Memoriam Otto J. Brendel. Essays in Archaeology and the Humanities*, ed. L. Bonfante and H. von Heintze, 13–20. Mainz.

Bonghi Jovino, M., ed.
1993 *Produzione artigianale ed esportazione nel mondo antico. Il bucchero etrusco. Atti del colloquio internazionale, 10–11 maggio 1990*. Milan.

Bouloumié, B.
1978 "Nouveaux instruments culinaires en céramique de Murlo (Poggio Civitate)." *Mélanges de l'Ecole française de Rome, Antiquité* 90:113–31.
1982 "Le bucchero nero d'Etrurie." *Latomus* 41:773–84.
1986 "Vases de bronze étrusque du service de vin." In *Artefacts*: 63–79.

Bouloumié-Marique, A.
1978 "La céramique communale de Murlo (Poggio Civitate)." *Mélanges de l'Ecole française de Rome, Antiquité* 90:51–112.

Brijder, H. A. G.
1976 *Griekse, Etruskische en Romeinse Kunst. Allard Pierson Museum, Amsterdam*. Culemborg.

Brumfiel, E., and T. Earle
1987 "Specialization, Exchange, and Complex Societies. An Introduction." In *Specialization, Exchange, and Complex Societies*, ed. E. Brumfiel and T. Earle, 1–9. Cambridge.

Bucchero nero
1979 *Le bucchero nero étrusque et sa diffusion en Gaule Méridionale*. Actes de la Table-Ronde d'Aix-en-Provence, 21–23 mai 1975. Collection Latomus 160. Brussels.

Camerini, G.
1985 *Il bucchero etrusco*. Rome.

Camporeale, G.
1962 "Considerazioni su un'anfora di bucchero." *Arte Antica e Moderna* 5:130–45.
1964 "Aggiunta alle 'considerazioni su un'anfora di bucchero." *Arte Antica e Moderna*:244.
1967 *La tomba del Duce*. Florence.
1969 *I commerci di Vetulonia in età orientalizzante*. Florence.
1970 *La collezione Alla Querce*. Florence.
1972a *I buccheri a cilindretto di fabbrica orvietana*. Florence.
1972b "Buccheri a cilindretto di fabbrica tarquiniese." *Studi etruschi* 40:115–49.
1991 *La collezione C. A. Impasti e buccheri I*. Rome.
1994 "Un gruppo di vasi bronzei chiusini di facies orientalizzante." *Studi etruschi* 59:29-37.
1995 "Un ceramista ceretano a Massa Marittima." *Studi etruschi* 60:69-77.
1997 *L'abitato etrusco dell'Accesa. Il quartiere B*. Rome.

Capecchi, G., and A. Gunnella
1975 "Calici di bucchero a sostegni figurati." *Atti e Memorie dell'Accademia Toscana La Columbaria* 40:33–116.

Caputo, G.
1962 "Gli Athyrmata orientali della Montagnola e la via dell'Arno e transappeninica." *Arte Antica e Moderna* 5:58–72.
1974 "Cultura orientalizzante della vallata dell'Arno." In *Aspetti e problemi:* 19–53.

Case e palazzi
1985 *Case e palazzi d'Etruria*. Ed. S. Stopponi. Milan.

Castenaso
1979 *La necropoli villanoviana di Ca' dell'Orbo*

a Villanova di Castenaso: problemi del popolamento dal IX al VI secolo a.c. Ed. S. Tovoli and D. Vitali. Bologna.

Cento preziosi
1984 *Cento preziosi etruschi: catalogo della mostra dal 7 settembre 1984; centro affari e promozioni; dal 20 ottobre 1984; anfiteatro romano arezzo.* Florence.

Cerveteri
1980 *Gli Etruschi e Cerveteri: nuove acquisizioni delle Civiche raccolte archeologiche: la prospezione archeologica nell'attività della Fondazione Lerici. Milano. Palazzo Reale, settembre 1980–gennaio 1981.* Ed. M. Bugli. Milan.
1986 *Gli Etruschi di Cerveteri: la necropoli di Monte Abatone.* Ed. B. Bosio and A. Pugnetti. Modena.

Cherici, A.
1988 *Ceramica etrusca della collezione Poggiali di Firenze.* Rome.

Chianciano
1986 *Le necropoli etrusche di Chianciano Terme.* Ed. A. Rastrelli. Montepulciano.

Cimino, L.
1986 *La collezione Mieli nel Museo Archeologico di Siena.* Rome.

Civiltà
1985 *Civiltà degli Etruschi.* Ed. M. Cristofani. Milan.

Civiltà di Chiusi
1993 *La civiltà di Chiusi e del suo territorio. Atti del XVII convegno di studi etruschi ed italici, Chianciano Terme, 28 maggio–1 giugno 1989.* Florence.

CLP
1976 *Civiltà del Lazio primitivo.* Rome.

Colonna, G.
1973 "Ricerche sull'Etruria interna Volsiniese." *Studi etruschi* 41:45–72.
1973–74 "Nomi etruschi di vasi." *Archeologia classica* 25–26:132–50.

Cortona
1992 *La Cortona dei Principes.* Ed. P. Z. Grassi. Cortona.

Costin, C.
1991 "Craft Specialization: Issues in Defining, Documenting, and Explaining the Organization of Production." In *Archaeological Method and Theory*, vol. 3, ed. M. Schiffer, 1–56. Tucson.

Cottier-Angeli, F.
1991 "Technical Notes on Impasto and Bucchero Wares." In Jucker 1991:292–94.

Cristofani, M.
1969 *Le tombe da Monte Michele nel Museo Archeologico di Firenze.* Florence.
1971 "Per una nuova lettura della pisside della Pania." *Studi etruschi* 39:63–89.
1972 "Contributi alla classificazione del più antico bucchero decorato a rilievo. II. Osservazioni sul kyathos di Monteriggioni." *Studi etruschi* 40:84–94.
1974 "A proposito della via dell'Arno." In *Aspetti e problemi*:67–69.
1975 "Considerazioni su Poggio Civitate (Murlo, Siena)." *Prospettiva* 1:9–17.
1987a "Duo sunt liquores." In *Alimentazione*: 37–40.
1987b "Il banchetto in Etruria." In *Alimentazione*:123–34.

Cristofani, M., and K. M. Phillips, Jr.
1971 "Poggio Civitate. Etruscan Letters and Chronological Observations." *Studi etruschi* 39:409–30.

Cristofani, M., and F. Zevi
1965 "La tomba Campana di Veio. Il corredo." *Archeologia classica* 17:1–35.

Crowfoot, J. W. and G. M. Crowfoot
1938 *Early Ivories from Sumuria.* London.

Cuomo di Caprio
1993 "Annotazioni tecniche circa la cottura del bucchero." In Bonghi Jovino:217–22.

Curtis, C. D.
1925 "The Barberini Tomb." *Memoirs of the American Academy at Rome*:9-52.

Damgaard Andersen, H.
1990 "The Feline Waterspouts of the Lateral

Sima from the Upper Building at Poggio Civitate, Murlo." Opuscula romana 18:61–98.
1992/1993 "The origin of the Potnia Theron in Central Italy." *Hamburger Beiträge zur Archäologie* 19/20:73-133.

De Puma, R. D.
1981[1984] "Etruscan Gold and Silver Jewelry from Poggio Civitate (Murlo)." *Archeologia classica* 33:78–92.
1986 *Etruscan Tomb-Groups: Ancient Pottery and Bronzes in Chicago's Field Museum of Natural History*. Mainz am Rhine.

De Puma, R. D., and J. P. Small, eds.
1994 *Murlo and the Etruscans: Art and Society in Ancient Etruria*. Philadelphia.

Dohan, E. H.
1942 *Italic Tomb-Groups in the University Museum*. Philadelphia.

Donati, L.
1967 "Buccheri decorati con teste plastiche umane. Zona di Vulci." *Studi etruschi* 35:619-32.
1968 "Vasi di bucchero con teste plastiche umane. Zona di Chiusi." *Studi etruschi* 36:319–56.
1969 "Vasi di bucchero con teste plastiche umane. Zona di Orvieto." *Studi etruschi* 37:441–62.
1977 "Skyphoi chiusini di bucchero con anse piatte." *Studi etruschi* 45:85–108.
1988 "Roselle (Grosseto): le ceramiche di due pozzetti in roccia sulla collina settentrionale." *Notizie degli scavi di antichità* 38–39 (1984–85):69–94.
1989 *Le tombe da Saturnia nel Museo Archeologico di Firenze*. Florence.
1991 "L'atelier delle rosette." *Studi e materiali* 6:82–99.
1994 *La casa dell'impluvium. Archittetura etrusca a Roselle*. Rome.

Donati, L., and M. Michelucci
1981 *La collezione Ciacci nel Museo Archeologico di Grosseto*. Rome.

EAA
1959 *Enciclopedia dell'arte antica, classica, e orientale*. Rome.

Edlund, I. E. M.
1980 *The Iron Age and Etruscan Vases in the Olcott Collection at Columbia University, New York*. Transactions of the American Philological Association 70, 1.
1987 *The Gods and the Place: The Location and Function of Sanctuaries in the Countryside of Etruria and Magna Graecia (700–400 B.C.)*. Stockholm.

Edlund-Berry, I. E. M.
1989 "Four Terracotta Heads from Poggio Civitate (Murlo). Towards a Definition of the 'Murlo Style'." *Opuscala romana* 17:21-32.
1992 *The Seated and Standing Akroteria from Poggio Civitate*. Rome.
1994 "Ritual Destruction of Cities and Sanctuaries. The 'Un-founding' of the Archaic Monumental Building at Poggio Civitate (Murlo)." In De Puma and Small 1994:16–28.

Enea
1981 *Enea nel Lazio: archeologia e mito. Mostra in occasione del bimillenario virgiliano, Roma, 22 settembre–31 dicembre 1981*. Rome.

ER 2
1956 E. Gjerstad. Early Rome. Vol. 2, *The Tombs*. Lund.

ER 3
1960 E. Gjerstad. *Early Rome. Vol. 3, Fortifications, Domestic Architecture, Sanctuaries, and Stratigraphic Excavations*. Lund.

ER 4
1966 E. Gjerstad. *Early Rome. Vol. 4, part 1, Synthesis of Archaeological Evidence*. Lund.

Etruria mineraria
1985 *L'Etruria Mineraria: catalogo della mostra Portoferraio-Massa Marritima-Populonia, 25 maggio–20 ottobre 1985*. Ed. G. Camporeale. Florence.

Etrusker
1987 *Etrusker in der Toskana. Etruskische Gräber der Frühzeit*. Ed. M. Cygielman. Florence.

Fairbanks, A.
1928 *Museum of Fine Arts, Boston: Catalogue of Greek and Etruscan Vases*. Cambridge.

Falchi, I.
1965 *Vetulonia e la sua necropolis antichissima*. Rome.

Falconi Amorelli, M. T.
1968 "Materiali di Ischia di Castro conservati nel Museo di Villa Giulia." *Studi Etruschi* 36:169–77.
1983 *Vulci. Scavi Bendinelli (1919–1923)*. Rome.

Falconi Amorelli, M. T., and E. Fabricotti
1971 "Materiali archeologici da Vulci." *Studi etruschi* 39:193–211.

Francaviglia, V., M. E. Minardi, and A. Palmieri
1975 "Comparative Study of Various Samples of Etruscan Bucchero by X-Ray Diffraction, X-Ray Spectrometry, and Thermoanalysis." *Archaeometry* 17:223–31.

Gierow, P. G.
1966 *The Iron Age Culture of Latium. Vol. 1, Classification and Analysis*. Lund.

Giglioli, G. Q.
1935 *L'arte etrusca*. Milan.

Gran-Aymerich, J. M.
1972 "Situles orientalisantes du VII siècle en Etrurie." *Mélanges de l'Ecole française de Rome, Antiquité* 84:7–59.
1979 "Bucchero, impasto et les tumuli Banditaccia 1 et 2 à Cerveteri." *Latomus* 38:3:597–636.
1982 *CVA France 31. Louvre 20*. Paris.
1992 *CVA France 34. Louvre 23*. Paris.
1993 "Observations générales sur l'évolution et la diffusion du bucchero." In Bonghi Jovino:19–42.
1995 "Le bucchero et les vases métalliques." In *Vaisselle métallique, vaiselle céramique. Productions, usages et valeurs en Étrurie*, ed. J. R. Jannot, *Revue des études anciennes* 97:1-2:45–76.

Gras, M.
1985 *Trafics tyrrhéniens archaïques*. Paris.

Gregori, D.
1991 "Una bottega vetuloniese di buccheri ed impasti orientalizzanti decorati a stampiglia." *Studi e materiali* 6:64–81.

Guzzo, P. G.
1969 "La collezione etrusca del Museo Nazionale di Atene." *Studi etruschi* 37:289–302.

Hayes, J. W.
1985 *Etruscan and Italic Pottery in the Royal Ontario Museum*. Toronto.

Hencken, H.
1968 *Tarquinia, Villanovans, and Early Etruscans. American School of Prehistoric Research Bulletin* 23. Cambridge.

Herrmann, G.
1986 *Ivories from Nimrud* (1949–1963). *Fasc. IV, 1–2, Ivories from Room SW 37, Fort Shalmaneser*. London.

Howes-Smith, P. H. G.
1984 "Bronze Ribbed Bowls from Central Italy and Etruria: Import and Imitation." *Bulletin antieke beschaving* 59:73–107.

Jannot, J. R.
1988 "Lieux de culte en Italie préromaine." *Journal of Roman Archaeology* 1:95–96.

Johansen, F.
1971 *Reliefs en bronze d'Etrurie*. Copenhagen.

Jucker, I.
1991 *Italy of the Etruscans*. Mainz.

Krauskopf, I.
1984 "Artumes" in *LIMC* II.1:774–92.

Leoni, M., and C. Trabucchi
1962 "Alcuni dati tecnici sulla colorazione nera dei buccheri etruschi." *Studi etruschi* 30:257–66.

Levi, D.
1936 "I canopi di Chiusi." *Critica d'Arte* 1:82–89.

Mangani, E.
1986 *CVA Grosseto* 2. Italy 63.
1990 "L'orientalizzante recente nella valle dell'Ombrone." *Annali. Istituto universitario orientale, Dipartimento di studi del mondo classico e del mediterraneo antico, Sezione di archeologia e storia antica (Napoli)* 12:9–21.

1992 "Castlenuovo Berardenga (Siena). L'orientalizzante recente in Etruria settentrionale:tomba A della necropoli princepesca del Poggione (1980)," *NSc* XLII–XLIII (1998–1999):5–84.

1987 *La ceramica degli Etruschi*. Novara.

Martelli, M.
1978 "La Ceramica Greco-Orientale in Etruria." In *Les céramiques de la Grèce de l'est et leur diffusion en occident*. Paris.

Materiali I–V
1962–66 *Materiali di antichità varia*. Vols. I–V. Rome.

Matteucig, G.
1951 *Poggio Buco*. Berkeley and Los Angeles.

Mengarelli, R.
1927 "Caere e le recenti scoperte: nuovi scavi nel selpocreto dellà Banditaccia." *Studi etruschi* 1:145–171.

Micozzi, M.
1989 *La collezione preromana del Museo Nazionale de L'Aquila. Biblioteca di Studi Etruschi* 18. Florence.

Miller, R. L.
1982 "A Late Villanovan Vase From Bologna." In *Artefacts*:267–71.

Mingazzini, P.
1930 *Catalogo dei vasi della Collezione Castellani*. Rome.

Minto, A.
1935 "Per la topografia di Heba etrusca nel territorio di Magliano in Toscana." *Studi etruschi* 9:11-59.
1943 *Populonia*. Florence.

Monaci, M.
1965 "Catalogo del Museo Archeologico Vescovile di Pienza." *Studi etruschi* 33:425–68.

Montelius, O.
1889 "Preclassical Chronology in Greece and Italy." *Journal of the Anthropological Institute of Great Britain* 26:79–106.
1904–1910 *La civilisation primitive en Italie*. Stockholm.

Naumann, R., and F. Hiller
1959 "Rusellae." *Mitteilungen des Deutschen Archäologischen Instituts, Römische Abteilung* 66:1–27.

Nicosia, F.
1972 "Un bucchero di Artimino." *Studi etruschi* 40:375–90.
1974 "Orientalizzante nella media valle del-l'Arno. Aspetti dell'artigianato artistico. Prima messa a punto sulla produzione del bucchero." In *Aspetti e problemi*:55–66.

Nielsen, E. O.
1974 "The Murlo Ivories." Ph.D. diss., Bryn Mawr College.
1984a "Speculations on an Ivory Workshop of the Orientalizing Period." In *Ancient Italy*:333–48.
1984b "Lotus Chain Plaques from Poggio Civitate." In *Studi di antichità in onore di Guglielmo Maetzke*:397–99. Rome.
1984c Review of P. J. Riis, Etruscan Types of Heads. A Revised Chronology of the Archaic and Classical Terracottas of Etruscan Campania and Central Italy. In *Archaeological News* 13:48–49.
1987 "Some Preliminary Thoughts on New and Old Terracottas." *Opuscula romana* 16:91–119.
1989a "Excavations at Poggio Civitate, Italy." *American Journal of Archaeology* 93:258.
1989b "A New Lateral Sima from Poggio Civitate (Murlo)." In *Secondo Congresso Internazionale Etrusco*, 26 maggio–2 giugno 1985, Atti, vol. 1 (Rome, 1989):509–15.
1991 "Excavations at Poggio Civitate." *Studi e materiali* 6:245–59.
1993 "Further Evidence for Metal Working

at Poggio Civitate." In *Antiche officine*:29–40.
1994a "Aspects of Bronze Production in Seventh-Century Etruria." *American Journal of Archaeology* 98:319.
1994b "Interpreting the Lateral Sima at Poggio Civitate." In De Puma and Small 1994:64–71.
1995 "Aspetti della produzione artigianale a Poggio Civitate." In *Preziosi in oro, avorio, osso, e corno. Arte e tecniche degli artigiani etruschi*, ed. E. Formigli, 19–26. Siena.
1996 "Seventh-Century Bronze Production at Poggio Civitate." *American Journal of Archaeology* 100:380.
1998 "Bronze Production at Poggio Civitate (Murlo)." *Etruscan Studies* 5:95–107.

Nielsen, E. O., and K. M. Phillips Jr.
1974 "Bryn Mawr College Excavations in Tuscany, 1973." *American Journal of Archaeology* 78:265–78.
1975 "Bryn Mawr College Excavations in Tuscany, 1974." *American Journal of Archaeology* 79:357–66.
1976 "Poggio Civitate (Siena)—Gli Scavi del Bryn Mawr College dal 1966 al 1974." *Notizie degli scavi di antichità* 30:113–47.
1977a "Bryn Mawr College Excavations in Tuscany, 1975." *American Journal of Archaeology* 81:85–100.
1977b "Murlo (Siena)." *Studi etruschi* 45: 464–66.
1986 "Excavations at Poggio Civitate, Murlo (Siena), 1976–1978." *Notizie degli scavi di antichità* 37 (1983):5–24.

Nijboer, A. J.
1998 *From Household Production to Workshops. Archaeological Evidence for Economic Transformation, Pre-Monetary Exchange and Urbanization in Central Italy from 800 to 400 B.C.* Groningen.

Palm, J.
1952 "Veiian Tomb Groups in the Museo Preistorico, Rome." *Opuscula archeologica* 7:50–86.

Paolucci, G.
1988 *Il territorio di Chianciano Terme dalla preistoria al medioevo*. Rome.

Pareti, L.
1947 *La tomba Regionali-Galassi del Museo Gregoriano Etrusco*. Vatican City.

Payne, H.
1931 *Necrocorinthia*. Oxford.

Pecchiai, I.
1967 "Catalogo dei buccheri del Museo Civico di Fiesole." *Studi etruschi* 35:487–514.

Pellegrini, E.
1989 *La necropoli di Poggio Buco—nuovi dati per lo studio di un centro dell'Etruria interna nei periodi orientalizzante ed arcaico*. Florence.

Phillips, K. M., Jr.
1968 "Bryn Mawr College Excavations in Tuscany, 1967." *American Journal of Archaeology* 72:121–24.
1969 "Bryn Mawr College Excavations in Tuscany, 1968." *American Journal of Archaeology* 73:333–39.
1970 "Bryn Mawr College Excavations in Tuscany, 1969." *American Journal of Archaeology* 74:241–44.
1971 "Bryn Mawr College Excavations in Tuscany, 1970." *American Journal of Archaeology* 75:257–61.
1972 "Bryn Mawr College Excavations in Tuscany, 1971." *American Journal of Archaeology* 76:249–55.
1973a "Bryn Mawr College Excavations in Tuscany, 1972." *American Journal of Archaeology* 77:319–26.
1973b "Two Archaic Bronzes from Poggio Civitate." *Opuscula romana* 9:177–82.
1980 "The Date of the Archaeological Terracottas from Poggio Civitate (Murlo, Siena)." *La parola del passato* 35:202–6.
1989a "Greek Objects at Poggio Civitate." *Analecta Romana Instituti Danici* 17–18:28–42.
1989b "Notes from Berlin on a Bronze Owl." *Opuscula romana* 17:97–122.
1993 *In the Hills of Tuscany: Recent Excavations at the Site of Poggio Civitate (Murlo, Siena)*. Philadelphia.
1994 "Stamped Impasto Pottery Manufactured at Poggio Civitate." In De Puma and Small:24–46.

Pieraccini, L.
1996 "A Storage Vase for Life. The Caeretane Dolio and Its Decorative Elements." In *Etruscan Italy. Etruscan Influences on the Civilization of Italy from Antiquity to the Modern Era*, ed. J. F. Hall, 93–113. Provo.

Pohl, I.
1981 "San Giovenale. The Semi-Subterranean Building in Area B. The Pottery." *San Giovenale* 2:4:19-84. Stockholm.

Pottier, E.
1897 *Vases antiques du Louvre. Salles A-E*. Paris.

Prayon, F.
1975 *Frühetruskische Grab- und Hausarchitektur*. Heidelberg.

Puglisi, M.
1959 *La civiltà apenninica*. Florence.

Ramage, N. H.
1970 "Studies in Early Etruscan Bucchero." *Papers of the British School at Rome* 38:1–61.

Rasmussen, T. B.
1979 *Bucchero Pottery from Southern Etruria*. Cambridge.

Rathje, A.
1983 "A Banquet Service from the Latin City of Ficana." *Analecta Romana Instituti Danici* 12:7–29.
1988 "Manners and Customs in Orientalizing Central Italy: Influence from the Near East." *Acta Hyperborea* 1:81–90.
1989 "Alcuni considerazioni sulle lastre da Poggio Civitate con figure femminili." In *Le donne in Etruria*, ed. A. Rallo, 75–84. Rome.
1990 "The Adoption of the Homeric Banquet in Central Italy in the Orientalizing Period." In *Sympotica: A Symposium on the Symposion*, ed. O. Murray, 279–88. Oxford.
1994 "Banquet and Ideology: Some New Considerations about Banqueting at Poggio Civitate." In De Puma and Small:95–99.

Reusser, C.
1988 *Antikenmuseum Basel und Sammlung Ludwig. Etruskische Kunst*. Basel.

Ricci, G
1955 "Caere. Scavi di Raniero Mengarelli. III. Necropoli della Banditaccía zona A 'del recinto'." *Monumenti Antichi* 42:202–1047

Riccioni, G., and M. T. Falconi Amorelli
1968 *La tomba Panatenaica di Vulci. Quaderni di Villa Giulia 3*. Rome.

Richter, G. M. A.
1936 "The Technique of Bucchero Ware." *Studi etruschi* 10:62–65.

Rizzo, M. A.
1990 *Le anfore da trasporto e il commercio etrusco arcaico. Vol. 1, Complessi tombali dall'Etruria meridionale*. Rome.

Roselle
1978 *Roselle: gli scavi e la mostra*. Ed. G. Maetzke. Pisa.

Rystedt, E.
1983 *Acquarossa. Vol. 4, Early Etruscan Akroteria from Acquarossa and Poggio Civitate (Murlo)*. Stockholm.
1984 "Architectural Terracottas as Aristocratic Display. The Case of Seventh-Century Poggio Civitate (Murlo)." *Opus* 3.2:367–76.

Salskov Roberts, H.
1974 "Five Tomb Groups in the Danish National Museum from Narce, Capena and Poggio Sommavilla." *Acta Archaeologica* 45:49–106.
1988 "Some Observations on Etruscan Bowls with Supports in the Shape of Caryatids or Adorned by Reliefs." *Acta Hyperborea* 1:69–80.

Scalia, F.
1968 "I cilindretti di tipo chiusino con figure umane (contributo allo studio dei buccheri neri a cilindretto)." *Studi etruschi* 36:357–402.

Serra Ridgway, F. R.
1986 "Impasto ceretano stampigliato: Gli esemplari del British Museum: Origini e affinità." In *Artefacts*:283–292.

SG
1967–72 *San Giovenale. Results of the Excavations Conducted by the Swedish Institute for Classical Studies at Rome and the Soprintendenza alle antichità dell'Etruria meridionale*. Ed. C. E. Östenberg. Stockholm.

Shefton, B. B.
1979 *Die "rhodischen" Bronzekannen*. Mainz.

Shuey, E. B.
1983 *Etruscan Maritime Activity in the Western Mediterranean*. Ann Arbor.

Small, J. P.
1971 "The Etruscan Banquet Frieze from Poggio Civitate (Murlo)." *Studi etruschi* 39:25–61.

Steingräber, S.
1985 *Catalogo ragionato della pittura etrusca*. Milan.

Stoddart, S.
1995 "Divergent Trajectories in Central Italy 1200–500 b.c." In *Centre and Periphery. Comparative Studies in Archaeology*, ed. T. Champion, 88–101. London.

Strøm, I.
1971 *Problems Concerning the Origin and Development of the Etruscan Orientalizing Style*. Odense.
1981 Review of T. B. Rasmussen, Bucchero Pottery from Southern Etruria (1979). In *Gnomon* 53:789–92.

Swaddling, J., S. Walker, and P. Roberts, eds.
1995 *Italy in Europe: Economic Relations 700 B.C.–A.D. 50*. British Museum Occasional Paper 97. London.

Szilágyi, J. G.
1981 *CVA Hungary* 1. Budapest 1.
1992 *Ceramica etrusco-corinizia figurata. Parte I, 630–580*. Florence.

Talocchini, A
1963 "La città e la necropoli di Vetulonia secondo i nuovi scavi (1959–1962)," *Studi etruschi* 31:435–51.

Thureau-Dangin, F., A. Barrois, G. Dossin, and M. Dunand
1931 *Arslan-Tash*. Paris.

TLE^2
1968 *Testimonia Linguae Etruscae*. Ed. M. Pallottino. Florence.

Tobey, M. H., E. O. Nielsen, and M. W. Rowe
1986 "Elemental Analysis of Etruscan Ceramics from Murlo, Italy." In *Proceedings of the 24th International Archaeometry Symposium*, ed. J. S. Olin and M. J. Blackman, 115–27. Washington, D.C.

Torelli, M.
1983 "Polis e 'palazzo.' Architettura, ideologia e artigianato greco in Etruria tra VII e VI sec. a.C." In *Architecture et société de l'archaïsme grec à la fin del république romaine. Collection de l'Ecole Française de Rome*, vol. 66. Rome, 1980.

Tuck, A.
1994 "The Villanovan Seated Banquet: Villanovan Ritual and Etruscan Iconography." *American Journal of Archaeology* 98:617-28.
1996a "Burials from Poggio Aguzzo: The Necropolis of Poggio Civitate (Murlo)." Ph.D. diss., Brown University.
1996b "New Burials from Poggio Aguzzo (Murlo): Economic and Cultural Development in Orientalizing-Period Etruria." *American Journal of Archaeology* 100:399–400.

Turfa, J. M.
1986 "International Contacts: Commerce, Trade and Foreign Affairs." In *Etruscan Life and Afterlife*, ed. L. Bonfante. Detroit.

Valentini, G.
1969 "Il motivo della potnia theron sui vasi di bucchero." *Studi etruschi* 37:413–40.

Versilia
1990 *Etruscorum ante quam Ligurum. La Versilia tra VII e III secolo a.C.* Ed. E. Paribeni. Pontedara.

Villard, F.
1962 "Les canthares de bucchero et la chronologie du commerce étrusque d'importation." In *Hommages à Albert Grenier. Collection Latomus* 58.3:1625–35. Brussels.

Villard, F., and G. Vallet
1955 "Megara Hyblaea, lampes du IIe siècle et chronologie des coupes ioniennes." *Mélanges de l'Ecole française de Rome, Antiquité* 67:7–34.

von Mercklin, E.
1936 "Etruskische Keramik in Hamburgischen Museum für Kunst und Gewerbe." *Studi etruschi* 10:387–98.

Vulci
1965 Vulci. Zona dell' "Osteria." *Scavi di Hercle*. Vol. 1. Rome.

Wadsworth, M.
1983 "A Potter's Experience with the Method of Firing Bucchero." *Opuscula romana* 14:65–68.

Walter-Karydi, E.
1973 *Samos. Band VI.1. Samische Gefässe des 6. Jahrunderts v. Chr. Landschaftsstile Ostgriechischer Gefässe.* Bonn.

Warden, P. G.
1982 "Two Archaic Bronzes from Poggio Civitate." *American Journal of Archaeology* 86:233–38.
1985 *The Metal Finds from Poggio Civitate (Murlo), 1966–1978*. Rome.
1993 "Copper, Iron, and Smelting Technologies in Iron Age Etruria: New Evidence from Poggio Civitate (Murlo)." In *Antiche officine*:41–51.

Warden, P. G., R. Maddin, T. Stech, and J. D. Muhly
1982 "Copper and Iron Production at Poggio Civitate (Murlo): Analysis of Metalworking By-Products from an Archaic Etruscan Site." *Expedition* 25.1:26–35.
1991 "Analysis of Metalworking By-Products from Poggio Civitate (Murlo)." *Studi e Materiali* 6 (1983):151–56.

Weinberg, S.
1954 "Corinthian Relief Ware: Pre-Hellenistic Period." *Hesperia* 23:109–37.

Wikander, C.
1981 *Aquarossa. Results of the Excavations Conducted by the Swedish Institute of Classical Studies at Rome and the Soprintendenza alle antichità dell'Etruria Meridionale. Vol. 1, The Painted Architectural Terracottas. Part 1, Catalogue and Architectural Context*. Stockholm.
1988 *Aquarossa. Results of the Excavations Conducted by the Swedish Institute of Classical Studies at Rome and the Soprintendenza alle antichità dell'Etruria Meridionale. Vol. 1, The Painted Architectural Terracottas. Part 2, Typological and Decorative Analysis*. Stockholm.

Wikander, Ö.
1990 "Archaic Roof Tiles: The First Generations." *Hesperia* 59:285–90.

Winter, N.
1977 "Architectural Terracottas with Human Heads from Poggio Civitate (Murlo)." *Archeologia classica* 29:17–34.

Wisseman, S. U.
1978 "Observations on the Technique of Etruscan Bucchero Pesante: Selected Examples from the University Museum, Philadelphia." *Archaeological News* 7.3:45–60.

FIGURE 9. Molded Oinochoe Fragment, 1

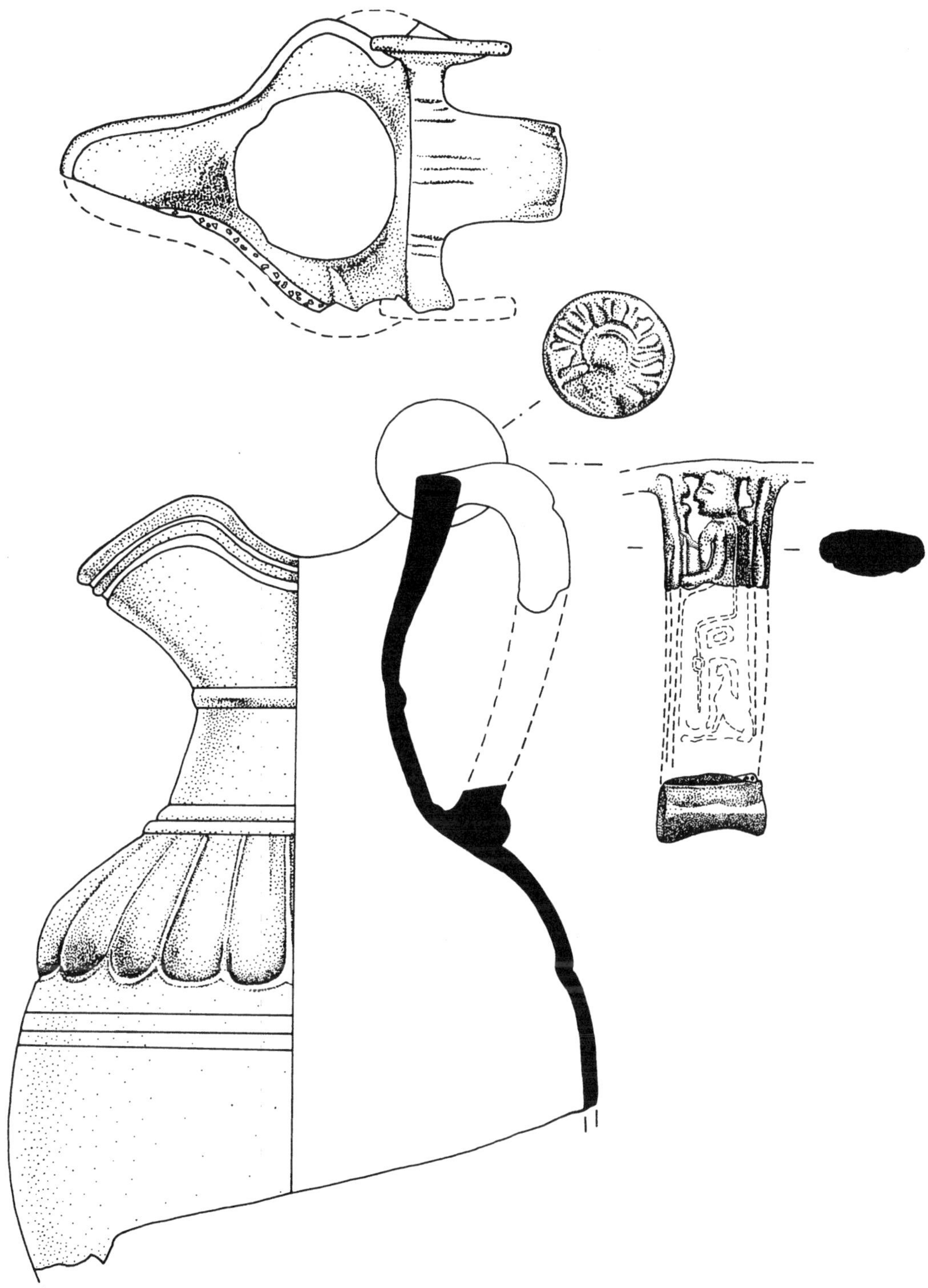

1

0cm 5cm

1:2

FIGURE 10. Oinochoe Handle Fragment, 3; Fragmentary Oinochoe, 4; Alabastron, 5; Kantharos, 6

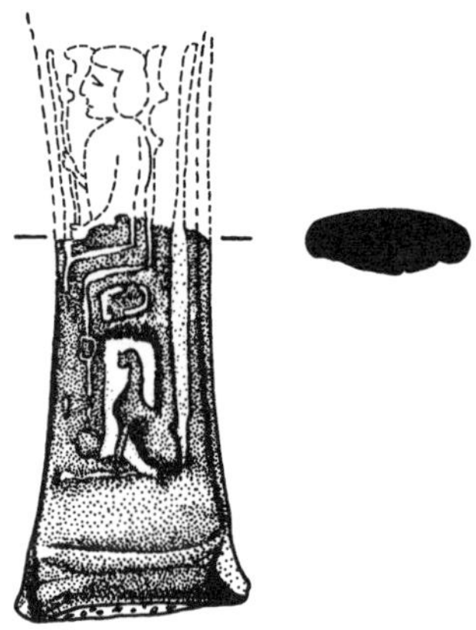

3

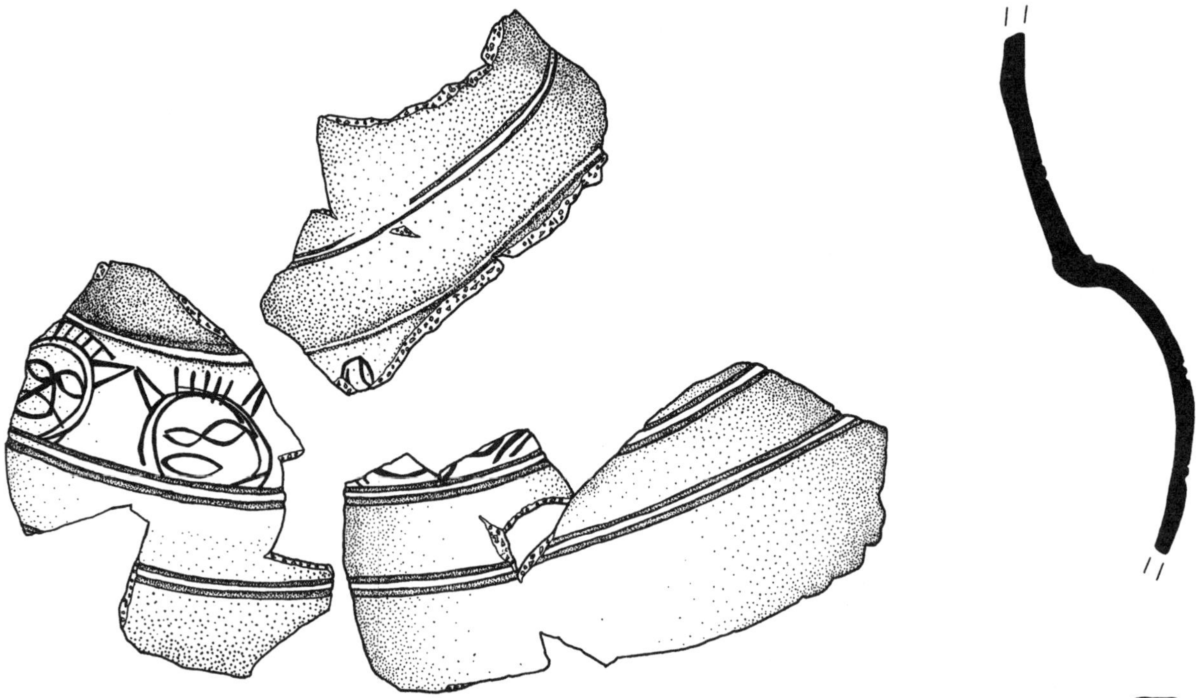

4

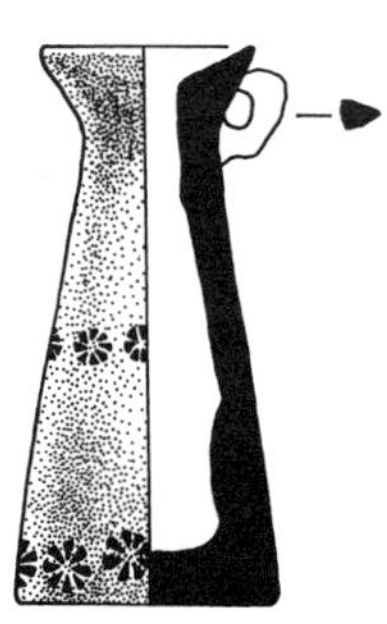

5

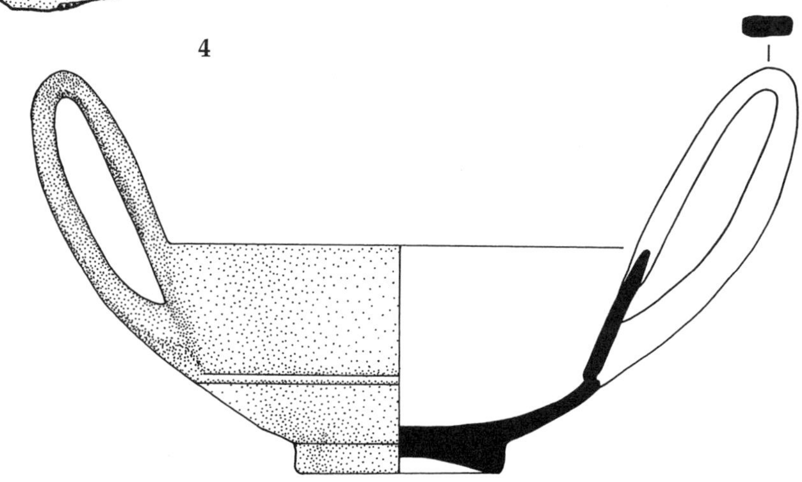

6

0cm 5cm

1:2

FIGURE 11. Kantharos Fragment, 7; Kantharos Fragment, 8; Kantharos Fragment, 9; Kantharos, 11

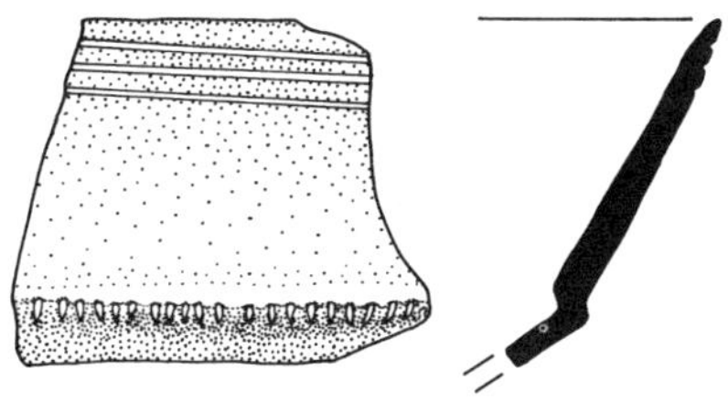

7

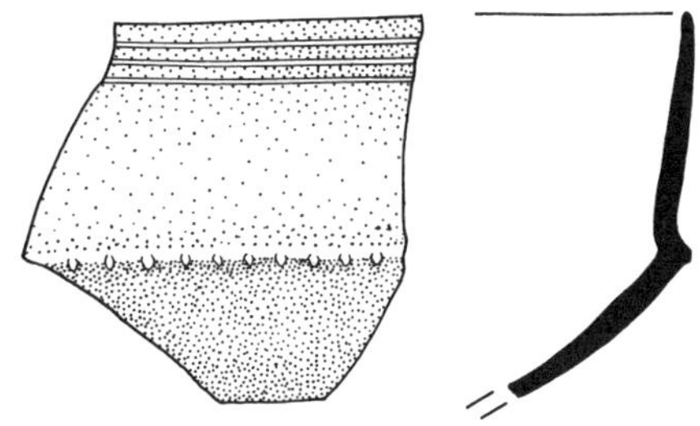

8

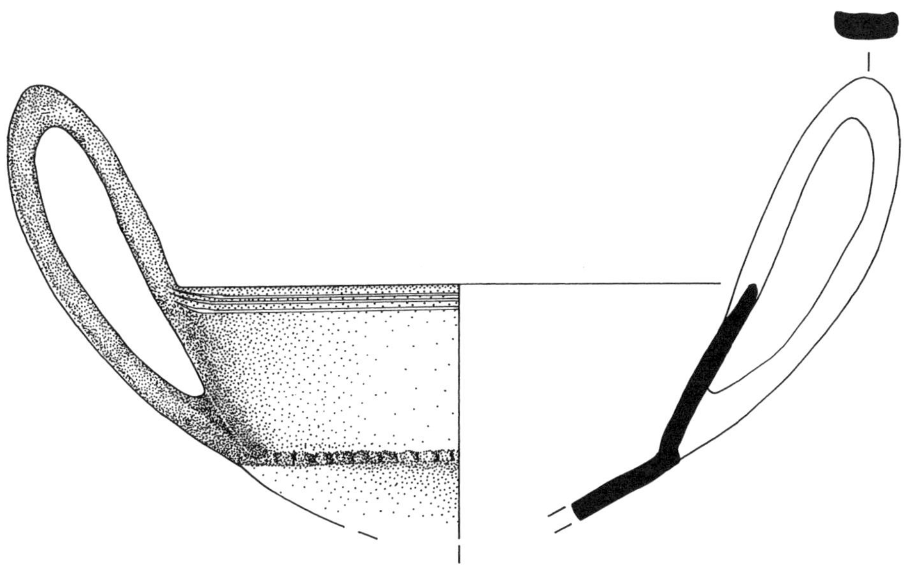

9

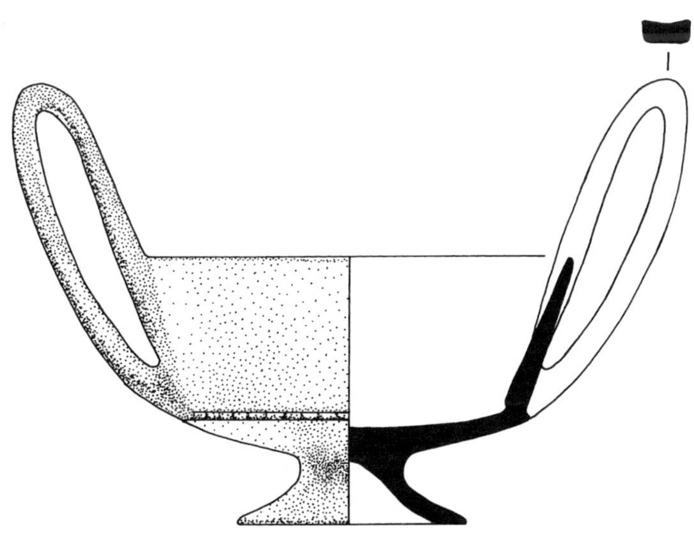

11

0cm 5cm

1:2

FIGURE 12. Kantharos 13; Kantharos, 15; Kantharos Fragment 17

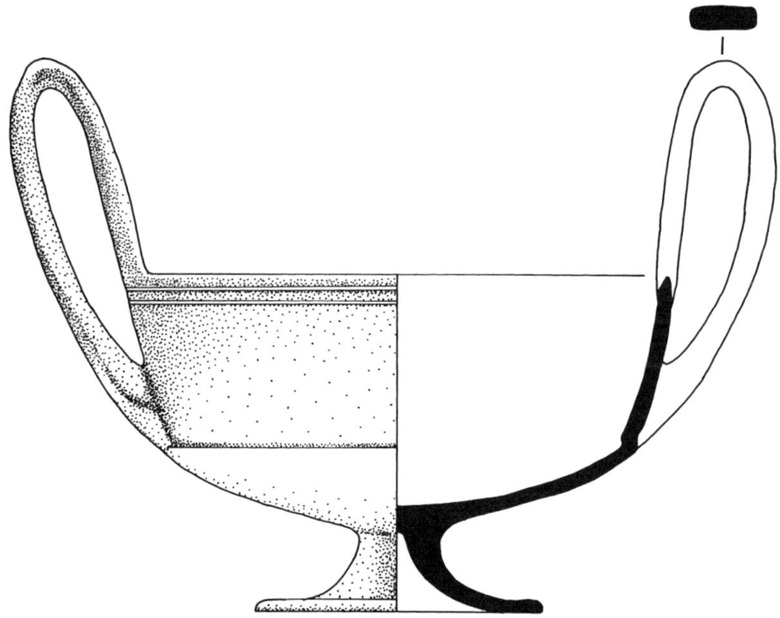

13

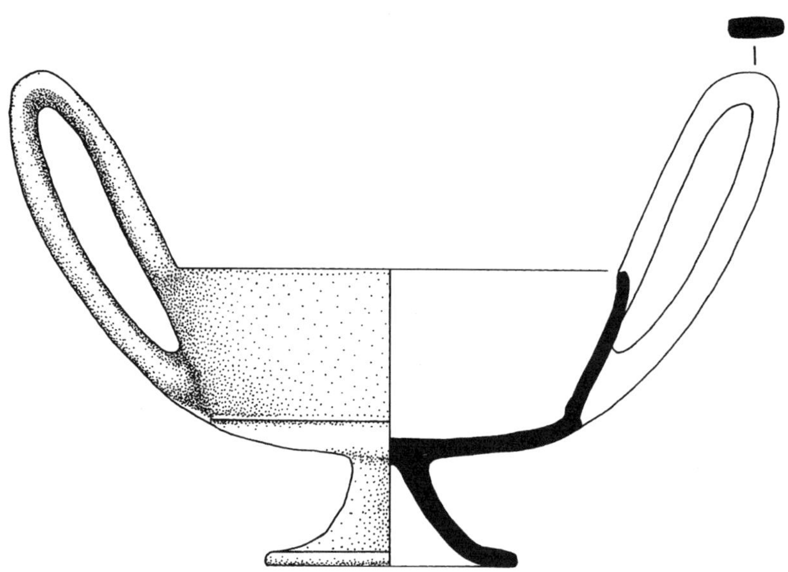

15

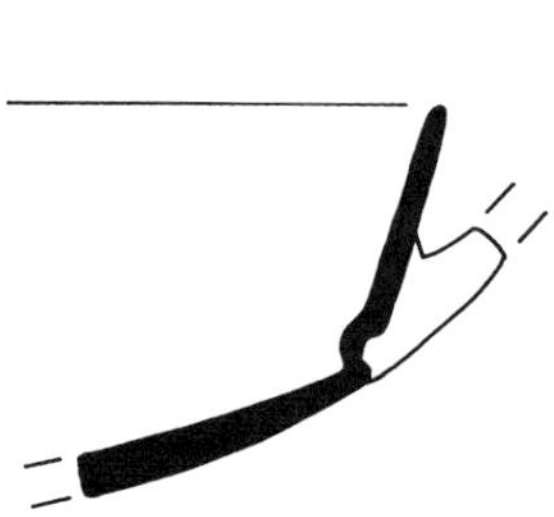

17

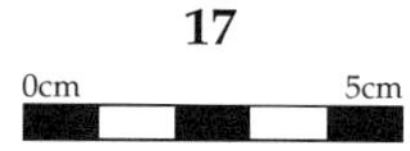

1:2

FIGURE 13. Kyathos Fragment, 22; Kyathos Handle Fragment, 23; Kyathos, 24

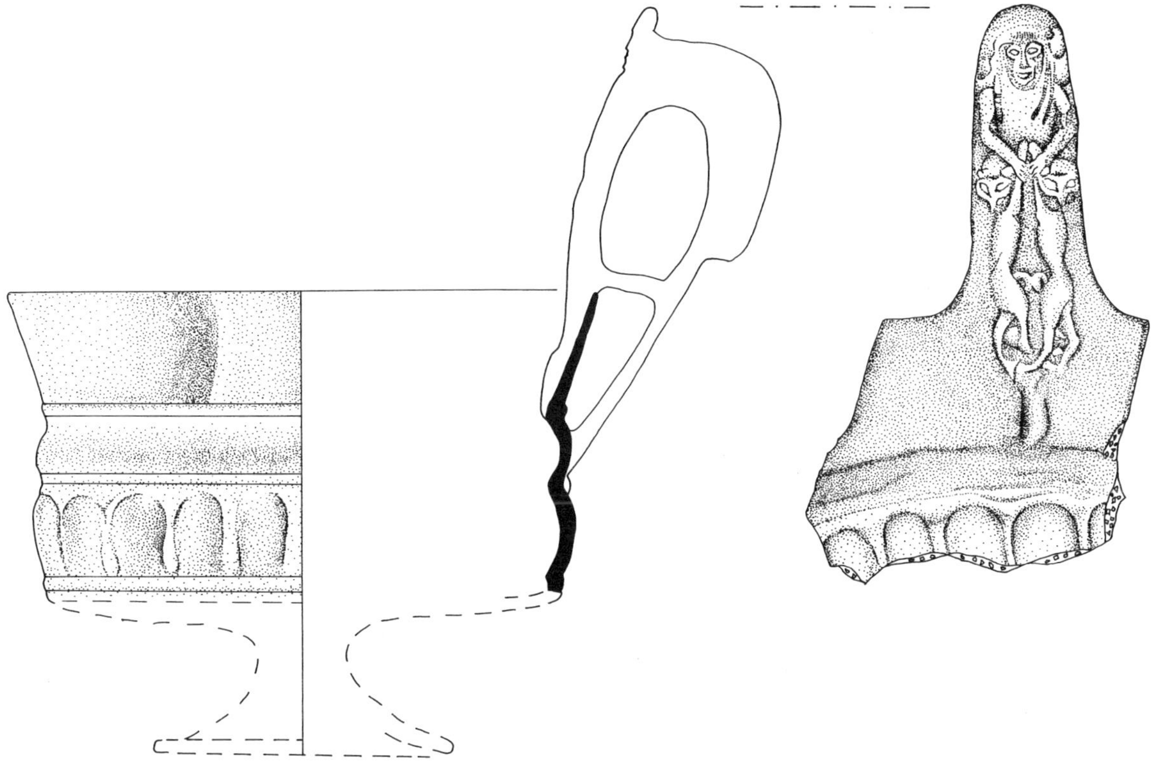

22

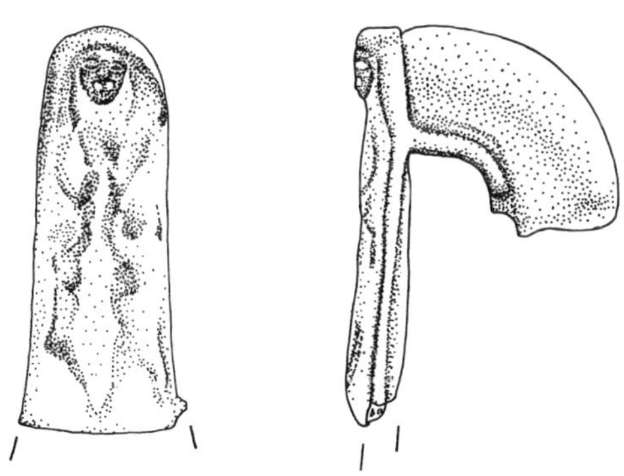

23

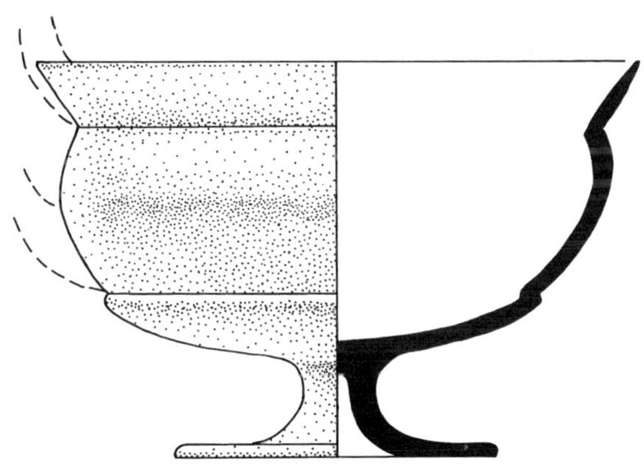

24

0cm 5cm

1:2

FIGURE 14. Scalloped Kyathos, 25; Scalloped Kyathos, 26; Scalloped Kyathos Fragment, 27; Kyathos Fragment, 29

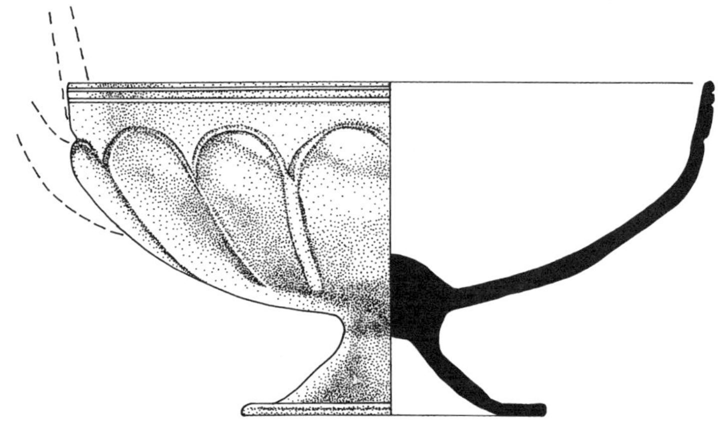

25

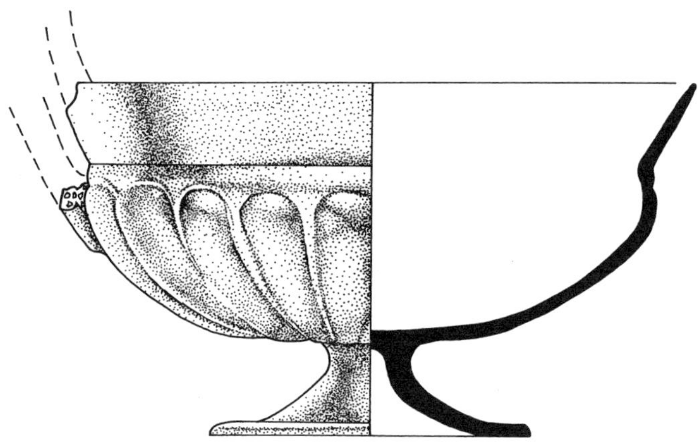

26

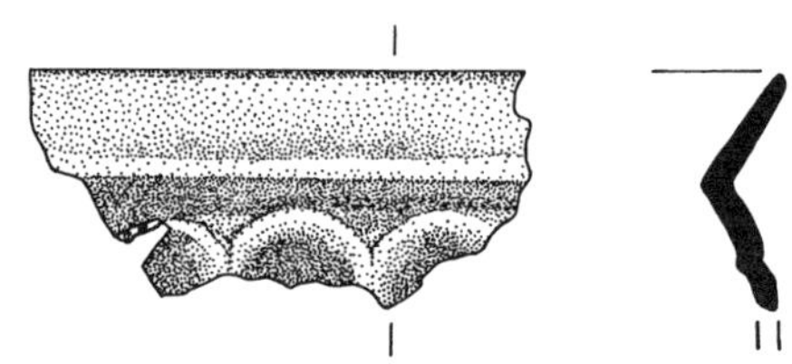

27

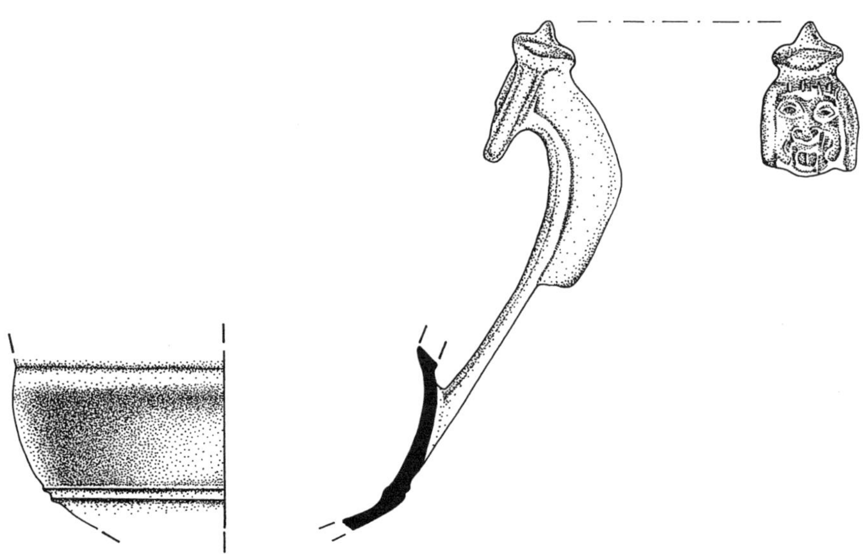

29

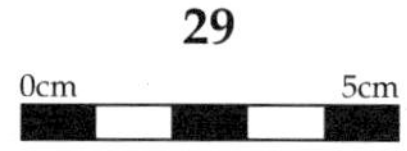

1:2

FIGURE 15. Kyathos Handle Fragment, 30; Scalloped Kyathos Handle and Body Fragment, 31; Kyathos Handle Fragment, 32

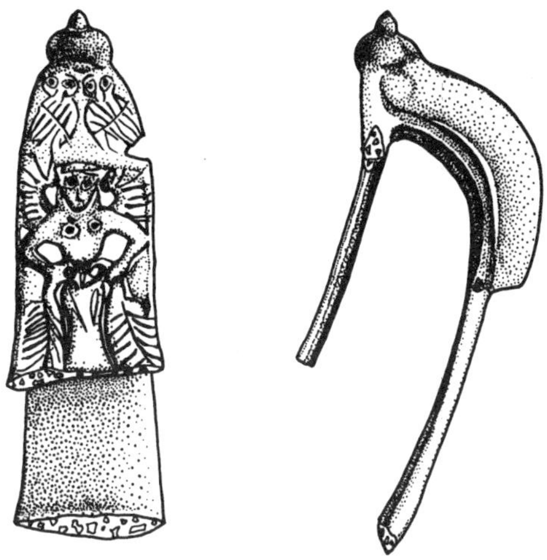

30

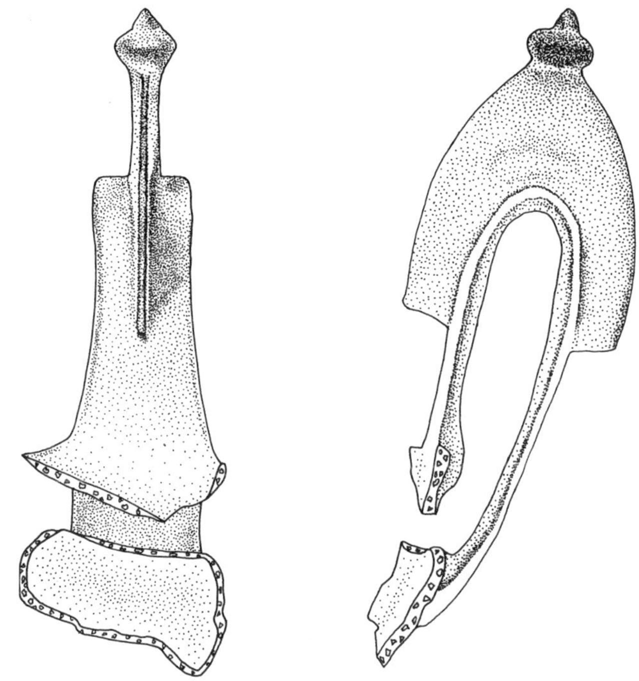

31

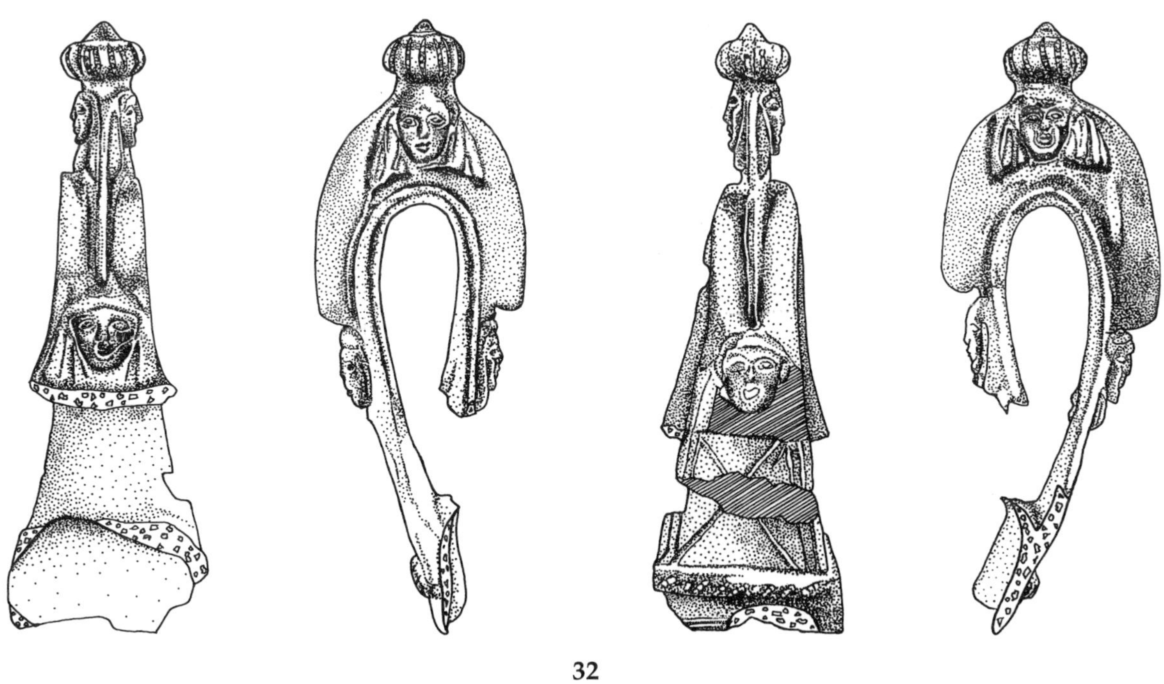

32

0cm 5cm

1:2

FIGURE 16. Kyathos Handle Fragment, 33; Scalloped Kyathos Handle and Body Fragment, 34; Kyathos Rim and Handle Fragment, 35

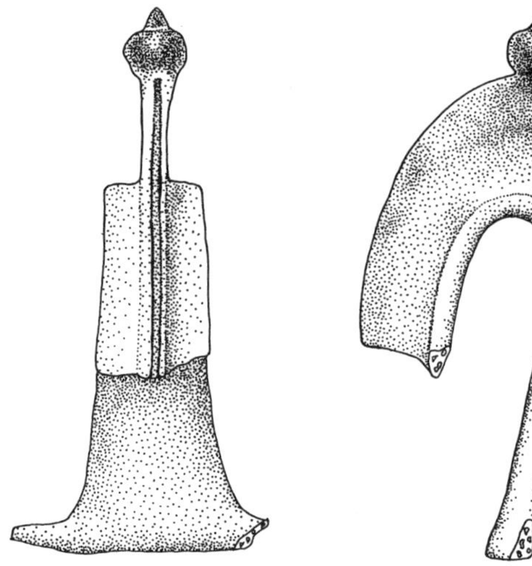

33

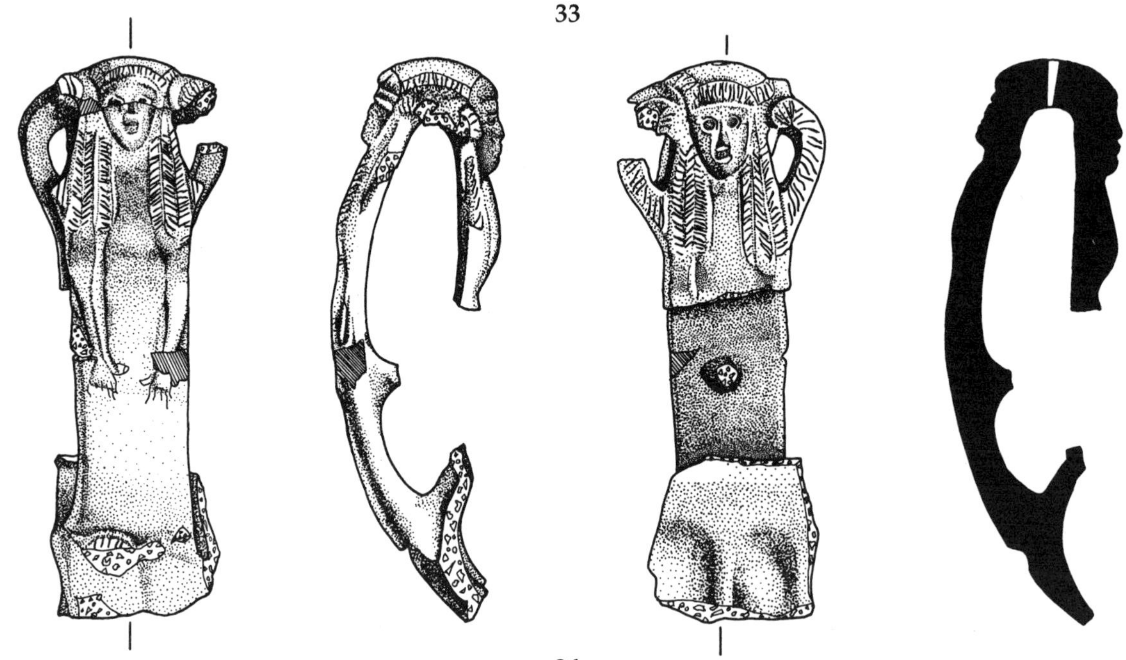

34

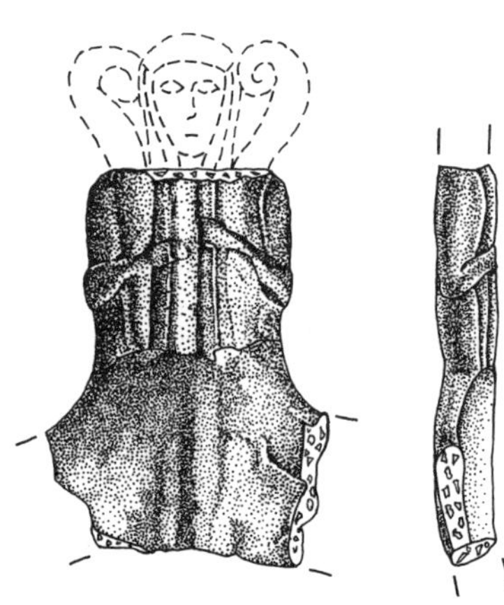

35

0cm 5cm

1:2

FIGURE 17. Kyathos Handle Fragment, 36; Kyathos Handle Fragment, 37; Cup, 38

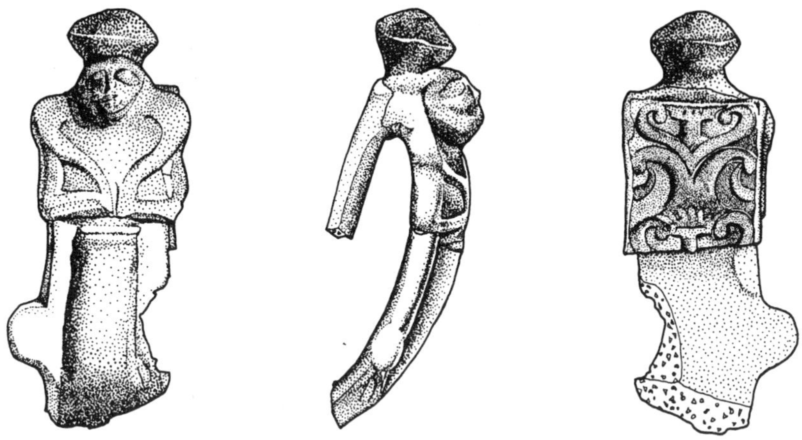

36

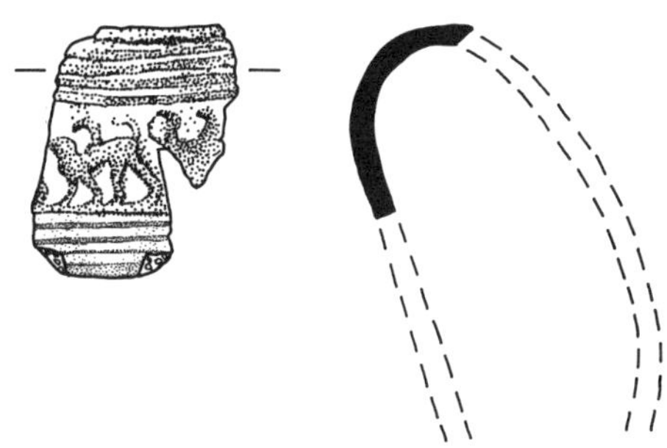

37

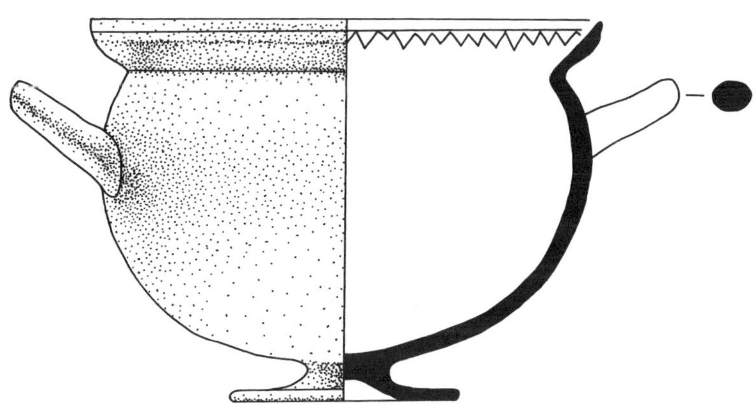

38

0cm 5cm

1:2

FIGURE 18. Cup, 39; Cup Fragment, 40; Cup Fragment, 41; Cup Fragment, 42; Cup Fragment, 43; Chalice, 44; Chalice Fragment, 45

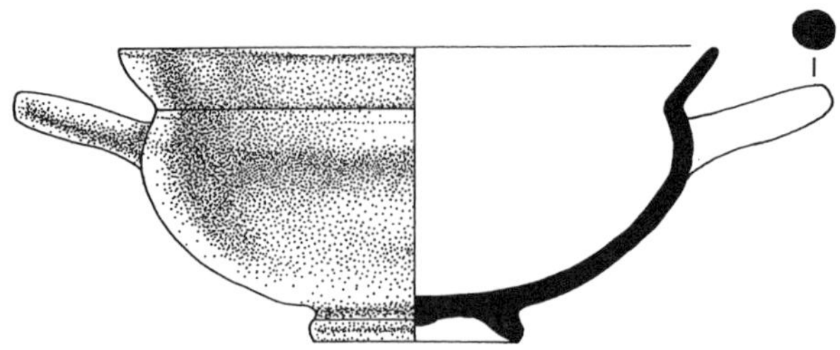

39

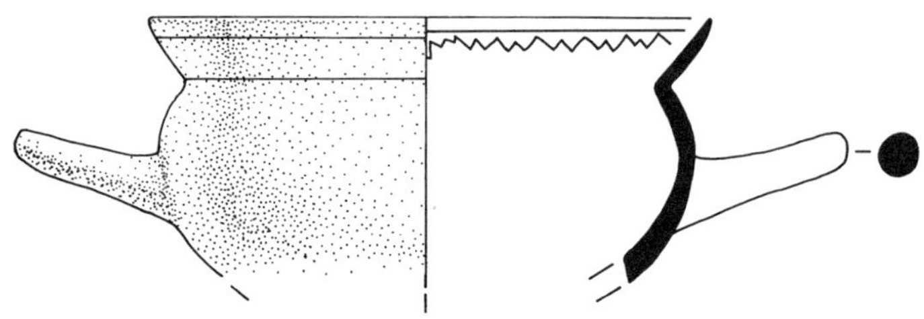

40

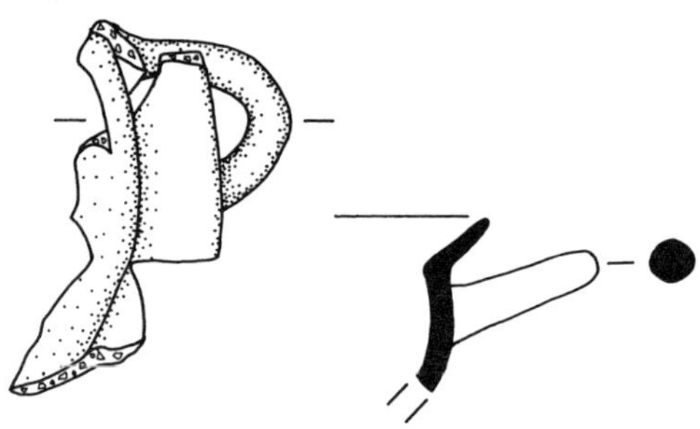

41

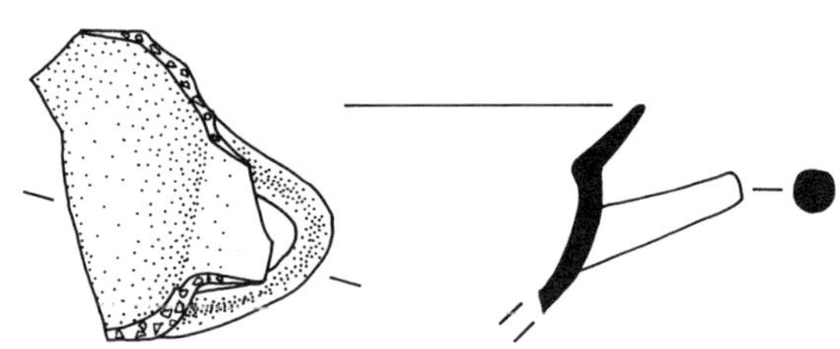

42

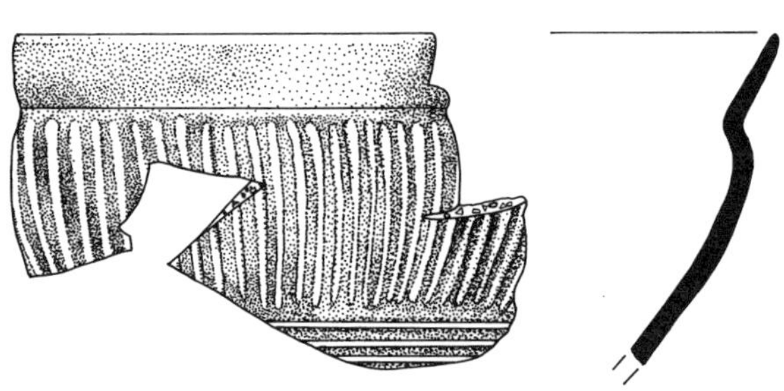

43

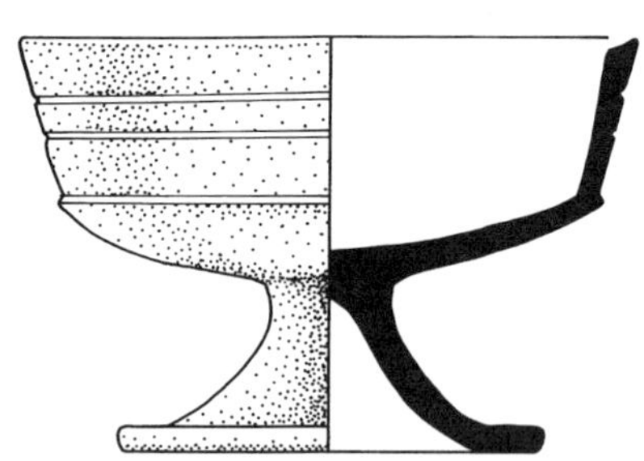

44

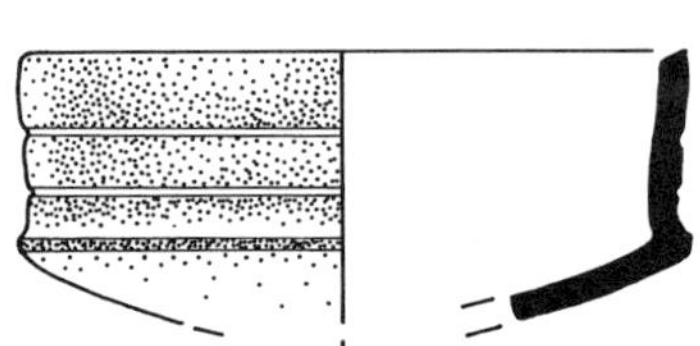

45

0cm 5cm

1:2

FIGURE 19. Chalice Fragment, 46; Phiale Fragment, 47; Fragmentary Jar, 48

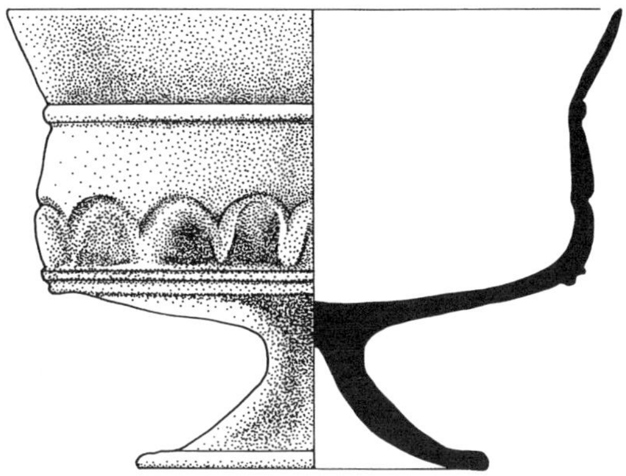

46

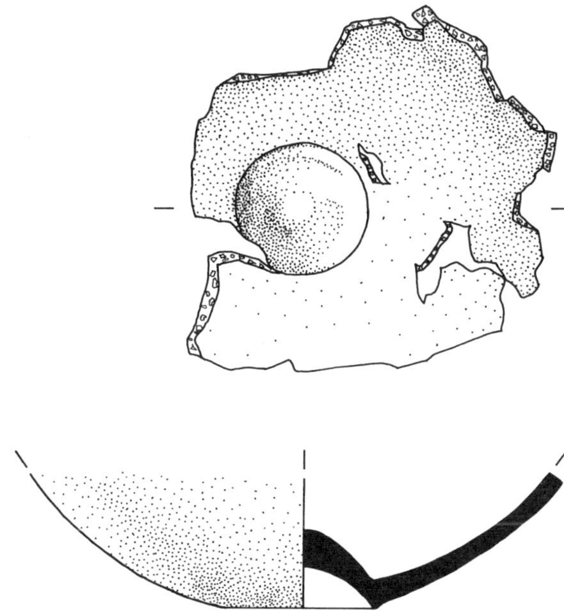

47

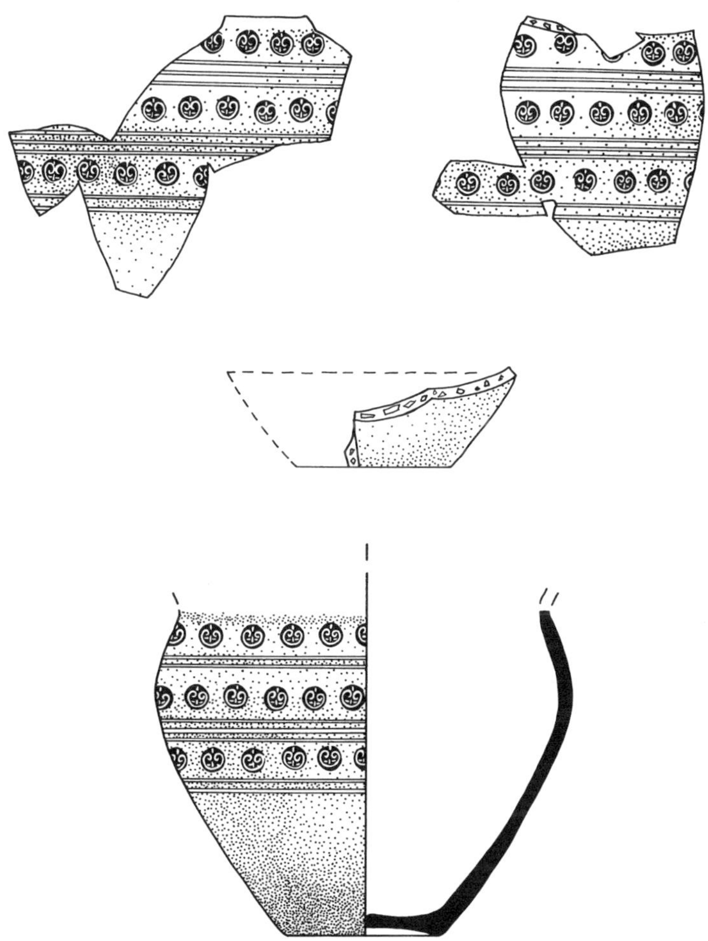

48

0cm 5cm

1:2

FIGURE 20. Fragmentary Jar, 49; Tripod Bowl, 50; Tripod Bowl Fragment, 51; Covered Footed Bowl, 53

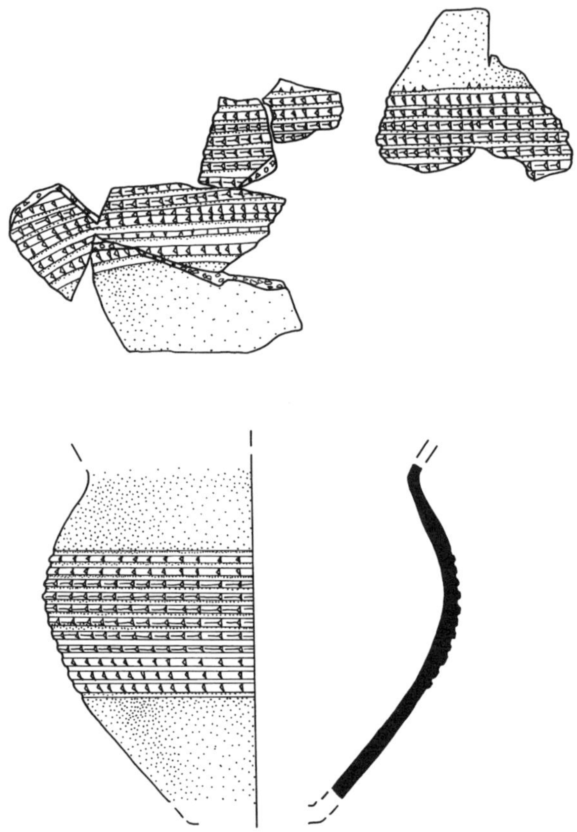

49

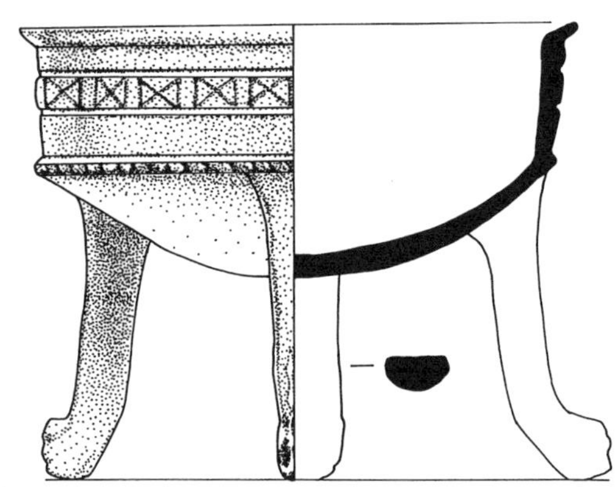

50

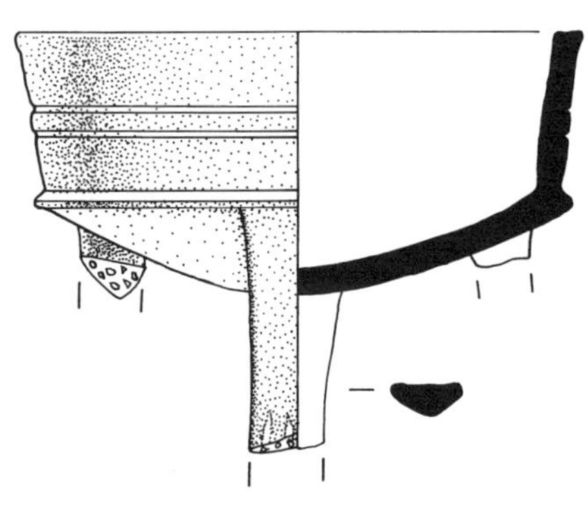

51

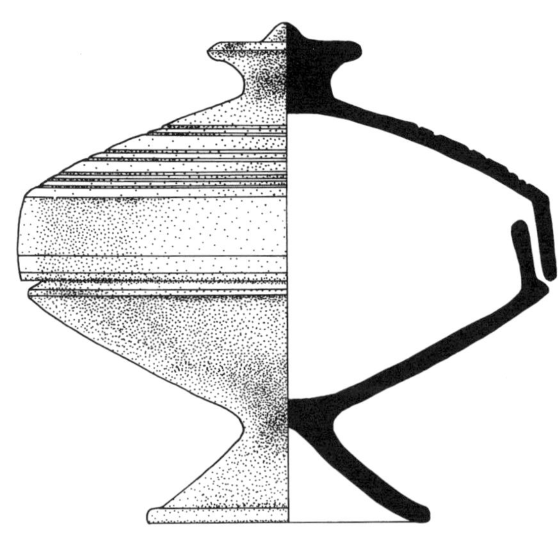

53

0cm 5cm

1:2

FIGURE 21. Footed Bowl, 54; Footed Bowl, 55; Bowl, 56

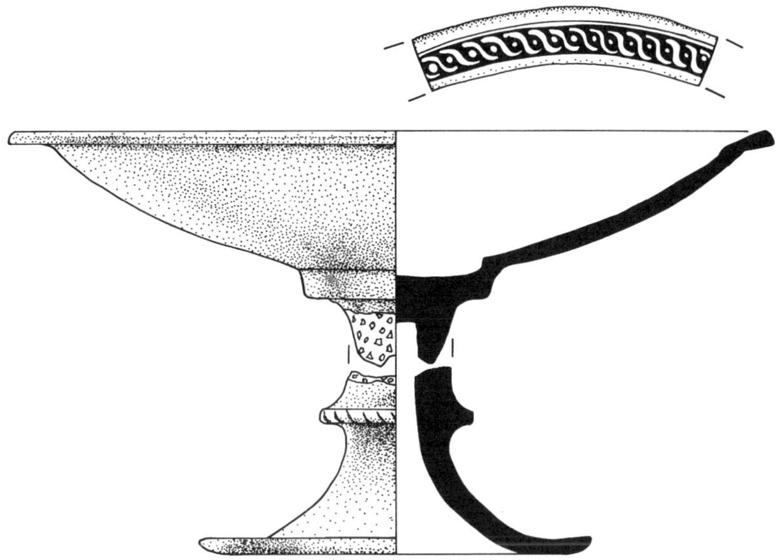

54

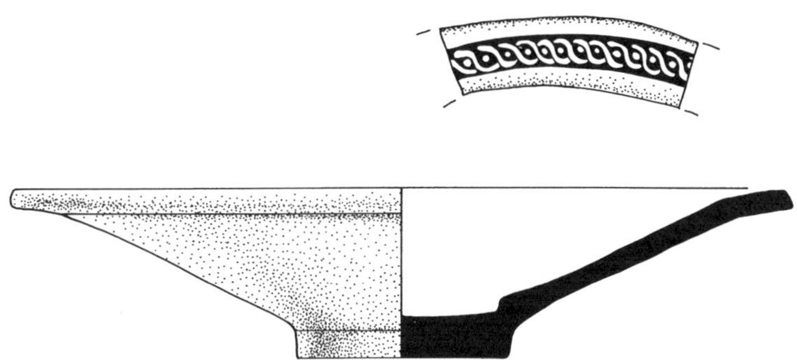

55

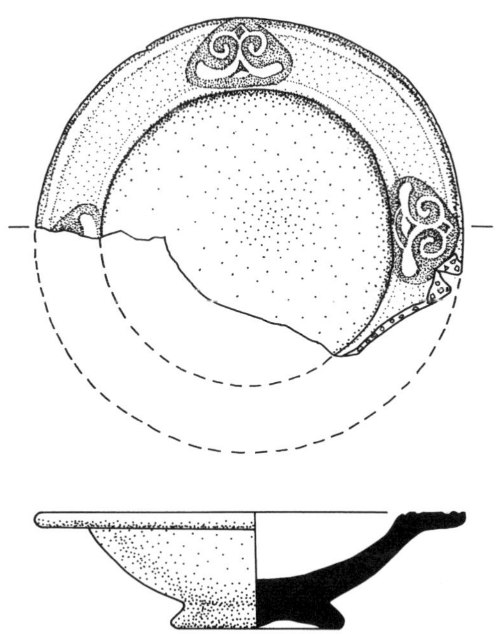

56

0cm 5cm

1:2

FIGURE 22. Bowl Fragment, 58; Bowl Fragment, 59; Bowl Fragment, 60; Bowl, 64; Bowl, 65

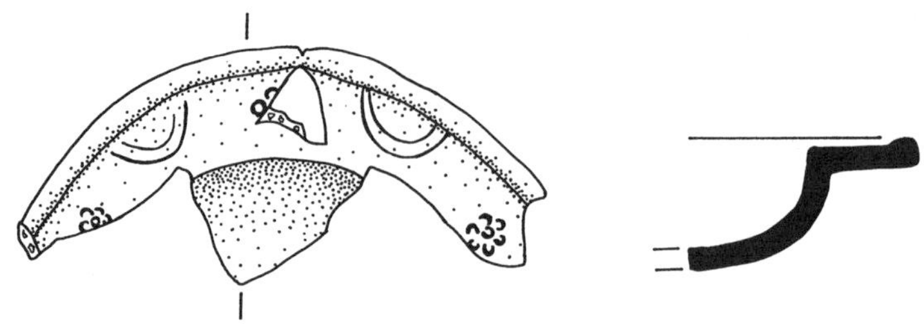

58

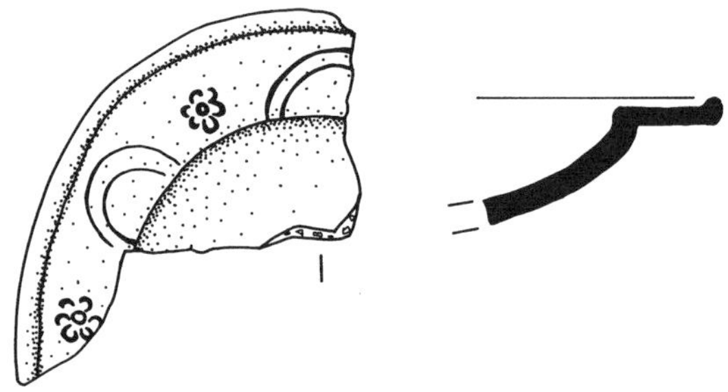

59

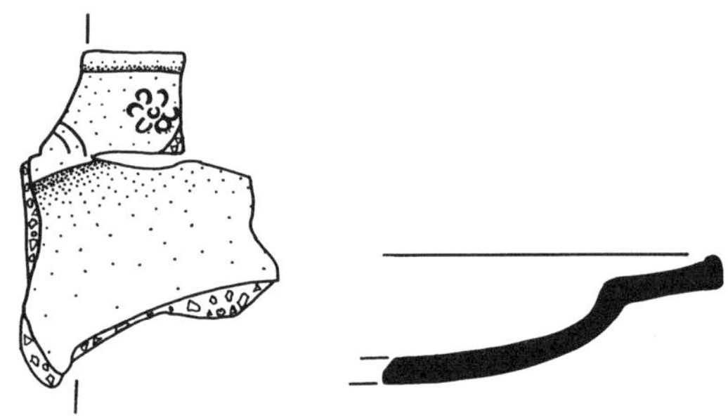

60

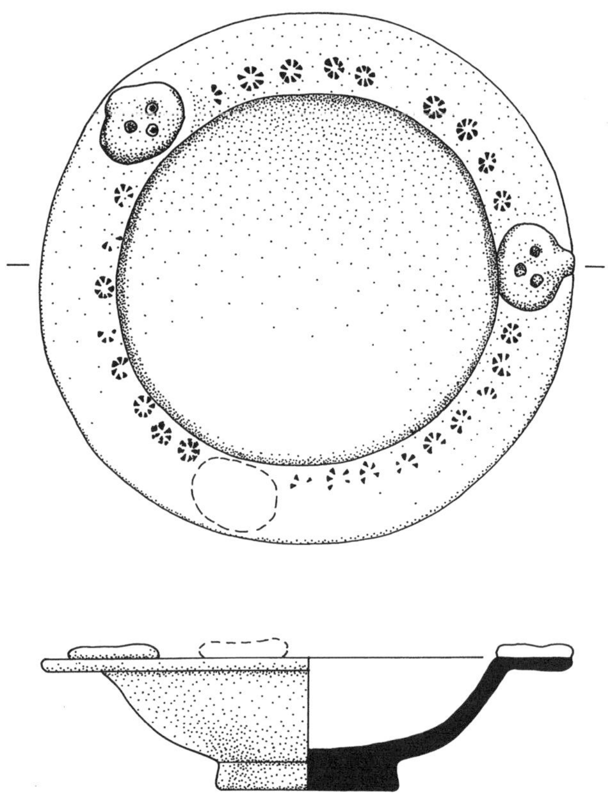

64

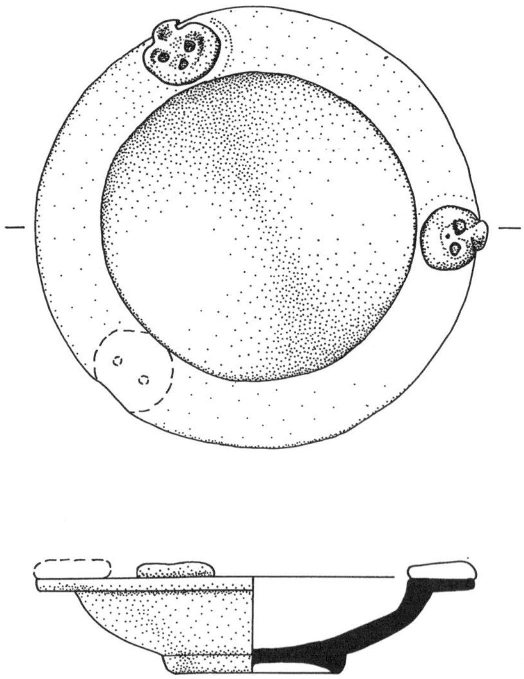

65

1:2

FIGURE 23. Bowl Fragment, 66; Bowl Fragment, 67; Bowl Fragment, 68; Plate, 69; Plate Fragment, 70

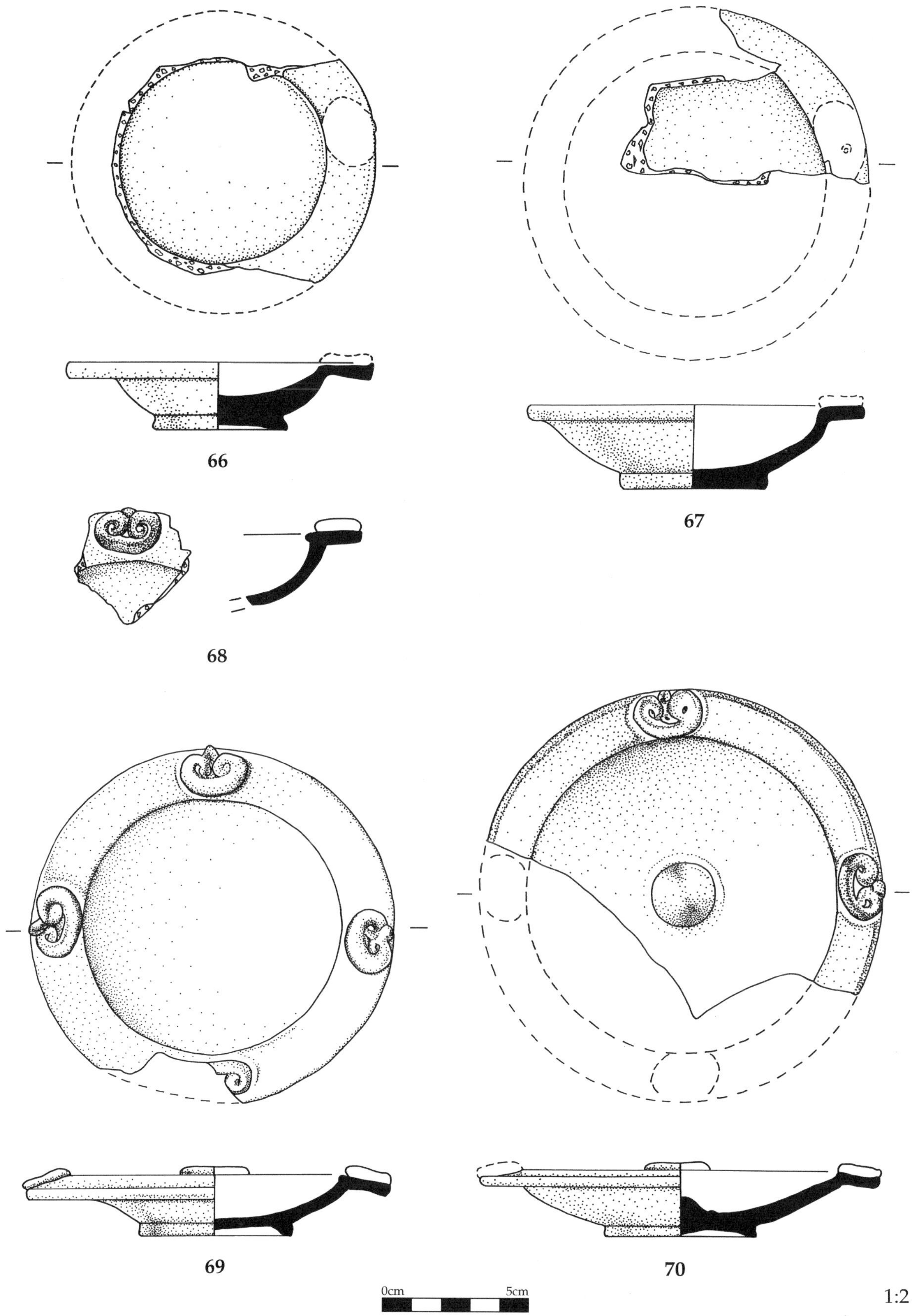

FIGURE 24. Plate Fragment, 72; Plate Fragment, 79

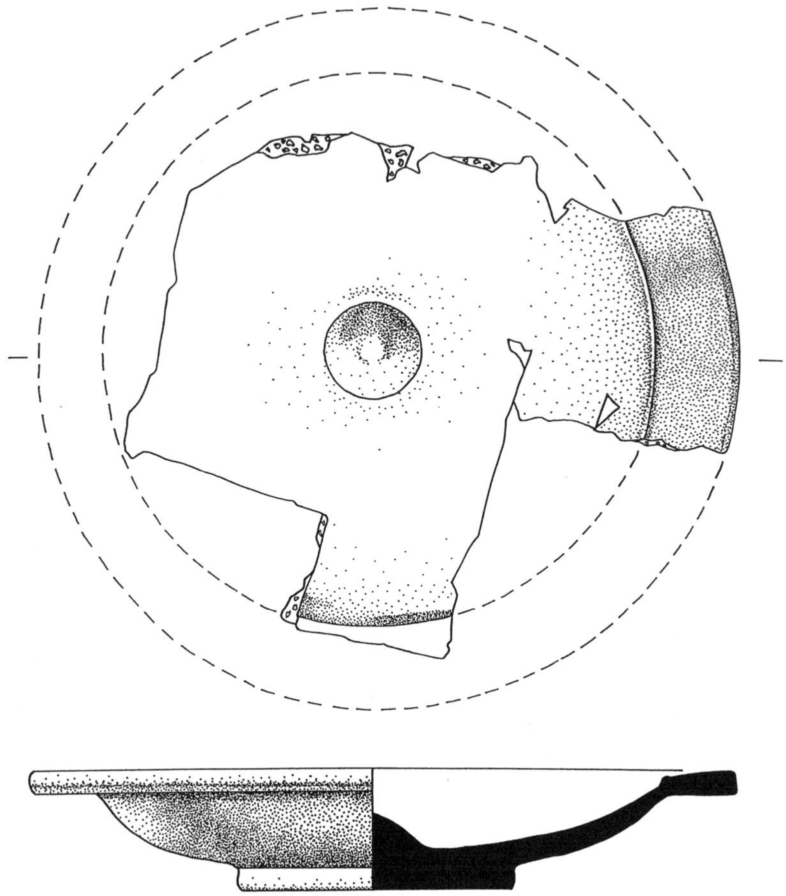

72

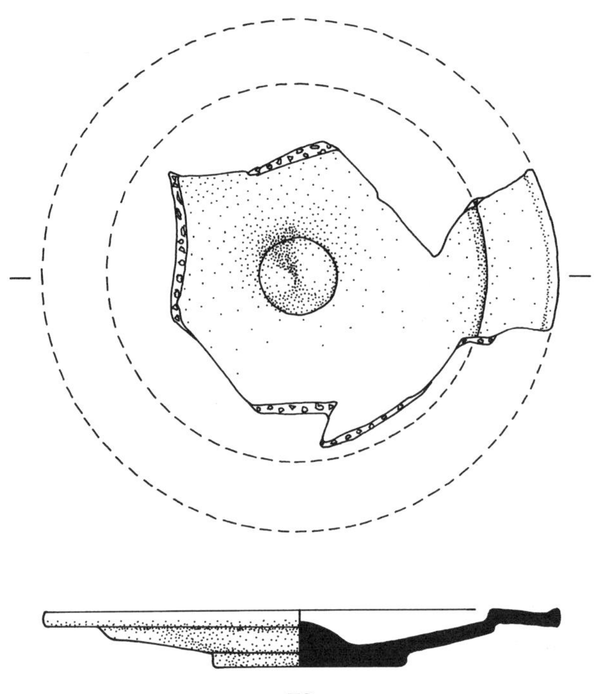

79

0cm 5cm

1:2

FIGURE 25. Plate Fragment, 90; Plate Fragment, 93; Rim and Handle Fragment, 102; Rim and Handle Fragment, 103; Rim and Handle Fragment, 104; Rim and Handle Fragment, 105; Rim and Handle Fragment, 106; Rim and Handle Fragment, 108; Rim and Handle Fragment, 110

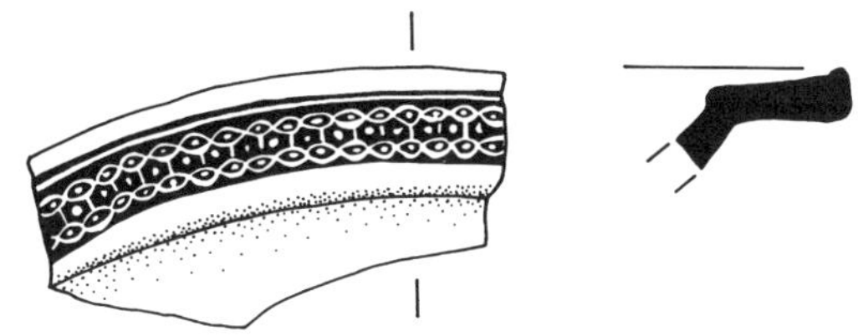

93

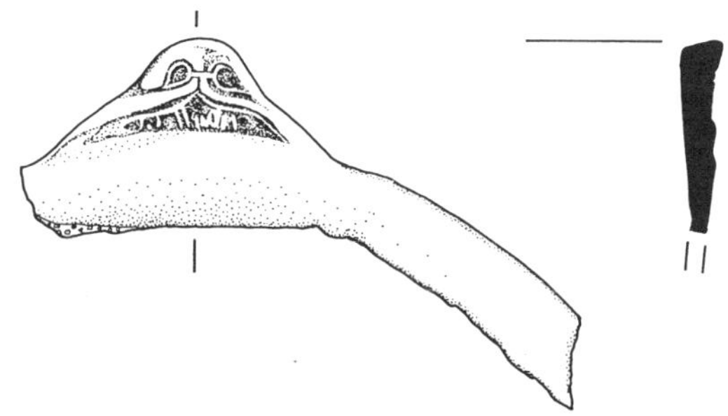

102

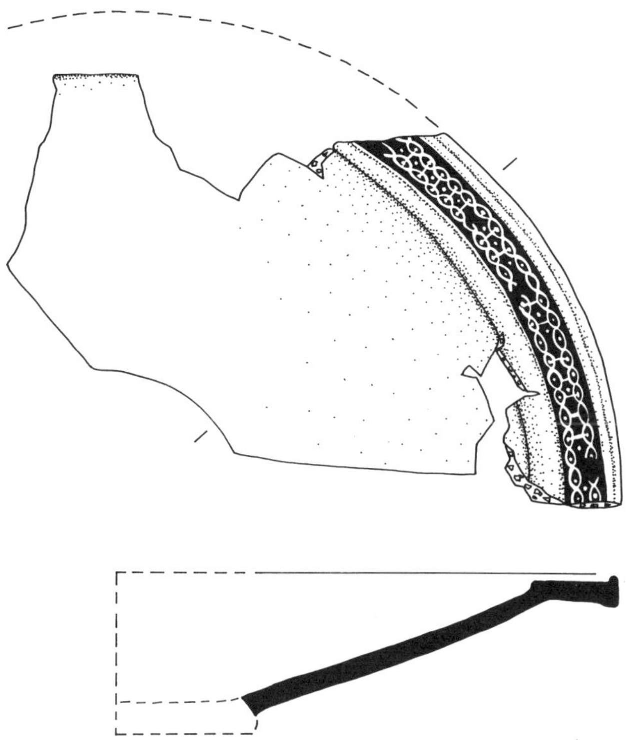

90

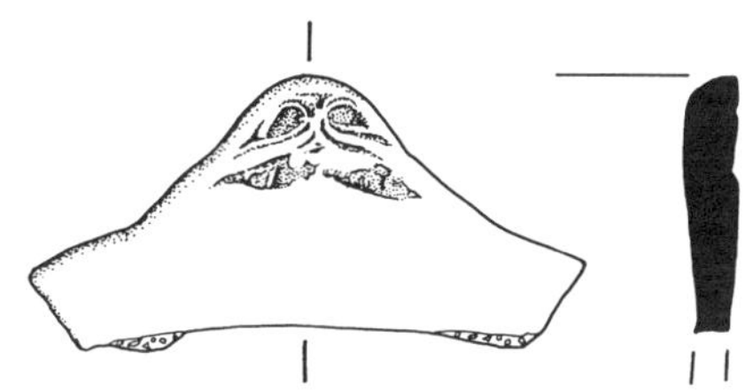

103

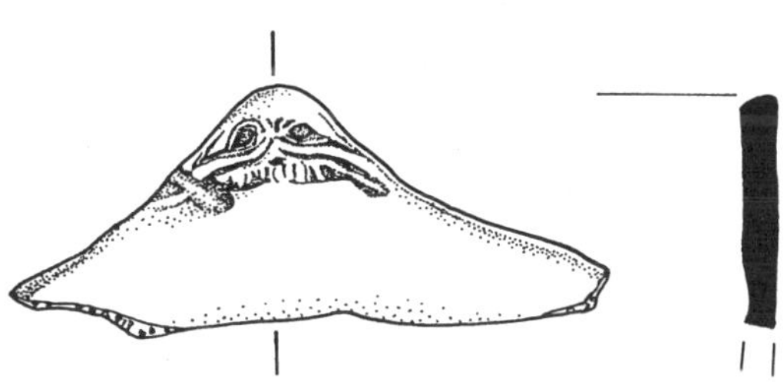

104

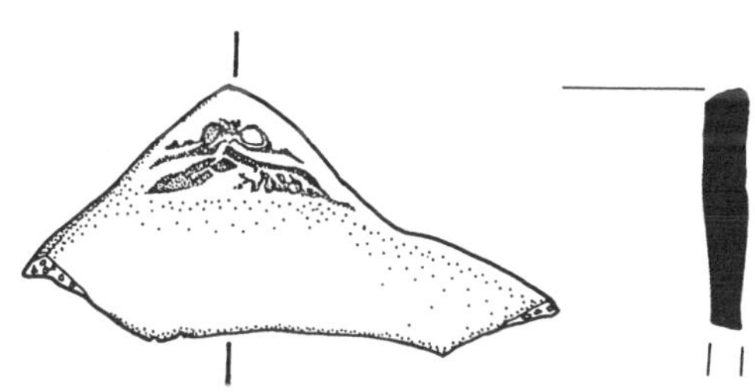

105

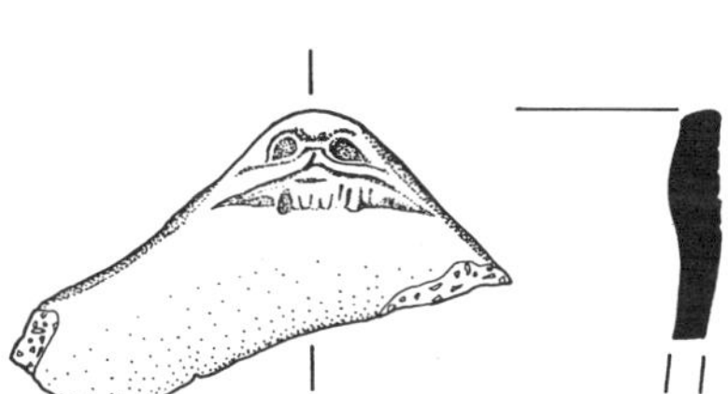

106

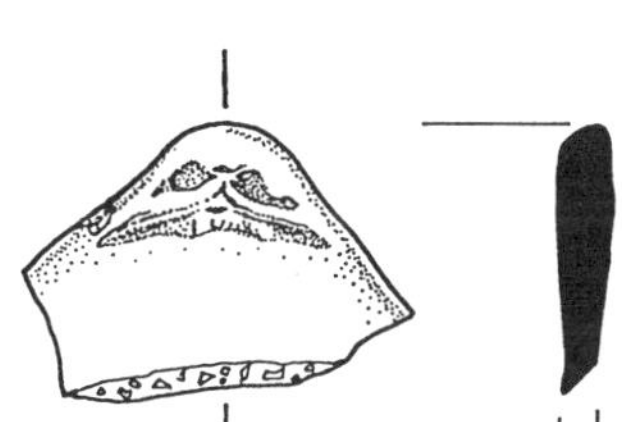

108

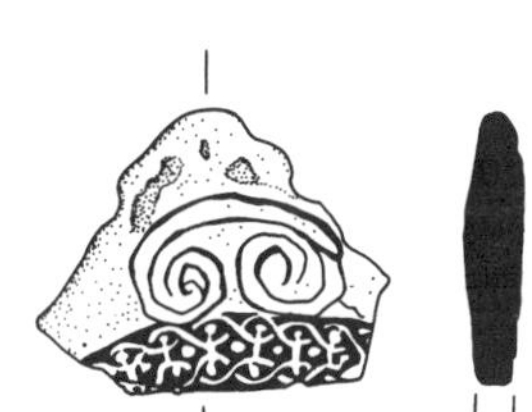

110

0cm 5cm

1:2

FIGURE 26. Plate, 111; Plate Fragment, 112

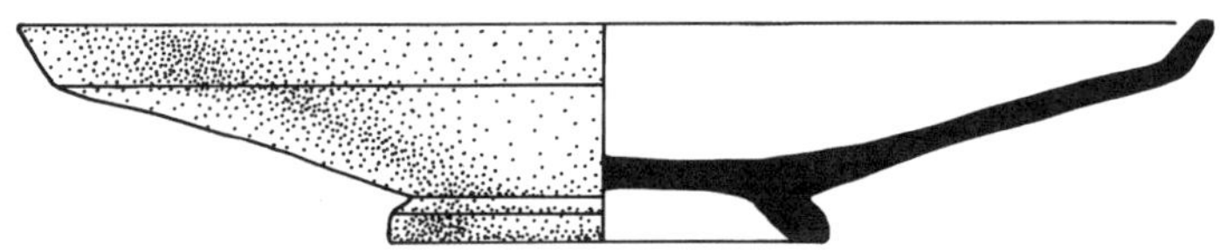

111

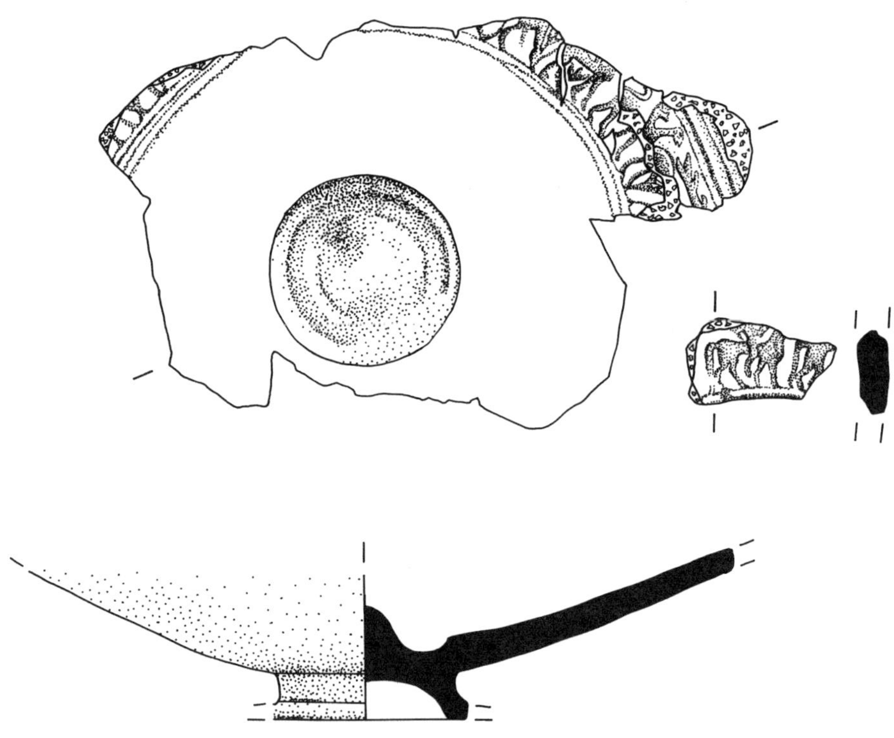

112

0cm 5cm

1:2

FIGURE 27. Lid, 113; Fragmentary Lid, 114; Fragmentary Lid, 115

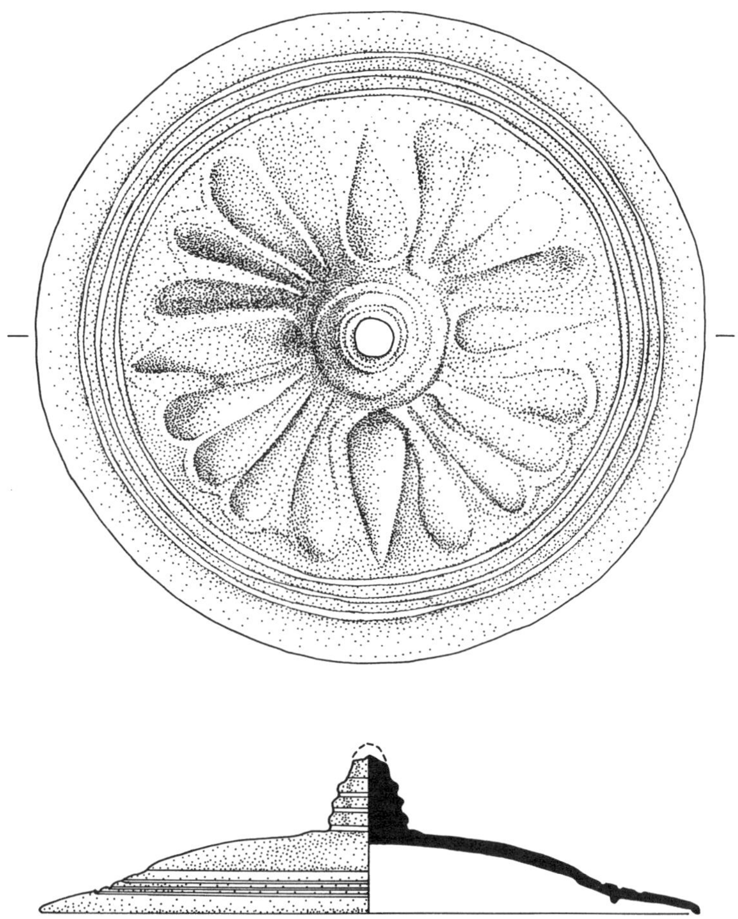

113

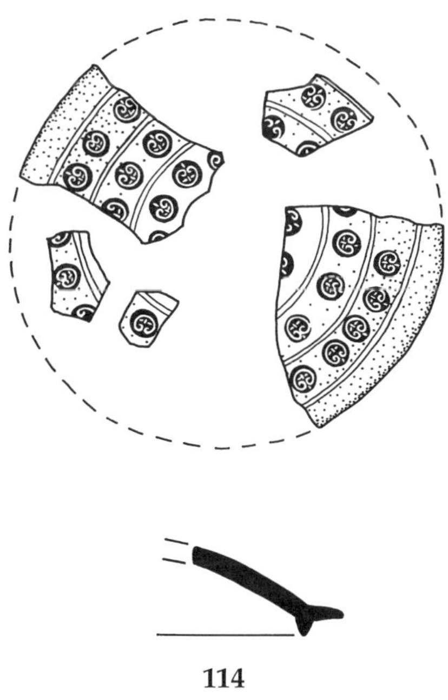

114

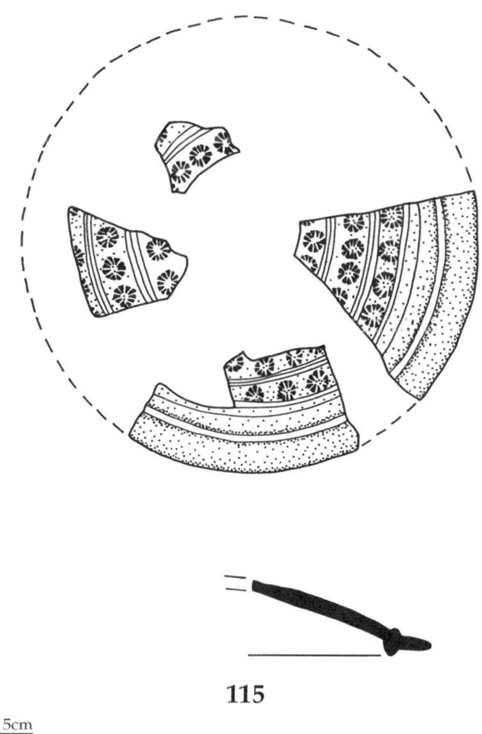

115

1:2

FIGURE 28. Lid Fragment, 116; Lid Fragment, 117; Fragmentary Lid, 118; Fragmentary Lid, 119; Lid, 120; Lid, 121; Lid Fragment, 122

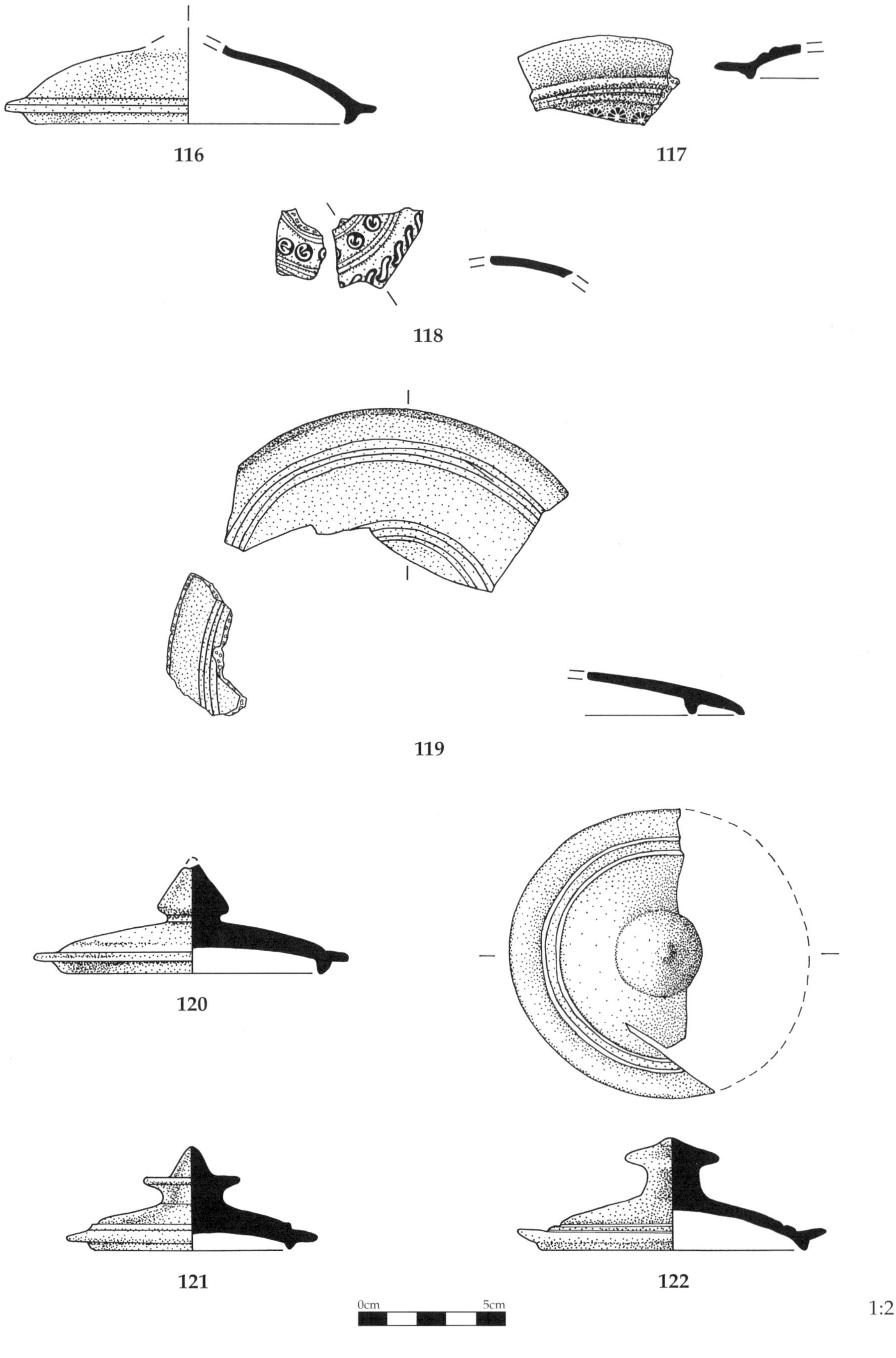

FIGURE 29. Lid, 123; Lid, 124; Lid Fragment, 127

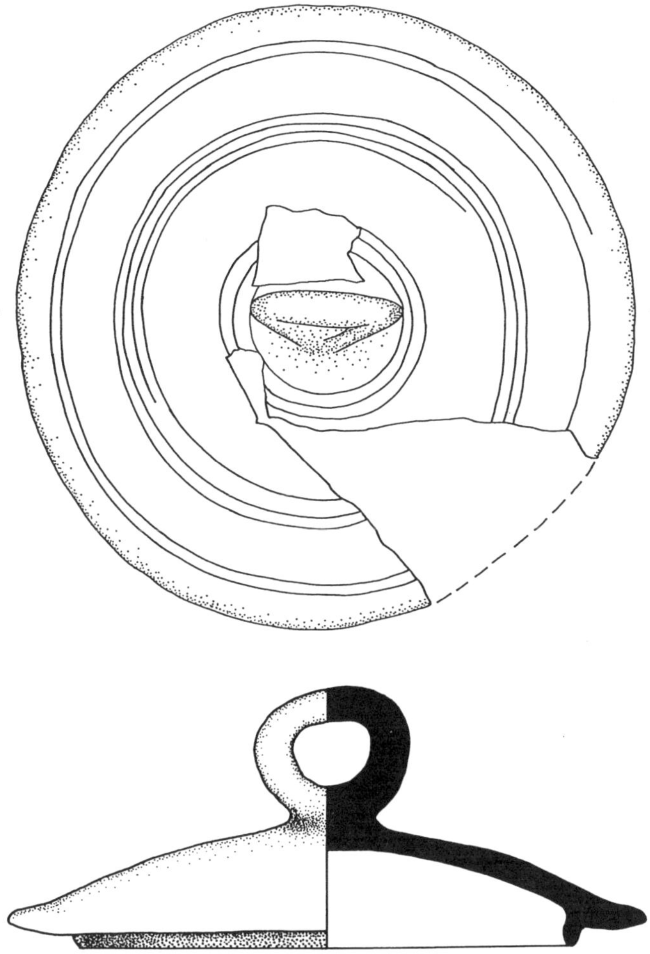

123

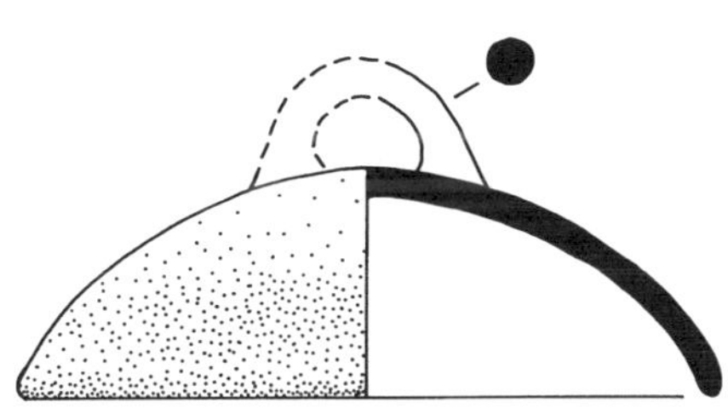

124

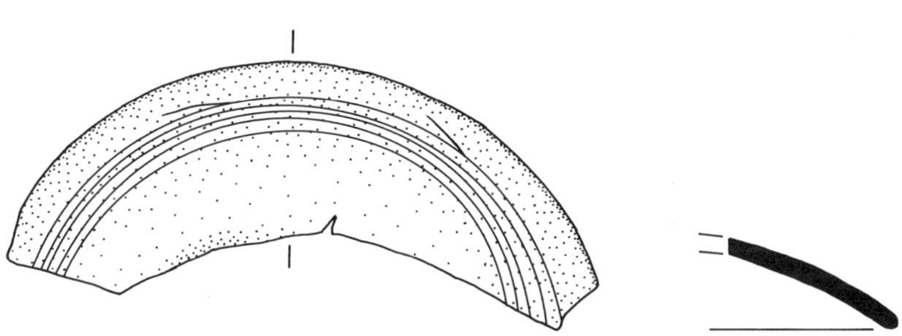

127

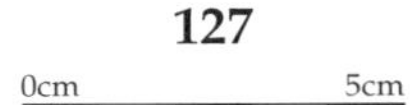

1:2

FIGURE 30. Lid Fragment, 128; Lid Finial, 129; Lid Finial, 131; Stamped Fragment, 132; Stamped Fragment, 133; Strap Handle Fragment, 134; Incised Cup or Bowl Fragment, 135; Inscribed Rim Fragment, 137; Inscribed Fragment, 138; Inscribed Fragment, 139

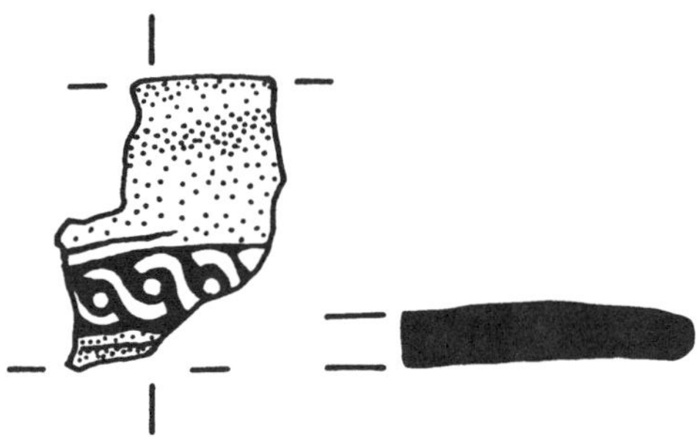

128

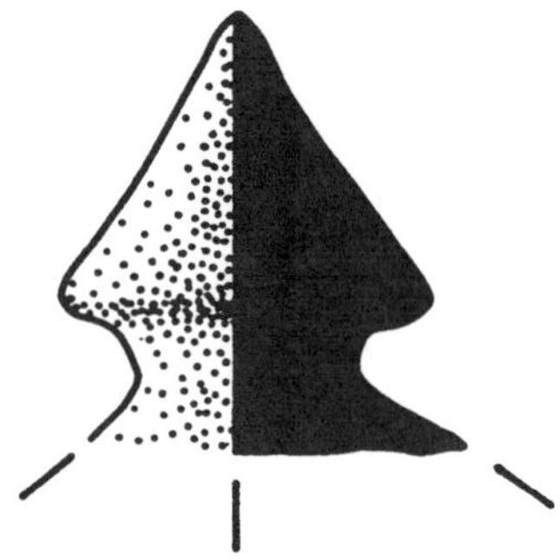

129

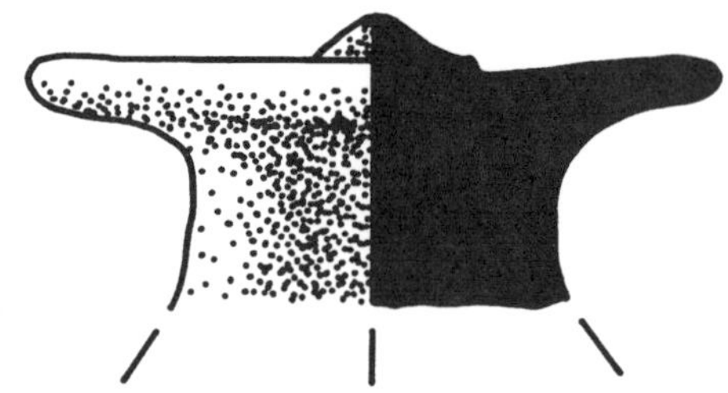

131

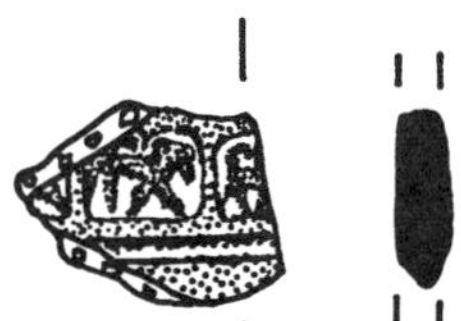

132

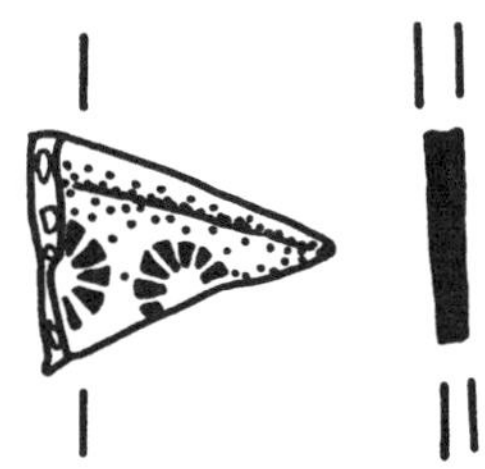

133

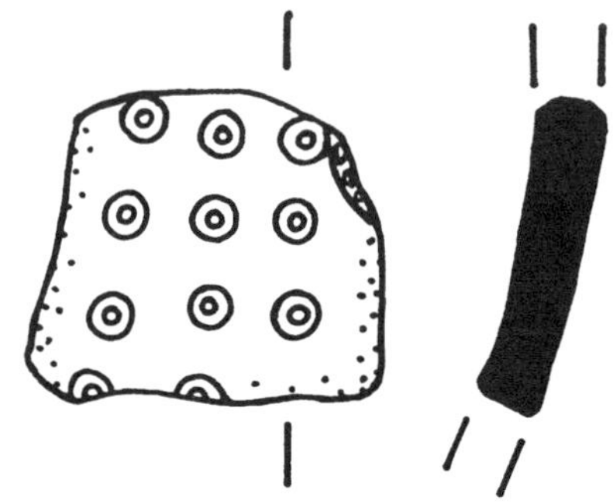

134

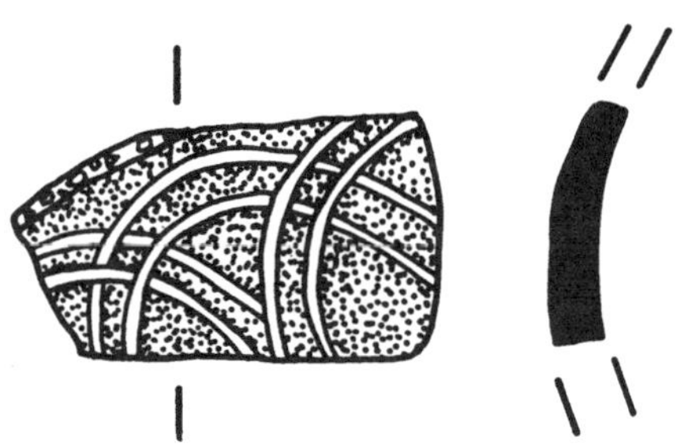

135

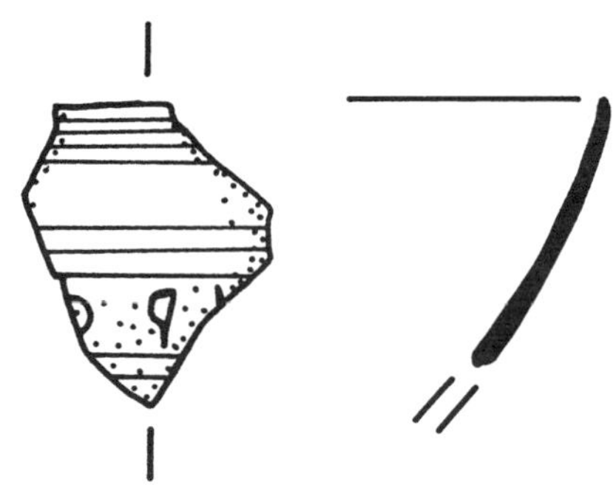

137

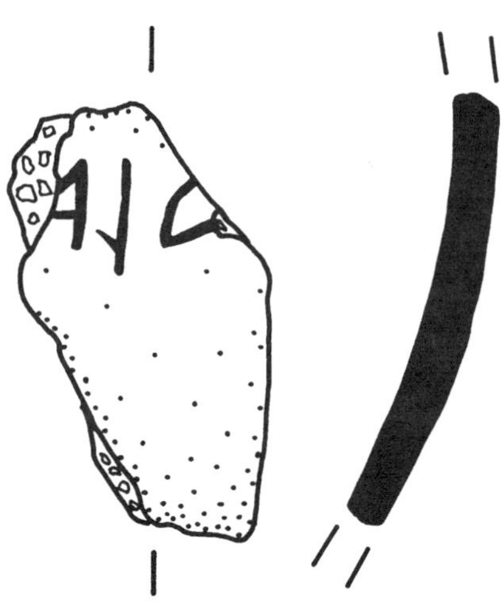

138

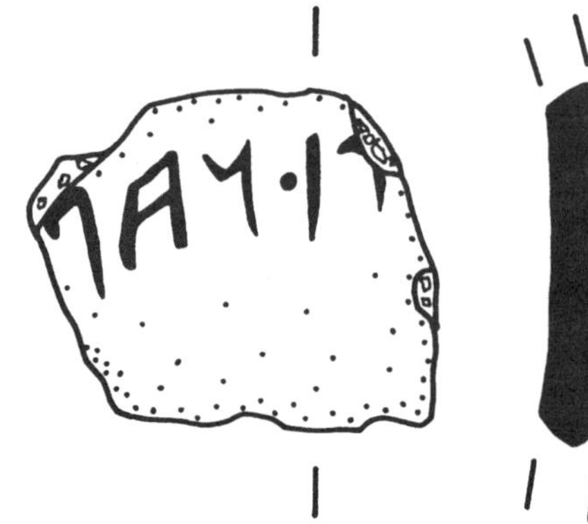

139

0cm 5cm

1:1

FIGURE 31. Selected stamped designs

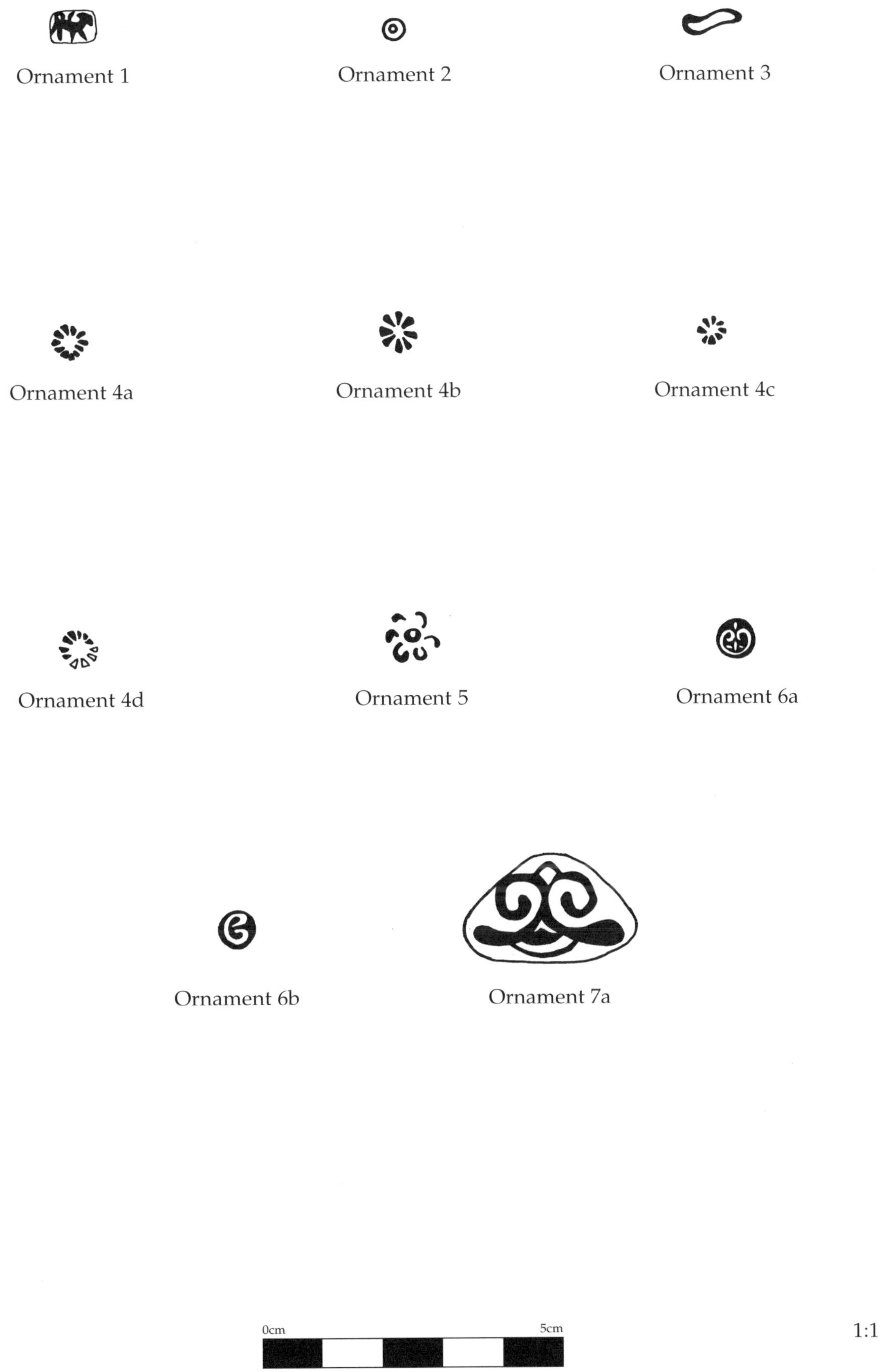

PLATE 1. Molded Oinochoe Fragment, 1

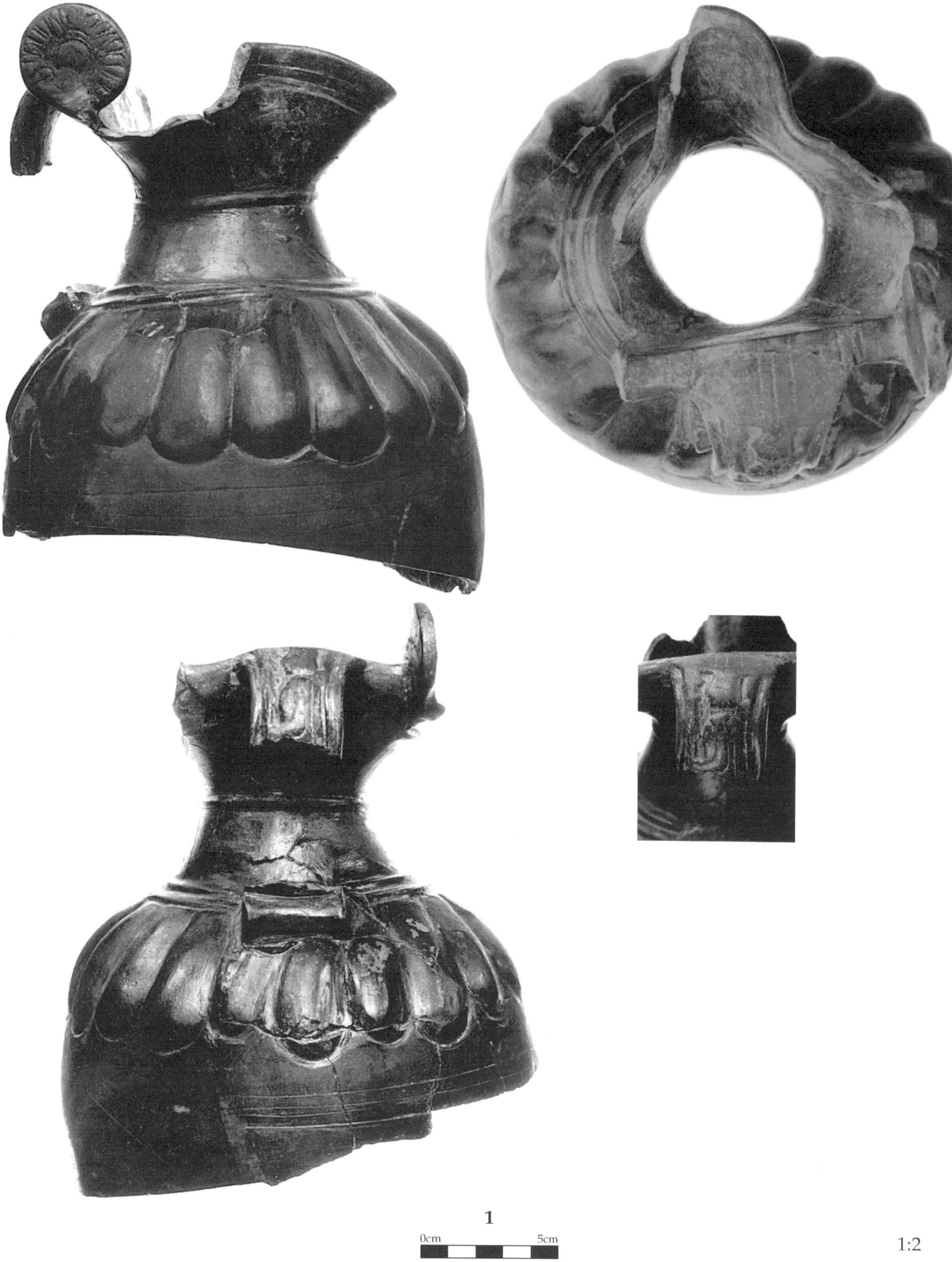

1

1:2

PLATE 2. Molded Oinochoe Fragment, 2; Oinochoe Handle Fragment, 3; Oinochoe Handle and Body Fragment, Murlo no. 73-317

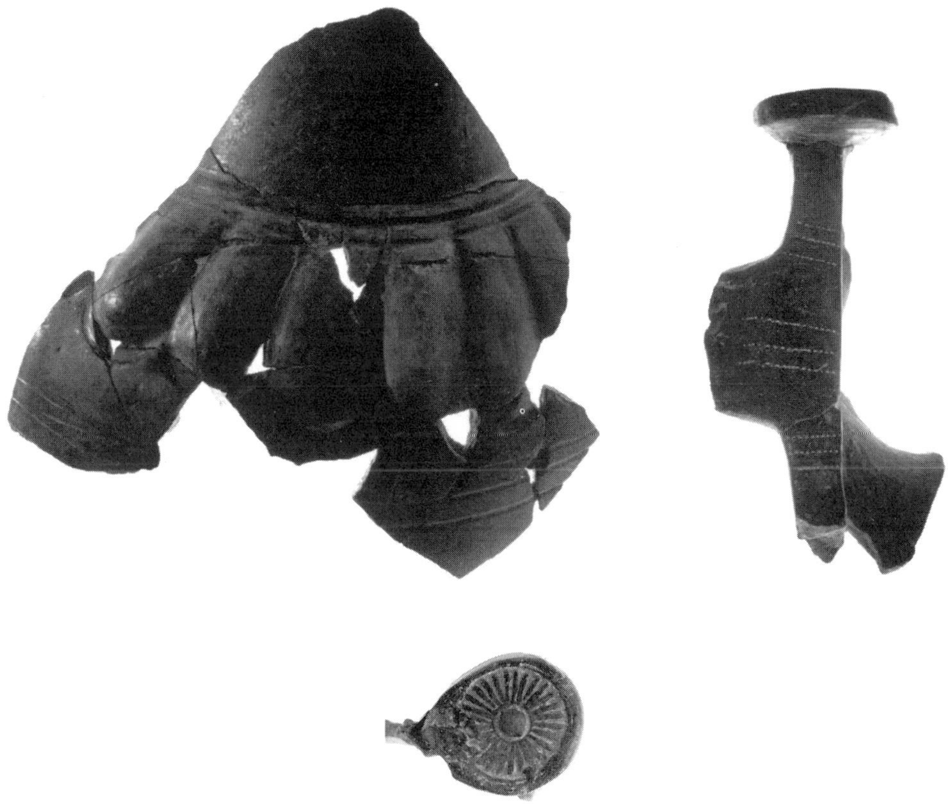

2

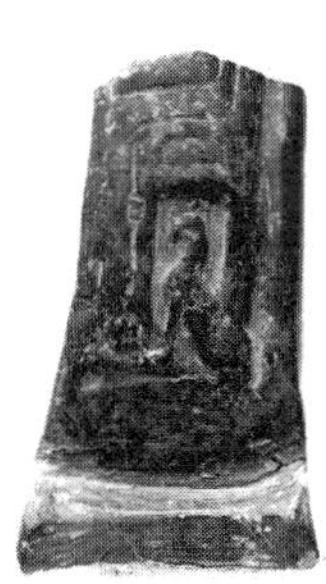

3

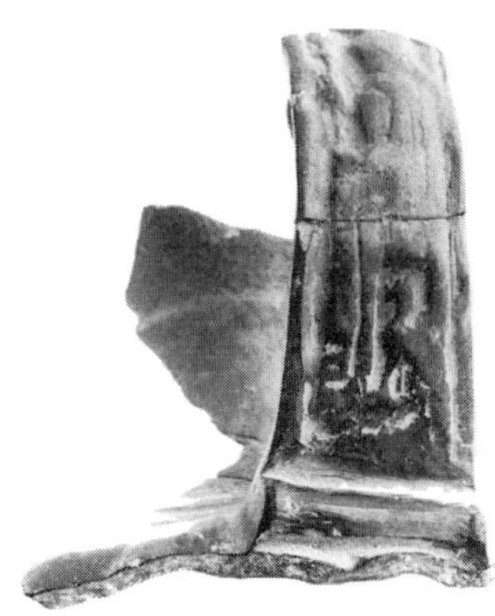

Murlo no. 73-317

0cm 5cm

1:2

PLATE 3. Fragmentary Oinochoe, 4; Alabastron, 5; Kantharos, 6; Kantharos Fragment, 7; Kantharos Fragment, 8

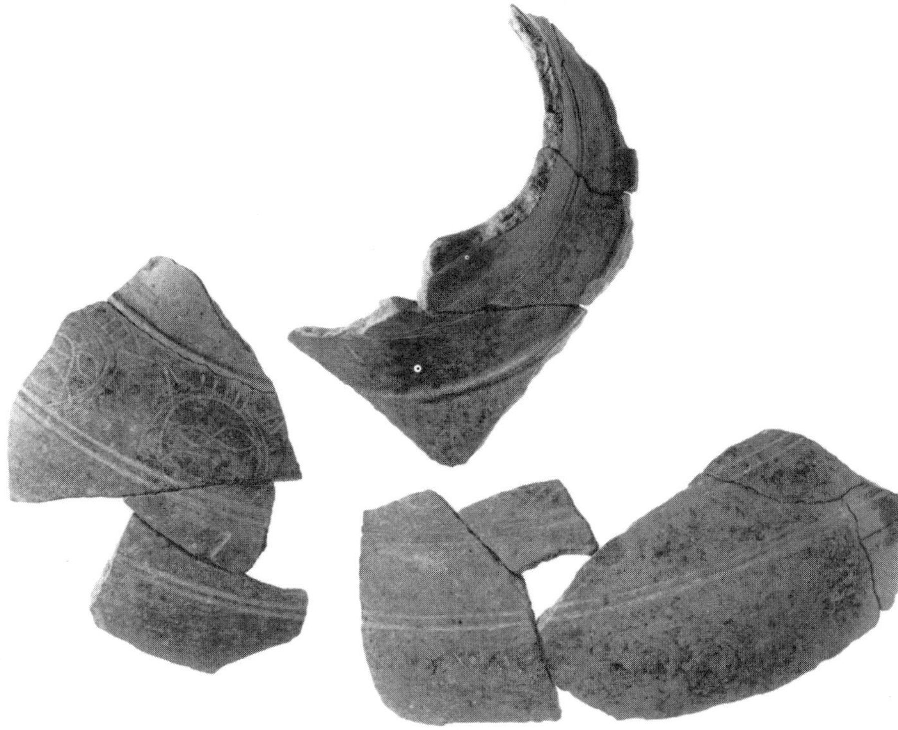

4

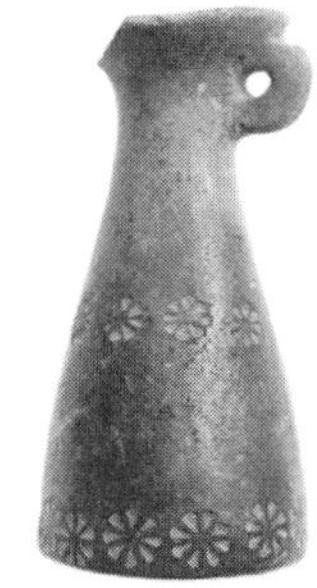

5

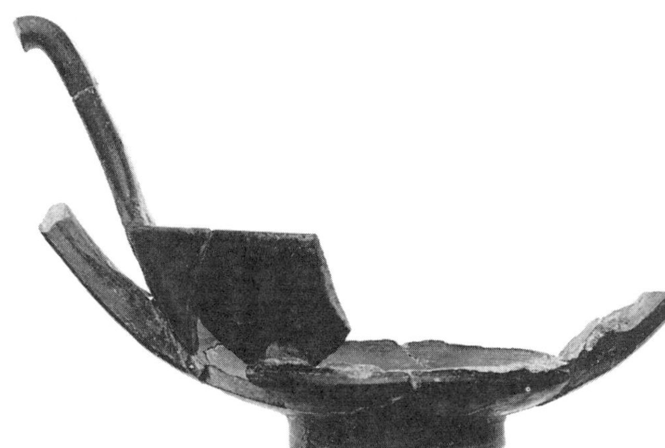

6

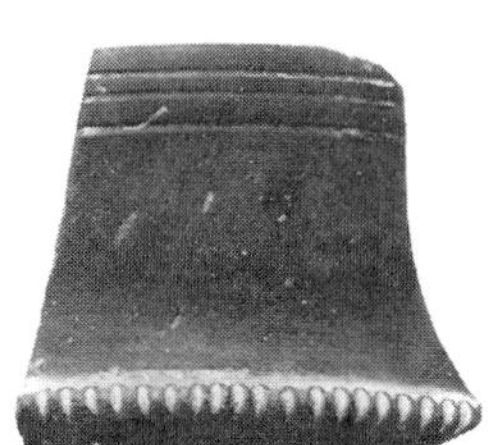

7

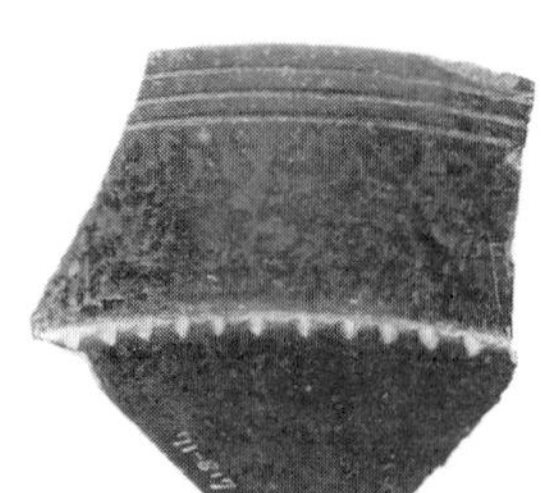

8

0cm 5cm

1:2

PLATE 4. Kantharos, 9; Kantharos Fragment, 10; Kantharos, 11; Kantharos Fragment, 12; Kantharos, 13

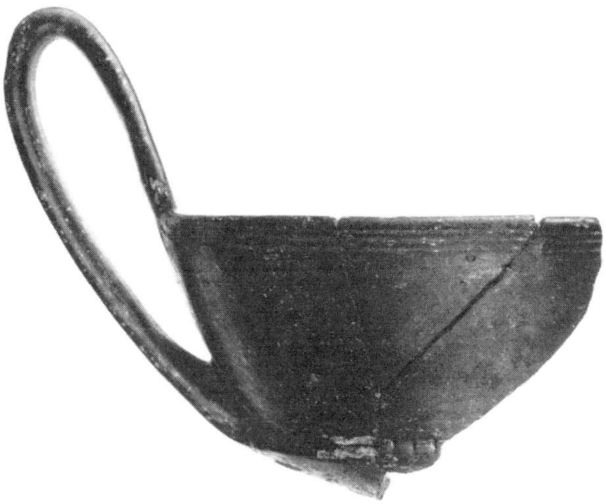

9

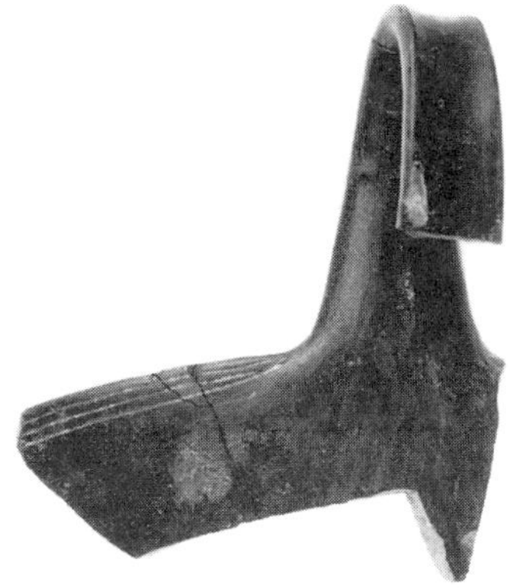

10

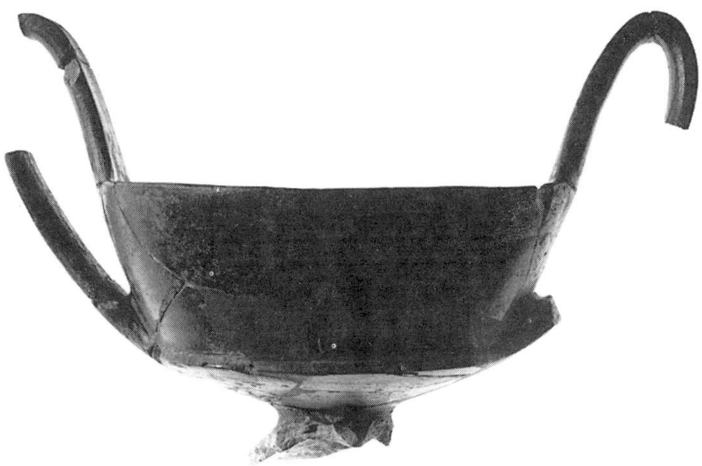

11

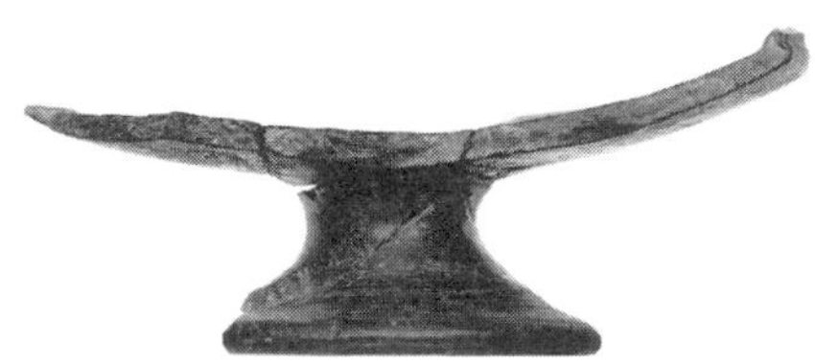

12

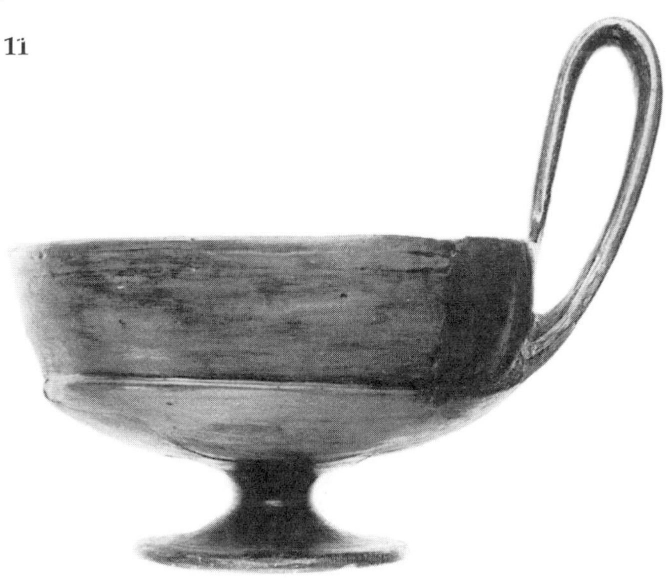

13

0cm 5cm

1:2

PLATE 5. Kantharos, 15; Kantharos Fragment, 16; Kantharos Fragment, 17

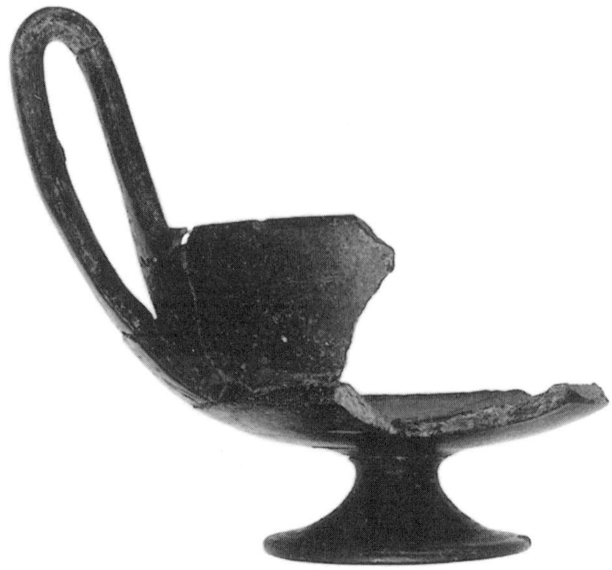

15

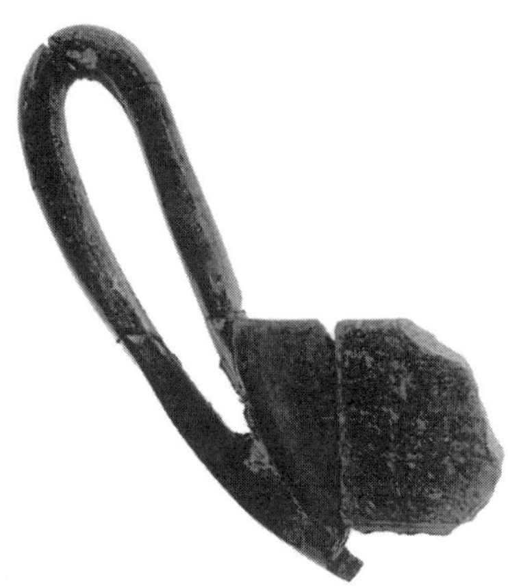

16

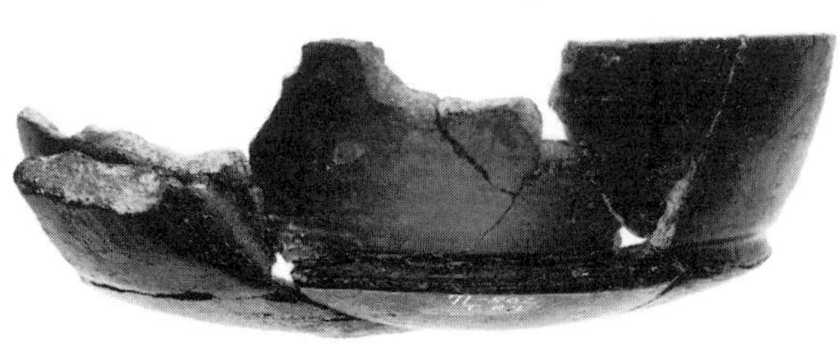

17

0cm 5cm

1:2

PLATE 6. Kantharos Handle Fragment, 18; Kantharos Handle Fragment, 19; Kantharos Handle Fragment, 20; Kantharos Handle Fragment, 21; Kyathos Fragment, 22

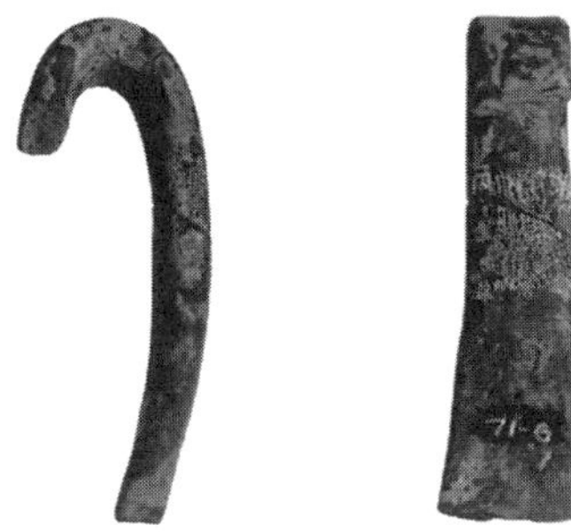

18

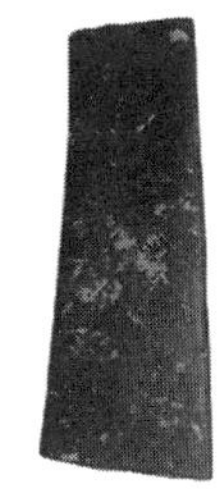

19

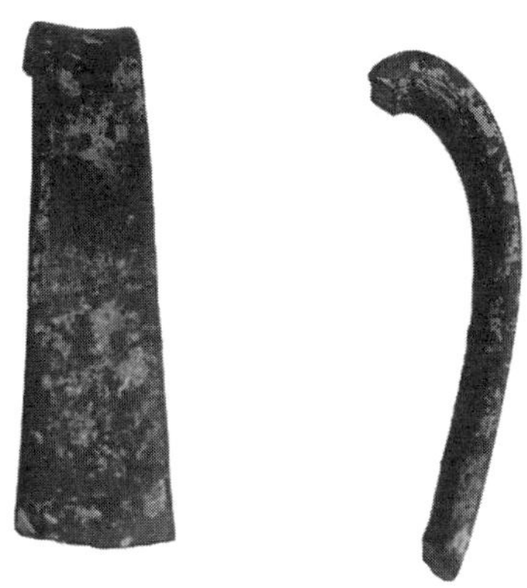

20

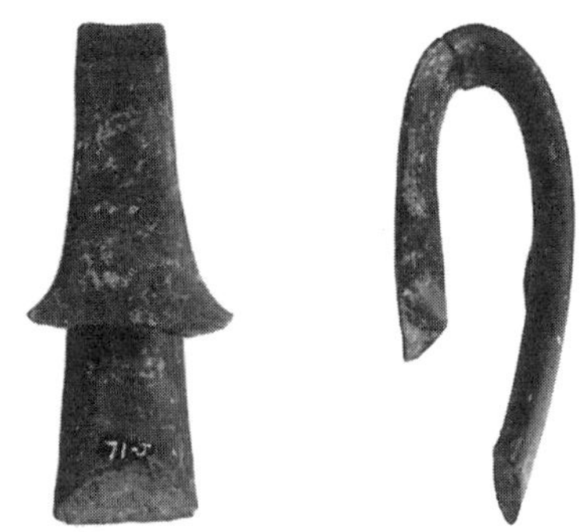

21

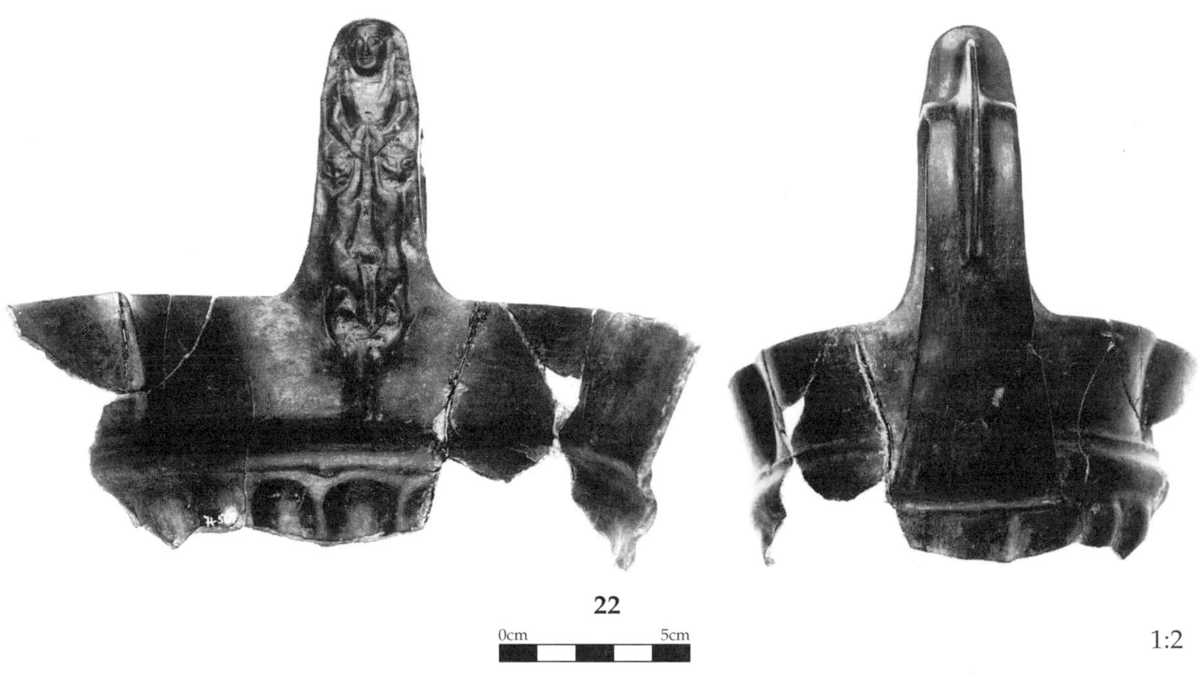

22

0cm 5cm

1:2

PLATE 7. Kyathos Handle Fragment, 23; Kyathos, 24; Scalloped Kyathos, 25

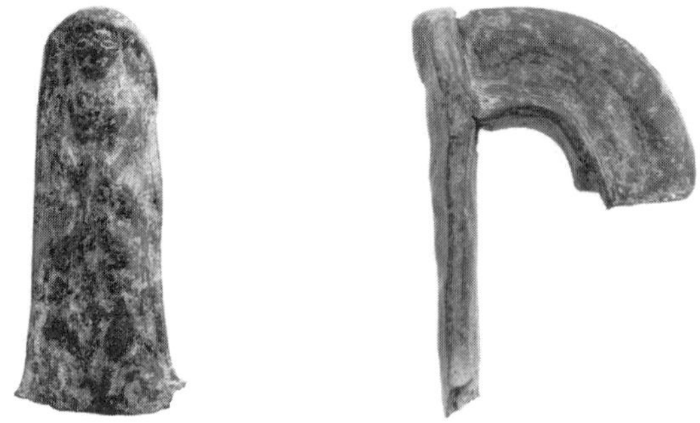

23

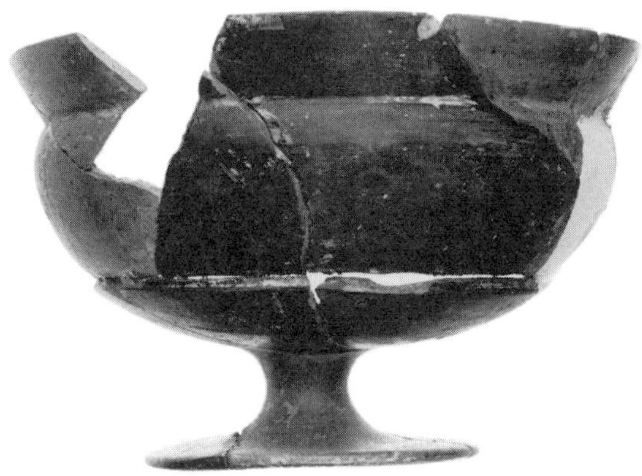

24

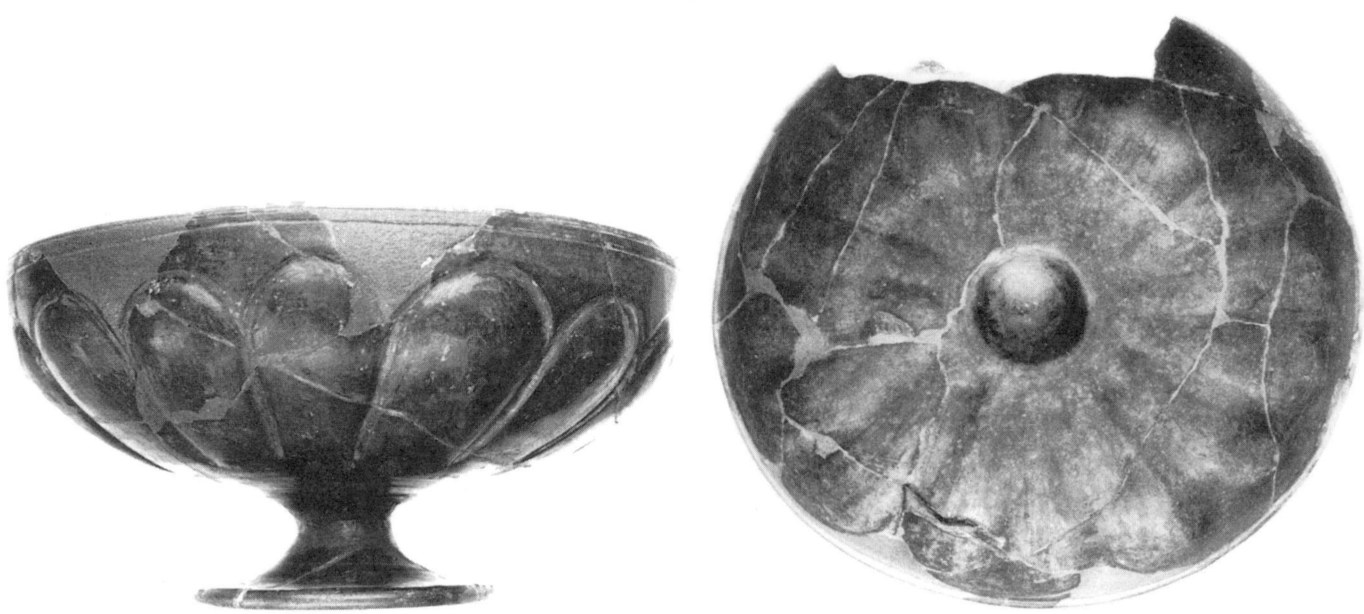

25

0cm 5cm

1:2

PLATE 8. Scalloped Kyathos, 26; Scalloped Kyathos Fragment, 27; Scalloped Kyathos Fragment, 28; Kyathos Fragment, 29; Ivory Inlay, Murlo no. 71-102

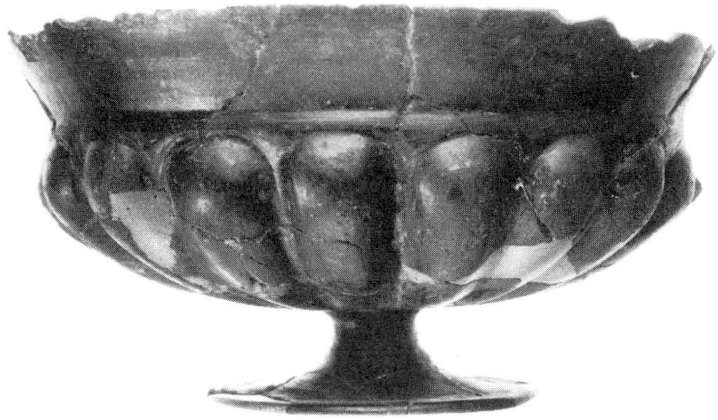

26

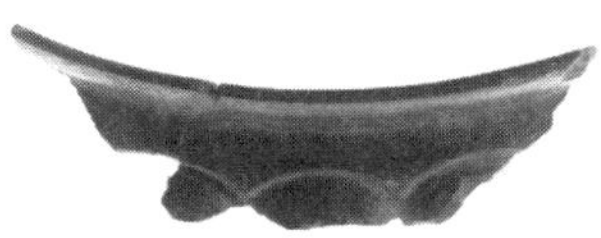

27

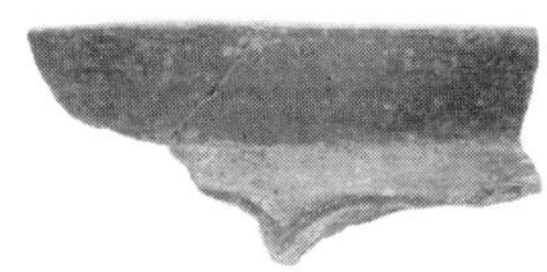

28

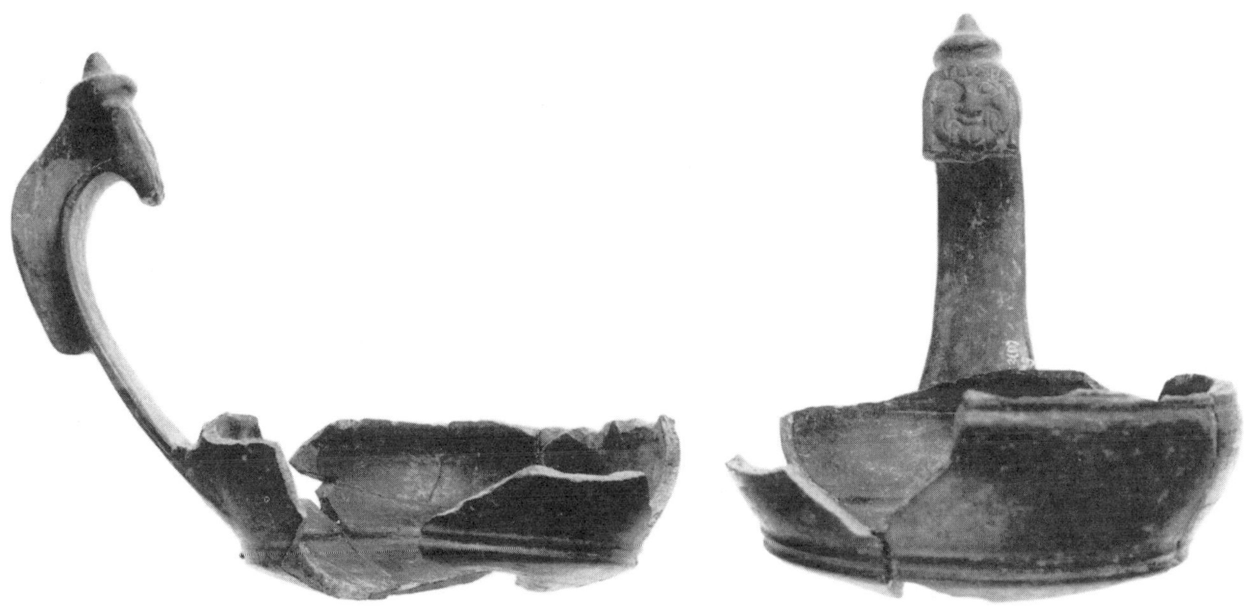

29

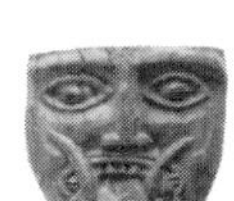

Murlo no. 71-102

0cm 5cm

1:2

PLATE 9. Kyathos Handle Fragment, 30; Scalloped Kyathos Handle and Body Fragment, 31; Kyathos Handle Fragment, 32

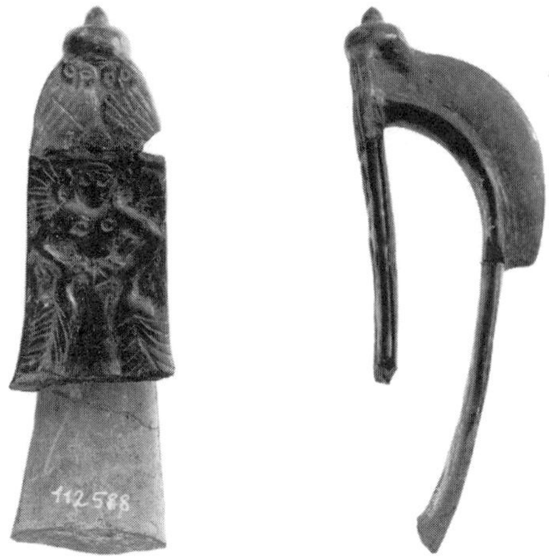

30

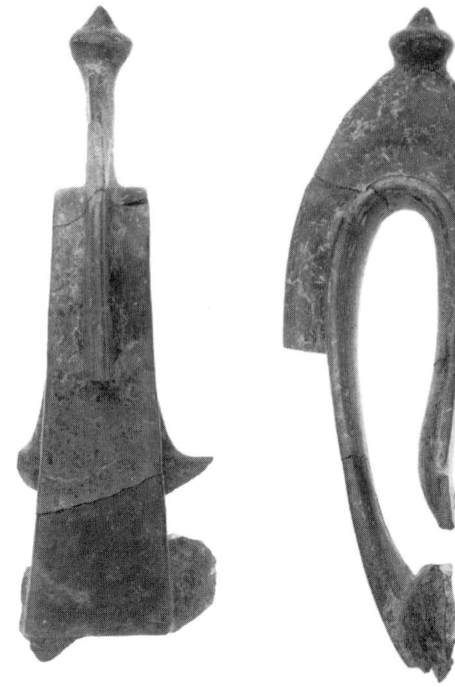

31

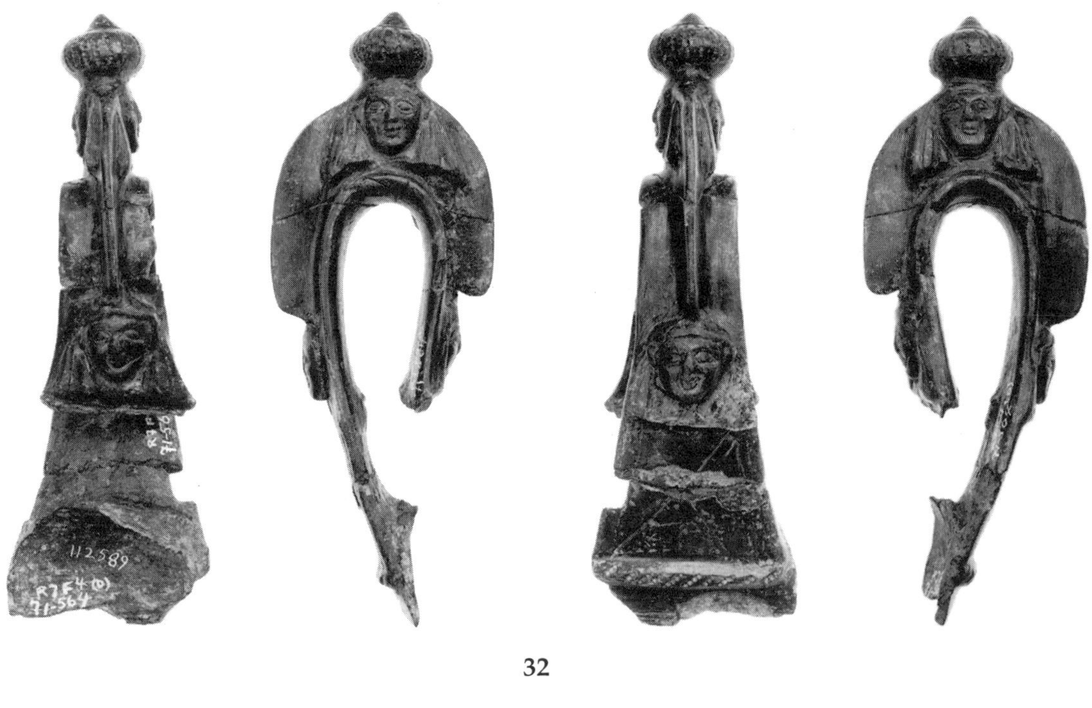

32

0cm 5cm

1:2

PLATE 10. Kyathos Handle Fragment, 33; Scalloped Kyathos Handle and Body Fragment, 34

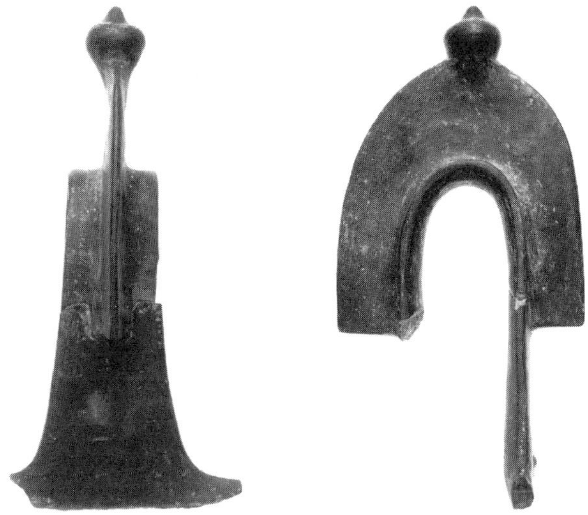

33

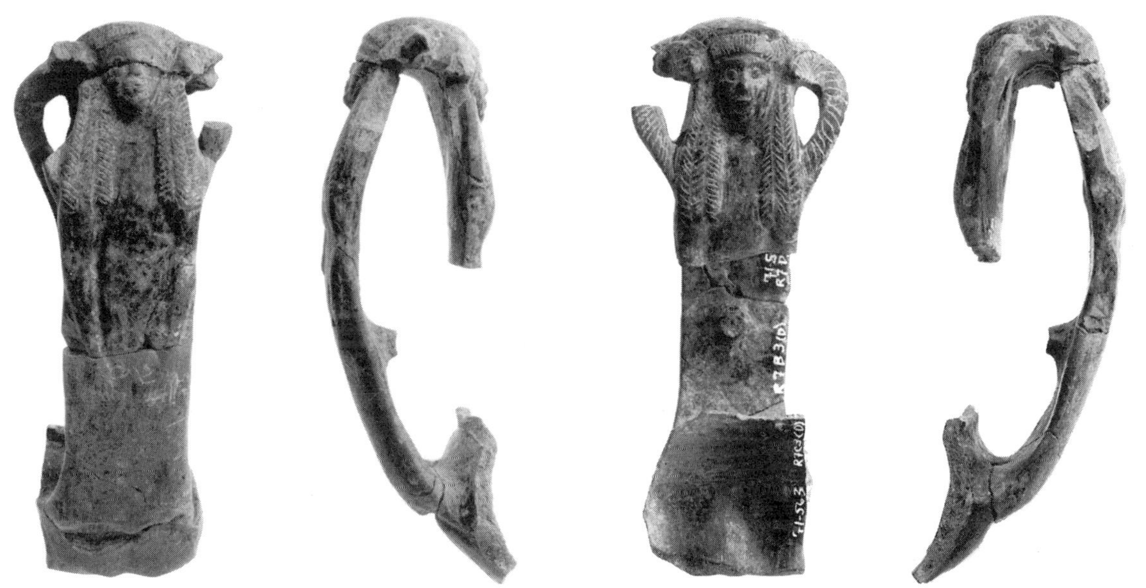

34

0cm 5cm

1:2

PLATE 11. Kyathos Rim and Handle Fragment, 35; Kyathos Handle Fragment, Murlo no. 73-268; Kyathos Handle Fragment, Murlo no. 73-269; Kyathos Handle Fragment, 36; Kyathos Handle Fragment, 37; Cup, 38

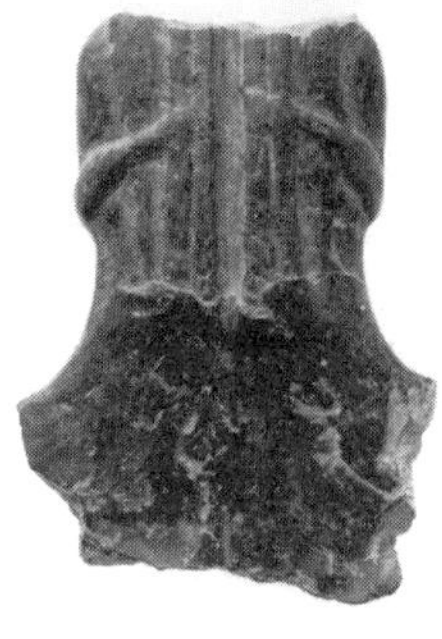

35

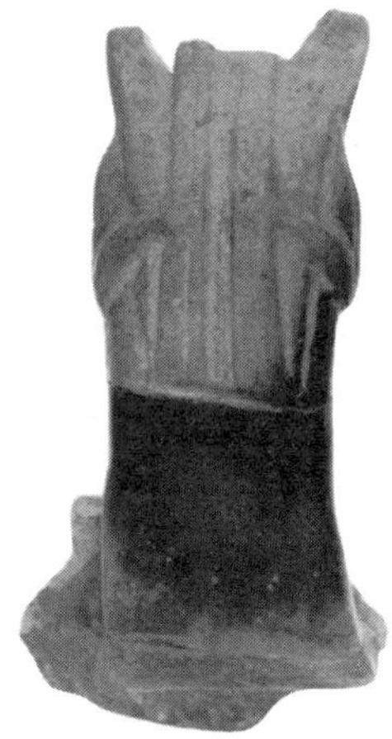

Murlo no. 73-268

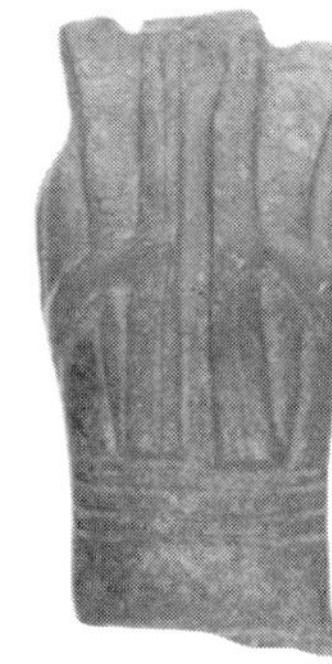

Murlo no. 73-269

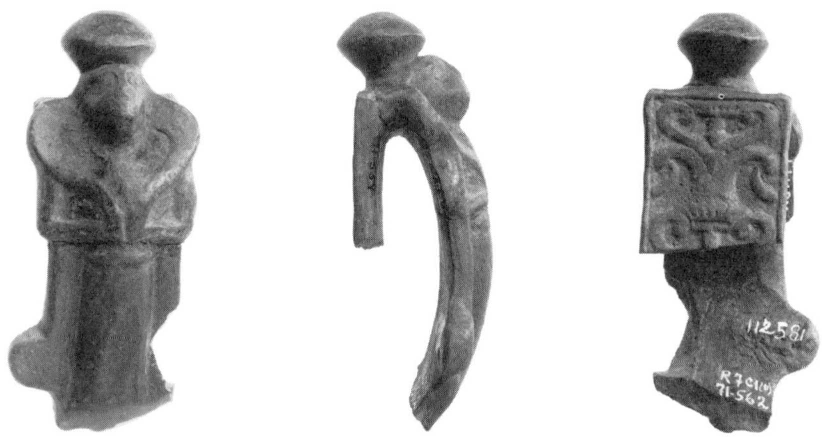

36

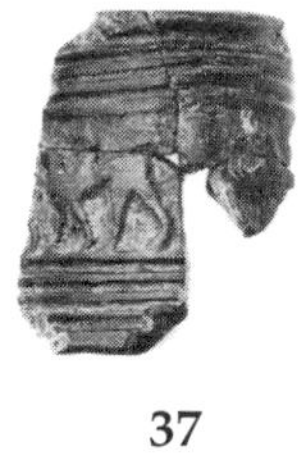

37

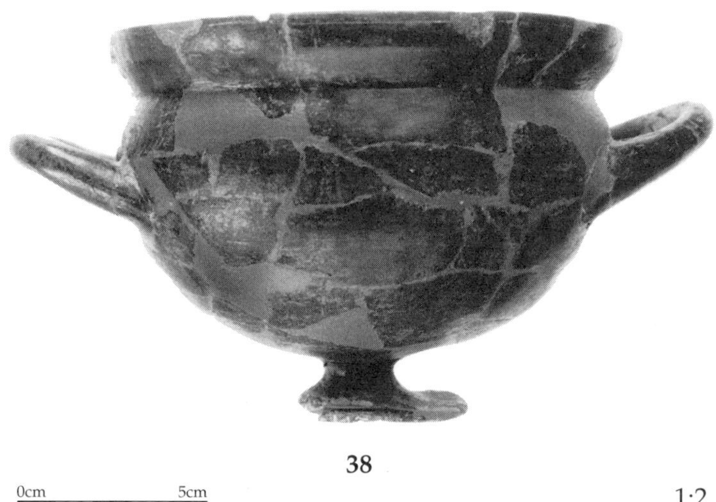

38

0cm 5cm

1:2

PLATE 12. Cup, 39; Cup Fragment, 40; Cup Fragment, 41; Cup Fragment, 42; Cup Fragment, 43; Chalice, 44; Chalice Fragment, 45; Chalice Fragment, 46; Phiale Fragment, 47

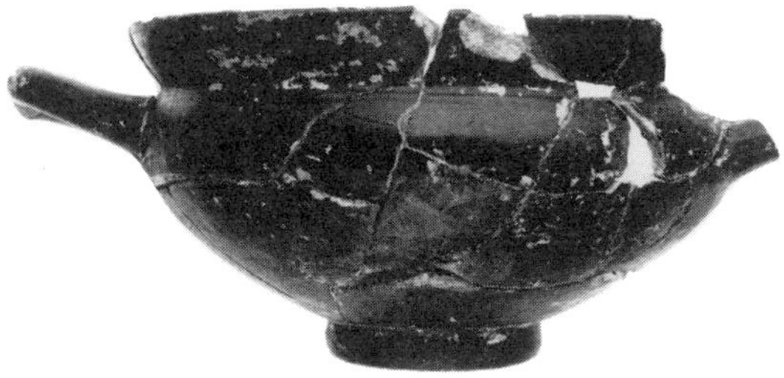

39

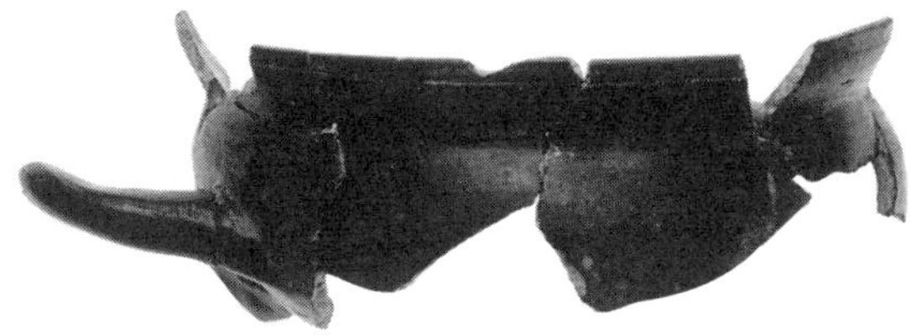

40

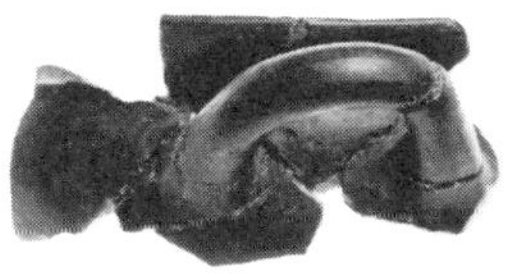

41

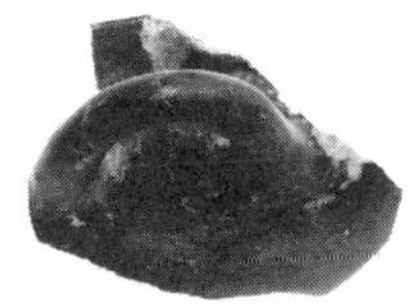

42

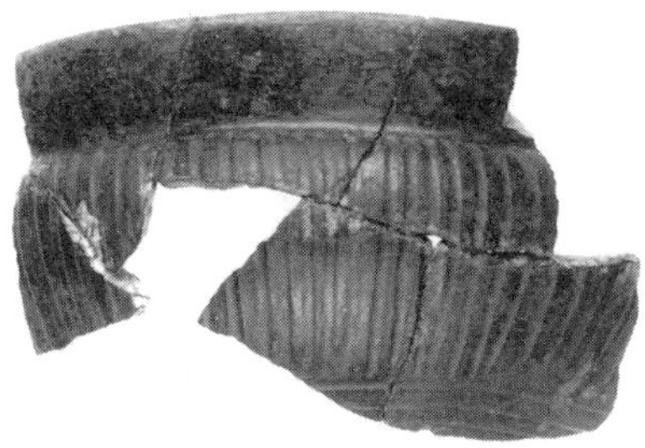

43

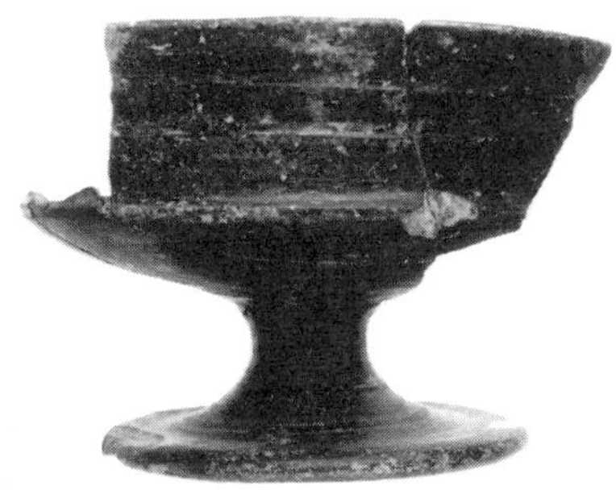

44

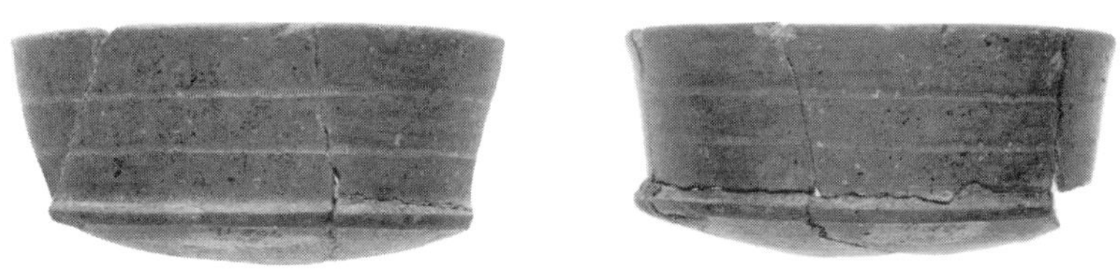

45

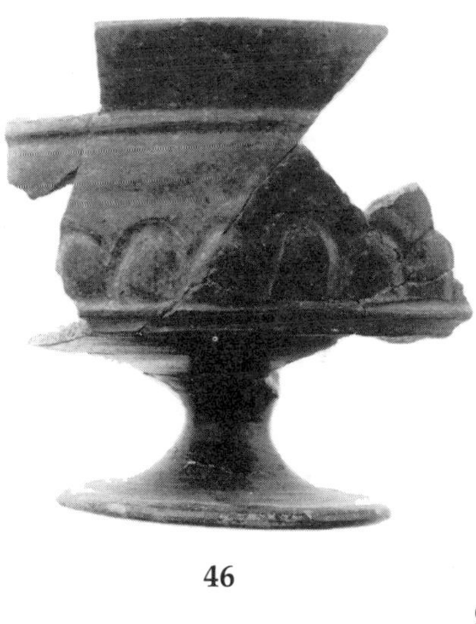

46

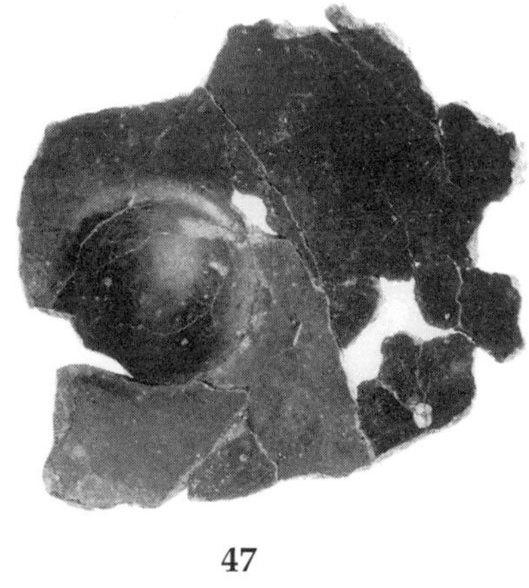

47

0cm 5cm

1:2

PLATE 13. Fragmentary Jar, 48; Fragmentary Jar, 49; Tripod Bowl, 50; Tripod Bowl Fragment, 51; Tripod Bowl Leg Fragment, 52; Covered Footed Bowl, 53

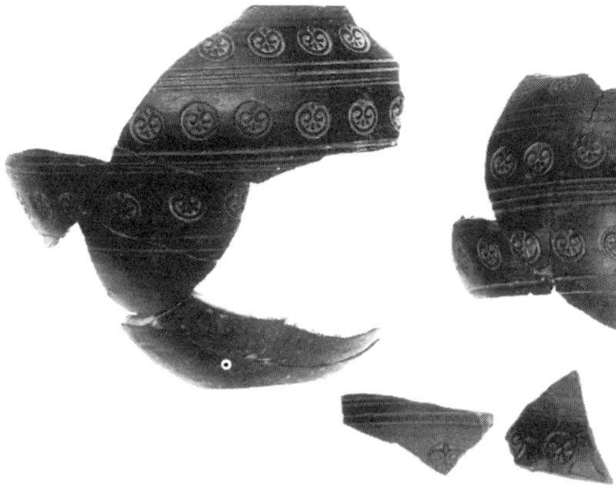

48

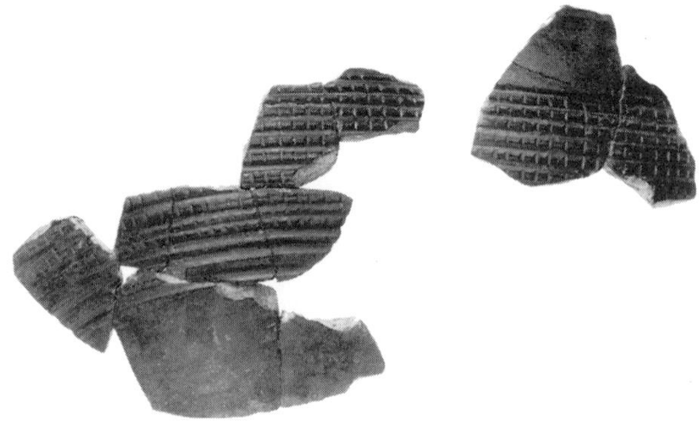

49

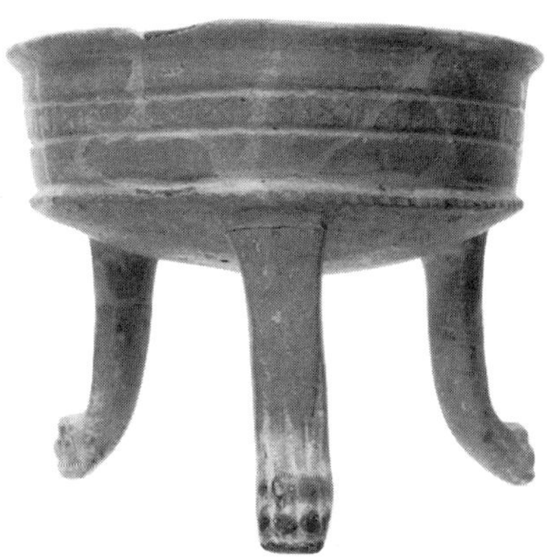

50

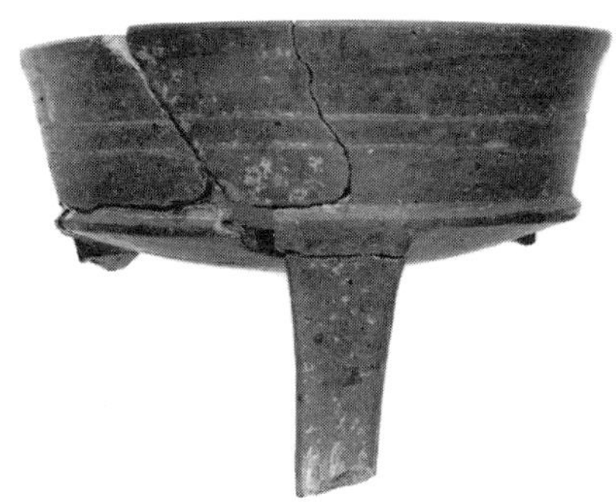

51

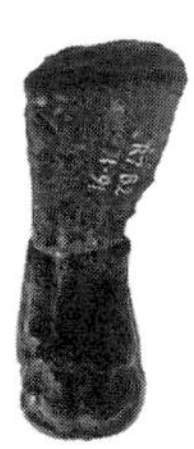

52

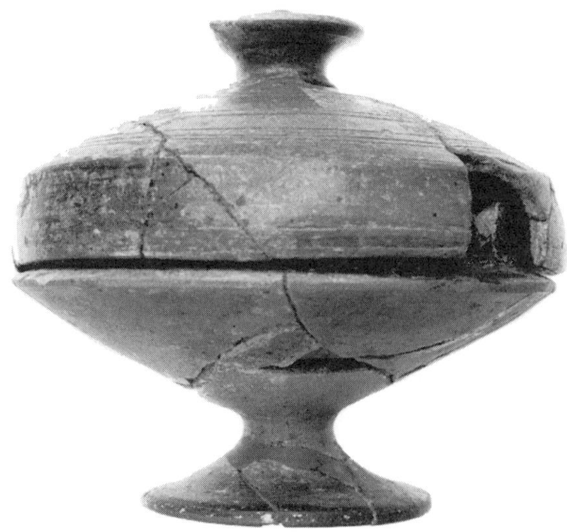

53

0cm 5cm

1:2

PLATE 14. Footed Bowl, 54; Footed Bowl, 55; Bowl, 56; Bowl Rim Fragment, 57

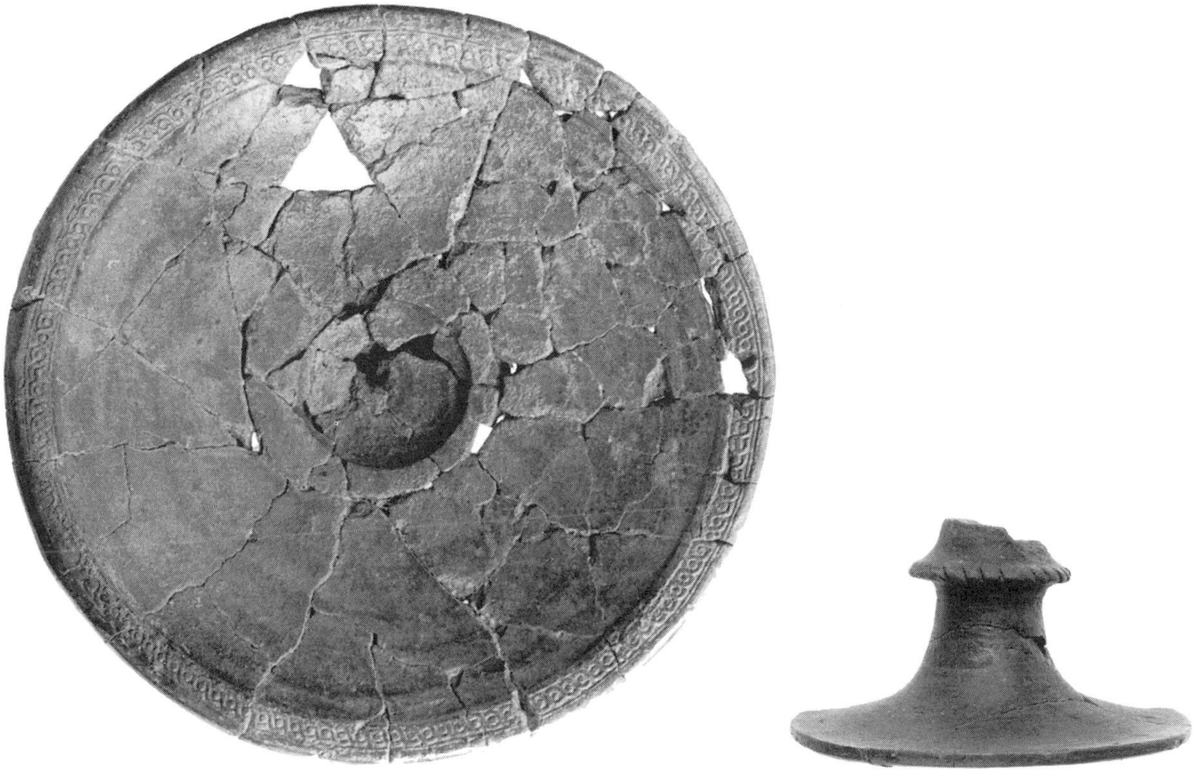

54

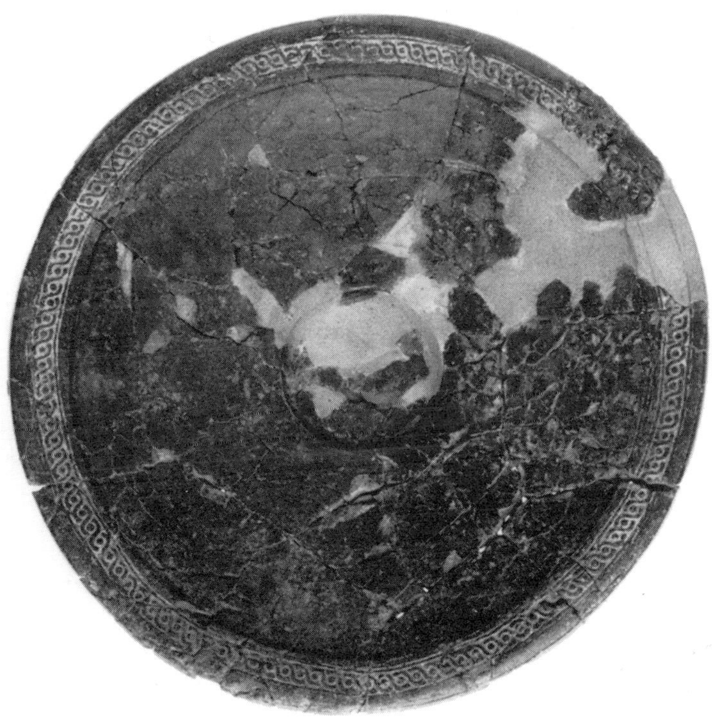

55

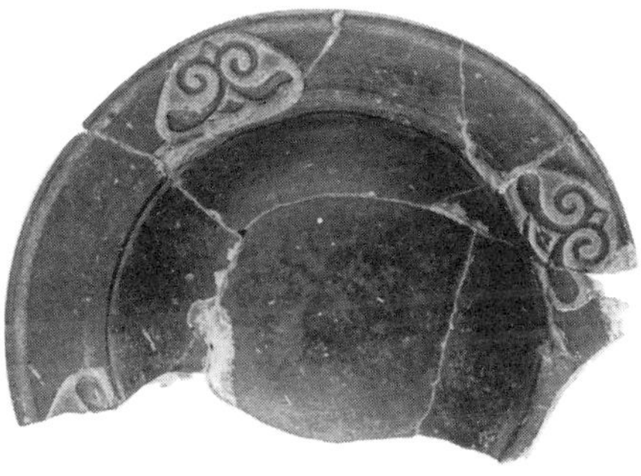

56

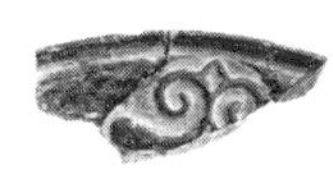

57

0cm 5cm

1:2

PLATE 15. Bowl Fragment, 58; Bowl, Murlo no. 70-100; Bowl Fragment, 59; Bowl Fragment, 60; Bowl Rim Fragment, 61; Bowl Rim Fragment, 62; Bowl Rim Fragment, 63; Bowl, 64; Bowl, 65

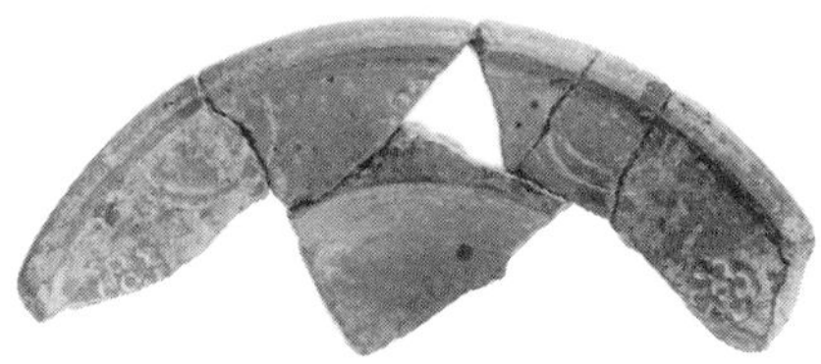

58

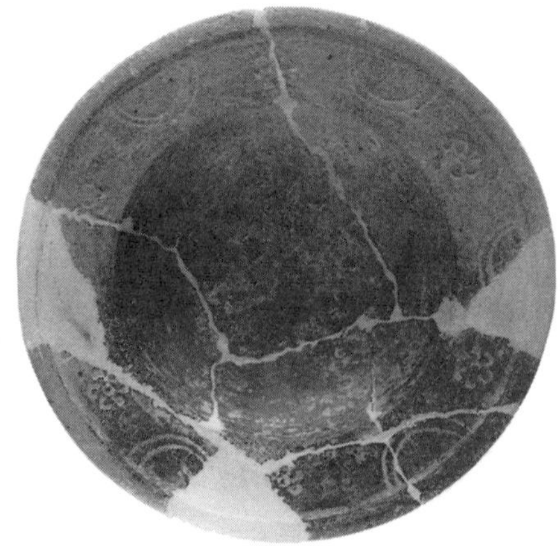

Murlo no. 70-100

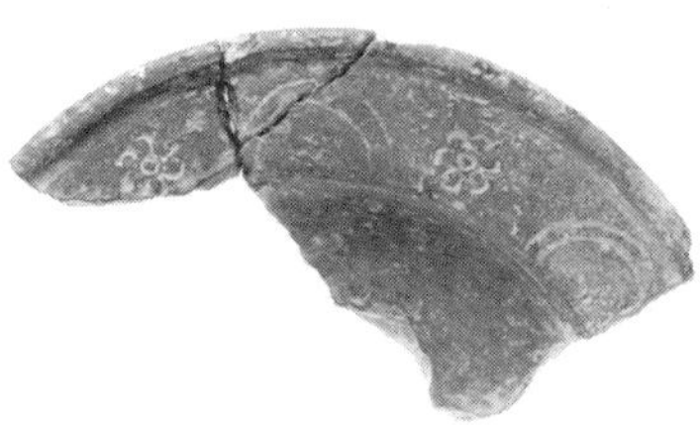

59

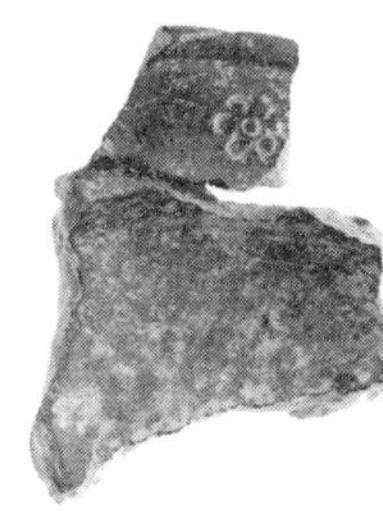

60

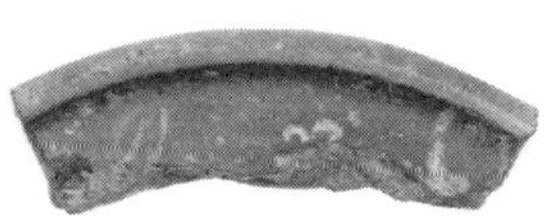

61

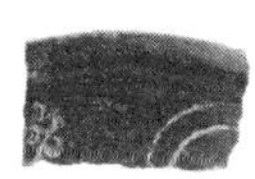

62

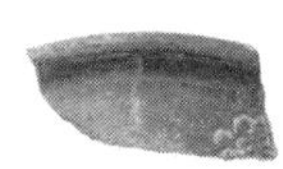

63

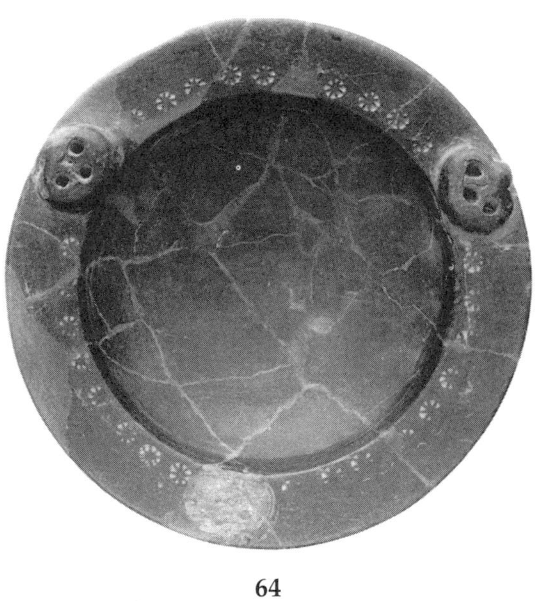

64

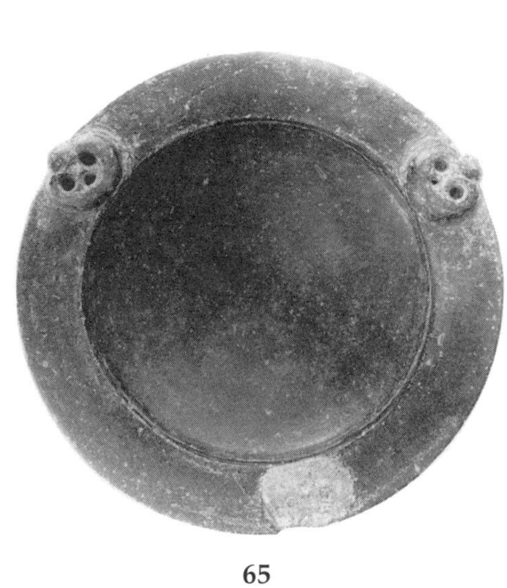

65

0cm 5cm

1:2

PLATE 16. Bowl Fragment, 66; Bowl Fragment, 67; Bowl Fragment, 68; Plate, 69; Plate Fragment, 70; Plate Fragment, 71; Plate Fragment, 72

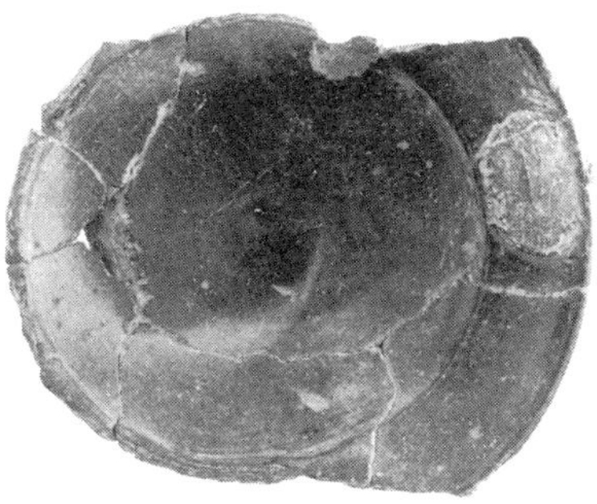

66

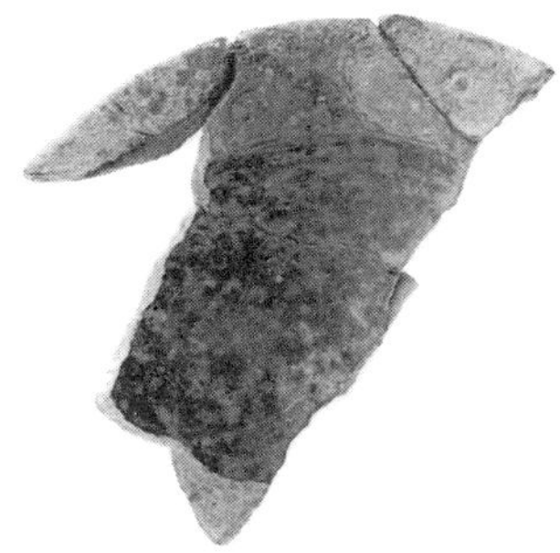

67

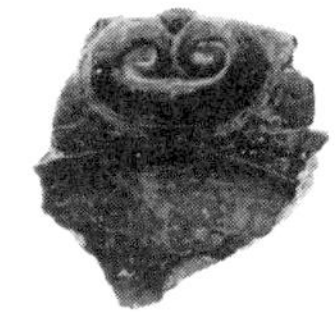

68

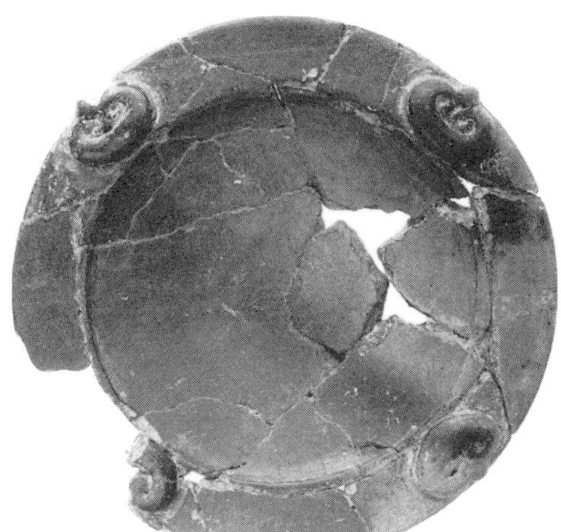

69

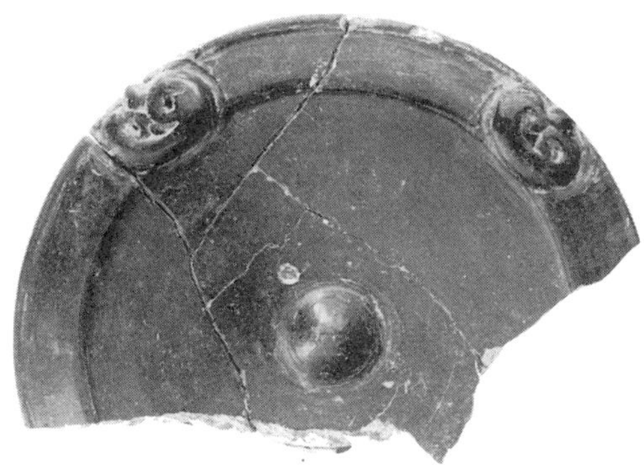

70

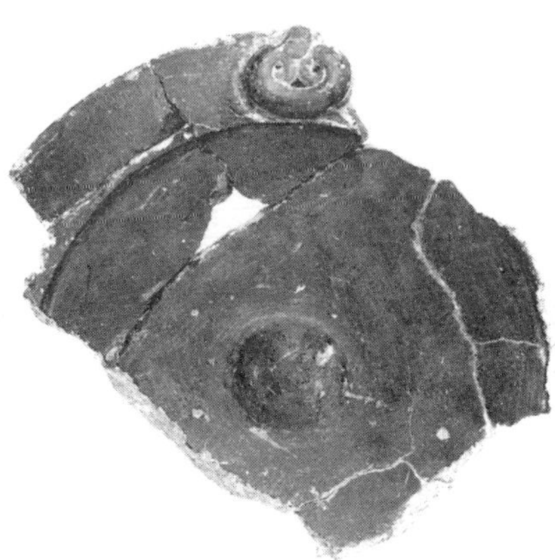

71

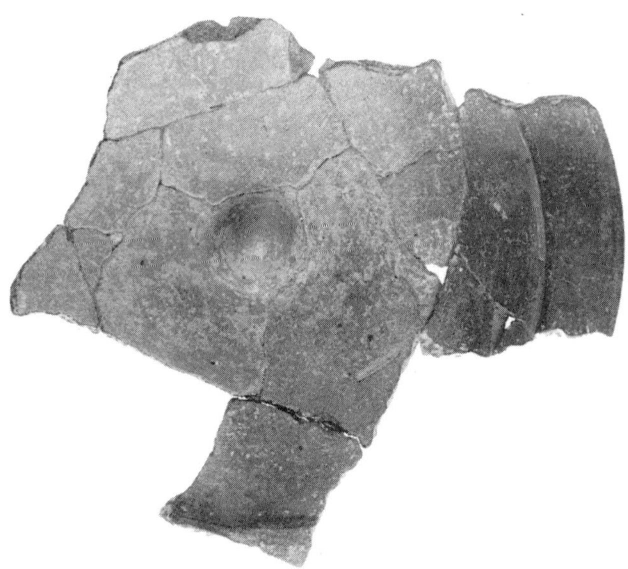

72

0cm 5cm

1:2

PLATE 17. Plate Fragment, 73; Plate Fragment, 74; Plate Fragment, 75; Plate Fragment, 76; Plate Fragment, 77; Plate Fragment, 78; Plate Fragment, 79; Rim Fragment with Applied Decoration, 80; Rim Fragment with Applied Decoration, 81; Rim Fragment with Applied Decoration, 82; Rim Fragment with Applied Decoration, 83; Rim Fragment with Applied Decoration, 84; Rim Fragment with Applied Decoration, 85; Rim Fragment with Applied Decoration, 86; Rim Fragment with Applied Decoration, 87; Molded Appliqué Fragment, 88; Molded Appliqué Fragment, 89

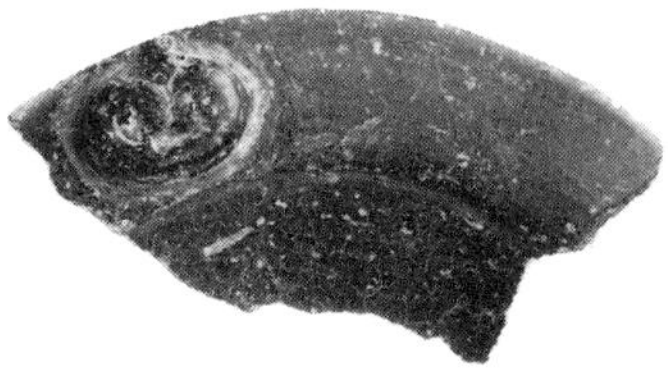

73

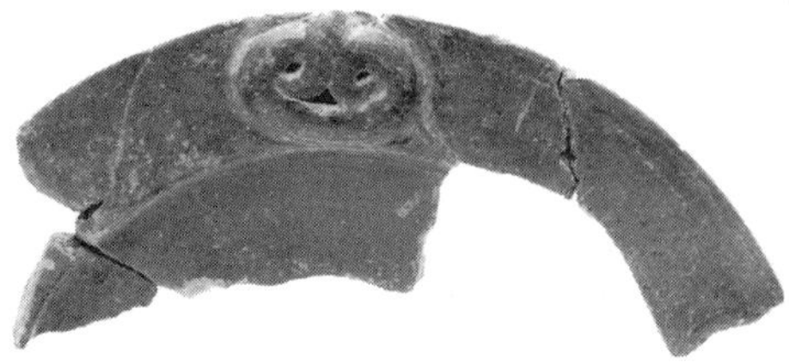

74

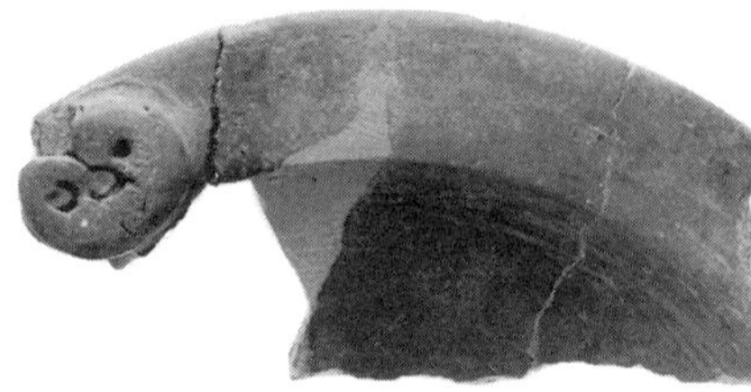

75

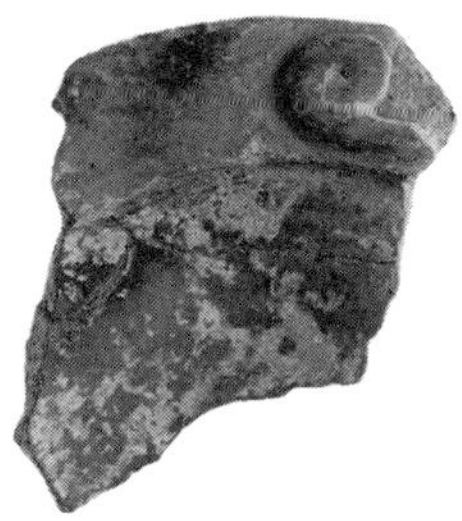

76

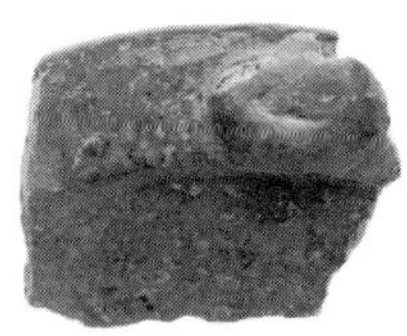

77

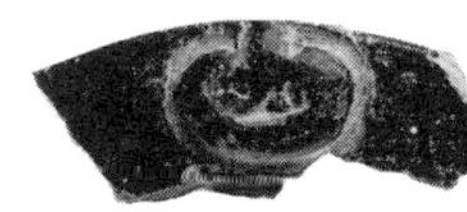

78

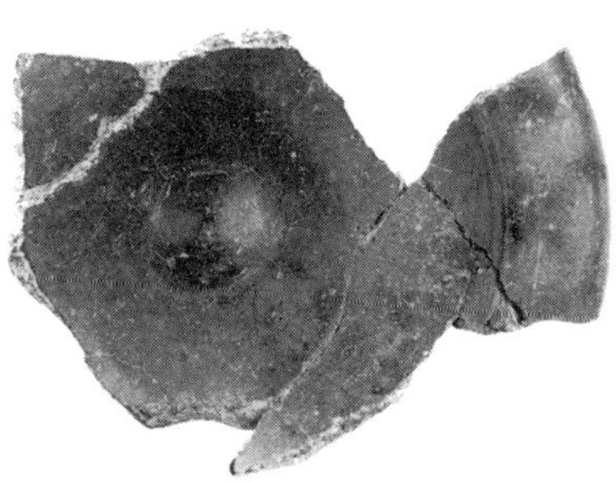

79

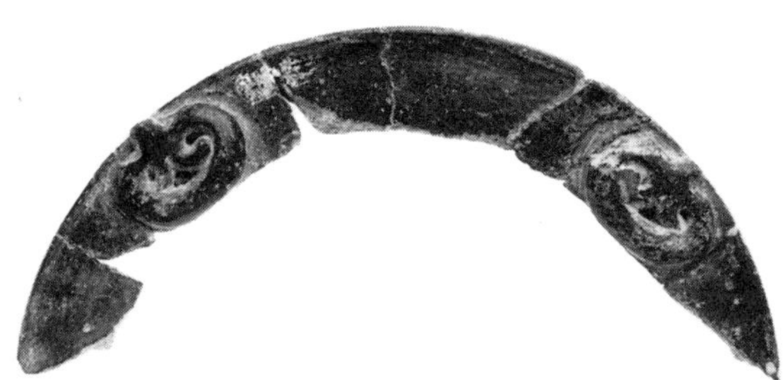

80

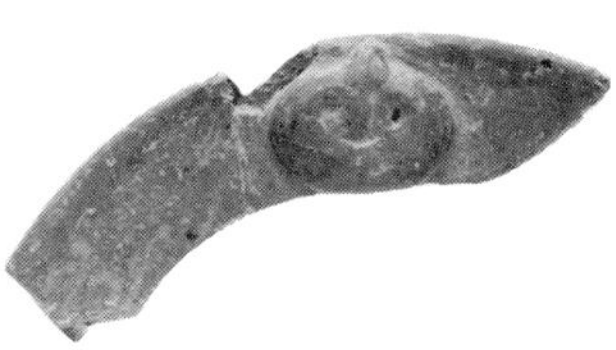

81

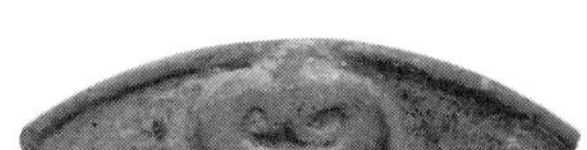

82

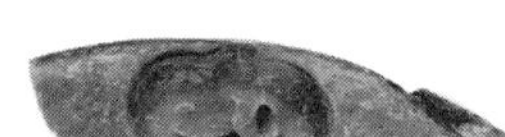

83

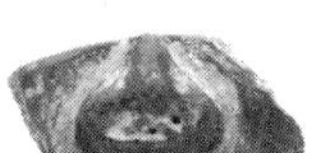

84

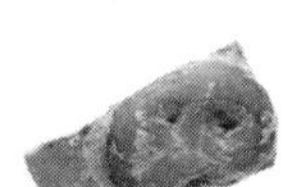

85

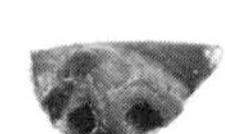

86

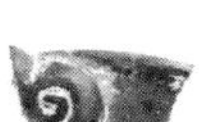

87

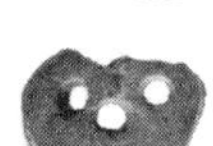

88

89

0cm 5cm

1:2

PLATE 18. Plate Fragment, 90; Plate Fragment, 91; Plate Fragment, 92; Plate Fragment, 93; Plate Fragment, 94; Cylinder-Stamped Rim Fragment, 95; Cylinder-Stamped Rim Fragment, 96; Cylinder-Stamped Rim Fragment, 97; Cylinder-Stamped Rim Fragment, 98; Cylinder-Stamped Rim Fragment, 99; Cylinder-Stamped Rim Fragment, 100; Cylinder-Stamped Rim Fragment, 101

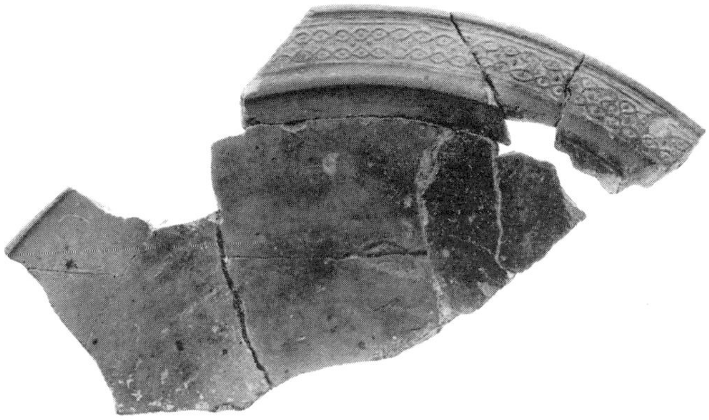

90

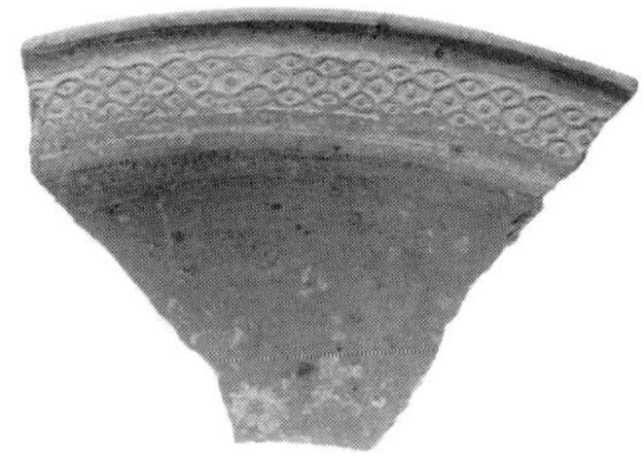

91

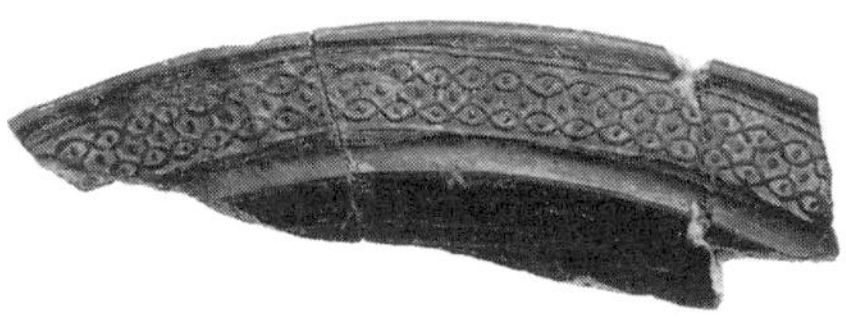

92

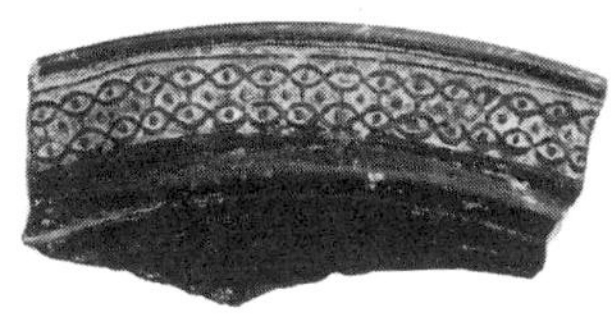

93

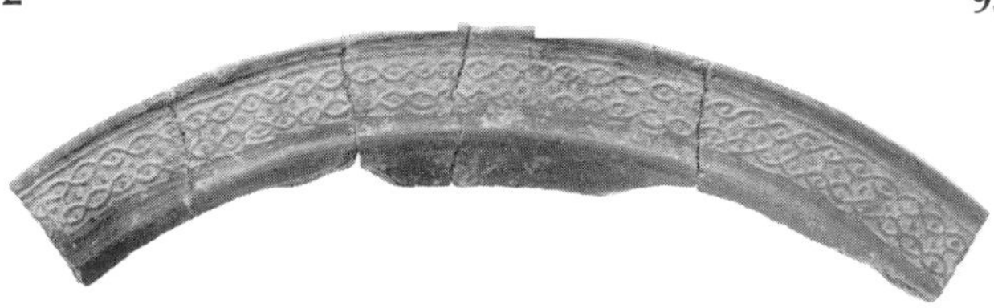

94

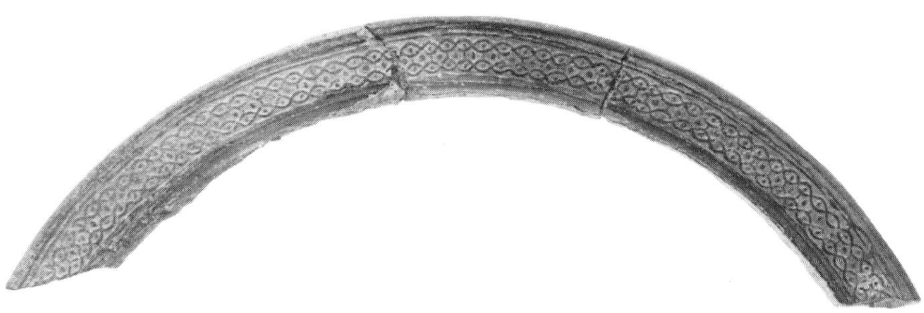

95

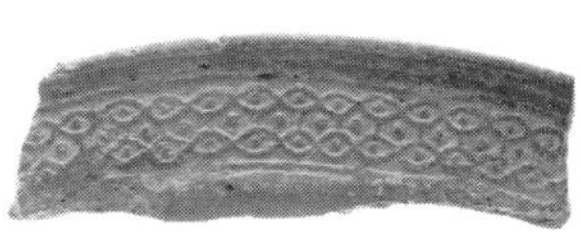

96

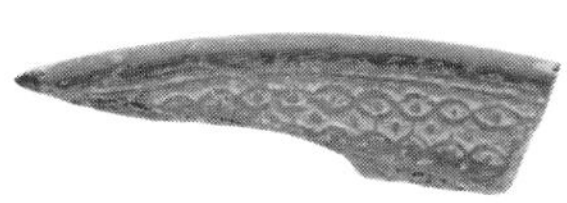

97

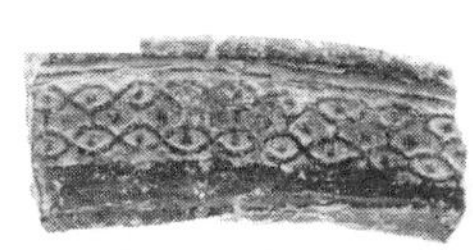

98

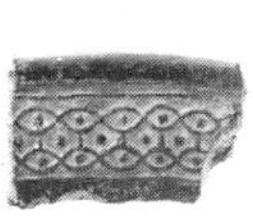

99

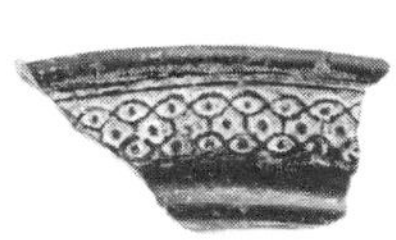

100

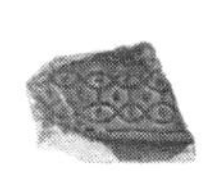

101

0cm 5cm

1:2

PLATE 19. Rim and Handle Fragment, 102; Rim and Handle Fragment, 103; Rim and Handle Fragment, 104; Rim and Handle Fragment, 105; Rim and Handle Fragment, 106; Rim and Handle Fragment, 107; Rim and Handle Fragment, 108; Rim and Handle Fragment, 109; Rim and Handle Fragment, 110; Rim and Handle Fragment, Murlo no. 72-427

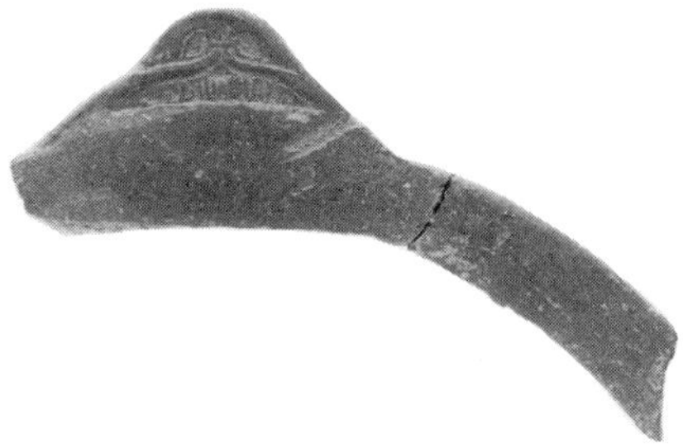

102

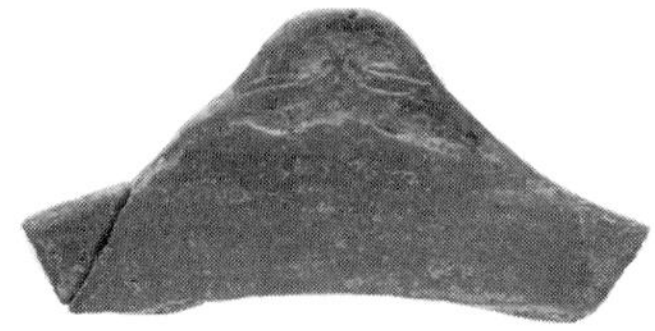

103

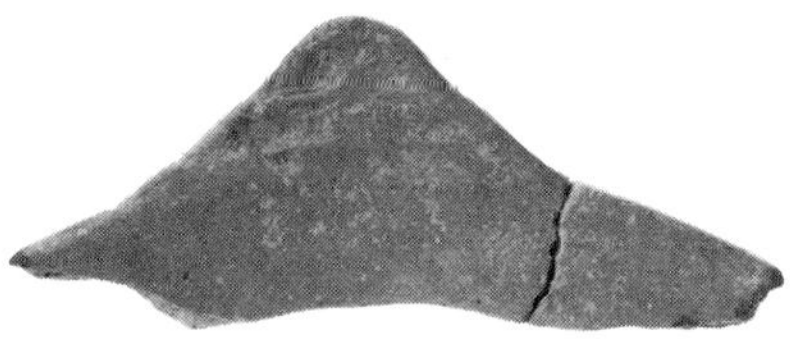

104

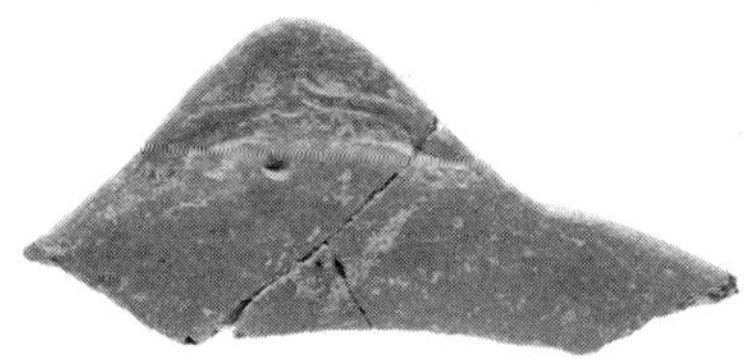

105

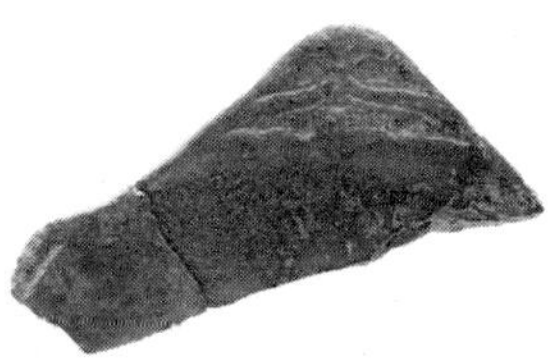

106

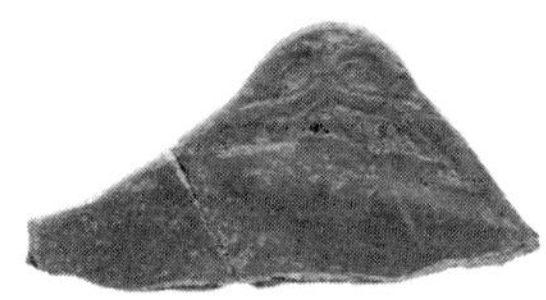

107

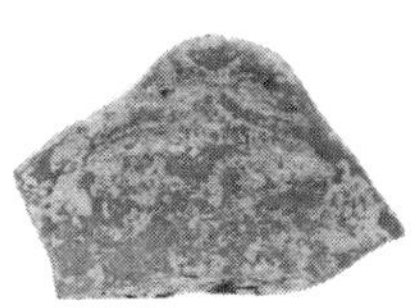

108

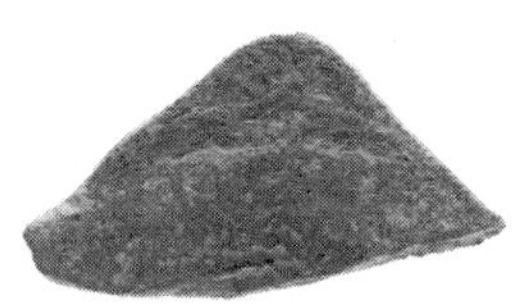

109

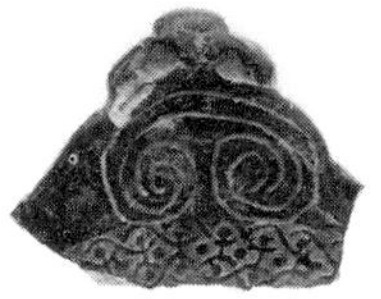

110

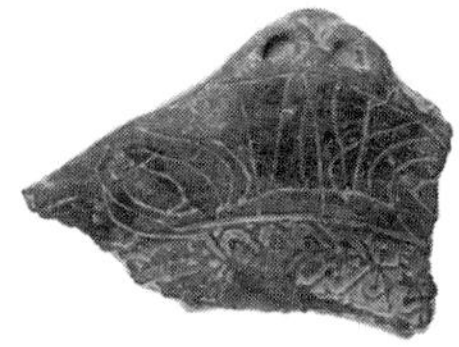

Murlo no. 72-427

0cm 5cm

1:2

PLATE 20. Plate, 111; Plate Fragment, 112

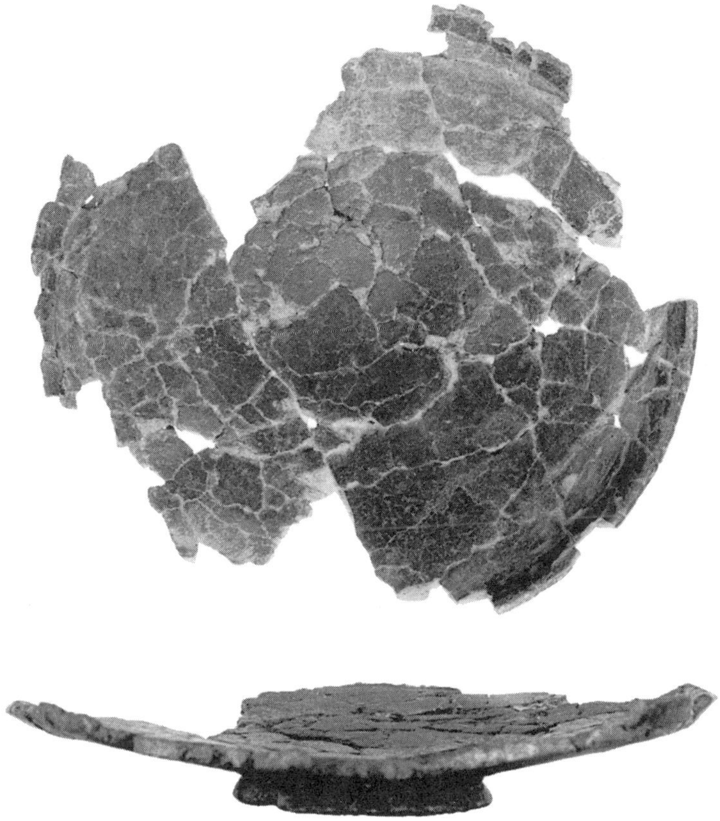

111

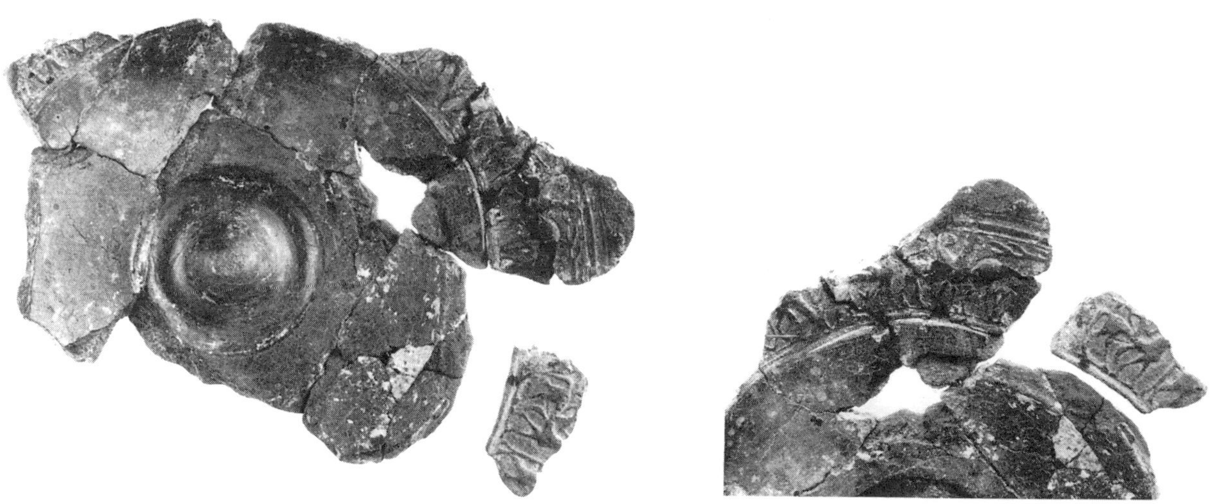

112

0cm 5cm

1:2

PLATE 21. Lid, 113; Fragmentary Lid, 114; Fragmentary Lid, 115; Lid Fragment, 116; Lid Fragment, 117; Fragmentary Lid, 118

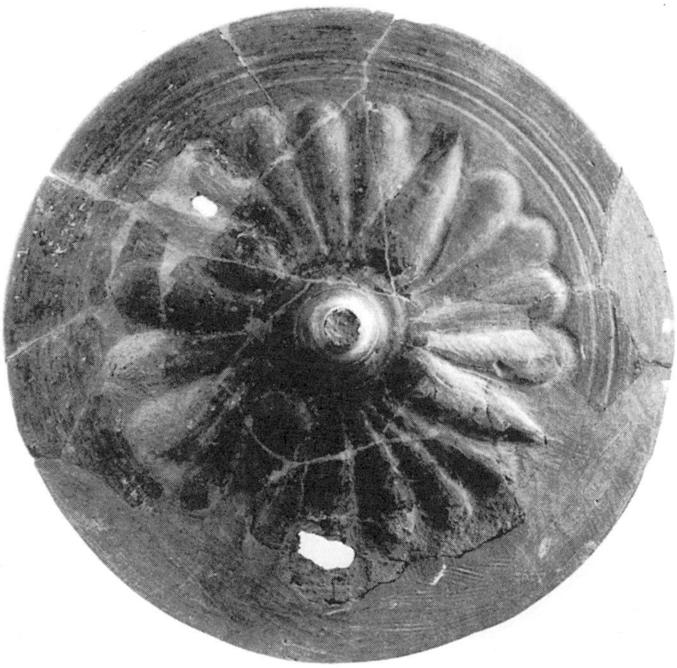

113

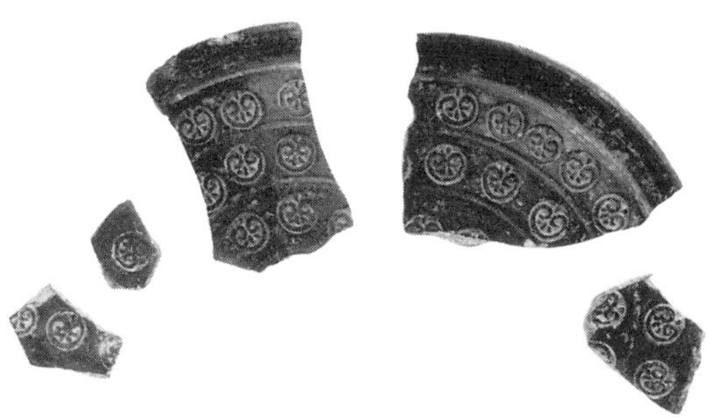

114

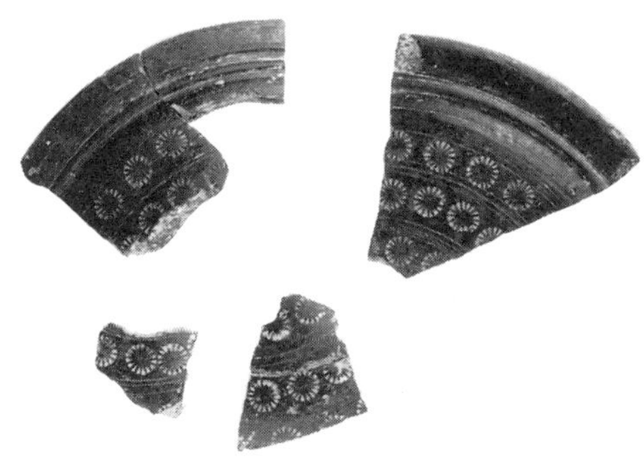

115

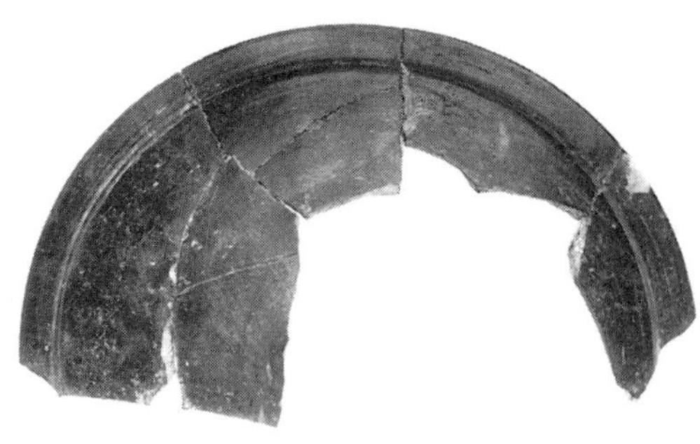

116

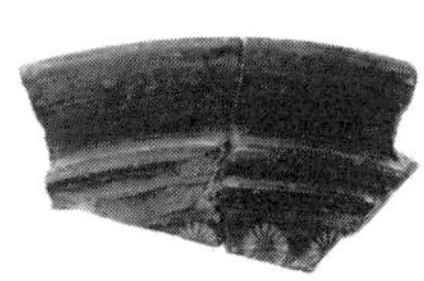

117

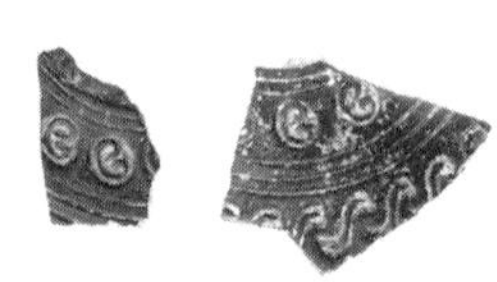

118

0cm 5cm

1:2

PLATE 22. Fragmentary Lid, 119; Lid, 120; Lid, 121; Lid Fragment, 122; Lid, 123

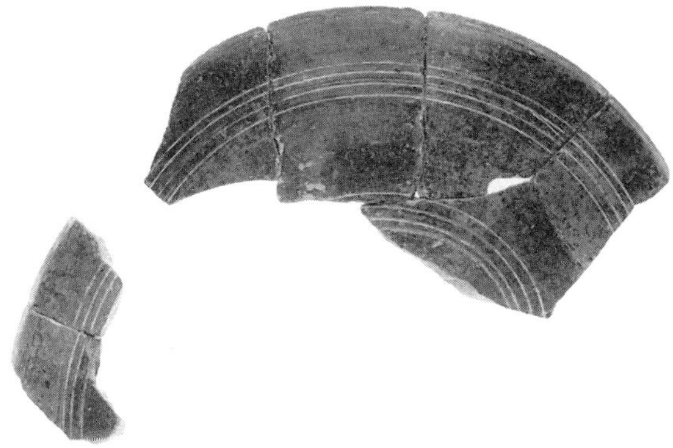

119

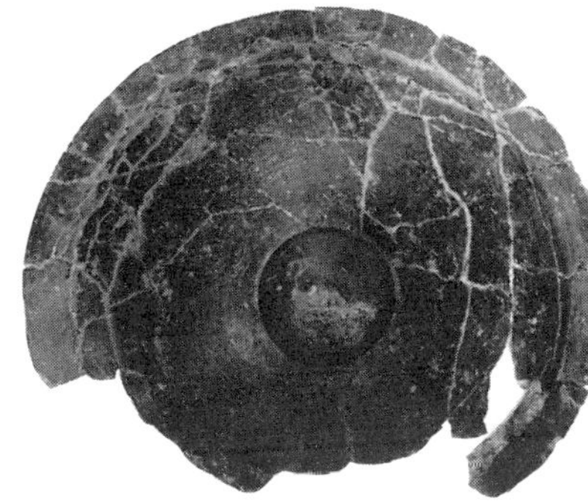

120

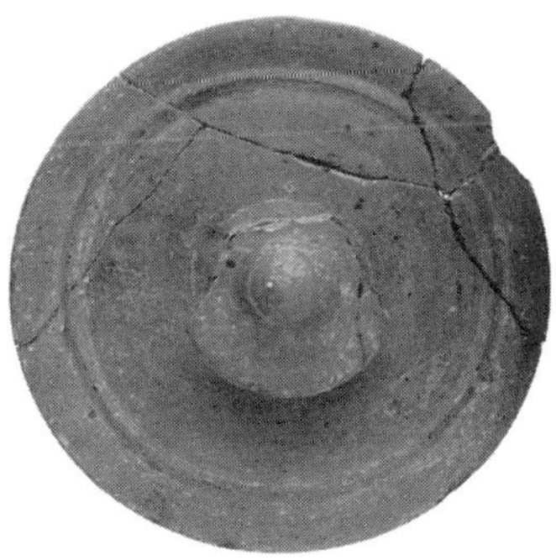

121

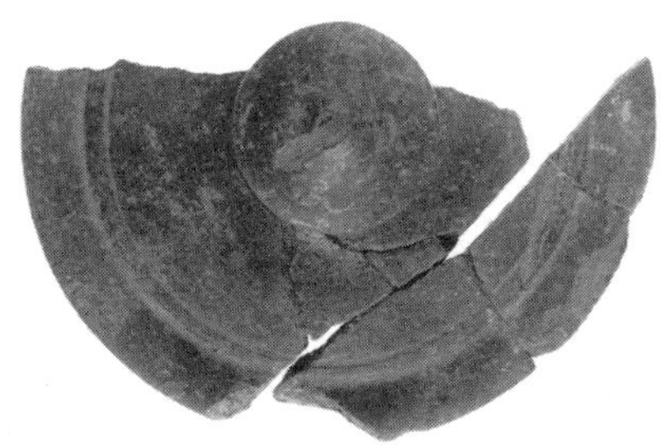

122

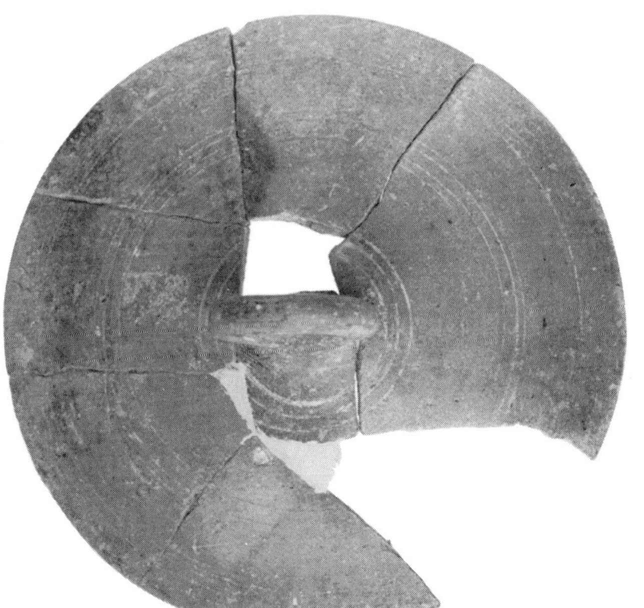

123

0cm 5cm

1:2

PLATE 23. Lid, 124; Lid Fragment, 125; Lid Fragment, 126; Lid Fragment, 127

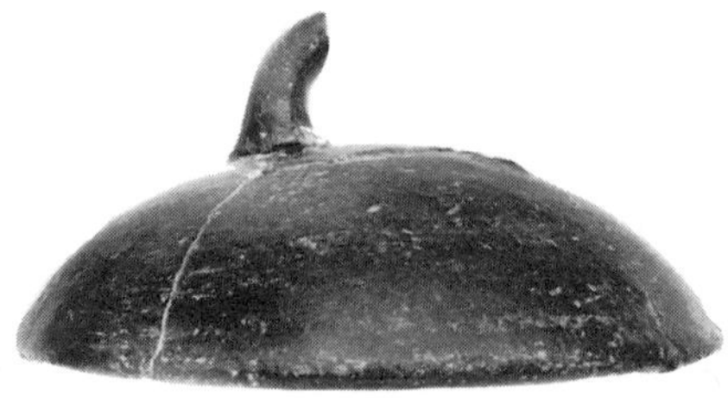

124

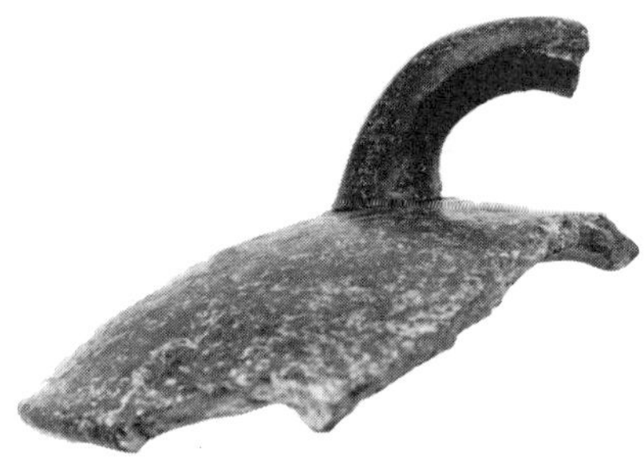

125

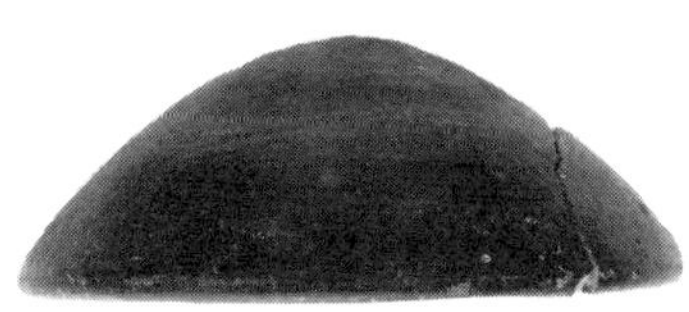

126

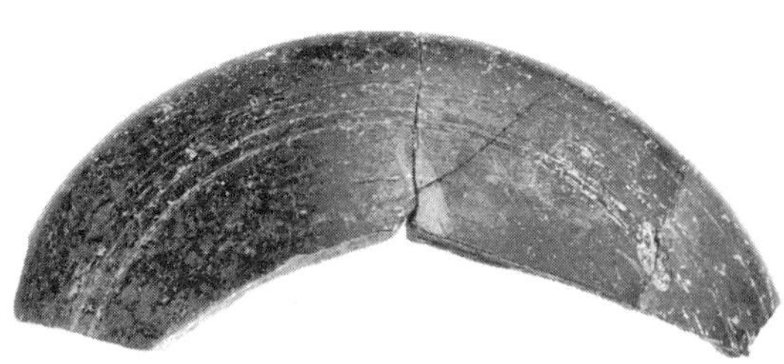

127

0cm 5cm

1:2

PLATE 24. Lid Fragment, 128; Lid Finial, 129; Lid Finial, 130; Lid Finial, 131; Stamped Fragment, 132; Stamped Fragment, 133; Strap Handle Fragment, 134; Incised Cup or Bowl Fragment, 135

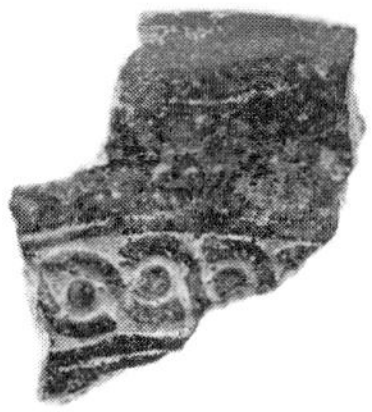

128

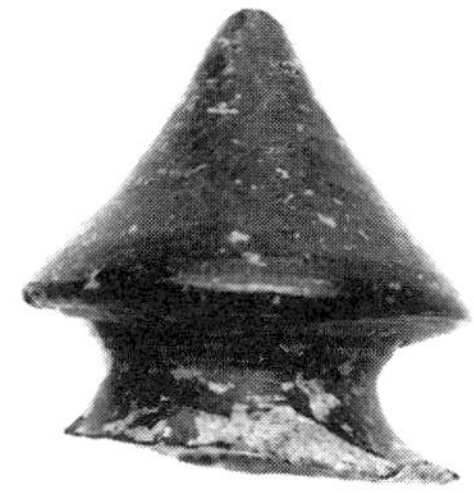

129

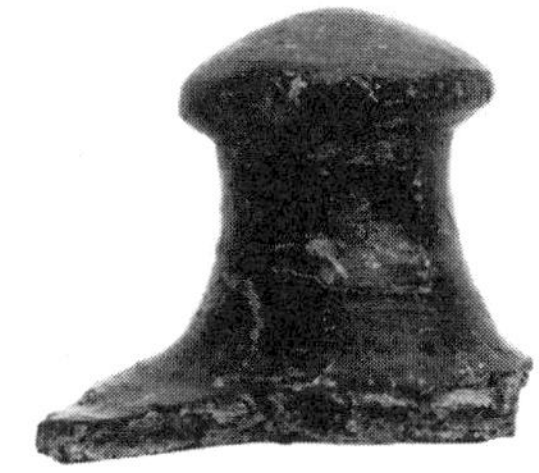

130

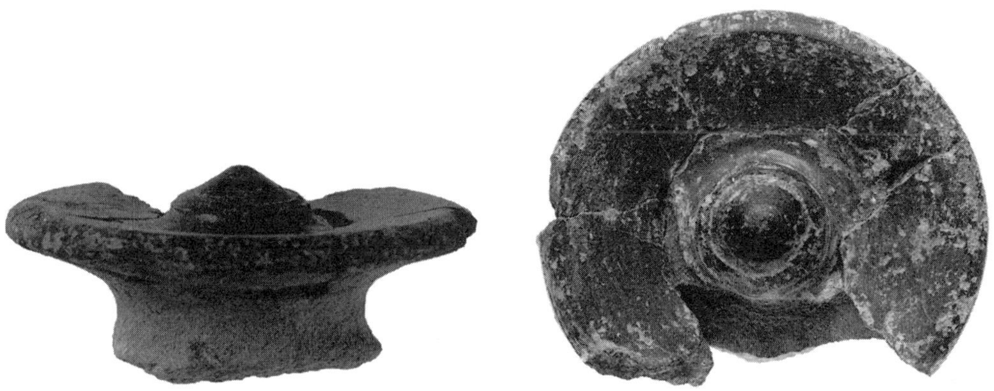

131

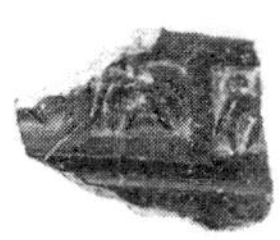

132

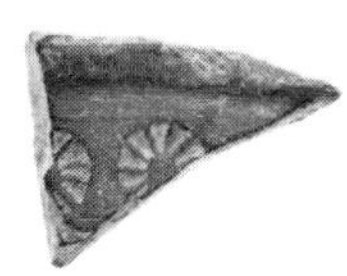

133

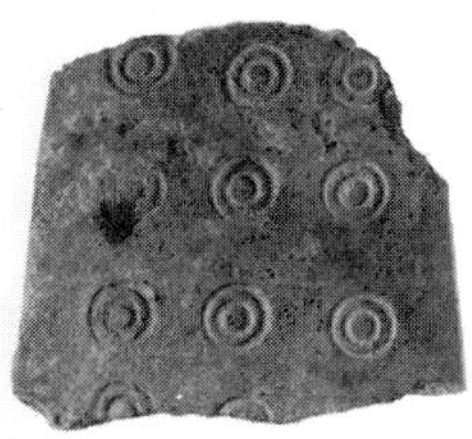

134

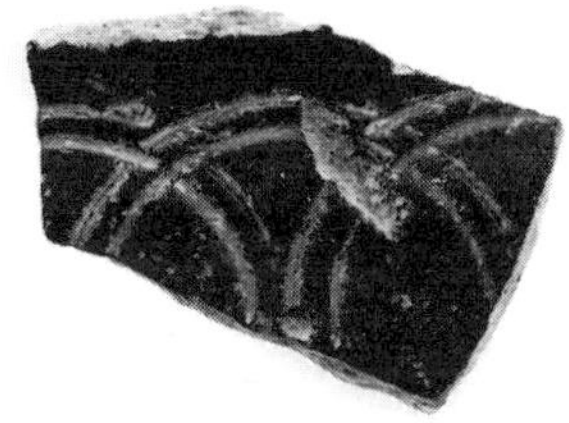

135

0cm 5cm

1:1

PLATE 25. Bowl or Plate Fragment, 136; Inscribed Rim Fragment, 137; Inscribed Fragment, 138; Inscribed Fragment, 139

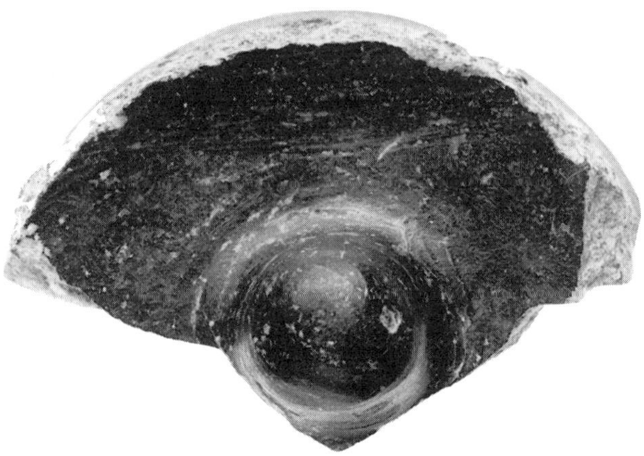

136

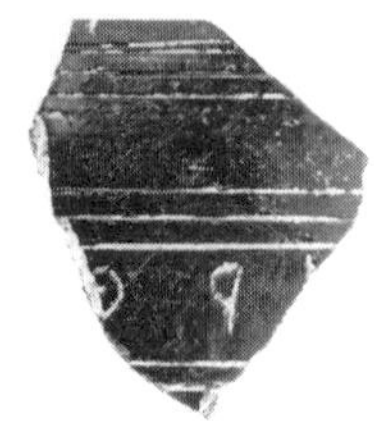

137

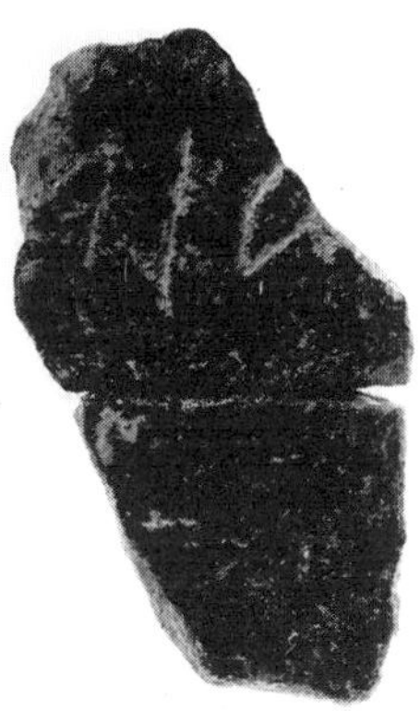

138

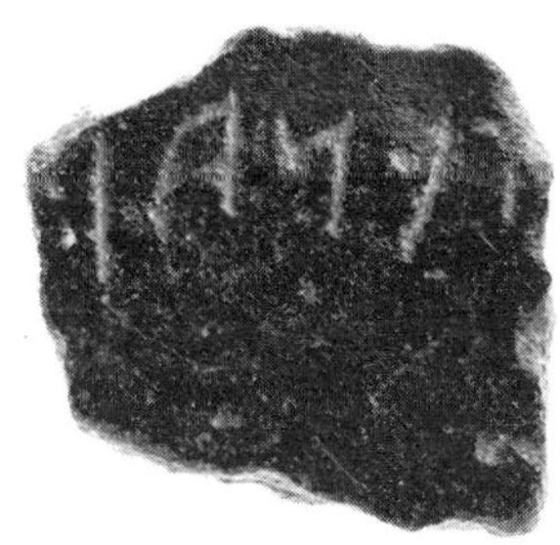

139

0cm 5cm

1:1